# Path to the Middle

# Path to the Middle

## *Oral Mādhyamika Philosophy in Tibet*

The Spoken Scholarship of Kensur Yeshey Tupden

Commenting on
Tsong-kha-pa's *Illumination of the Thought, Extensive Explanation of (Candrakīrti's) "Entrance to (Nāgārjuna's) 'Treatise on the Middle Way'"*

*(dbu ma dgongs pa rab gsal)*

The Sixth Chapter, "Perfection of Wisdom" verses 1-7

Collected, translated, edited, annotated and introduced
by
Anne Carolyn Klein

Translation of Tsong-kha-pa's text by Jeffrey Hopkins and Anne Klein, annotations by Jeffrey Hopkins

STATE UNIVERSITY OF NEW YORK PRESS

Published by
State University of New York Press, Albany



Printed in the United States of America



For information, address State University of New York Press,
State University Plaza, Albany, N.Y., 12246

Frontispiece photo by Armen Elliot
Production by Marilyn P. Semerad
Marketing by Nancy Farrell

SUNY Series in Buddhist Studies
Matthew Kapstein, editor

**Library of Congress Cataloging-in-Publication Data**

Kensur Yeshey Tupden.
Path to the Middle : oral Mādhyamika philosophy in Tibet : the spoken scholarship of Kensur Yeshey Tupden commenting on Tsong-kha-pa's illumination of the thought, extensive explanation of (Candrakīrti's) "Entrance to (Nāgārjuna's) 'Treatise on the middle way'" : (dbu ma dgongs pa rab gsal), the sixth chapter, "Perfection of wisdom" verses 1-7 / collected, translated, edited, annotated, and introduced by Anne Carolyn Klein ; translation of Tsong-kha-pa's text by Jeffrey Hopkins and Anne Klein ; annotations by Jeffrey Hopkins.
p. cm. — (SUNY series in Buddhist studies.)
Includes index.
ISBN 0-7914-2043-4 (HC). — ISBN 0-7914-2044-2 (pb)
1. Tsoṅ-kha-pa Blo-bzaṅ-grags-pa, 1357-1419. Dbu ma la 'jug pa 'i rnam bśad dgoṅs pa rab gsal. 6. Don dam pa'i sems bskyed pa drug pa 'i bśad pa. 2. Candrakīrti. Madhyamakāvatāra. 3. Mādhyamika (Buddhism) 4. Wisdom—Religious aspects—Buddhism. I. Klein, Anne C., 1947- . II. Hopkins, Jeffrey. III. Tsoṅ-kha-pa Blo-bzaṅ-grags-pa, 1357-1419. Dbu ma la 'jug pa 'i rnam bśad dgoṅs pa rab gsal. 6. Don dam pa 'i sems bskyed pa drug pa 'i bśad pa. English. Selections. 1994. IV. Title. V. Series
BQ2910. M365T77235 1994
294.3'83—dc20 93-39863
CIP

10 9 8 7 6 5 4 3 2

*To the flourishing and freedom of wisdom traditions everywhere, and the furthering of the peoples who speak, write, and live them.*

# Contents

PART III: TSONG-KHA-PA'S TEXT
Translated by Jeffrey Hopkins and Anne Klein,
annotated by Jeffrey Hopkins

# ACKNOWLEDGMENTS

Like most endeavors, this one required a constellation of funds, friendship, scholarly advice, and encouragement. It is a pleasure to thank those who provided any of these elements.

I am grateful to the National Endowment for the Humanities for a summer grant in 1987 to complete the initial translation and transcription of this material, and to the Fulbright Foundation, which, in funding my dissertation research in 1980, also gave me the possibility of beginning this work with Yeshey Tupden in India that same year. I am grateful to the Department of Religious Studies, Stanford University, which, under the chairmanships of Van Harvey and Lee Yearley, countered harsher and more prevalent academic customs by generously granting released time despite my very junior status.

I am delighted to refresh my memory of my earliest introduction to Tsong-kha-pa's text in 1971 through the kindness of Doboom Tulku, then a student at Banaras Sanskrit University and now Director of Tibet House in New Delhi. After working with him for five months, I moved for nine months to Dharamsala, where Lati Rinboche, now abbot emeritus of Shardzay College, Ganden, was kind enough to guide me through the last chapters of Tsong-kha-pa's text; his oral commentary was translated into English by Georges Dreyfus, now a professor at Williams College, and Daniel Coffman, whose current whereabouts I would be most interested to discover.

I warmly thank the late Geshe Wangyal, founder in 1958 of the first Tibetan Buddhist institution in this country, known today today as the Tibetan Buddhist Learning Center, in Washington, New Jersey, for inviting Kensur Yeshey Tupden in 1982. In a similar vein I thank the Center's present Director Joshua Cutler and Assistant Director Diana Marks Cutler, for their work in sustaining vitality there after Geshe-la's death and for inviting Kensur back in 1985 and again 1987. These visits made possible the third and most detailed sweep of the material that follows.

I am grateful for the hospitality I received at Gomang College, Drebung, in Mundgod, India, and especially to Geshe Tupden Gyatso, now at the Center in New Jersey, who supervised the excellent food and other necessities that sustained me through a meteorologically difficult season, and to Geshe Mönlam, now at the Kalmuk Society Temple in Philadelphia, who not only aided in these matters, but also travelled by bicycle over several hot miles to bring me help during a brief but violent sickspell.

I am grateful to Professor Jeffrey Hopkins for introducing me to Tibetan Mādhyamika philosophy in 1970, both through his own teaching and his translation of lectures by Kensur Ngawang Lekden, abbot emeritus of Gyu-mey, the Tantric College of Lower Lhasa. I thank Jeffrey also for his careful review of this manuscript at various stages.

For their helpful comments on the introduction I thank Harvey Aronson, Carl Bielefeldt, José Cabezón, Steven Goodman, Janet Gyatso, Martin Jaffee, Werner Kelber and Donald Lopez. For her impeccable and most gracious assistance in proofreading the manuscript and preparing the glossary I am grateful to L. Annette Jones. B. Jill Carrol provided crucial help in typing the index. Michele Martin, formerly Acquisitions Editor at SUNY, gave me much appreciated encouragement in the early years of this project. I am especially fortunate that Leah Zahler, a scholar in her own right, was able and willing to copy edit in the three languages required.

I want here especially to mention my late colleague at Stanford, Lawrence V. Berman, a well-known specialist in what he liked to call West Asia, more often referred to as the Middle East. He took a special interest in this book, stemming from his awareness of the importance of scholarly oral traditions in Islam and early Judaism. Even on his deathbed he made a point of asking about the work's progress and assuring me of its importance. "I can appreciate its significance better than most," he added, implying that the significance of oral scholarship was yet to be widely recognized. As I continued to work on this, with the inevitable doubts about such an atypical way of producing a book in Buddhist studies, his kind words remained the source of much encouragement.

# Technical Note

Standard Wylie transliteration is used for word-equivalents. For a description of this system, see Wylie, "A Standard System of Tibetan Transcription," *Harvard Journal of Asiatic Studies* 22 (1959), 261-67.

Where appropriate, a phonetic rendering is also offered to aid pronunciation (Lhasa dialect); these phonetics are an adaptation of the system formulated by Jeffrey Hopkins (see his *Meditation on Emptiness*, pp. 19-21).

# PROLOGUE

In the spring of 1968, I enjoyed a college semester abroad at the University of Neuchâtel, Switzerland. While admiring the sun's sparkling effects on that city's famous lake during a morning class on Kierkegaard, I was seized by a powerful desire to go to India. Nothing diminished this inviolable urge, even when I understood it would take some doing and several years to accomplish the journey.

I returned home determined to find a path to India. This led me to graduate school at the University of Wisconsin, where I arrived in the fall of 1969 with a vague expectation that I would find a project to engage me in India and perhaps a companion to travel with. At my first class, I sat on the floor toward the back of a crowded room as the professor asked our names and the program in which we were enrolled. When I called out that I was in Buddhist Studies, two heads in the front row swiveled in my direction. One was that of Jeffrey Hopkins, who subsequently introduced me to Tibetan thought and language and invited to Wisconsin the teacher who helped me formulate a project for my first trip to India. The other was that of my future husband, Harvey Aronson, who, on our first evening out a few months later, brought up the subject of travel to India and whose American Institute of Indian Studies Dissertation Fellowship would unofficially fund my initial Indian sojourn and my first efforts to study the text elaborated in these pages.

The Tibetan monk, scholar, and tantric master Kensur Ngawang Lekden arrived in Wisconsin in the spring of 1970. I attended his classes on Prāsaṅgika philosophy at the University, and also his extracurricular meditations on Sunday afternoons, where he based his instructions on the early chapters of Candrakīrti's *Entrance to the Middle Way (dbu ma la 'jug pa, madhyamakāvatāra).* During my second year at Wisconsin, I lived at "Tibet House," an arrangement created by the late Richard Robinson and Jeffrey Hopkins, whereby a few graduate students could share a house with Rinboche, enabling us to form a more personal relationship with him. Kensur was then seventy years old. Before he walked out of Tibet in 1959 in search of a safe route for the Dalai Lama, he was abbot of the Tantric College of Lower Lhasa, an incumbent to the Throne of Tsong-kha-pa, and famous throughout Tibet for his lectures and learning. As he liked occasionally to point out, his title of "Rinboche" ("Precious One") came to him not through birth, in that he was not seen as an incarnation or *tulku*, but through the learning and other qualities he cultivated in his lifetime.

He was totally unassuming. A man who in Tibet could be approached only with bowed head and lowered eyes, and to whom anyone within speaking distance would immediately prostrate themselves, contentedly put away the cutlery and picked up carpet lint in this old Wisconsin farmhouse. He knew also how to foster a relationship without much reliance on the language I could not yet understand. Once he gestured firmly that we leave the warm house and walk uphill over hard Wisconsin snow to share for a simple moment a view he enjoyed.

I completed my M.A., worked for a few months, and then, with their encouragement, sold the car my parents had given me and bought a ticket to India. Shortly before leaving Wisconsin, I consulted with Kensur Ngawang Lekden. Much as I respected him, I felt comfortable with him by now and confidently asked his advice regarding what I might study in India. To my surprise, he balked. He said he couldn't really say. He had no advice. Taking courage from our friendly relationship, I persisted. Wasn't there something he might suggest? Please? I would really appreciate it. Finally, he paused in his nay-saying, and when the pause ended he was suggesting that I read Candrakīrti's *Entrance to the Middle Way* . Next day, I xeroxed the Tibetan text and Poussin's French translation of Candrakīrti's commentary on it.

I was off! I had an extended visa, very hard to get in those days, thanks to Prof. Robinson, who, some weeks before the terrible and ultimately fatal accident that befell him in the spring of 1970, had written to a colleague at the University of Delhi. That letter paved the way for a university affiliation and the treasured year-long student visa.

Now that I had determined what I would study, the challenge was to find someone who both spoke English and was trained in the philosophical background and oral traditions of the text, regarded by Tibetan scholars as a most difficult work. I was fortunate to make a connection with Doboom Tulku, then a student at Banaras Sanskrit University, living in Sarnath, and interested in improving his English by teaching a foreigner. We worked together for several hours every afternoon, I struggling with the Tibetan, he helping me with it and adding occasional explanations from Tsong-kha-pa's *Illumination of the Thought* which lay open on his desk.

The room we worked in was a large dormitory, shared by several monks. When I entered for our first session, Doboom Tulku introduced me to the older monk who sat near the table where we read. "This is Guru-ji," he said. Guru-ji, with whom I could not speak much because we did not know each other's language, sat on his cushion, reading, reflecting, or affably looking on, during most of my classes over the next five months. When I showed him, in the fall of 1971, a letter saying that Kensur Ngawang Lekden had died, he looked at me with his characteristic clear and quiet gaze and said simply, "A sun has set."

I did not speak with Guru-ji again until 1980, when I returned to India on a Fulbright Dissertation Fellowship. My actual dissertation focused on other texts, but I had never given up my commitment to study fully the *Entrance* and its commentarial tradition. This meant engaging with oral commentary as well as the written word. After my preliminary work on the text with Doboom Rinboche, and now that I could speak Tibetan, reading Tsong-kha-pa's commentary with a scholar who could illuminate it orally was a natural next step. Jeffrey Hopkins had already translated the first five chapters of Tsong-Kha-pa's *Illumination*, which meant I would start with the sixth chapter, itself more than half the entire work, on the perfection of wisdom.

When I arrived in India for my Fulbright year I went south to the new Drebung Monastic University in Karnataka State to pursue my long-cherished goal. Everyone told me that Kensur Yeshey Tupden, a senior scholar and former abbot of Loseling College, Drebung, was the person to study it with. When we met, Kensur Yeshey Tupden turned out to be none other than Guru-ji, whose real name I never learned while he oversaw my studies in Sarnath. Despite a teaching schedule that often kept him sitting on his cushion, lecturing a roomful of students for six or eight hours a day, Kensur met with me daily to read Tsong-kha-pa's text.

Reading a text in the Tibetan monastic environment is never an engagement with words or ideas only. It is also a human encounter and one that for me, in practice and in memory, permeates the text and the intertwined traditions of ritual, conversation, meditation, and analytical debate which the text embraces. Other intangibles also come into play. It has, for example, indelibly impressed me that no matter how dense the philosophical content of our text or the technical minutiae on which our discussions focused (and the reader will soon encounter both in the body of this book), Kensur's physical posture and personal ambience was always relaxed, with no sign of the breathy or obsessive air one often sees associated with rigorous thinking. Similarly, no matter how many hours had passed since he began his teaching, his manner was always the same: kindly, patient, with a quiet enjoyment in what he was doing. The soothing quality of his demeanor was reflected in a soothing coolness of the air, rare in that climate in the summer months, which surrounded us as we worked. There seemed always to be a breeze in his rooms. It was a relief to step inside his door and out of the sun that blazed ovenlike over the several hundred yards I traversed from my quarters to his. I came to experience this blend of personal and atmospheric comfort as a metaphysical refreshment which fused clarity with caring, physical groundedness with abstract thinking, and abstract thinking with human engagement. Indeed, my entire chain of association with this text, from Kensur Ngawang Lekden to Doboom Tulku to Kensur Yeshey Tupden himself, as well as the association of those who made these interactions possible—such as Richard Robinson, Jeffrey Hopkins, Harvey Aronson, my parents, and Geshe Wangyal—links this work, hard abstractions and all, with human kindness and the pleasure and privilege of human interaction.

By the end of my six months' stay at Drebung monastery we had completed most of Tsong-kha-pa's Perfection of Wisdom Chapter. In December 1980, I returned to the States, finished my dissertation, and then took up where I had left off, listening to, translating, and editing the first forty-five or so hours of tape-recorded commentary. Many questions developed from this process. Luckily, I was able to continue our discussions when Kensur was invited to the University of Virginia as Visiting Lecturer in 1982, and during his visits to the Tibetan Buddhist Learning Center as Resident Teacher later that year and again in 1985 and 1986. On all these occasions, I was able to add more detail and context, through approximately twenty more hours of oral discussion on issues that had emerged during our first readings. I completed a penultimate draft of the compiled and edited oral "text" in 1987, thanks to a summer grant from the National Endowment for the Humanities. In between other projects, I have continued to edit and annotate the material until now. In a kind of karmic coda, two weeks before sending this to press, I was able to ask a last round of questions on oral and written commentarial genres in discussion with Kensur's senior student, Gen Yeshey Thabkey (*ye shes thabs mkhas)* of the Tibetan Studies Institute, Sarnath, during his visit to the Tibetan Buddhist Learning Center in July 1993.

Thus, the discussion you find here is actually several layers of commentary gathered over a period of six years. The latter two layers were garnered mostly in response to issues and questions that I pursued. In most cases the questions are blended into the text, but I have let parts of the dialogue remain to give something of the flavor of our interaction. The result is, I believe, the densest presentation of Tibetan oral philosophy yet committed to written English; that is, the proportion of oral comment to printed text is unprecedentedly high. At the same time, this volume represents only the first third of the oral commentary I received from Yeshey Tupden on this text; there are still about eighty hours of tape to be transcribed and edited. The luxury of asking him further questions is not ours, however, since another sun set when Kensur Yeshey Tupden died in New Delhi in the fall of 1988.

I regret very much that I did not manage to finish this volume during my teacher's lifetime, as he would have liked. In 1986, some months before he was discovered to have intestinal cancer, he told me it would be good if I could finish it soon. I'm sorry it took me so long, Kensur, but here it is.

# PREFACE

The *Illumination of the Thought (dbu ma dgongs pa rab gsal)* is one of two major works by Tsong-kha-pa to comment directly upon and incorporate an Indian Mādhyamika text. It is also the last of his five works on Mādhyamika, written in 1418, the year before his death, when he was sixty-one years old.[1] This text, among the last in a lifetime of writing that produced over two hundred separate titles occupying eighteen Tibetan volumes, can be located in other ways as well. On the one hand, it takes its place in a lineage of textual commentary considered to link the turn-of-the-millennium Nāgārjuna and the seventh-century Candrakīrti with the fourteenth-century Tsong-kha-pa. Innumerable other voices, including a wide of range of Buddhist scriptures and the opponents whose views he debated, also surface in this text. The other locus, and the one to which this volume directly addresses itself, is the place of Tsong-kha-pa's work in the living oral philosophical traditions of Tibet. It is in this latter context that Tibetans encounter texts such as this, whether as monastic scholars listening to it from their teachers and debating its fine points with their peers, or more rarely as members of the lay public who gather on special occasions to hear discourses on it from renowned lamas.

Nāgārjuna, the initial systemizer of Indian Mādhyamika, formed the basis for virtually all subsequent Indo-Tibetan Mādhyamika studies with his *Treatise on the Middle Way (dbu ma'i bstan bcos, mūlamadhyamakaśāstra).* Candrakīrti, who studied and then became abbot at the famous Buddhist Monastic University of Nālanda in the post-Gupta period, marked a turning point in Indian Mādhyamika. His *Entrance to the Middle Way*[2] (*dbu ma la 'jug pa, madhyamakāvatāra)* expanded greatly on Nāgārjuna's writing and paved the way for a new vision of Mādhyamika known as Prāsaṅgika-Mādhyamika. Candrakīrti organized his discussion around the ten Bodhisattva grounds (*sa, bhūmi*), and his interweaving of practical guidelines—such as detailed descriptions of the perfections of giving, ethics, and patience—as well as philosophical analysis, struck a deep chord in Tibet, where a whole class of literature outlining the stages of the path *(lam rim)* grew up on this model, with Tsong-kha-pa's own work one of its supreme exemplars.

Nāgārjuna's *Treatise on the Middle Way* lies at the heart of both Tsong-kha-pa's Indian-based texts on Mādhyamika. In the *Ocean of Reasoning, Great*

*Commentary on (Nāgārjuna's) "Treatise on the Middle Way" (rigs pa'i rgya mtsho rtsa shes tik chen),*[3] Tsong-kha-pa comments directly on Nāgārjuna's work and incorporates it into his text in the manner characteristic of Tibetan commentarial tradition. In the *Illumination*, Tsong-kha-pa takes as his focus Candrakīrti's famous commentary on Nāgārjuna's *Treatise,* the *Entrance to the Middle Way* (*dbu ma la 'jug pa, madhyamakāvatāra).*[4] Here Tsong-kha-pa not only incorporates Candrakīrti's verses into his own prose but draws extensively from Candrakīrti's *[Auto]Commentary to "Entrance to the Middle Way" (dbu ma la 'jug pa'i rang 'grel, madhyamakāvatārabhāṣya)* as well. In this way, Tsong-kha-pa's work is elaborately intertextual, not only incorporating and addressing significant portions of Candrakīrti's work but also quoting from or implicitly referring to a wide variety of Indian and Tibetan texts. For the Gelukba (*dge lugs pa*) order, which regards Tsong-kha-pa as its founder and reveres him as teacher of the first Dalai Lama, Tsong-kha-pa's corpus is a high mark in the formidable enterprise of making a coherent presentation of the Mādhyamika perspective, an enterprise that had begun approximately four hundred years after Śākyamuni Buddha's death with the writing of Nāgārjuna's *Treatise on the Middle Way.*

During the reign of the eighth-century religious king Tri-song-day-tsen *(khri srong lde brtsan),* Tibetans seem to have taken an approximately equal interest in Chinese and Indian Buddhist traditions, with ongoing translation projects rendering Sanskrit and Chinese works into Tibetan, and Tibetan into Chinese.[5] Gradually, however, things changed, and much of Tibet came to regard India as the major, if not the sole, source of teachings on Buddhism. This tendency was hastened to a significant extent by the so-called debate, which may actually have been merely an exchange of documents, between the Chinese Ha-shang and the Indian pandit Kamalaśīla. In the aftermath of this exchange, King Tri-song-day-tsen decided against the Chinese position and the monks who promulgated it, who were then "driven from the land."[6] This decision may have been for political as much as doctrinal reasons, but from that time the prestige of Indian Buddhism was virtually unchallenged in Tibet.

The *Illumination* remains to this day an important focus of Mādhyamika studies in the Gelukba monastic universities. It is approximately ten times the length of Candrakīrti's *Entrance* and follows Candrakīrti's structure in setting forth the ten grounds by which a Mahāyāna Bodhisattva progresses to the eleventh ground, Buddhahood. These ten grounds are occasions for completing or enhancing, respectively, the ten perfections of giving, ethics, patience, effort, concentration, wisdom, skillful means, aspirational prayer, power, and exalted wisdom. The first five are accomplished in order to facilitate the sixth, the perfection of wisdom, and the last four are subdivisions of it. The discussion of the sixth ground constitutes more than half the entire text of eleven chapters.

Kensur weaves into his discussion of Tsong-kha-pa's work reflections on numerous difficult and interesting issues. He considers in some detail the interplay between concentration and analysis, comments on the relationship between ordinary study and a Buddha's omniscience, as well as on the way in which emptiness inspires religious life, and in the later chapters devotes particular care to the crucial philosophical nuances that distinguish the major schools' discussions of emptiness.

Nāgārjuna warned that emptiness misunderstood is as dangerous as a snake held by an inexperienced snake-handler. Tsong-kha-pa, as Robert Thurman has noted,[7] responded to this warning by dedicating much of his literary effort to clarifying the meaning of emptiness. In the *Illumination*, his attention to this task is interwoven with his efforts to examine the relationship of that understanding to other aspects of the Bodhisattva's path. Tsong-kha-pa, like Candrakīrti, is said to have had direct meetings and conversations with Mañjuśrī, the embodiment of all Buddhas' wisdom. This wisdom is considered the central inspiration of the *Illumination,* and the hope of attaining wisdom animates its traditional readers to this day. Thus, Tsong-kha-pa's work, like most Buddhist texts, is regarded as a medium by which one contacts the mind of the Buddhas that inspired it, even as one reads about the wisdom and other qualities that enable oneself to experience such a mind, first vicariously and then actually. Such is the larger religious vision in which this work abides. Tsong-kha-pa's text, therefore, in addition to the philosophical reflections it offers, also provides a basis for entering into the world of oral commentary, wherein human speech creates multiple webs and layers of connection. Among the most important of these are the links between teacher and student, which also involve relationships between teacher and text, student and text, as well as between text and personal reflection, and which engage students and teachers with a wide variety of other texts cited in the reading, or quotes that simply come to mind in the course of reflection and conversation.

Let us begin then, by considering the oral genres and other Tibetan scholarly traditions that contextualize Kensur's discussion.

# Introduction

## Oral and Textual Genres: Buddhist Philosophy and the Many Dimensions of Reading in Tibet

> The word in its natural, oral habitat is part of a real, existential present. . . . Spoken words are always modifications of a total situation which is more than verbal. They never occur alone, in a context simply of words.
>
> —Walter Ong, *Orality and Literacy*

> The evidence is substantial that it is only in relatively recent history, and specifically in the modern West, that the book has become a silent object, the written word a silent sign, and the reader a silent spectator.
>
> —William Graham, *Beyond the Written Word*

Kensur Yeshey Tupden's oral scholarship on a major text of his tradition invites us to consider the place of orality in Tibetan scholarly traditions, and especially the relationship between oral genres and the philosophical categories and ritual expressions of Tibetan Buddhism. I see Tibetan oral genres as falling into two broad categories. The first is explanatory, such as the oral philosophy translated here, and its primary purpose is to amplify the meaning of a text. The second is more ritualistic, for it includes vocalizations in which sound rather than meaning is paramount, such as the recitation of mantra or other rhythmic chanting.

Tibetan oral performances vary considerably in how they balance explanatory and ritual power, some utilizing one genre almost to the exclusion of the other, some having both but emphasizing one or the other. In practice, therefore, these two genres are often intertwined.

The variety of Tibetan oral genres, their relationship with written texts, and the meditative use of both oral and written media can all be brought to bear on a single question: what does it mean to *read* a text such as Tsong-kha-pa's in a Tibetan context? Do contemporary Western concepts of *reading*, especially as practiced in Western academies or seminaries, which are modern Western culture's closest analogues to Tibetan monastic universities, suffice to explore the variety of activities encompassed by textual engagement in a traditional Tibetan setting?

We begin with a brief survey of the oral genres associated with textual engagement in Tibet, especially in the Geluk and Nyingma orders, respectively the newest and oldest forms of Tibetan Buddhism. In the second segment of this introduction we consider central philosophical principles of Tsong-kha-pa's text, focusing on how its discussions of subjectivity are compatible with textual practices that include oral, conceptual, meditative, and sensory processes. The final segment of this introduction illustrates how these processes intermingle in a widely used meditation text from Tsong-kha-pa's tradition. I will propose that this intermingling produces a practice that includes but is not fully encompassed by modern concepts of reading, and that "reading" in the Tibetan context intertwines oral and literary orientations in a manner reflective of Tibet's situation as a powerfully oral culture with a highly developed and highly respected circle of literary achievement at its center.

## I. GENRES OF ORALITY

### A. Explanatory Forms

> Speech is seen as in direct contact with meaning: words issue from the speaker as the spontaneous signs of his present thought. Writing, on the other hand, consists of physical marks that are divorced from the thought that may have produced them.
>
> —Jonathan Culler, *On Deconstruction*

1. *Textual Commentary.* Kensur Yeshey Tupden's reflections here are an example of "textual commentary" *(gzhung khrid).*[1] In this genre, a work like Tsong-kha-pa's serves as a basis for lectures by a teacher or, in more intimate circumstances, for a series of discussions between student and teacher.[2] Such oral philosophy replicates, questions, and expands on the text at hand, partly by bringing related texts into the discussion, partly through the teacher's own reflections on the text. The richness of this oral scholarship derives in large measure from its capacity to integrate the major genres of *written* textual commentary. Therefore, we can best consider this and other explanatory oral genres if we pause briefly to take account of the five main

genres of written textual commentary from which they draw inspiration.

A written "word commentary" *(tshig 'grel)*, as its name suggests, comments on every word of a text; for example, Mipham's *Word Commentary on the "Wisdom" Chapter [of Śāntideva's 'Engaging in the Bodhisattva Deeds'] "The Norbu Ketaka" (shes rab le'ui tshig don go sla bar rnam par bshad pa nor bu ke da ka).* A "meaning commentary" *(don 'grel)* does not comment on every word but expands on a text's central issues, for example Panchen Sönam Drakba's *(pan chen bsod nams grags pa) General Meaning of [Maitreya's] 'Ornament for Clear Realization' (phar phyin spyi don).* A "commentary on the difficult points" (*dga' 'grel)* is narrower than either of these, focusing only on the most vexed matters of a text, for example Tsong-kha-pa's *Explaining Eight Difficult Points in [Nāgārjuna's] "Treatise on the Middle Way"* (*rtsa ba shes rab kyi dka' gnas chen po brgyad kyi bshad pa).* "Annotations" *(mchan 'grel)* is a form that provides either interlinear notes within the text itself, or comprises a separate discussion *(zur mchan)* of the text, often moving between a narrow focus on particular issues and a broader perspective on their import. A famous example of this is Ngawang Belden's (*ngag dbang dpal ldan) Annotations for (Jam-yang-shay-ba's) "Great Exposition of Tenets," Freeing the Knots of the Difficult Points, Precious Jewel of Clear Thought* (*grub mtha' chen mo'i mchan 'grel dka' gnad mdud grol blo gsal gces nor).* Well known as these genres are in the Geluk and other orders, they are not strictly defined, and often have overlapping functions; for example the genre known as "analysis" *(mtha' dpyod)* is like a meaning commentary in the form of a debate[3]—for instance, Panchen Sönam Drakba's *Analysis of (Candrakīrti's) "Entrance to the Middle Way" (dbu ma 'jug pa'i mtha' dpyod).* Another instance of overlapping functions is the *Annotations* mentioned above, which is also a commentary on the difficult points of its focal text.

The broadest genres of written commentary are known as "explanatory commentary" *('grel bshad)* and "instructions on the explanation" *(bshad khrid).* Jayānanda's *Explanatory Commentary on the "Entrance," a Clarification of Meaning (dbu ma 'jug pa'i 'grel bshad)* can be given as an example of both types—that is, though the names of these forms differ the actual instances of them (*mtshan gzhi, lakṣya)* are the same.[4] Explanatory commentaries and instructions on the explanation can be quite detailed but maintain an interest in the text as a whole. Both rubrics can also be applied to oral commentary with similar characteristics.

Oral commentarial genres also include *smar khrid*, meaning "rich, detailed" exposition, and *dmar khrid*,[5] translated here as "essential instructions" but literally meaning "naked instruction" or, even more literally, "instructions getting to the red," and glossed as "getting behind the flesh, naked, getting inside the meaning,"[6] suggesting that like a surgeon's knife these instructions open onto the red blood at the heart of a text. The meditation text discussed below, for exmple, calls itself a *dmar khrid* on the path to enlightenment. This oral form, important in Nyingma and Bön as well as Geluk, is considered especially lucid and is often more condensed than the genres just mentioned. An oral genre associated especially with meditation texts is "instructions of experience" *(myong khrid)* which incorporates the meditation of both students and teachers into the discussion. Although the names of these genres are widely used, their boundaries are not clearly fixed, nor are they necessarily used in the context of enacting the oral genre itself. I consider Yeshey Tupden's commentary an explanatory commentary within the larger genre of textual instructions, but Yeshey Tupden himself never used any of these labels in our years of working together. He simply called our activity "looking at the book" *(dpe cha lta).*

What marks Yeshey Tupden's style as "oral"? Certainly, Tibetan text-based oral commentary departs dramatically from the "classical" characteristics of the oral noted by Walter Ong.[7] Contrary to the works of "oral cultures" as Ong describes them, neither Tsong-kha-pa's writing nor Kensur Yeshey Tupden's discussion of it is marked by reliance on mnemonics, formulas, or rhythm.[8] Further, Yeshey Tupden's words do not "carry a load of epithets";[9] they are not redundant (though they *are* copious).[10] The material here does not express its oral nature by being overly empathetic or situational, and it is not experience-near. Kensur's commentary also stands in adamant contradiction to Ong's puzzling claim that "an oral culture has no vehicle so neutral as a list."[11] Nor are the written and oral expressions recorded here "highly polarized" or revelatory of "the agonistic dynamics of oral thought."[12] In short, the scholarly oral material with which we are dealing here is far more "literary" than its rubric of "orality" might suggest. For all their literariness, however, explanatory genres of scholarly oral commentary are intricately intertwined with ritual oral genres, wherein, as Ong would put it, the sacredness and power of sound are crucial elements. Further, though often as technical in vocabulary and overall topic matter as the written text in question, scholarly oral commentary is marked by a more expansive style, a willingness to try out ideas in a more experimental fashion than textual rigor allows.

To the extent that a culture is oral, the immediacy with which it entertains its past[13] dissolves some of the distance between past and present. Ong, following Goody, describes oral cultures as homeostatic in that elements contradictory with or irrelevant to contemporary ideas fall into disuse, leaving little evidence that they ever existed.[14] This is to some extent descriptive of oral philosophical commentary in Tibet, and even of textual commentary, which often had its origins in oral discourse. For example Gelukba scholars today are extraordinarily erudite regarding diverse viewpoints within their own order, but they have largely lost the Indian origins and various Tibetan permutations of many of their tenets. Oral or written, their commentary is highly nuanced philosophically, but the relatively small emphasis on intellectual history is more akin to an oral orientation.

In addition, philosophical analysis is "homeostatic" in that, while texts and their commentators frequently inquire into the logical consistency of various constructs, they do not erode the basic principles on which the argument is based. For example, there is much discussion regarding the compatibility between the doctrines of rebirth and of emptiness (how can the selfless person be reborn?) but I have never encountered a questioning of the fundamental principles of rebirth, or doubt in the possibility of highly developed states of concentration which aid one in ending the process altogether. In a traditional Tibetan context, one hears about these with faith, with a mind that skillfully questions the logical outcome of specific propositions but is unburdened or ungifted by a skepticism that would undermine the basic philosophical principles involved (much as the European Enlightenment did not question the value of reason).[15]

Oral textual commentary is typically just as rigorous syntactically and conceptually as the text on which it is based. In giving it, the teacher draws on material from other texts which supplement, or are supplemented by, his own analyses developed over a lifetime. What chiefly distinguishes it from the explanations contained in texts are its responsiveness to questions asked, its reflection on a wider range of topics than any one text is likely to include, and the insertion of unique examples, often from the lives of teacher or student, to illustrate the teacher's points. In addition the Lama adds to the reading an aura of kindliness, humor, excitement, or severity, depending on his demeanor. This much is common wherever teachers lecture on texts. However, in Tibet, texts such as Tsong-kha-pa's are rarely left to speak for themselves as texts so often are in modern secular contexts. Moreover, the "distance" between texts and persons is formulated differently than in the West. The traditional Lama "represents" the text in several senses: as often as not he has memorized it and may spontaneously recite portions of it or related texts in the course of oral commentary. In addition, as a representative of the Buddha, his teaching, and his community of followers, the Lama embodies the text in concrete ways. He can in a very real sense be considered a "living text," and he teaches the texts he lives in order to produce more living approximations of the traditional values and forms of knowledge they elaborate. At the same time, the Lama whom the student regards as embodying the text also stands outside it, always taking a position of reverence toward it as he conveys to the student its meaning, whose profundity he may claim only partially to comprehend, much less embody.

In the Gelukba monastic setting, oral philosophical commentary is closely connected with another form of oral training, the daily and hours-long debates which foster an intellectual and social context for developing a community of knowledge.[16] Whereas oral commentary transmits knowledge from one generation to another, debate solidifies learning among members of the same generation.[17] Debate aims primarily to clarify the meaning of terms and textual passages; yet even this most technical and information-based form of speech typically begins with a ritual incantation of the syllable "*dhīḥ,*" which every Tibetan knows to be the "seed syllable" of Mañjuśrī, the Bodhisattva of wisdom. Indeed, ritual and explanatory forms are rarely wholly separate.

In addition, focusing one's attention on the spoken word of the teacher typically takes place in an arena suffused with sound. In a monastery, for example, the air is periodically filled with the reverberations of deep chanting, accompanied by drums and bells, or the incessant roar of verbiage from the debating courtyard. This barrage of sound lends richness to a setting otherwise relatively free of gifts for the senses (with the exception of elaborately adorned meditation halls which, however, one must enter to be affected by). The sound, by contrast, is everywhere. As I listened to the commentary of Kensur Yeshey Tupden on this work by Tsong-kha-pa, for example, our attention to the textual words and my intent focus on his spoken commentary were contextualized by rhythmic and melodic emanations from other quarters of the monastery, and by the saturation with vocalized sound that one lives in day by day. It may even be that such a holistic experience with sound provides psychic nourishment which facilitates the long hours of textual study for which Tibetan monastic life is justly famous.

My point is that nonconceptual and ritual aspects of orality mingle in all areas of literary activity. Yet, Geluk understands spoken language to affect the mind quite differently than mere sound. Sound as such is an object of direct sense perception, whereas meaningful speech must be processed by conceptual thought. That is, words and thoughts do not themselves directly get at actual objects, but produce meaning through the medium of an image *(don spyi, arthasāmānya)* which serves to exclude all objects but the one or ones in question.[18] Oral explication also operates by way of such exclusion. Sound alone, however, including the sound of speech, is full of itself, with no need to proffer anything other than what it is.[19] In practice these epistemological processes[20] are often combined, just as ritual and explanatory sound are inevitably intertwined. Thus, in sitting for oral commentary, or in chanting the verses of a ritual, one engages in conceptual images and ideas, and also bathes in the positive manifestation of the sound that conveys these.

2. *Advisory Speech.* Oral textual instruction (*gzhung khrid)*[21] can be considered a form of advisory speech *(gdams ngag, upadeśa/ avadāna ādeśa),* though advisory speech also includes discussions not directly linked with textual explication.[22] Advisory speech is associated with a wide range of philosophical, ritual, and meditational texts, and includes extemporaneous reflection

independent of specific texts. A defining characteristic of advisory speech is its simple effectiveness; it is described as "an especially quick and facile way of eliminating of doubt."[23] This facility does not lie with the informative value of speech alone. As if underscoring this point, the great fourteenth-century Nyingma scholar and meditation master Longchenba, contemporaneous with Tsong-kha-pa, notes that advisory speech has a particular connection with kindness.[24] A person without such kindly intention cannot convey the same potent effect, even using the very same words.

In its most specialized sense, "advisory speech" is said to be something which the Lama holds as secret, revealing it only to a heart-disciple who, on hearing it, can develop an understanding not previously accessed. This, too, occurs because of its special ability to cut off doubt.[25] How much this "facile" elimination of doubt owes to the clarity of explanation and how much to timing and the charismatic presence of a teacher is an open question. In any case, the economy associated with such treasured precepts is the kind of economy usually associated with something alive, whose limited energy needs to be preserved for just the right occasion. "If a teacher has a dearly held precept, giving this precious thing to a student who then wastes it would be sad. When one finds a special student with faith, confidence, and understanding, then the teacher gives all these to that student."[26]

An important sub-genre of advisory speech is known as direct speech (*man ngag*). Gen Yeshey Thabkey glossed this genre as something easy to understand and capable of taking you through to complete understanding of a particular topic. He emphasized also that such direct speech must not be idiosyncratic to a particular Lama but must accord with the Kangyur, Tangyur, and the great books. A Nyingma text describes it like this:

> Its hardship is small, its import great,
> Its approaches are multiple.
> Easy to enact, difficult to encompass,
> This is direct speech.[27]

"Focus your mind on tantra, scripture, and direct speech," writes Longchenba, in which case "Buddhahood will be imminent."[28] In his *Treasure of Precious Direct Speech (man ngag rin po che'i mdzod)*, Longchenpa also lists "listening to the kindly *(brdzal)* direct speech of a Lama" first in a list of six helpful activities.[29]

Direct speech, like advisory speech, often involves something which is usually held secret—something, in short, that is usually *not* spoken. Whatever its informative value, it has other sources of power as well. This is indicated by two different etymologies of "direct speech" *(man ngag)*. In one, the first syllable, *man*, is said to signify "mantra"; the second syllable, *ngag*, signifies "speech," including instructional speech. According to another explanation, the first syllable of the term, *man*, is related to the Tibetan word *sman,* spelled differently but pronounced the same, meaning "medicine."[30] In both etymologies, a potency beyond conceptual import is indicated. As with anything potent, words or medicine, the effect can be good or bad. Thus one can speak of helpful direct speech *(phan ba'i man ngag)* as well as harmful or evil speech *(ngan ngag).*[31]

Whereas in the modern West the term "speech" refers almost exclusively to informative or conceptually communicative vocalization, the Tibetan term here translated as "speech" (*ngag*, *vāca*) is defined (in the oral tradition, at least) in such a way as to account for both expository and ritual significance: "Because the Lama's speech is the supreme eliminator of doubt, it is called *ngag*."[32] In short, the ritual power of words does not preclude, but also does not depend on, their explanatory capacity.

## B. Ritual Oral Genres

> Sound is a special sensory key to interiority . . . [that] . . . has to do with interiors as such, which means with interiors as manifesting themselves, not as withdrawn into themselves, for true interiority is communicative.
>
> —Walter Ong, *The Presence of the Word*

Advisory speech is a form that incorporates both explanatory and ritual aspects. There are also oral genres which do not "explain" at all. These genres are far less concerned with *what* the mind knows than with the *kind* of mind in question. For example, there are forms of oral expression primarily concerned with producing concentration rather than understanding. Such expressions tend to find their greatest usage outside of the Geluk and sutric context of the Tsong-kha-pa's text. They are significant aspects of tantric practice, and prominent also in Nyingma practices.

1. *Scriptural Transmission.* Most textual encounters begin with an oral practice known as *lung*. This term translates the Sanskrit word *āgama*, literally meaning "scripture," and *lung* is in fact the scriptural text itself in oral presentation, read aloud by a teacher to a student in order to create a connection with the entire vocal, scholarly, and ritual lineage of the text.[33] Only after receiving *lung* is one ready to hear oral commentary on the text, to study and debate its meaning and, if one chooses, to incorporate it into a meditation practice. It is clear from the importance placed on this practice that, written or oral, a text is not words or meaning alone. Texts also include sound, power, and blessings. Unlike the purely visual text, which is distinctly "out there," causing the reader to shift continuously between the external physical text and his or her own

internal responses, the sonorous text occupies inner and outer space simultaneously, but not necessarily conceptual space. During the transmission of *lung*, the text is read so rapidly that conceptual grasp of it is minimal; this is a time when the spoken word must be heard, not necessarily understood. Complete *lung* is achieved when recited by a teacher out of compassion for a student who has faith in that teacher and focuses full attention on the reading. Merely hearing the words, or mere unfeeling articulation of them, does not fully accomplish the giving of *lung*, although there may still be some effect.[34]

In a looser interpretation it is said that as long as one has a "consciousness which apprehends sound" (*sgra 'dzin gyi shes pa)* one has received *lung*. This is because blessings are received through the sound itself, even though one has not understood the words.[35] To have the blessings means one has some power or capacity *(nus pa, śakti)* to engage the text profitably. Blessings and power are materially inseparable, both are united with sound.[36]

I did not receive a formal *lung* on Tsong-kha-pa's text, although Kensur Yeshey Tupden did read each passage aloud before discussing it, and according to his senior student Gen Yeshey Thabkey, this too constitutes *lung*, as long as all the words are included. *Lung*, it is said, can be transmitted by anyone who has received it properly. Does this mean that I could read aloud Tsong-kha-pa's work and bestow *lung* on someone else? Gen Yeshey Thabkey and his student, Losang Tsayden laughed, perhaps uncomfortably, when I asked this. They may have laughed because this is not something a Tibetan layperson, especially a laywoman, would even think about in relation to himself or herself. Nevertheless, they responded that if I should do this it would indeed be *lung*, and that it would qualify even if I myself had not understood what I had heard, because the power *(nus pa, śakti*) and latencies *(bag chags, vāsanā),* aids to future practice carried by the sound, would still be imparted. However, since blessings in general depend both on the faith of the recipient and the good qualities of the giver, the issue of an ordinary layperson giving *lung* would not arise in Tibetan culture; there would always be qualified lamas whose bestowal would be more effective.

At the same time, *lung* is not considered equally important for all texts, but is most significant for works directly related to practice, such as meditation texts or specific rituals. Denma Lochö Rinboche, who gave formal *lung* prior to his *khrid* (instruction) on the meditation text discussed below, had himself received *lung* on the *Stages of the Path (lam rim)* texts by Tsong-kha-pa, but not, as some Tibetans do, on the entire Canon of Buddha's word and its commentaries. He said,

> I have not received *lung* on the Kangyur and Tangyur. I did not place tremendous importance on that. . . . I have had it many many times on *The Path of Well-Being (bde lam)* and also on the books of Tsong-kha-pa

> and his spiritual sons. But not the Kangyur and Tangyur. I have faith that there is *lung* and that it is good to receive it. Yet some hold it as extremely important in ways that I do not.[37]

2. *Chanting.* There are forms of orality still less grounded in informative values than textual instruction, scriptural transmission, and advisory or direct speech. "Chanting" is a term I use to emphasize the focus on the musicality and rhythm of vocalized texts, as well the repetitive chanting of mantras during ritual performance by a group or individual, or during a session of meditation.[38]

Insofar as Buddhist philosophy is directed toward the nonconceptual and not only toward producing conceptual pyrotechnics (though these are present in abundance), the *tone* of philosophical expression is very important. The importance of recitation is a reminder that textual engagement does not always focus solely on a written text. In Tibet, as in many traditional cultures, the most essential religious, philosophical, or meditational texts are recited aloud from memory. Candrakīrti's *Entrance*, for example, would be memorized by monks in childhood or adolescence; when they come upon quotations years later embedded in a commentarial text, Candrakīrti's words ring in their ear like the familiar lyrics of a song whose meaning is only now coming clear. Lugubrious as these texts often sound in English, most of them are poetry in Sanskrit and Tibetan. They can be recited rhythmically, making complex ideas music to the ears of those who hear and repeat them habitually. Memorized texts are said literally to be "held in mind" (*blo la 'dzin*). Such texts are also, in an important sense, held in the body. Chanting vibrates one's vocal cords and even some bones.[39] It can also take over one's inner "voice" and thereby mute or transform the inner chatter that interferes with the concentration from which all meditative endeavor must flow.[40]

In meditative rituals the chanting of liturgical texts or mantras has physical and mental effects which in some contexts (especially Nyingma) override their conceptual impact. Mantras in particular are important not simply for what they mean, but for how they sound and for how that sound resonates with the chanter's mind and body. It is well known that human organisms are profoundly affected by sound. If one sings along with or even just listens to Mick Jagger bellowing "I Can't Get No Satisfaction," the effect is quite different than if one participates in a rendition of "Amazing Grace." The difference is real: palpable and physiological. The Tibetan way of expressing something similar to this is to observe that because the body's inner currents *(rlung, prāṇa/vāyu),* affect the mind, one way to alter or subdue the mind is through breathing-and-chanting practices that, in conjunction with the proper posture, help smooth out the movement of these currents by straightening the channels through which they move.

Meditation texts frequently alternate between descriptions of qualities cultivated, prayers to achieve those qualities, and depictions of visualizations done in tandem with the recitation. All are chanted during the meditation session itself, and during such recitation the words of the text may seem to pass before the mind's eye, making it simultaneously an oral and a visual text.

Tantric meditation involves an intense visual, visceral, and spiritual identification with a particular deity. That deity is understood to body forth from a particular sound—namely, the mantra which one recites as part of the practice. There are three styles of practice by which one enhances oral and visual emulation of the deity: (1) the "great emulation," so called because it is done in a group *(bsgrub chen)*; (2) recitation done alone (*dpa' bo gcig)*, and (3) alternating between solitary and group practice (*bsgrub sogs*).[41]

Chanting is also done as a practice on its own, with concentration focused through the medium of sound itself. A particularly important form of recitation in Nyingma, and not present in Geluk,[42] is known as *dzab dbyangs*. This word is the Tibetanized form of the Sanskrit *jāpa,* meaning "recitation of mantra." Here it is considered crucial to be precise about the rhythm, the melody, and, perhaps most of all, the junctures at which one takes breath.[43] Such vocalization[44] is significant for its association with breath and other, subtler forms of physical energy (*rlung).* In this sense it mediates between mind and body and participates in both. The use of breath and *rlung* is primarily significant in tantric practice and is also an important principle in oral recitation and mantric chant.

Many practices which emphasize sound are done in groups. Chanting with others makes sound a palpable element in ways not replicable in solitude. It is no wonder that, worldwide, song or other forms of vocalization are important expressions of community. Joining one's voice with others, one is both an individual and part of a unity, and yet not quite either.

There are also sound practices done in solitude, often outdoors, which yield a different kind of experience. One's own sound emanates outward into space. As it fades away, the practitioner, still imaginatively extended over that space, is left in pithy silence. This silence is not an utter absence of sound but the evanescent vanishing of the sound on which one's energy and attention had been focused. One rests the mind in this vivid and particular absence, a sensory analogue to settling the mind on emptiness, a practice which lies at the heart of both sutra and tantra. Emptiness, too, is a specific absence; it is not the lack of things in general but of a characteristic which Tsong-kha-pa, following other Mādhyamika sources, explains as a lack of inherent existence.

Chanting practices are premised on the efficacy of vocalized sound rather than on explication, on vocality over orality. Nevertheless, these are text-based practices, and instruction on them is received through a combination of scriptural transmission, or *lung,* and initiation (*dbang, abhiṣeka)*, which is bestowed in part through speech. Such speech includes the recitation of mantras and prayers, sometimes accompanied by drums, bells, or symbols, as well as textual instruction. In addition, initiatory speech includes both advisory and direct speech. Again, no oral genre in Tibet is completely independent of the others.

## II. PHILOSOPHICAL ASSUMPTIONS ABOUT SUBJECTIVITY

The structure of Tsong-kha-pa's *Illumination* is that of the *lam rim* or Stages of the Path genre that he helped make famous. Taking its inspiration in part from Candrakīrti's *Entrance, lam rim* literature attempts to organize numerous topics and styles of Buddhist practice into a meaningful trajectory, a step-by-step movement from the ordinary to the enlightened state. However, unlike his own and other *lam rim* texts, this one begins with the Bodhisattva's initial direct realization of emptiness.

The first direct cognition of emptiness is one of the great transitions of the Buddhist path. It marks the end of one's career as an "ordinary" person and the beginning of one's life as a Superior or āryan practitioner. It marks also the move from a conventional to an ultimate Bodhisattva intention. Prior to this moment one has sought enlightenment for the sake of all but has not yet fully understood the emptiness that makes this possible. This initial direct cognition of emptiness is the first of the ten Bodhisattva grounds.

Like the first ground, all the subsequent Bodhisattva grounds are characterized by a direct cognition of emptiness. This much is clear. But since each "ground" of understanding is, like the first, a nonconceptual and complete realization of emptiness, and since therefore there is nothing "more" to be understood about emptiness, what is it exactly that distinguishes the grounds from one another? What "improves" along the path to enlightenment? Since the Bodhisattva has already directly cognized emptiness on the first ground, why is the sixth ground known as an "enhanced" perfection of wisdom? Herein lies a mystery that this book seeks to explore.

Method and wisdom are often said to be the two wings of the bird flying to Buddhahood; in the Mahāyāna the special method is compassion, and the wisdom is the understanding of emptiness. Despite the fame of these two "wings," it is neither compassion nor an understanding of emptiness that most markedly increases over the Bodhisattva grounds. What changes most dramatically is not one's understanding as such but rather *the kind of mind* that understands. As Kensur puts it, "The difference between grounds is not made in terms of their realization of emptiness; it is measured in terms of the true or final cessation of obstructions that accompanies each." With the initial insight into emptiness come increased magical powers and also the virtuous power to overcome the coarser misconceptions known as the artificial conceptions of inherent existence *(bden 'dzin kun btags, *satyagrāhaparikalpita),* but the more subtle and harder-to-eradicate misunderstandings are not be discarded until the higher stages. A central issue that emerges early in the wisdom chapter of Tsong-kha-pa's *Illumination* is the way that concentration, or how the mind *is*, affects insight, or what the mind *knows.*[45]

The role of concentration and mental agility on the Bodhisattva path have often been overlooked in academic discussions of Buddhist path structure and categories of mind. Kensur Yeshey Tupden's expansion on Tsong-kha-pa's discussion of a type of concentration known as the uncommon absorption of cessation provides an important counter to that neglect. This uncommon absorption of cessation (*thun mong ma yin pa'i 'gog snyoms, *asādāranirodhasamāpatti)* is what primarily distinguishes the initial direct cognition of emptiness from the sixth ground's "enhanced" perfection of wisdom.

The detailed enumerations of subtly distinguished types of minds often seem far more elaborate than personal experience can support. Few of the descriptions are experience-near. In not finding these doctrines descriptive of their own experience, Western readers are not so very different from traditional Tibetan students of this text. The architecture of the book is, therefore, primarily intellectual; it speaks to that which many monastics will learn, but few will do. Unlike in his *lam rim* texts, Tsong-kha-pa here gives no meditation instructions; this work does not touch on Tsong-kha-pa's own meditation practice. At the same time, the significance of what the text has to say can only, by the lights of this tradition, be truly understood through considerable meditation practice.

In some ways the message and the medium of Tsong-kha-pa's work, like those of many scholastic texts of the Buddhist tradition, are at odds. The *Illumination* is a highly elaborate textual scheme dedicated to describing nonconceptual insights. The elements that mediate this dissonance are fourfold: (1) the teacher who brings the words to life by way of his respect for them and his own personal example; (2) the actual contents of his explanation; (3) the traditional ritual, meditative, and social context of which the text is an integral part, and finally, (4) the emphasis on forms of subjectivity which are nonconceptual, intense, and stable. Oral expression is crucially related to all of these.

## A. Kensur Yeshey Tupden's Commentary

One of the major soteriological concerns throughout Buddhist history has been to distinguish mere calming or concentration from actual special insight (*lhag mthong, vipaśyanā).* Kensur's discussion, as well as Tsong-kha-pa's text, addresses this issue by considering the matter of concentration in some detail, distinguishing the special forms of absorption associated with the sixth ground from other forms of mental quiescence, and describing the insight associated with this ground and the way in which concentration facilitates its development. The subjective states of calming (*zhi gnas, śamatha*), concentration (*bsam gtan, dhyāna*), and cessation (*'gog pa, nirodha)* are central to the Geluk path, as they are to much of Buddhist soteriology. At the same time, if we wish eventually to relate Buddhist categories of mental functioning to Western ones, calming and concentration are among the most difficult to place.[46] Here we consider the status of concentration as a philosophical category of analysis, and in this light note its specific significance in Tsong-kha-pa's work and related texts.

Kensur's discussion, like Tsong-kha-pa's, is loosely organized around three reasons for calling the sixth ground "the Manifest." At this ground (1) the illusory nature of phenomena becomes manifest because (2) the Bodhisattva has on the fifth ground manifested a nonconceptual state known as an enhanced perfection of concentration with which he observed the four noble truths. Because of this fifth ground concentration, (3) the Bodhisattva is drawing near to being capable of manifesting a Buddha's perfect qualities. All these qualities emerge because of the strengthened state of concentration on the fifth ground, which makes possible the uncommon absorption of cessation's particular experience of emptiness and dependent arising on the sixth ground. This movement between the fifth and sixth grounds repeats the pattern of a calm mind providing a basis for insight that occurred in relation to the path of preparation (*sbyor lam, prayogamārga*), when a minimum level of concentration known as calm abiding (*zhi gnas, śamatha*) was required for the initial direct cognition of emptiness on the path of seeing (*darśanamārga*).

1. *Mental Calm and the First Bodhisattva Ground.* The most obvious places to explore the significance of concentration on the Bodhisattva path are the first and sixth Bodhisattva grounds, since at these junctures the importance of concentration for special insight is foregrounded in traditional Indo-Tibetan expositions. Candrakīrti's *Entrance,* Tsong-kha-pa's discussion of it in *Illumination,* and Kensur's oral commentary on this provide particularly detailed accounts of the issues involved.[47]

In the early and intermediate stages of practice, one stabilizes concentration through observing a mental object. Among Gelukbas, unlike in some other Tibetan and non-Tibetan Buddhist traditions, calm abiding is not cultivated through focusing the eyes on an external object but by setting the mind on an internal object such as one's own breath, or on a visualized object such as the image of a Buddha. In visualizing a Buddha, one imagines the Buddha in front of oneself. This mimics but does not replicate the subject-object distancing of sight, since a visualized object is neither quite external nor quite internal; in this sense concentration moves outside the structure of the visual. Once calm abiding is achieved, the sense that subject and object are separate is relaxed to a significant degree; the meditator feels as if he or she could see through objects—a visual experience that has some of the unobstructed nature of sound. Calm abiding is the minimum level of concentration needed to proceed to the nondualistic and direct experience of emptiness known as the path of seeing when subject and object appear united, "like fresh water poured into fresh water."

In Gelukba Prāsaṅgika, an understanding of emptiness is said to result from analysis. For this reason an explanation of the compatibility between analysis and calming is considered critical. In order to make the case that conceptual analysis leads to nonconceptual experience, it becomes necessary to soften the boundaries around the functions of calming and insight. It is said that when one is properly trained, analysis *itself* induces a state of calm abiding on emptiness. This profound compatibility between calming and insight culminates in the apparent unification of these two into a single consciousness, whether as a union of calm abiding and special insight on the first ground or as the direct cognition of emptiness by the uncommon absorption of cessation (*thun mong ma yin pa'i 'gog snyoms, *asādāranirodhasamāpatti)* on the sixth ground.

The time of the initial direct cognition of emptiness, as we have noted, is called "the path of seeing"; yet this is the moment when the most salient characteristics of ordinary sight are superseded. The name "path of seeing" is almost ironic insofar as its dynamics are more suggestive of the dynamics of hearing. Direct cognition of emptiness is not, like sight in general, a sequentially ordered scanning in which objects are viewed by turn or in which subject and object are mutually distanced. All emptinesses are perceived at once, simultaneously. Emptiness suffuses experience in the all-around seamless manner of sound. Thus, the Gelukba account of the progressive stages leading to Buddhahood invokes two mental gestures which must be reconciled: opening consciousness to encompass the space-like, unconditioned emptiness, and withdrawing the mind from sense objects through cultivating various stages of concentration *(bsam gtan, dhyāna)* and absorption *(snyoms 'jug, samāpatti).* However, even when "united," calm abiding and special insight remain functionally distinct; they are not one entity *(ngo bo gcig, ekadravya/*ekarūpatā).* Wisdom does not *become* calming, and calming does not *become* insight. Panchen Sönam Drakba himself points out that those who say these become one at the time of attaining a Bodhisattva ground are mistaken. The two mental gestures of withdrawing the mind in one sense and expanding its horizons in another are entwined, not blended. Moreover, at this advanced stage of practice, *both* the calming and wisdom functions can be characterized by both gestures. Calming takes one into oneself, and yet developed concentration leaves one with a sense of mental expansiveness. Wisdom, as the direct cognition of emptiness on the Bodhisattva grounds, withdraws the mind from conventional appearances and at the same time engages one in knowledge of the nature of all phenomena everywhere. Moreover, the oral tradition offers a delicate *caveat* here: whereas, in earlier stages of the path, analytical and stabilizing meditation are different, they later become as if one entity insofar as they neither manifest different functions nor require different forms of effort.[48]

On the first Bodhisattva ground, which is also the path of seeing, the wisdom realizing emptiness *(stong nyid rtogs pa'i shes rab)* is united with calm abiding, and no conceptual or other perceptual errors are operative. It might seem that any tensions between concentration and insight are resolved by this point on the path. To a certain extent they are. However, the nature of their relationship again becomes an issue on the sixth ground, where a further integration of calming and wisdom is required. At this time one gains an enhanced perfection of wisdom that makes possible a new type of mental focus known as the uncommon absorption of cessation, a category unique to Prāsaṅgika, and probably to Gelukba Prāsaṅgika. Whereas on the first ground one newly interfused the state of calm abiding with a direct experience of emptiness, on the sixth ground one newly unifies the uncommon absorption of cessation with that experience. The movement from the fifth to the sixth Bodhisattva ground is said to occur in a single extensive meditation session which can last as long as seven days. During this time, one attains the uncommon absorption of cessation through the power of this enhanced concentration.

The sixth-ground Bodhisattva's perfection of wisdom is an enhanced form of the nonconceptual, nondualistic experience of emptiness of the first ground. Candrakīrti uses the term "cessation" to express the attainment unique to the sixth ground; Tsong-kha-pa glosses this as an "uncommon absorption of cessation," a term he uses only at the beginning of his three-hundred-page discussion of the sixth ground.[49] Virtually the only significant sources for the topic of an uncommon absorption of cessation come from monastic texts centered on Candrakīrti's *Entrance* or Tsong-kha-pa's discussion of it.[50] Tibetan works on the grounds and paths *(sa lam, *bhūmimārga),* tenets *(grub mtha', siddhānta)* and in the *Collected Topics* genre *(bsdus grva)* do not discuss this category. The uncommon absorption of cessation, a rubric that apparently gained attention after Tsong-kha-pa's day,[51] is thus a category to which only a limited, albeit important, group of texts calls attention. Kensur Yeshey Tupden's discussion of it here is probably the most elaborate in print in any language.

Tsong-kha-pa explains that on the fifth ground the Bodhisattva's concentration, no longer impeded by distraction and other faults incompatible with the perfection of concentration, becomes surpassing. This surpassing concentration enhances the wisdom which facilitates the uncommon absorption of cessation. The category of the uncommon absorption of cessation appears to exist at least in part as a way of exploring how wisdom simultaneously (1) unites with its object, and (2) knows that object, as well as (3) what kind of "improvement" occurs in between the first and sixth grounds. It is not a question of having a better conceptual understanding of emptiness, because one has already experienced it directly. The developmental trajectory here occurs without the benefit of conceptualized "differences"—that is, without the apohic, exclusionary process by which terms and thoughts operate. There is no indication that the referent conceptual image of emptiness "improves." Improvement is nonetheless possible because concentration improves or develops irrespective of thought-imagery.

The "surpassing, fully developed perfection of wisdom" begins at the sixth ground. At this time, one "sees emptiness to be like a reflection in the sense that it exists but is not truly established."[52] It is a dependent arising in the sense that the emptiness of a table, for example, depends on the emptinesses of the parts of the table. However, emptiness itself is "unconditioned" because it does not change from moment to moment in dependence on causal conditions, and thus does not exhibit the most telling symptoms of conditionality: production, aging, and destruction. This means that, although it does not depend on causality, emptiness is not independent in general, nor is the "inexpressible" mind that cognizes it. Inexpressibility here has to do with a new relationship between subject and object, and between certain of the subject's cognizing functions, such as the full complementarity between concentration and insight. It has also to do with the ascendance of concentration, a mental state even less moored in language than the "inexpressible" wisdom it makes possible.

The uncommon absorption of cessation on the sixth and higher grounds has as its mental basis the highest form of concentration within cyclic existence. Thus, the calming side of the insight/calming equation is considerably more developed than at the initial union of calm abiding and direct experience of emptiness on the first ground.[53] Both calm abiding and absorption have emptiness as their object, but because their relationship to that object is different from that of most other subject-object relationships, the object is important as a support (*rten, āśraya*) rather than as an observed object (*dmigs pa, ālambana).* Thus, unlike in ordinary sensory and mental perception, the object is not a *cause* of subjective experience during the higher stages of concentration; rather the subjective process unfolds through a power of its own. The wisdom consciousness can exist only when conjoined with such a calmed mind.

Progress from the sixth through the tenth grounds is very much a function of the mind's increased facility due to its further independence from thought-images. The increased mental agility which characterizes the seventh ground comes about through a cultivated dexterity that now allows one to move in and out of direct realization of emptiness very quickly—not because one has grasped some clearer understanding of emptiness but because one has acquired a more direct route to the nonconceptual mind itself. One no longer needs to be prompted by a concept or image of emptiness on the way to a direct cognition of it—that is, for the first time one no longer needs to enter direct cognition of emptiness by way of a mental image of emptiness. Thus one is able to enter into and arise from meditative equipoise *(mnyam bzhag, samāhita)* on emptiness far more swiftly than on the sixth ground. This skillful means *(thabs, upāya)*, the special perfection of the seventh ground, is a subcategory of the sixth ground's perfection of wisdom. It consists of "a wisdom of meditative equipoise induced by the surpassing method and wisdom which are of the entity of the uncommon absorption of cessation."[54] Thus, over and over again on the path described by Tsong-kha-pa and his commentators, the power of what we might call a language-associated faculty—namely, insight—is increased through the development of a faculty not associated with language at all—namely, mental calming and concentration. To put this another way, calming, though it forms part of a cognitive process, is not itself altered by "ideas." The factors that make a difference in relation to concentration—one's own training, immediate surroundings, physical well-being, and so forth—are not necessarily conceptual. The deeper levels of mental stabilization affect how the mind relates to its own understanding, rather than what it understands. Let us look at this claim more closely.

2. *Mental Calm and the Sixth Bodhisattva Ground.* A crucial epistemological issue here is the extent to which consciousness can become distanced from usual modes of sensory, conceptual, and other culturally or conceptually specific input and still function as consciousness in some meaningful way. In the *Entrance*, Candrakīrti writes (VI.1d): "By dwelling in wisdom [the Bodhisattva] attains[55] cessation." His own commentary elaborates:

> Because on the fifth ground the Bodhisattva attained the completely pure perfection of concentration, on the sixth ground the Bodhisattva dwells in a mind of meditative equipoise and sees the nature of the profound dependent arising; due to the thoroughly pure perfection of wisdom, the Bodhisattva achieves a cessation that did not occur previously.[56]

Tsong-kha-pa develops this briefly:

> Because [the Bodhisattva] attained the thoroughly pure perfection of concentration on the fifth ground, on the sixth ground, the Approaching or Manifest, s/he dwells in a fully developed mind of meditative equipoise. With this as a basis s/he abides on the sixth Bodhisattva ground seeing the profound suchness which is mere conditionality, or dependent arising, whereby s/he attains cessation. Prior to this, on the fifth ground and below, s/he did not attain cessation because of lacking the surpassing form of the

> fully developed perfection of wisdom. One cannot attain cessation merely through the five fully developed perfections of giving and so forth.[57]

Immediately following this statement, Tsong-kha-pa identifies the cessation in question as "an uncommon absorption of cessation."[58] Commenting on this passage two centuries later, Jam-yang-shay-ba (*'jam dbyangs bzhad pa*) points to Candrakīrti's emphasis on the sequential relationship between the sixth-ground attainment of wisdom and this form of cessation:

> The Bodhisattva, seeing the suchness of profound dependent arising, attains [the uncommon absorption of] cessation through the thoroughly pure perfection of wisdom, not before, because s/he did not have the surpassing form of the perfection of wisdom.[59]

As a type of meditative equipoise, the uncommon absorption of cessation is a form of the calming-and-focusing function; it is also, by definition, a wisdom consciousness.[60] For example, Panchen Sönam Drakba defines an uncommon absorption of cessation as "a wisdom of meditative equipoise that is directly poised equally on reality, [and] induced by the surpassing practice of the perfection of wisdom."[61] One gets the impression of two mounting spirals of mental functioning, each supporting and furthering the other. This internally stimulated energy reveals and expresses something about the nature of consciousness, just as a bird that flies at the sight of a cat reveals and expresses something about the nature of bird. It is an implicit principle in the literature on calming and concentration that consciousness does not have to be affected *by* an object in order to express its own characteristics of clarity and knowing.

Kensur is careful to distinguish between common and uncommon absorptions of cessation. He observes that coarse mental exertion ceases from the time of first Bodhisattva ground, when it yields to an experience of the *common* absorption of cessation. This cessation however does not realize emptiness of inherent existence, whereas the uncommon absorption of cessation does. The uncommon absorption of cessation, first occurring on the sixth ground, is a highly developed form of meditative equipoise. Only Prāsaṅgika asserts it, because only Prāsaṅgika discusses the lack of inherent existence which is said to be the object of this cessation. Although Bodhisattvas do not have an uncommon absorption of cessation until the sixth ground, they do have meditative equipoise. A true cessation of the artificial conception of inherent existence is achieved on the first ground; an uncommon absorption of cessation, on the sixth. This is one of the critical differences between the two types of wisdom. Again, this has more to do with the type of mind involved than with what that mind knows.

The uncommon absorption of cessation associated with the sixth ground's "surpassing wisdom" is to be distinguished from the cessation of discrimination and feeling *('dus shes dang tshor ba 'gog pa, saṃjñāvedyitanirodha)* described by Buddhaghosa in the *Path of Purification (Visuddhimagga)*, wherein nothing mental endures. Nor is this the cessation described by Vasubandhu in the *Treasury of Knowledge* (*chos mngon pa'i mdzod, abhidharmakośa)* as neither mind nor form. In contrast to both of these, the absorption of cessation *is a consciousness.*[62] It is, moreover, a consciousness no longer governed by the linear, and subject-distancing, characteristics of the visual senses.

The uncommon absorption of cessation is a rubric that further interfuses the functions of calm abiding and special insight which first combined on the path of preparation *(sbyor lam, prayogamārga)*. To call the union of these "special insight" (*lhag mthong, vipaśyanā)* is to assimilate the function of calming to insight; by contrast, on the sixth ground, the name "meditative equipoise" assimilates, or even masks, the function of wisdom.

Just as the path of seeing *(mthong lam, darśanamārga)* is only possible when calm abiding has been accomplished, the sixth ground's perfection of wisdom becomes possible only upon completing the surpassing concentration on the fifth ground. The perfection of wisdom in turn, makes possible the uncommon absorption of cessation: one cannot gain such a cessation merely through the five perfections of giving, and so forth.[63] Calm abiding, the surpassing concentration of the fifth ground, and the uncommon absorption of the sixth ground, each provide an increased level of concentration that frees the mind from its dependence on an object. As concentration and insight develop, the subject becomes increasingly free from a differentiation between itself and the emptiness that is its special object.

It is interesting to consider the two gestures of expansion and withdrawal in terms of the characteristics of oral and literary orientations. In the descriptions above, the relative linearity of the analytical side of practice is assimilated to the more mentally and physiologically global model of stabilizing. There is a sense, albeit limited, in which concentration coalesces with the experience of sound, and wisdom, with the experience of sight. One cannot take this analogy too far, however, before it breaks down and, in the process, reveals the artificiality of the boundaries between "sight," and "hearing," "oral," and "written." The point is that the interplay of oral and visual, of concentration and insight, is complex. This complexity is the focus of our next section.

## III. MEDITATION TEXTS: SIGHT AND SOUND

> The sensorium is a fascinating focus for cultural studies. Given sufficient knowledge of the sensorium exploited within a specific culture, one could probably define the culture as a whole in virtually all its aspects.
>
> —Walter Ong, *The Presence of the Word*

Having summarized a variety of oral and vocal genres associated with texts and the types of subjectivity discussed in Tsong-kha-pa's and related works, let us consider the meditative context in which Tsong-kha-pa's text is positioned. We take as our focus the First Panchen Lama's *Path of Well-Being for those Traveling to Omniscience, Essential Instructions [dmar khrid] on the Stages of the Path to Enlightenment (byang chub lam gyi rim pa'i dmar khrid thams cad mkhyen par 'brod ba'i bde lam),* usually referred to simply as the *Path of Well-Being (bde lam).*[64] This is an early seventeenth-century meditational text based on traditional Gelukba *lam rim* teachings which coalesce recitation, visualization, physical gesture, and the nonverbal interiority of concentration. All these functions can be incorporated into a Tibetan concept of "reading" because all are directly related to the texts that provide focus and structure in meditation. In another sense, "reading" is too limited a term because the primary modern Western (and therefore secular) use of this term typically excludes gestures central to the Tibetan context. The tension between these two readings of the act of reading is itself instructive and interesting.

The *Path of Well-Being,* or similar works, are familiar to all traditional readers of Tsong-kha-pa's order. In a manner typical of Tibetan meditation texts, and in contrast to philosophical works such as Tsong-kha-pa's *Illumination,* the *Path of Well-Being* intersperses sections of general instruction or explanation with lines to be recited. In some meditation texts, the portions to be recited appear in larger typeface than the instructions, which, once they become habit, recede to the background. For a Tibetan engaged with such a text, the purpose is not to interpret the various understandings of wisdom and compassion it offers, nor to compare these with other texts familiar to him or her, even though such activity might indeed occupy one for time. Insofar as one approaches this text as a meditator, the wisdom and other qualities it describes are meant to be internalized. One's attention is, therefore, directed through the text to oneself, and not only to oneself as an intellect, or as one is at present, but as one can imagine oneself becoming and endowed with qualities that, aided by the text, one now takes steps to manifest.

The oral genre most closely associated with this and other meditation texts is known as "instructions of experience" (*myong khrid*),[65] mentioned above as a form of advisory speech unique to meditation texts. In the course of oral instruction, the entire text is commented on by the teacher and read silently by the student. In meditation sessions, done alone or with a group, one recites the appropriate portions and puts the instructions on compassionate motivation, visualization, and so forth, into practice during recitation. Instructions of experience have a particular structure.[66] In session A, the teacher discusses a portion of the text and closes with a summary of what has been said. In the interval before the next session, the student meditates on the meaning of that segment of the text as illuminated by oral instruction and tries to gain an experiential taste of what has been discussed. In session B, the teacher opens with a summary of the previous day's discussion, now perhaps heard differently because of the intervening meditation, and then about midway through the lecture turns to new material, which is then summarized at the close of the lecture. This new material becomes the focus of meditation prior to lecture C.

Like many texts used in meditation, the First Panchen Lama's work contains a liturgy that is chanted rhythmically during a meditation session, and also offers instructions or observations that shape the meditation session but are not themselves recited during it. Before one attempts to perform the text in meditation, one receives scriptural transmission (*lung, *āgama),* and instruction *(khrid)* and then studies the work in its entirety, usually with the benefit of oral commentary.

A. The Meditator and the Text

Once one has received instructions on a text such as the *Path of Well-Being*, one is ready to use it in private sessions of meditation. In addition to recitation of the text and reflection on its meaning, these will involve periods of visualization and concentration. Knowledge of the words will not suffice; one must know the melody and rhythm with which to chant them, as well as the posture, gestures, and visualized images that accompany them. Doing this properly involves both conceptual understanding and focused concentration.

A Gelukba trainee would have studied and orally debated the topics of meditation, and listened to oral philosophical commentary on them as well. In addition, one would have studied and heard oral commentary on Tsong-kha-pa's *lam rim* texts and the *Illumination.* Like these and other texts modeled on Candrakīrti's chronicling of the Bodhisattva stages, the *Path of Well-Being* presents an ordered series of meditations for the practitioner to follow. The multiplicity of media involved here—vocal, intellectual, nonconceptual, kinesthetic, visual, and olfactory (often incense will be burned)—and even gustatory (in longer group recitations monks are usually served tea at specific junctures)—is obvious. Their interplay is altogether typical of Tibetan religious practice.

The text proceeds through the stages of practice common to the *lam rim* cycle. Each of its topics[67] is presented in a four-part segment: preparation, actual session, conclusion, and instructions on what to do between meditative sessions. One is instructed to sit on a "comfortable cushion" in the lotus or other posture "that puts you at ease." As the practitioner knows from other texts and from the example of those around him, this posture requires, above all, that the back be straight, the shoulders even and relaxed, the neck slightly arched, the chin lowered, and the mouth relaxed. This is the kinesthetic frame for the rest, providing, among other things, a maximal echo chamber for vocalization as well as a stillness of body likely to facilitate stillness of mind and clarity of attention.

The body accounted for, one next examines one's mind and develops a virtuous intention. This intention is itself "textualized" through the many written and oral commentaries the practitioner would have heard regarding the compassionate motivation that sustains all Mahāyāna practice. In other words, one's reflection at this point, even if neither a reading nor a recitation, would most likely echo standard Mahāyāna phrases such as "for the benefit of all beings," "May all beings have happiness," and so forth, which appear throughout Gelukba and other Tibetan Mahāyāna literature.

Next comes instruction on visualization: in the space directly before one's eyes the image of one's own teacher or teachers—including the one who gave instructions on the text—appear in the form of Śākyamuni Buddha. Here the meditator must call upon visual texts, paintings or statues familiar since childhood and perhaps recently studied again to refresh memory of particular details. Śākyamuni Buddha is in this visualization surrounded by the entire lineage of figures associated with the *Path of Well-Being* and its traditions. In front of each of these many teachers, "upon marvellous tables are their own verbal teachings in the form of volumes which [like all visualizations] have the nature of light." Texts are visualized as part of a tableau that is itself a text. In its visualized presence one reflects on and recites the appropriate words.

While still sustaining this image, the practitioner is instructed by the text to "offer the seven branches of worship along with the mandala. . . ." The text does not elaborate because anyone trained in this tradition would know, from other texts as well as personal instruction, how to enact the recitation, hand gestures, and visualization that these seven branches involve.[68] Thus, the simple words "offer the seven branches of worship along with the mandala" encompass a considerable range of oral and textual traditions. The "inter-orality" implied here is compounded insofar as these seven branches themselves incorporate verses from the eighth-century Indian Buddhist poet, scholar, and meditation master Śāntideva.

Rays of light are then visualized arising from one's own heart and reaching the figures imagined before oneself, who thereby transform into light and dissolve onto the Lama visualized above one's head. Then, imagining one is reciting in unison with the vast array of beings on whose behalf one altruistically undertook the practice, several verses of supplication to the visualized Buddhas are rhythmically chanted. As chanting ends, five-colored rays extend their radiance through infinite space to purify oneself and all living beings. In particular, they purify those limitations which would interfere with accomplishing the purpose of that particular session—for example, with the development of compassion, calm abiding, or special insight.[69]

With minor differences, the same preparation of posture and visualization is used for all the meditation topics of this text.[70] In between the meditation sessions described in the *Path of Well-Being*, one is asked to study relevant scriptures and commentaries, or to engage in other appropriate activities such as restraining the senses through mindfulness and introspection, or "eating moderately and making effort at the yoga of not sleeping and of bathing and eating." In other words, "really" engaging the text means not only reading but incorporating such nonliterary agendas as posture, recitation, movement, and nonconceptuality. At the same time, one is engaged in a complex intertextuality that assumes knowledge of other ritual, philosophical, or oral texts. Performing these is in Tibet the time-honored way of fulfilling the purpose of the "reader" and believer who engages with that text.

## B. The Context of the Senses

> Whereas sight situates the observer outside what he views, at a distance, sound pours into the hearer.
>
> —Walter Ong, *Orality and Literacy*

If, as Walter Ong suggests, sight is the sensory mode most associated with literacy, and hearing, with orality, then the intertwined practices of reading, recitation, chanting, accompanying gesture, and visualization suggest the unique situation of Tibet's monastic and literary communities as sites dedicated to literacy and flooded with orality/vocality. At moments when the hands and voice are still, however, visualization practices in Tibet typically include a phase in which visions themselves literally pour into the meditator, or the meditator may visualize herself as dissolving into the figure imagined before her. In this way the visual, which in general entails some distance between observer and observed, takes on characteristics usually associated with sound: one is situated in the midst of it, is gradually suffused by it, and then experiences the fading of visualized images into space, much as one hears sound drift toward silence. This consonance between sensory experiences which are ordinarily different has its own affective power.[71]

These visualizations, formalized and embedded in verbal descriptions, emerge as a kind of illuminated text that is "read" not just with ears or eyes, but with the entirety of one's mind and body, which themselves become imaginatively transformed in the process of visualization. The meditators to whom such texts are addressed thus interact with them in a manner neither altogether writerly nor readerly, but physiologically and meditatively.

In visualization one's most private, profound, and "interior" experiences—those of meditation—are expressed and elicited through visualized images. As with the kind of reading attributed to "writerly" texts, there is an ongoing process of interaction and mutual change between the reader/meditator and the texts/images. The visualized images are in some sense experienced as "out there," as if available to all,[72] though at the same time they are understood to be the effect of one's own mind. My point is that whereas Tsong-kha-pa's *Illumination* is studied as a philosophical text, and the oral commentary associated with it is valued primarily for its explanatory value, these other forms of orality, especially the conjunction of oral performance with chanting and visualization, would be well known and would be part of what the hearer/student brings to any textual encounter.[73]

The process of embodied visualization, like the textual and oral orientations that contextualize it, engages several dimensions of experience. The person is constructed by the text and its accompanying oral traditions as both a meditator and a reader and also—given the related emphasis on posture, breath, and chanting, and the receiving of *lung* and initiation through sound and gesture—as an embodied meditator. He or she is also, however, constructed as a philosopher who has read, debated, and understood a variety of interrelated texts and brought their ideas to a level of visceral understanding. The same person, engaged in visualization, can also be constructed as an artist. Like an artist who uses a trained imagination rather than a brush, with a visualized expanse as canvas, one creates the image one has seen in paintings and whose descriptions one has read in texts. Ong observes that peoples from primary oral cultures are likely to externalize their psychological imbalances whereas literate cultures create persons who, regarding their own interior consciousness as private, like the pages of a text read silently and in solitude, experience themselves as "holding" individual characteristics unseen by others.[74] Traditional Tibet was *not* a primary oral culture; yet its oral orientation was sufficiently strong that if Ong is right about how such an orientation can shape interiority, the visualizations and associated textual practices just described would resonate differently for traditional Tibetans than for modern Westerners.

The visualized figures, male or female, Buddha or Bodhisattva, are experienced as embodying the qualities one seeks to incorporate, especially compassion and wisdom in unity. But this visualized figure is not a symbol only; he or she is a reflection of one's own mind as well as a projection from one's own mind. One relates to him or her as a person, pouring out faith, respect, joy, in some cases even desire, to that person.[75]

The meditator and visualized image come to resemble each other more and more, finally dissolving one into the other and thus leaving the practitioner in a nonconceptual contemplation of their absence. Language, whether the written language of texts or words orally recited, does not in the end so much govern the process of visualization and meditation as dissolve into it. In this sense visualization, like the cultivation of concentration, though initiated through language, proceeds on a trajectory that moves further and further away from governance by language.[76] Yet all this is encompassed by traditional forms of engagement with texts—texts that may describe the subject state of concentration or form part of the basis for cultivating it.

### *C. Summary: Reading in Tibet*

We have seen that Tibetan texts are typically performed in multiple ways. They can be read, silently or aloud, and if aloud either in a drone or musical incantation; their descriptions can be visualized, their instructions enacted in silent meditation, or accompanied by chants and music. Sound and words enliven not simply textual performances but the larger environment in which this typically takes place.

For all these reasons, the modern secular construct of "reading" seems inadequate to describe Tibetan textual engagement. The face-to-face and often ritualized encounter with the person whose oral commentary is integral to the experience of text is one differentiating factor; another and even more significant difference is what occurs through repeated practice of the text, that is, through performing the procedures it teaches, including recitation, visualization, and conceptual training. One is not so much reworking the written text—although this is a crucial and fundamental practice in many quarters—as reworking the self. Nor does the usual meaning of "reading" illuminate the nonconceptual processes of calming, breathing, concentration, and mental intensity so central to meditative textual practices.

Further, such meditation texts are never really extractable from the oral forms that make them part of interpersonal as well as intrasubjective communication. Partly because of the pervasive intermingling of oral and written orientations, one is rarely left alone with a text as is the custom in Western contexts. Perhaps the western enthusiasm for interpreting texts is an attempt to break out of that lonely encounter, even though the result is often simply to be alone with another text. The oral forms discussed here produce a field in which "reading" engages multiple media, senses, and persons, becoming an experience that reverberates through one's body as well as through various types of subjectivity, and engages one in social community as well.

The investigation of orality's place in the process of "reading" provides a pertinent cross-cultural perspective from which to consider the kind of reciprocity between reader and text which is a hallmark of contemporary literary theory. In Euro-American literary circles, this reciprocity in general means that texts are not produced only by their authors, but that a reader too is, in Roland Barthes' phrase, "the producer of a text."[77] This refers primarily to the way in which a reader "produces" texts through a process of *interpretation,* and what is produced is another text, different in meaning but not in form from the first. But in the Tibetan religious context the object of production is not a new reading or interpretation, and thus not precisely a new text, but a new experience or insight, even new ways of breathing and being. ("New," however, means "new for the individual involved"; the production of a "novelty" that expresses one's new and unique interpretation is not the goal.)[78] It is also clear that the meditator-chanter-philosopher is not treated as a disembodied mind, as the reader of Western texts most typically is constructed, but very much as both a material and a spiritual being. It is partly the interplay between oral and written gestures, as well as between concentration and insight, that in Tibet allows the faithful[79] to produce a multimedia text and new forms of subjectivity through various kinds of *activities* done in connection with that text.

We have noted that oral explanations of meditation texts are typically repeated three times; between lectures one meditates on the topic discussed. For the person alternately constructed as a meditator and a listener, each hearing is a different experience. Within the Buddhist tradition, this is probably the most important way in which a text, in Barbara Johnson's phrase, "differs from itself." Such differences may be described as experiential rather than textual, involving nuanced shifts in social, physical, and mental states.

The text's table of contents, usually memorized at the beginning of one's study, lists the stages of practice. Reading or reciting this, the practitioner unfolds a description of her own future as a meditator, and then begins to enact this future by "meditating" the text, a process embedded in the traditional Buddhist formula of "hearing, thinking, and meditating." Like a reader, a meditator's experience is not preordained by the nature of the text; there are bound to be resistances, complications, or shifts in perspective that the text precipitates but does not explicitly anticipate or acknowledge.

In addition to being "read" differently by one's present and future self, the text is felt differently by different aspects of oneself engaged in practice, and by internal elements which are opposed to the discipline, goals, or other elements of practice. Contemporary Western literary theorists tease out with great skill the hidden but implicit perspectives which contradict the overt message of the text. This difference, Barbara Johnson explains, is how a text differs from itself. Such reading makes it possible to experience the multiplicities that exist within an apparently singular text. As Johnson puts it, "A text's difference is not its uniqueness, its special identity, but its way of differing from itself. And this difference is perceived only in the act of rereading."[80] Similarly, but differently, there are "differences" that appear only through the act of performing and reperforming the practices described in a meditative text.

In brief, the boundaries taken for granted in reading, writing, and other forms of creativity performed in a print-oriented environment seem not to obtain here. The philosophical texts on which Yeshey Tupden comments here, and his own exposition, is often dense and turgid, yet these qualities are much mitigated, in my experience, by being embedded in traditions of interpersonal communication and meditative enactment. Textual expression in Tibet should always be understood as part of this larger system of the visual and the aural. To take account of this context, and especially of the variety of oral genres that supplement the written, is to be aware that the ideal "reader" is not addressed only as a disembodied mind. She or he is evoked also as a physical presence, seated erectly and breathing deeply, vocalizing with rhythmic precision chosen words received not only from texts, but personally transmitted in the voice of one's own teacher, thereby connecting one with a dimension not encompassed by the textual or conceptual, and thus reinforcing one of the central premises of the text to which Kensur Yeshey Tupden's commentary is about to introduce us, that the mind of the subject is not enhanced through words alone. Also required is the art of concentration, the only subjective dimension in which wisdom can thrive.

We turn now to Kensur's spoken scholarship.

# PART I

## Kensur Yeshey Tupden on Emptiness and the Bodhisattva Path

# 1

# Introduction to the Sixth Bodhisattva Ground

The ten chapters of Tsong-kha-pa's *Illumination of the Thought* discuss, in order, the ten Bodhisattva perfections *(pha rol tu phyin pa, paramitā)* of giving *(spyin pa, dāna)*, ethics *(tshul khrims, śīla)*, patience *(bzod pa, kṣānti)*, effort *(brtson 'grus, vīrya)*, concentration *(bsam gtan, dhyāna)*, wisdom *(shes rab, prajñā)*, skillful means *(thabs, upāya)*, aspirational prayer *(smon lam, praṇidhāna)*, power *(stobs, bala)*, and exalted wisdom *(ye shes, jñāna)*. The sixth chapter, on the Bodhisattva's perfection of wisdom, consists of four main sections:

1. an etymological discussion of the name of the sixth ground *(sa, bhūmi)* and its special perfection
2. praise of the perfection of wisdom
3. an explanation of suchness in which [context] the profound dependent arising is seen, and
4. a conclusion stating the good qualities of this ground.

The first section explains why the sixth ground is called the Manifest *(mngon du gyur pa, abhimukhī)*; the second praises the perfection of wisdom and indicates why it is unlike the other perfections and superior to them. Each of these sections has multiple subdivisions, which will be considered in order. The sixth-ground perfection of wisdom is a consciousness whose object is the profound emptiness; therefore, in describing this perfection it is necessary to explain in detail the meaning of emptiness, as is done in the third and largest section of this chapter, which discusses emptiness, or suchness, in the context of seeing or understanding the profound dependent arising. The final section sets forth the good qualities of the sixth Bodhisattva ground.

## ETYMOLOGICAL DESCRIPTION OF THE SIXTH GROUND AND ITS SPECIAL PERFECTION

A Bodhisattva's initial direct cognition of emptiness occurs at the beginning of the first Bodhisattva ground, attained simultaneously with the Mahāyāna path of seeing. More specifically, upon attaining the consciousness of an uninterrupted path of seeing *(mthong lam bar chad med lam, darśanānantaryamārga)*, a Bodhisattva directly cognizes emptiness for the first time. Prior to this, on the Mahāyāna path of preparation, one understood emptiness by means of a meaning generality *(don spyi, arthasāmānya)*, or mental image.

On the first of the four levels comprising the path of preparation, known as heat *(drod, uṣmagata)*, it is as if the object being understood, emptiness, is far away. Over the next three levels—peak *(rtse mo, mūrdhan)*, forbearance *(bzod pa, kṣānti)*, and highest mundane phenomenon *('jig rten pa'i chos kyi mchog, laukikāgryadharma)*—one is as if approaching closer and closer to the object. At the same time, the meaning generality, or mental image, recedes, and the sense of dualism between subject and object becomes more and more subtle. On the last two stages of the path of preparation the refined dualism that still exists is no longer ascertained. When one is about to attain the uninterrupted path of seeing, it is as if subject and object—the mind and emptiness—are almost touching. However one does not think, "They are now almost touching," in the manner of dualistic perception. The mind is now very subtle, and the meaning generality, or mental image, has nearly vanished.[1]

In short, one establishes and then cultivates the meaning of emptiness. One meditates on the emptiness of one particular thing until, as the consciousness becomes clearer and clearer, the image of emptiness dissolves and the dualistic appearance vanishes. When this happens, the empty nature of everything, the meaning of everything [as empty], comes forth.

When the path of seeing has actually developed in one's mental continuum, subject and object seem to be mixed. There is no dualistic sense that the observing mind is here and the observed emptiness is there. During such direct perception of emptiness, all the appearances of the object of negation—inherent existence—have ceased for one's own mind. There is no appearance of the negated object; only the aspect of its negation appears. As coarse dualistic appearances *(gnyis snang)* vanish [over the path of preparation], the sense of subject and object as different continues to decrease until there is an appearance in which these seem to be fused.[2]

As one continues to meditate, the clear appearance of emptiness *(stong nyid gyi gsal snang)* increases more and more. Does the mind itself become emptiness? No; the mind realizing emptiness is the realizer, and emptiness is the object realized.[3] Earlier in the *Illumination* Tsong-kha-pa quoted Nāgārjuna's example of a garment made of stone [probably asbestos], observing that if this is placed in fire, its dirt and so forth are burned, but not the garment itself.[4] Our consciousness is like the garment; the cleansing fire like the consciousness that realizes emptiness. Such realization burns away mental defilements but does not do away with the mind. What is this mind doing? It directly realizes emptiness, though we cannot [fully] express its manner of doing so. Some scholars wrongly assert that there is no consciousness at all at this time. This is incorrect; however, there is no conceptual thought, no need to reflect, "It is like this." The aspect of the way of abiding of phenomena—their emptiness of inherent existence—is simply cast toward the perceiving consciousness.[5]

In general there are two types of meditative minds: analytical *(dpyad sgom)* and stabilizing *('jog sgom)*.[6] The mind on the uninterrupted path of seeing is engaged in analytical meditation. However, this is not at all the sort of analysis that reflects, "This is," or "This is not." Like an eye consciousness it just sees what it sees and, because it is a yogic direct perceiver, it ascertains all that appears to it. There are no conventional appearances and no movement *(rgyu ba, cāraṇa)* of conceptual thought. Such a mind is very strong. Although there is no movement of thought, this mind has great activity and comprehends many reasons. Such cannot come about except through meditation, which refines the mind until it becomes the entity of yogic direct perception. Not a single factor of a mental image or meaning generality appears to this mind—only emptiness. It is thus possible to have analytical meditation without conceptualization. The path of seeing is the first instance of a nonconceptual analytical meditation on emptiness, although there is a union of analytical and stabilizing meditation prior to this [on the path of preparation]. In fact, the uninterrupted path of the Mahāyāna path of seeing is the best type of analytical meditation. Its subtle analysis operates only with respect to its object [emptiness]. No appearances of "one" or "many" or "object of knowledge, agent, action," and so forth, can occur in the absence of conceptual thought. In association with this analytical realization, one has a calm abiding concordant *(mtshung, anukūla)* with one-pointedness on emptiness. Such calm abiding is [the lowest level of] a stabilizing meditation which accompanies the Mahāyāna uninterrupted path of seeing.[7]

The path of seeing is the first instance of a nonconceptual analytical meditation. Uninterrupted paths of meditation are later instances of nonconceptual analytical meditation. To be nonconceptual *(rtog pa med pa, nirvikalpaka)* does not necessarily mean that a consciousness is also free of any [mistaken] conceptual aspect. For example, a yogic direct perception of impermanence is "without conceptual thought" *(rnam rtog med, avikalpaka)*, but it has a [mistaken] conceptual aspect because it is mistaken regarding the appearance [of its object] *('khrul snang yod mkhan)*. Even a direct realization of impermanence has a mistaken appearance because [that impermanence] appears to inherently exist. Such appears because predispositions for the conception of inherent existence still remain. All consciousnesses except for direct realizers of emptiness are involved with mistaken *('khrul ba, bhrānta)* appearances *('khrul snang yod pa red)*. Therefore, to say that "a conceptual aspect exists" *(rnam rtog yod)* does not definitively indicate that conceptual thought *(rtog pa, kalpanā)* is present.[8] In general, the factor *(cha, aṃṣa)* of superimposition *(sgro 'dogs, samāropa)* is called conceptuality. Here however [conceptuality] has to do with a mistaken appearance of an object. Is a yogic direct perception of impermanence an unmistaken consciousness? It is not. Is it yogic direct perception? Yes. Thus, we can speak of mistaken yogic direct perception.[9] However, a yogic direct perceiver of emptiness is not mistaken [regarding the appearance of emptiness].[10]

On the path of seeing, the artificial conceptions of inherent existence become utterly nonexistent. All superimpositions made by thought are gone. In this way, analysis operates by way of direct perception. One has a special insight or wisdom, which is one entity with the uninterrupted path; one also has a meditative stabilization of the level of the fourth concentration, which is also one entity with the uninterrupted path.[11]

The mind directly cognizing emptiness, like all directly perceiving consciousnesses, is a mind of complete engagement *(sgrub 'jug gi blo, *vidhipravṛttibuddhi)*.[12] Such a mind operates or engages its object by the power of the object itself[13]—that is, by the aspect being cast toward it, and not by the power of a sign or reason as occurred on the path of preparation, where emptiness was known by way of a mental image. Thus, a consciousness directly perceiving emptiness depends on the aspect [of emptiness]. It depends on it in the sense that at the time of the great, or final, fourth portion of the path of preparation *(sbyor lam chos mchog chen po, prayogamārgalaukikāgryadharma)* [one's consciousness] does not have the aspect of all emptinesses. One has established emptiness through reasoning, then meditated, and as this meditation reaches completion, all appearances decrease more and more, and [emptiness] becomes very clear. When one moves from this path to the uninterrupted path of seeing, the aspects of all emptinesses are there for it. This mind of collective or complete engagement is one that knows all aspects of its object. In this it is unlike conceptual thought [a mind of partial engagement].

There are as many emptinesses as there are phenomena; everything that exists is connected with [its own] emptiness. All these emptinesses are established through reasoning at the time of the path of preparation and, as one meditates on their import, the meaning of emptiness becomes clearer and clearer. Because emptiness has only one aspect which is the same for all emptinesses, the mind on the path of seeing knows directly not just one emptiness but all emptinesses. This does not mean that it knows all the objects in all world-systems which are qualified by those emptinesses.

Thus, there are many emptinesses that do not exist as objects of a [conceptual, dualistic] mind. [However] when one comes to the Mahāyāna uninterrupted path of seeing, all these emptinesses become one's objects. This occurs because the appearance of the meaning generality [or mental image of emptiness] has vanished. Object and subject become like water poured in with water; they appear as one. [Nevertheless,] one is the object, and one is a consciousness; one is impermanent, and one is permanent. Although not actually one, they are not distinguished [from the viewpoint of experience]. One can speak of an emptiness, a nonaffirming negative or an object of negation, in connection with all objects whatsoever. In every case this is a way of getting at the nature of the object.

Through seeing the nature [emptiness] of a single thing, one thereby directly sees the nature of all things.[14] It is not necessary to know all phenomena; the emptiness of phenomena that one does not know also appear. [This emptiness] is like space [in encompassing whatever phenomena exist]. Such a consciousness has no conceptualized aspect *(rnam par mi rtog pa)* and thus no area of mistake regarding appearances. In brief, no conventional objects and all ultimates, which is to say all emptinesses, appear [to the mind] on the uninterrupted Mahāyāna path of seeing. Even the [image of its] negated object does not appear to it; no image or meaning generality [even of emptiness] appears to it either. The [emptiness or] way of being *(gnas lugs)* of all things that exist is all that appears to it. It is as if their aspects come toward or are cast [to the perceiving consciousness]. These are not cast by their own force *(nus pa, śakti)*; it is [simply] their nature [to appear or] be cast in this way.[15] Such aspects are cast toward it and the consciousness engages *('jug)* with its object through the power of the object *(dngos dbang)*. Subject and object appear as one. The subject itself is a consciousness, a conventional phenomenon. Its own aspect [as consciousness] does not appear to it. Does the person then realize emptiness? The person does, for what the consciousnesses realizes, the person also realizes. And such a mind has tremendous power. If an atom bomb were dropped at that time, it probably would not disturb the mind of a person on the uninterrupted path of seeing.

*Question:* When, for example, one speaks of the eye consciousness apprehending a table, we say that the table casts its aspect, and that the eye consciousness takes on the aspect of the object. The aspect of the table's impermanence is also cast. Can one say that the aspect of emptiness is cast in the same way?

*Answer:* When an object is seen by an eye consciousness, all factors existing as one entity of establishment and abiding *(grub bde rdzas gcig)* with that object are seen. Can all these be [fully and simultaneously] expressed by terms? They cannot. Terms, like conceptual thought, proceed discretely, one by one. Similarly, if aspects of emptiness appeared, they would have to be discrete [as is not the case when emptiness itself appears directly].

[The table's] impermanence also casts its aspect, as does its productness. Terms cannot simultaneously express such [detailed appearance]. On the uninterrupted Mahāyāna path of seeing one cognizes emptiness, not the aspect of emptiness. The aspect of emptiness and the aspect of impermanence are different [in that whereas the aspect of impermanence can be considered as impermanence] it must be said that the aspect of emptiness is not emptiness. Its aspect is a conventional object. [At this time] there is no object expressed by a term (*sgra'i brjod bya, *śabdasya-abhidheya* [a mental image appearing to the consciousness]) because that would be something coarse.[16]

Still, it is perfectly suitable to say that the consciousness on the uninterrupted Mahāyāna path of seeing takes on the aspect of emptiness. If it is essential to say this [as in the context of debate], it is suitable enough. However, to say that the consciousness directly cognizing emptiness takes on the aspect of emptiness [as is said in the case of ordinary direct perception] does not have much meaning. [Moreover] if we have to go on to finalize the meaning of this, it will be difficult. [Still] if one states that [the consciousness] takes on the aspect of emptiness, it will not be refuted, but there are some difficulties with this [such as how the mind could engage or see through such a multiplicity of such aspects, just as] we cannot see to the bottom of a cup filled with tea. The consciousness on the uninterrupted path of seeing sees all emptinesses [though] we cannot express the manner in which it does so.

Conventional objects have many different aspects, none of which—except emptiness—appears in direct cognition of emptiness. Although the subjects are different, their [empty] nature is the same. Thus, when you cut away superimpositions with respect to the emptiness or reality of one phenomenon, the nature of that and all other phenomena come to the mind. It is like learning the letter *a*; you do not have to learn it again with respect to every piece of writing you see. Whether it is large or small, you will understand it to be *a*. This is just an example, however, for when you learn the letter *a*, except for gaining the capacity to recognize all letters *a*, you do not actually see all *a*'s; the different aspects related with all the different letter *a*'s do not appear. By contrast, the emptiness which is the object of direct perception on the uninterrupted path of seeing has only the one aspect [of a lack of inherent existence] which is identical with all emptinesses.

This is a mind for which all appearances of true existence have ceased. Not a single one remains; thus, the mind operates with respect to all emptinesses. This is not true on the path of preparation. There, one still has conceptual thought and does not cognize all emptinesses. Just as when you turn on a light, the light itself and all the objects in the room simultaneously become visible to the eye consciousness, so on the path of seeing, when the mental image [of emptiness] and all conventional appearances are eliminated, there is direct cognition of the mere negation of the [inherent existence] of all emptinesses.

The wisdom that directly cognizes emptiness is synonymous with a non-conceptual wisdom *(rnam par mi rtog pa'i ye shes, nirvikalpajñāna)* or a knower of individual emptinesses. These individual emptinesses are not variegated in any way; they are as one. They do not differ except in that the objects they qualify are different. In terms of the emptinesses themselves and the consciousness that directly cognizes them, they are one. To be variegated or different is a quality only of conventional truths, not of ultimate truths, and only ultimate truths are objects for the mind during the uninterrupted path of seeing. Just emptiness is cognized, the mere absence of what is negated. The factor of [emptiness] being an object of consciousness, or being an object of knowledge, and so forth, is not an emptiness; even the factor of emptiness being an ultimate truth is probably not an emptiness. Moreover, the production, cessation, disintegration, and whatever else is posited in relation to a given [object qualified by] emptiness is not an emptiness, nor are any of these [factors] objects of the wisdom directly realizing reality. Only the very emptiness itself is cognized by such a mind.

This emptiness cannot be taught or expressed in just the way that it is directly cognized. Some wrongly think that because emptiness is not an object of expression in this way, it does not exist. Yet, emptiness is the best of existents! The above wrong view arises if one does not know how to posit the specific way in which emptiness is an object of expression. Emptiness can be taught and can be expressed; but it cannot be expressed exactly as it is known in non-dualistic direct cognition.

Although one directly cognizes emptiness on the path of seeing—that is, on the first Bodhisattva ground—one does not yet have a special, or enhanced, practice of the perfection of wisdom. This cannot occur until the sixth Bodhisattva ground, for its accomplishment depends on the completion of the special perfection of concentration that occurs on the fifth ground. Unless one first attains the enhanced perfection of concentration, one is unable to develop the enhanced perfection of wisdom but, on the contrary, remains far from it.

Through having attained an enhanced perfection of concentration on the fifth ground, the sixth-ground Bodhisattva is able to attain an uncommon absorption of cessation *(thun mong ma yin pa'i 'gog snyoms, asādhārananirodhasamāpatti)* that has as its object the emptiness of inherent existence. Only the highest system of Buddhist tenets, Prāsaṅgika-Mādhyamika, describes this meditative state because only it posits the subtle emptiness of inherent existence that is its object. The lower tenet systems—Svātantrika, Cittamātra, Sautrāntika, and Vaibhāṣika—do not assert this type of absorption, which is different from the common absorption of cessation that they do discuss.

The entity of [the wisdom which is the uncommon absorption of cessation] has the capacity both to enter into and to reverse [from meditative stabilization] on emptiness in a single session and is the agent which does this. This [mind on the sixth ground] is an entity consisting of the practice *(nyams len)* of the surpassing perfection [of wisdom].

A common or ordinary absorption of cessation occurs when coarse thought and coarse exertion *(rtsol ba, vyāyāma)* have ceased. Coarse exertion signifies [the operation of] those minds that do not realize [some type of emptiness]. Consciousnesses that know the various types of objects—forms, and so forth—are instances of coarse exertion. During a common absorption of cessation all coarse feelings and discriminations cease.[17]

Only a nonassociated compositional factor *(ldan min 'du byed, viprayukta-saṃskāra)*—something that is neither mind nor matter—is established in the mind. This nonassociated compositional factor itself is the cessation of all coarse exertion: that which has ceased is coarse exertion. This transpires from the time of the first Bodhisattva ground.

A common absorption of cessation is not a mind realizing the emptiness of inherent existence. Only an uncommon absorption realizes this most subtle emptiness; therefore, the Buddhist tenet systems from Svātantrika on down, which do not assert a lack of inherent existence because they maintain that phenomena inherently exist, cannot posit the uncommon absorption of cessation.

Although a Bodhisattva does not attain an uncommon absorption until the sixth ground, he or she has meditative equipoise on the emptiness of inherent existence long before attaining the sixth ground. Such a meditative equipoise—which is neither a common nor an uncommon absorption of cessation—first occurs on the uninterrupted path *(bar chad med lam, ānantaryamārga)* and path of release *(rnam grol lam, vimuktimārga)* of a Mahāyāna path of seeing.[18] According to Prāsaṅgika-Mādhyamika, both subject and object—the mind and emptiness—are directly cognized as lacking inherent existence.

According to Prāsaṅgika, any phenomenon's lack of inherent existence and its lack of ultimate existence are synonymous. Svātantrika-Mādhyamika, however, makes a distinction between a thing's lack of inherent existence and its lack of ultimate existence; they affirm the former and negate the latter.[19] Thus, although the Svātantrikas, like all Mahāyāna tenet systems, maintain that on the sixth ground one attains the perfection of wisdom, they cannot fully posit the special qualities of this ground because their tenet system cannot encompass an uncommon absorption of cessation that cognizes a lack of inherent existence. The Svātantrika assertions on emptiness, though not considered the final word on the subject, are greatly valued by Prāsaṅgika as a means of easing into the more difficult discussion and realization of a lack of inherent existence. Prāsaṅgika maintains that a person who is presently capable of understanding Svātantrika tenets will later become able to take up the Prāsaṅgika view.

The uncommon absorption attained on the sixth ground is a type of meditative equipoise *(mnyam bzhag, samāhita)* on emptiness [different from the meditative equipoise achieved on the path of seeing]. This word in Tibetan literally means "placed equally," with "equally" referring to the fact that in equipoise consciousness and object are equal or coextensive in the sense that any emptiness is necessarily the object of an uninterrupted Mahāyāna path of seeing, and any object of such a consciousness is necessarily an emptiness. In terms of the ten Bodhisattva grounds, only the first one is a path of seeing; the other nine are levels of the path of meditation *(sgom lam, bhāvanāmārga)*.[20] Thus, this etymology strictly applies only to the first Bodhisattva ground. For, on the uninterrupted paths of the path of meditation—and hence of the second through tenth Bodhisattva grounds—it is possible to have true cessations as an object. In other words, whatever is an object of equipoise on those grounds is not necessarily an emptiness. For example, the true cessation of afflictions that occurs on the first ground can be an object of the uninterrupted path of the second ground.

With respect to the second part of the etymology, to say, "Whatever is a consciousness of meditative equipoise on emptiness directly cognizes emptiness," means that whatever is one entity with that mind—for example, virtuous mental factors like faith, conscientiousness, and so forth—is also said to directly cognize emptiness. Specifically, what directly cognizes emptiness is the main mind *(sems, citta)* and twenty-three of the fifty-one mental factors—all of these being [associated with] a main consciousness that directly cognizes emptiness, which makes them cognizers of emptiness as well. These mental factors are:

5 omnipresent mental factors *(sems byung kun 'gro, sarvatraga-caitta)*: feeling, discrimination, intention, mental engagement, and contact

5 determining mental factors *(sems byung yul nges, *viśayapratiniyama-caitta)*: aspiration, belief, mindfulness, stabilization, and wisdom.

11 virtuous mental factors *(sems byung dge ba, kuśala-caitta)*: faith, shame, embarrassment, non-attachment, non-hatred, non-ignorance, effort, pliancy, conscientiousness, equanimity, and non-harmfulness

2 changeable mental factors *(sems byung gzhan 'gyur, *anyathābhāva-caitta)*: investigation and analysis.[21]

Thus, there are twenty-three mental factors in all that directly cognize emptiness. These are each one entity with the consciousness of the uninterrupted

Mahāyāna path of seeing. Each has emptiness as its object and, moreover, each mental factor realizes all emptinesses. This is a special feature of a consciousness directly perceiving emptiness that does not apply to minds which understand emptiness conceptually. The most subtle type of conceptual consciousness realizing emptiness occurs on the highest of the four levels of the path of preparation, that of highest mundane phenomenon, but whatever is a consciousness of this level does not necessarily have emptiness as its object, for a mental image or meaning generality also appears to such a consciousness, since any conceptual consciousness necessarily has a mental image as its appearing object. That mental image represents emptiness, and thus emptiness itself is an object for a consciousness on the path of preparation, but it is not the only object. [Nor is emptiness here an appearing object *(snang yul, *pratibāsaviṣaya)* for that consciousness because emptiness itself does not fully appear to it.]

Only factors of mind that are one entity with the wisdom consciousness cognize emptiness. Other qualities, such as the impermanence and emptiness of the wisdom consciousness, do not realize emptiness, for they are not minds. Moreover, although all qualities or factors which are minds and are one entity with the wisdom cognizing emptiness cognize emptiness, there are also good qualities of, for example, the sixth ground, which are not one entity with that wisdom and thus do not realize emptiness. For example, the mind of enlightenment *(byang chub kyi sems, bodhicitta)*—which is the compassionately motivated intention to attain Buddhahood in order to help others become enlightened—is a different entity from the wisdom consciousness. Yet it is a quality of mind possessed by a sixth-ground Bodhisattva in the sense that both it and the enhanced perfection of wisdom are good qualities of the same mental continuum. Still, the compassionate mind of enlightenment does not realize emptiness, whereas the wisdom consciousness does.

It should be emphasized that all Bodhisattva grounds are consciousnesses directly realizing the subtle emptiness of inherent existence. The difference between grounds is not made in terms of their realization of emptiness but is measured in terms of the true or final cessation of obstructions that accompanies each. The higher grounds are superior to the lower because of the afflictions or obstructions they are able to overcome.

## True Cessations and Absorptions of Cessation

A true cessation is the cessation of adventitious mental stains or defilements such that they will not return again in any lifetime. When these undesirable qualities cease, they simply stop.

There is a difference between true cessations which are the third of the four noble truths and an absorption of cessation, for, from the first ground, one has a true cessation—the cessation of the artificial conception of inherent existence—but one does not have an uncommon absorption of cessation until the sixth ground is attained. Thus, a true cessation is not necessarily an absorption of cessation, just as any direct cognition of emptiness is not necessarily an uncommon absorption of cessation.

A true cessation itself is not an emptiness, although there are scholars who say otherwise.[22] In any case, there is an important distinction between true cessations and emptinesses. True cessations are a negation or cessation of something that exists—a specific affliction or obstruction. More technically, this means that the objects which cease are included among existent phenomena. The greatest true cessation, the nirvana of a Buddha, is a complete extinguishment of all obstructions to liberation and omniscience; it is a negation of existent objects. However, the inherent existence which is the negated object of the most subtle emptiness is not included among existents. Inherent existence does not exist; thus, emptinesses are not true cessations.

Those scholars who, despite the above, maintain that emptinesses are true cessations, hold that because true cessations are objects of the wisdom of meditative equipoise, they must be emptinesses. They consider that whatever is the object of a wisdom in meditative equipoise is necessarily an emptiness. We who hold true cessations and emptinesses to be different maintain that whatever is the object of a wisdom in meditative equipoise need not be an emptiness, for, as mentioned above, although the object of an uninterrupted Mahāyāna path of seeing is necessarily an emptiness, the object of a Mahāyāna release path of seeing *(rnam grol lam, vimuktimārga)*[23] or of an uninterrupted path of meditation, can be a true cessation—the absence of a certain mental defilement. For example, the true cessation of afflictions that comes about on the first Bodhisattva ground can be an object of the uninterrupted path of the second ground.

## Special Attainments on the Sixth Ground

On the fifth ground the Bodhisattva gained an enhanced perfection of concentration. This is a prerequisite to attaining the enhanced perfection of wisdom. In a sense, the attainment of such concentration is all that stands between a fourth-ground Bodhisattva and achievement of the sixth ground. However, this does not mean one attains the enhanced perfection of wisdom in the second moment following attainment of the enhanced perfection of concentration.

The perfection of wisdom is the most difficult of all the perfections. Once one has attained the fifth ground, it is necessary to complete the uninterrupted and release paths related to that ground and the state following the meditative equipoise *(rjes thob, pṛiṣṭhalabdha)* of that ground. This causes the collections of wisdom and merit to increase, empowering one to develop the sixth ground. Through the power of having attained the practice of a wisdom directly cognizing emptiness and the enhanced perfection of concentration, the Bodhisattva is able to develop the enhanced perfection of wisdom. Thus, there is still much to be accomplished between the attainments of the enhanced perfection of concentration and the sixth ground's enhanced perfection of wisdom. Although it is not easy to move to the sixth ground, since one is a Bodhisattva Superior the two collections of merit and wisdom necessary for it will not decrease. Indeed, they increase by their own power. Such Bodhisattvas have great force; they are not limited by laziness and afflictions as are ordinary persons. Moreover, once one has attained the fifth ground, one proceeds to the sixth with [only] very subtle exertion.

The movement from the fifth to the sixth ground occurs within a single extensive meditative session. First one enters meditative equipoise, after which for a long time there is no thinking. The length of this period is indefinite; it can last for three, five, or seven days. The point is that no matter how accustomed the mind becomes to the perfection of concentration, one cannot attain the enhanced perfection of wisdom through concentration alone. Subsequently, one attains the uncommon absorption of cessation [realizing] the emptiness of inherent existence; through the power of this enhanced concentration [i.e., the absorption of cessation] the Bodhisattva passes to the sixth ground during the meditation session.[24]

# 2

# THREE FEATURES OF UNDERSTANDING

The consciousness of a sixth-ground Bodhisattva is enhanced by the manifestation of three types of skill or understanding:

1. completion of the understanding that emptiness—the nature of illusory phenomena—is itself like an illusion in that it exists but does not inherently or truly exist
2. completion of skill with respect to the coarse and subtle aspects of the four noble truths
3. approaching the attainment of Buddhahood.

All three of these relate to the manner in which the enhanced perfection of wisdom consciousness cognizes the nature of phenomena.[1]

## UNDERSTANDING EMPTINESS

All things that exist are dependent arisings. A thing would exist inherently or by way of its own nature only if it existed without depending on anything else, and thus a dependent arising necessarily lacks true or inherent existence. Moreover, just as conventional phenomena are qualified by an emptiness of inherent existence, so emptiness—an ultimate truth in the sense that its way of appearing and way of abiding are concordant—is also a dependent arising which lacks or is empty of inherent existence.

When emptiness is first cognized directly on the uninterrupted Mahāyāna path of seeing, one has a spacelike meditative equipoise.[2] One does not at this time think, "This emptiness is like an illusion," for a nonconceptual consciousness cannot reflect in this way. However, once one attains the illusion-perceiving state subsequent to meditative equipoise[3] [at which time one is still on the path of seeing], one can reflect, "Emptiness is like a dream, an illusion." Thus, during the state subsequent to the meditative equipoise of the first ground, one understands that emptiness itself is illusion-like. Why, then, does Tsong-kha-pa consider the understanding that emptiness is like an illusion to be a quality of the sixth ground? This understanding is completed [or more strictly speaking, enhanced], at this time in the sense that it becomes an antidote that can eliminate mental obstructions more subtle than those abandoned previously. On the sixth ground emptiness itself is manifestly realized to be a dependent arising and thus to lack being established by way of its own nature. Due to this understanding the Bodhisattva newly attains a true cessation of the obstructions abandoned on the sixth ground. More specifically, when Tsong-kha-pa states that the illusory nature of emptiness becomes manifest on the sixth ground, he means that at this time one becomes skilled in the twelve links of dependent arising. These twelve are:

1. ignorance *(ma rig pa, avidyā)*
2. action *('du byed kyi las, saṃskārakarma)*
3. consciousness *(rnam shes, vijñāna)*
4. name and form *(ming gzugs, nāmarūpa)*
5. six sources *(skye mched, āyatana)*
6. contact *(reg pa, sparśa)*
7. feeling *(tshor ba, vedanā)*
8. attachment *(sred pa, tṛṣṇā)*
9. grasping *(len pa, upādāna)*
10. existence *(srid pa, bhava)*
11. birth *(skye ba, jāti)*
12. aging and death *(rga shi, jarāmaraṇa)*.

Just as there can be no smoke without fire, so when ignorance, the first link, is abandoned, the subsequent eleven links do not arise; this is the reversal of the twelve links of dependent arising. However, just as, when there is smoke, there will necessarily be fire and burning, if ignorance is present, the others will also occur.[4]

*Question:* Tsong-kha-pa states (115.9 ff.) that when the reflection-like nature of phenomena becomes manifest because of the sixth-ground Bodhisattva's surpassing wisdom, this signifies that one has "skill in the process of entry [into cyclic existence]." What does this mean, since skill or training is not necessary for entry into cyclic existence?

*Answer:* To enter cyclic existence is indeed not a skill; it means one has come under the power of a mind which is itself under the sway of afflictions. The root of these is ignorance.

Those who perceive the danger of cyclic existence wish to leave it. To do so involves understanding the root from which [cyclic existence] is derived—the process by which one comes into cyclic existence. The beginningless ignorance at the root of this process is the conception of inherent existence [which stands in direct opposition to knowing phenomena as illusory]. Seized by the power of this conception, we succumb to it helplessly, accumulating actions by which we again and again wander in cyclic existence, only to accumulate and wander over and over again. Thus, if we do not wish to remain in cyclic existence, ignorance must be eradicated, and this involves knowing the stages by which one enters into and exits from cyclic existence. This is what is meant by understanding the stages involved in the process of entry into cyclic existence.

There are three increasingly subtle meanings of "dependent arising." The first and least subtle refers to the fact that all impermanent phenomena are dependent arisings in the sense that they depend on causes and conditions. For example, to travel from India to the United States, one depends on an airplane or other conveyance; similarly, our present comfort and health depend on resources such as food and shelter. Without these we could not live comfortably, if at all. In this way, we depend on many external things, and we can exist only by depending on them. We therefore exist dependently and not inherently. The twelve links of dependent arising are a presentation of the causes of being reborn in cyclic existence and the effects of these. Thus, all products or impermanent phenomena are dependent arisings in the sense of being dependent on the completion of concordant causes and conditions which foster their existence and [being dependent on the absence of] discordant conditions which interfere with their existence.

The second and third meanings of dependent arising are considered more subtle than this and apply to both permanent and impermanent phenomena. The second meaning refers to the dependence of all existents on their own valid bases of designation. For example, all the different parts of a tape recorder form the basis for designating your tape recorder. They are a valid basis of designation [because they actually do function as a tape recorder]. The bases of designation of a person are the mind and body. Just as none of the parts of the tape recorder is itself a tape recorder—the microphone is not, the volume switch, the motor, and so forth—so no portion of the mind or body is the person. Nevertheless, as with the tape recorder, it is suitable to designate a person on the basis of mind and body. For example, if I see Diana's hand, it is correct to think, "Diana is here," even though I am only seeing a small portion of her form. To designate means to apply the name "Diana" or "tape recorder" to an appropriate basis of designation.

All phenomena other than emptinesses are conventional truths. Emptinesses are ultimate truths. Conventional and ultimate truths both exist conventionally or imputedly. They are dependent arisings in the sense that they depend on imputation by thought. This is the third and most subtle meaning of dependent arising; it is a tenet unique to Prāsaṅgika-Mādhyamika. According to Prāsaṅgika, things that exist conventionally necessarily possess the three attributes of being:

1. well known to the the world; that is, they are known to nonanalytical conventional consciousnesses and are posited by being well known to them
2. not undermined by another conventional valid cognizer
3. not undermined by a reasoning consciousness analyzing the ultimate [i.e., emptiness].

Objects of knowledge, existents, established bases—in short, everything that exists— exists conventionally. [Phenomena such as] the horns of a rabbit [which are nonexistent] do not exist conventionally.

The Prāsaṅgika-Mādhyamika system [in accordance with] Candrakīrti's *Entrance to the Middle Way* sets out a conventional mode of existence and an ultimate one. Both existent phenomena and nonexistent ones may be well known to a conventional consciousness [but only the former conventionally exist]. However, what is well known to a nonanalytical [conventional] consciousness [a mind that does not analyze the ultimate] does not conventionally exist if it is undermined by another conventional valid cognizer. The horns of a rabbit or flowers in the sky, for example, are undermined [because they are not perceived] by valid conventional consciousnesses. Therefore, even though such things may be well known to a conventional consciousness, they do not conventionally exist. To give another example, the distant water that appears in a desert is known by a conventional consciousness—namely, the eye consciousness. When one approaches that place, however, the presence of water is contradicted by another valid consciousness, the new eye consciousness that views the area from nearby.

[The third attribute of conventional existence pertains to] a reasoning consciousness realizing emptiness. This is known as a valid reasoning consciousness [analyzing the ultimate]. Reasoning consciousnesses in general are of two types: those analyzing the ultimate and those analyzing conventionalities. The term "analyze" in Tibetan combines two syllables: *spyod* and *byed*, meaning to analyze *(spyod)* what is out there *(phar)* and to take in or understand *(tshur byed)* the object. A consciousness analyzing the ultimate realizes and posits the way a thing exists. Such a consciousness realizes, for example, the mode of existence of the pillar—its lack of inherent existence. This mind is a knower analyzing the conventional with respect to emptiness. When it takes emptiness as the subject and analyzes its way of abiding, then it is a knower analyzing the ultimate.[5] Anything undermined by such an ultimate analytical consciousness does not exist. What is so undermined? An inherently existent pillar, or a pillar established from its own side. A [conventionally existent] pillar, however, is not undermined by a reasoning consciousness analyzing emptiness.

There are two kinds of analysis [associated with valid cognition]: that which investigates to discover the entity [which is the conventional object] and that which analyzes again after the entity has been established [to discover, not what it is, but how it exists]. For example, when one uses [conventional] analysis to find a watch that has been missing, the entity of that watch is not [yet] established [for one's own mind]. However, this is not an [ultimate] analytical mind in relation to that [entity]. When you find the watch, you take it in hand: "The watch is here." You do not search for it [further]. If you did, this would be a mind of analysis and investigation. Without analysis, you were easily able to find what you sought, but if you analyze once the entity is established [that is, once you have the watch in front of you], you will not find it.[6] Prior to locating it, the watch is not established by valid cognition in [the limited sense] that it is not establisblished by *your* valid cognition. It is, however, established by valid cognition in general. [The *Collected Topics* textbooks define "existent thing" as "that which is observed by valid cognition."] In short, if you search for something prior to establishing it by valid cognition, you can find it. Once it is found, if you analytically search it out, it is not there. The consciousness analyzing conventionalities does not realize the mode of abiding [of an object]; thus, its object is necessarily a conventional truth. Therefore, the two [types of analytical or reasoning consciousnesses, ultimate and conventional] are different.[7]

*Question:* What distinguishes a nonanalytical conventional consciousness (*ma dpyod pa'i tha snyad pa'i shes pa*) from any consciousness analyzing the conventional?

*Answer:* A non-analytical conventional consciousness (*tha snyad pa'i shes pa*, **vyavahāravijñāna*) and the consciousness analyzing the conventional (*tha snyad spyod byed gyi shes pa*) are a little bit different. A consciousness analyzing conventionalities is necessarily a conventional consciousness that does not analyze [the ultimate mode of abiding]. However, a conventional consciousnesses is not necessarily a consciousness analyzing conventionalities because [a consciousness] analyzing the ultimate—an inferential valid cognizer realizing emptiness, or a yogic direct cognition of emptiness, or a path of preparation, and so forth—is a conventional consciousness.

*Question:* How can this be?

*Answer:* A conventional consciousness (*tha snyad pa'i shes pa*) is a valid realizer (*tshad ma rtogs mkhan*). A conventional consciousness is, for the most part, a subject that has a conventionality as its object (*kun rdzob pa'i yul can*). An ultimate consciousness is one which posits the ultimate. To say that it analyzes the ultimate means that it is an analyzer of [an object's] way of being (*gnas lugs*). However, it is in my opinion suitable to call the consciousness on the Mahāyāna uninterrupted path of seeing, and so forth, a conventional consciousness. Such a yogic direct perceiver is a conventional consciousness with respect to emptiness. It is a knower that analyzes the entity of emptiness.

*Question:* Why is this a conventional consciousness? Doesn't it realize the mode of abiding of emptiness as empty?

*Answer:* It understands all emptinesses. It knows the emptiness of emptiness and thus knows the mode of abiding of emptiness. However, merely realizing emptiness does not produce a realization of its mode of abiding. From this point of view, the consciousness realizing emptiness is a [nonconceptual] reasoning consciousness analyzing a conventionality.[8]

There is a great deal of discussion on this issue. This is how I see it; whether it should be so stated or not I cannot say. If this [conventional consciousness] were not an analyzer of conventionalities, there is no other [consciousness] which [would reflect on] whether emptiness conventionally existed or not. Emptiness does conventionally exist; it does not exist ultimately. It is an object of valid cognition, is it not? Valid cognition and conventional consciousness are as one. Whatever is an object of valid cognition is necessarily conventionally existent. Whatever is not an object of valid cognition does not conventionally exist. Whatever is established by valid cognition is necessarily realized by a conventional consciousness. Whatever is realized by a conventional consciousness is necessarily established by valid cognition.

Since emptiness conventionally exists, what is the [consciousness in relation to which it is a] conventional existent? Only the valid cognizer realizing emptiness. It exists as the object of that valid cognizer, and [such a mind must be posited because] if [emptiness] existed for a consciousness *not* realizing emptiness [this would not signify that] emptiness [exists]. Therefore it seems to me necessary to posit the consciousness that realizes emptiness [as the consciousness in relation to which emptiness conventionally exists]. However, the texts do not seem very clear about this. I have looked into this a great deal. The Svātantrikas do say that the uninterrupted path is [a consciousness analyzing conventionalities]. They understand it in this way; I have not seen a clear Prāsaṅgika discussion on this. There is only our own reflection [to go on].

[In short,] the consciousness directly realizing emptiness is a conventional consciousness, but conventional subjects *(kun rdzob pa'i chos can)* do not appear to it.[9] [In general] a conventional consciousness is a nonanalytical, nonsearching conventional consciousness; it is nonanalytical with respect to the ultimate, emptiness, although it may do the conventional analysis by which it conventionally [distinguishes] object and agent. Such nonanalytical consciousnesses [designate] eating, drinking, moving, staying, permanent, and impermanent. All such things are designated without [ultimate] analysis. Nonanalytically speaking, these exist. An analytical consciousness, as we have seen, is one that engages in analysis with respect to reality.

The *Illumination of the Thought* states that the meaning of emptiness is well known to a conventional consciousness. Although discussed in the context of Svātantrika tenets, this assertion also carries over to Prāsaṅgika. Is the meaning of emptiness as a lack of inherent existence well known to a nonanalytical conventional consciousness? Yes, it is. Does such a consciousness posit it? Yes, because it is posited by the conventional consciousness to which it appears.[10] We have said that any established base *(gzhi grub)*, even emptiness, is necessarily conventionally established.

Thus, emptiness conventionally exists because any consciousness realizing emptiness is [from the perspective described above] a nonanalytical conventional consciousness. The emptiness [which is its object] is established by valid cognition; that is, because of being apprehended, it is asserted as established by valid cognition. Only its mode of abiding, not its entity, is being analyzed; the entity [of emptiness] must be posited as existing just through this [that is, nonanalytically].

Therefore, a realizer of emptiness—whether an inferential valid cognizer or a direct valid cognizer—does realize emptiness. Indeed, [as indicated above,] emptiness can be posited as existent just because of being established by such valid cognition. Therefore, it conventionally exists and is posited by the power of the consciousness that takes it as an object—that is, by the power of a convention *(tha snyad pa'i dbang gi bzhag pa red)*.

Objects such as cars and houses appear to conventional consciousnesses and are not undermined by other valid cognizers. They, too, exist conventionally. Truly existent houses, cars, or persons are a different matter. They are well known to conventional thought and are not undermined or contradicted by other conventional valid cognizers. They are, however, undermined by a consciousness analyzing the ultimate. This means that when one searches to find whether there is a referent object—that is, a phenomenon which corresponds to the conception of an inherently existent house, car, or person—this analytical consciousness—an analyzer of the ultimate—undermines or refutes the existence of such a truly existent phenomenon. It does not, however, undermine the *appearance* of such. Thus, although truly existent houses, for example, do not exist, the appearance of a truly existent house does exist. The conventional or imputedly existent house is what is left over once the inherently existent house is refuted.

This imputedly existent house or person conventionally exists. The inherently existent house or person does not exist at all, even conventionally. Thus, the imputedly existent house is a dependent arising in the sense of being (1) dependent on causes and conditions, (2) dependent on its own parts, and (3) imputed by thought. Moreover, the very existence of phenomena is posited in dependence on a valid cognizer; this is what being conventionally or imputedly existent means. Thus, according to Prāsaṅgika Mādhyamika, all phenomena—conventional and ultimate—are posited in dependence on valid cognition.

Does it follow that anything that exists must be known by some consciousness? Not exactly. To say that phenomena exist imputedly is a measure of their type of existence, and they fulfill this measure whether they are perceived or not. For example, if you have a pound of butter and weigh it, it can be designated as a pound of butter. But whether you actually weigh it or not, it is a pound of butter. The measure or amount is there. Similarly, except for being merely posited by a conventional valid cognizer, houses, and so forth, do not exist.

A conventional consciousness is one that establishes the measure of [an object's] being existent or nonexistent. When we say that phenomena exist conventionally, meaning that they exist for a conventional consciousness, this conventional consciousness is not just the consciousness of an ordinary person.[11] A conventional consciousness does not necessarily have to posit conventional phenomena; it is not necessarily a consciousness analyzing or distinguishing a conventionality. Even a consciousness analyzing the ultimate—emptiness—in the continuum of a yogi can probably be considered a conventional consciousness.

For an object to be established or posited by valid cognition, it is sufficient that it be realized by valid cognition. It is not necessary that the consciousness realize the object's existence or realize that it is established by valid cognition. For example, when one sees a house, one realizes neither the existence of the house nor that it is established by a valid cognizer. Nevertheless, one does realize the house. It is the same with emptiness. The emptiness of inherent existence exists and is realized by valid cognition, but that valid consciousness need not realize *that* emptiness exists or *that* it is established by valid cognition.

The objects known by valid cognition are dependently arisen phenomena. They exist conventionally, not ultimately or inherently. Once one has understood the lack of true or inherent existence, one understands dependent arising. That is, once you have understood the lack of true existence, you realize that a conventional truth such as a house is false and deceptive. Once you establish a lack of true existence, you know that there is no referent object (*zhen yul, *adhyavasāyaviṣaya)*, for the conception of true existence. The conception of true existence exists in the mental continuums of all ordinary persons. It is the root cause of cyclic existence—the ignorance that is the first of the twelve links of dependent arising. One must investigate carefully to find whether or not there is a truly existent object that corresponds to this conception. If one reflects on this a little, it gradually helps. It is a difficult contemplation, yet extremely important. Although there are many things which should be done quickly, practice of the teaching is to be done slowly. In this way one can cultivate the first type of skill completed on the sixth ground, skill with respect to dependent arising and specifically, the understanding that emptiness, like all other phenomena, is a dependent arising and, therefore, illusory.

## THE COARSE AND SUBTLE FOUR TRUTHS

The second type of skill which becomes manifest on the sixth ground is a Bodhisattva's understanding of the four noble truths. As a second reason for calling the sixth ground "the Manifest," Tsong-kha-pa states that on the fifth ground the Bodhisattva observed true paths. True paths are the fourth of the four noble truths. To say, therefore, that on the fifth ground Bodhisattvas are skilled with respect to the fourth truth means that they have completed skill with respect to the preceeding three as well. That Bodhisattva has a knower which understands all four truths.

*Question:* Why does Tsong-kha-pa quote Jayānanda's comment that the sixth ground is "the manifestation of a path in which knower and known are not observed?"[12] It seems to contradict Tsong-kha-pa's position.

*Answer:* Jayānanda's *Commentarial Explanation*, from which Tsong-kha-pa is quoting, is a commentarial discussion of Candrakīrti's *[Auto]Commentary on the "Entrance to (Nāgārjuna's) 'Treatise on the Middle Way'" (dbu ma la 'jug pa'i rang 'grel, madhyamakāvatārabhāṣya).* It is a worthwhile text but not entirely correct on this point. Jayānanda maintains that the sixth-ground Bodhisattva, on the basis of having observed true paths on the fifth ground, now has complete wisdom regarding the four truths because "knower and known are not observed." This is incorrect because a path which merely realizes knower and known as unobserved [that is, as lacking inherent existence] occurs even on the first Bodhisattva ground. Therefore, merely [stating] this factor does not give the complete meaning of the sixth ground's feature of fully knowing the four truths on account of following upon the fifth-ground observation of true paths. Moreover, on the fifth ground one already had skill regarding the coarse and subtle aspects of the four truths. The difference on the sixth ground comes because now, for the first time, skill with respect to the four truths occurs by way of an attainment of the special enhanced perfection of wisdom, whereas on the fifth ground one's skill regarding the four was by way of an enhanced perfection of concentration. Just as it is necessary to attain calm abiding before special insight [on emptiness] can be achieved, so, in order to attain the special insight which observes the coarse and subtle forms of the sixteen aspects of the four noble truths, one must first achieve the calm abiding which observes these.

There is always a cause-and-effect relationship between the coarser and more subtle [attainments]. Thus, in order to attain the [sixth ground's] complete special insight which observes the coarse and subtle sixteen aspects of the four noble truths, it is necessary to attain the complete [perfection of] concentration. In dependence, therefore, on the surpassing perfection of concentration achieved on the fifth ground, one subsequently—never simultaneously—achieves the surpassing practice of the perfection of wisdom which observes the coarse and subtle sixteen aspects of the four noble truths.

On the sixth ground, true paths themselves become manifest. They were not manifest on the fifth ground but were objects of an enhanced perfection of concentration. This difference can be likened to completing and handing in an examination. The study is finished. But if someone asks, "Did you get an A?" you do not yet know. Although the work is done, the result is not yet manifest. Similarly, on the fifth ground, one has skill with respect to the four noble truths, and on the sixth ground this skill becomes manifest.

On the sixth ground, moreover, one manifests skill regarding the coarse and subtle sixteen aspects of the four noble truths. Each of the four truths has four aspects associated with it, making sixteen; each of the sixteen has both a coarse and a subtle form. The first truth, sufferings, has the four aspects of being

1. impermanent
2. miserable
3. empty
4. selfless.[13]

Coarse impermanence here refers to the fact that a chair, for example, cannot remain stable for a second moment after the time of its own establishment. The entity disintegrates in the very next moment. Here "disintegration" and "impermanence" are equivalent. Subtle momentariness refers to the momentariness that is qualified as lacking inherent existence. Our texts[14] define impermanence as "momentary," but this does not define subtle impermanence. Thus, the more subtle form of impermanence has to do with the fact that phenomena do not exist from their own side. The conception that they do so exist is a beginningless form of ignorance due to which one accumulates a conditioning action, the second of the twelve links of dependent arising. This is an action which impels the taking up of mental and physical aggregates in another rebirth.

Coarse misery, the second aspect of true sufferings, refers to the suffering which comes about due to the conception of a substantially existent, self-sufficient *(rang rkya ba)* self of persons, as a result of which one is reborn in cyclic existence. Subtle misery is the effect of the conception of inherent existence. Impelled into cyclic existence by such misconception, one experiences the three types of suffering [that of pain, change, and being under the influence of contaminated actions and afflictions]. Some scholars do not consider a presentation of coarseness and subtlety in relation to the first two aspects of true sufferings; yet it can be posited and is helpful to consider.[15] It is easier, however, to explain the coarse and subtle forms of the next two aspects, emptiness and selflessness.

In the context of the four aspects of true sufferings, selflessness signifies the lack of a self of persons, and emptiness, the selflessness of the objects used by such persons. The coarse aspect of this selflessness is the lack of a substantially existent, self-sufficient person. An example of the conception of such a self is the thought, "My aggregates [mind and body]," within apprehending the person as having sovereignty over the aggregates. The lack of [persons and other phenomena] existing from their own side *(rang ngos nas grub pa, svarūpasiddhi)* is their subtle selflessness. The coarse and subtle emptinesses are the lack of phenomena existing as objects used, respectively, by (1) a substantially existent, self-sufficient self or (2) an inherently existent self. The lack or emptiness of persons and other phenomena existing from their own side is [also] a subtle emptiness.

As long as one has not ascertained the lack of inherent existence, actions are accumulated as a result of conceiving it. Moreover, the conception of inherent existence is the root of misconceiving both coarse and subtle impermanence.

In dependence on the coarse and subtle conceptions of self, we experience coarse and subtle suffering. Whenever one is experienced, the other is [in principle] experienced also. However, you cannot identify them separately in terms of your own experience. They are one entity but different for thought.

## True Causes of Suffering

One accumulates actions in dependence on both the coarse conception of a substantially existent self-sufficient self and the subtle conception of inherent existence. Just as these conceptions differ in coarseness and subtlety, so do the actions accumulated due to them. Only Prāsaṅgikas are able to make such a presentation; Svātantrikas, as well as the lower systems [Cittamātra, Sautrāntika, and Vaibhāṣika] do not state the necessity for realizing the lack of inherent existence; they maintain that phenomena do inherently exist, at least conventionally, if not ultimately. They identify only the conception of a substantially existent self as the motivator for contaminated actions. The fact that Prāsaṅgika distinguishes two motivating conceptions sets their presentation apart from that of the lower tenet systems.

[Thus, Prāsaṅgika speaks of] two forms of ignorance; the conception of a substantially existent self-sufficient person is coarse ignorance, and the conception of inherently existent persons and other phenomena is subtle ignorance. There are also coarse and subtle forms of attachment, the eighth of the twelve links of dependent arising (see above). The division of ignorance and existents into coarse and subtle forms is clearly stated in the texts. In the case of ignorance, the coarse and subtle forms are actually different entities and, being different entities, they are necessarily different for thought. One is a conception of substantial self-sufficient existence, the other a conception of existence from a phenomenon's own side. These are different consciousnesses.[16] The coarse and subtle forms of attachment and grasping, the eighth and ninth links of dependent arising, are probably [different] entities and not just different [for thought]. Svātantrikas and the lower systems consider attachment and grasping to be coarse. The Prāsaṅgikas also discuss the coarse forms of these and, in addition, posit an uncommon subtle form of them which exists even in the continuum of those whom the Svātantrikas and below consider Arhats. Unlike the lower systems, Prāsaṅgika maintains that the manifestation of subtle ignorance sets up the impelling actions *(phen byed kyi las)* for the aggregates [of mind and body]. Thus, [anyone not actually liberated] accumulates actions on the basis of these two forms of ignorance. [Subsequently] grasping and existence-karma become manifest, and wandering in cyclic existence continues.

It would be difficult to talk about the aggregates [in terms of which type of ignorance each depends on]. A person accumulates actions in dependence on both [types of ignorance] and thus wanders in cyclic exisence. Therefore, the impelling action itself must be [due to] both coarse and subtle ignorance.

Indeed, one can posit coarse and subtle forms with respect to each of the twelve links of dependent arising, and with respect to the sixteen aspects of the four noble truths, such as impermanence, and so forth. In some cases, the coarse and subtle forms are different entities; in others, they are only differentiated conceptually. It is a bit difficult [to establish a full presentation] regarding the existence of those that are of different entity. This requires some thought. [The essential point here is that] one accumulates actions in dependence on both coarse and subtle forms of ignorance, but the conception of inherent existence is the deeper one; it is the root.

In general, we are not aware that such conceptions motivate actions. It is like watching someone perform an activity without knowing that this action is actually being motivated by someone else. We see only the external and cannot know what lies beneath. It is important to recognize what the deep cause of the prison of cyclic existence is. Worldly beings do not understand it and in this way are like a dog who, upon being hit by a stone, becomes angry at the stone rather than at the person who threw it. They do not understand the actual cause of their pain.

In brief, as regards the coarse and subtle aspects of the true origins of suffering, the apprehension of a substantially existent or self-sufficient self has the four aspects of being:

1. cause
2. source
3. strong producer, and
4. causal condition [of suffering].

The subtler apprehension of inherent existence also has these four aspects.

### True Cessations

The four coarse aspects of true cessations are these:

1. cessation
2. pacification
3. being highly auspicious, and
4. being definitely liberating.

These come about through the abandonment of the conception of a substantially existent or self-sufficient self. The four subtle aspects are the abandonment of a conception of inherent existence.

### True Paths

True paths are the direct realization of the lack of an [inherently existent] self, a realization that the ignorance [conceiving of inherent existence] has no referent object. This realization reverses beginningless ignorance by means of the reverse process of dependent arising.

The path which is a direct realization of the lack of a substantially existent or self-sufficient person has four coarse aspects. It is

1. a path
2. suitable
3. an achieving, and
4. a deliverer.

The path which has the subtle forms of these four aspects is the direct realization of the lack of inherent existence.

Although there are many who maintain it is unsuitable to present coarse and subtle forms of all sixteen aspects of the four noble truths, Panchen Sönam Drakba has explained the suitability of such as described above.

## APPROACHING THE ATTAINMENTS OF BUDDHAHOOD

The third reason for calling the sixth ground "The Manifest" is that the Bodhisattva is drawing near the attainment of a perfect Buddha's qualities; for the first time, fewer than half the ten grounds remain to be accomplished. Six grounds have been achieved, and only four remain. One will not now fall to the fifth ground, just as from the fifth one would not fall to the fourth, nor from the fourth to the third, and so on.

The sixth-ground Bodhisattva's perfection of wisdom is enhanced, not only because of the special absorption of cessation, but because both phenomena and their emptinesses are understood to be like illusions or reflections in a mirror. In brief, on the sixth ground one is skilled from two points of view: in terms of the forward procedure and reversal of the twelve links of dependent arising, and in terms of the four noble truths. Because the four truths and the twelve links become actualized or manifest at this time, the sixth ground is called "The Manifest."

## PRAISE OF THE PERFECTION OF WISDOM (116.1)

This perfection is different from the other perfections practiced by Bodhisattvas. Without wisdom, the other five—giving, ethics, patience, effort, and concentration—do not act as causes of highest enlightenment. The other perfections are as if blind, and the perfection of wisdom is like an eye. A group of a hundred or a thousand blind persons cannot make their way to a desired destination unless someone with sight leads them. Similarly, without wisdom [these other perfections] are unable to proceed to the ground [of enlightenment]. The *Condensed Perfection of Wisdom Sutra ('phags pa sdud pa/ shes rab kyi pha rol tu phyin pa sdud pa, sañcayagāthāprajñāpāramitā)* says:

> How could billions of blind and guideless persons,
> Not even knowing the path, enter the city?
> Without the perfection of wisdom, these five sightless perfections
> Lack a guide and, thus, cannot reach enlightenment.[17]

[Similar] statements are made in the *Diamond Cutter Sutra* and in Candrakīrti's *Entrance to the Middle Way.*

The perfection of wisdom is to be joined with each of the preceeding perfections. For example, in order for the perfection of giving to be a direct cause of Buddhahood, the Bodhisattva must understand that the three spheres of gift, giver, and recipient do not inherently exist but are only dependently arisen. Except for being dependently arisen, they have no existence whatsoever; they are like reflections in a mirror.

At night, in the absence of light, even those with good eyes can see nothing and go nowhere. Although the various types of object exist nearby, they remain unseen, but when the sun rises, all become visible, and we can go where we choose. Similarly, if someone [in mental darkness] thinks that there is inherent existence, he or she also considers giving and the other perfections to exist inherently. This is what falling to a conception of "things" [i.e., as inherently existent] means. By cultivating the perfection of wisdom, one understands that all phenomena are without true or inherent existence. Giving is done within this understanding. For example, if I give you money within understanding that I, you, and the money do not inherently exist, that is very good.

The same understanding also applies to the perfection of effort. If one exerts effort within thinking that oneself, the effort exerted, and the object with respect to which effort is made inherently exist, this does not become a cause of Buddhahood. Practiced within a conception of inherent existence, the other virtues will not become causes of Buddhahood, no matter how much difficulty one undergoes to perform them.

If such wisdom is lacking, then even though one has a Bodhisattva's motivation, one is not engaging in faultless Bodhisattva activity. If one practices giving within construing the gift, giver, and recipient as inherently existent, one will not reach the stage of Buddhahood. The same is true for the practice of ethics, patience, effort, and concentration. In this sense, the perfection of wisdom is like an eye leading the other blind perfections to the state of perfect enlightenment. Without wisdom, the perfections of giving, and so forth, will not lead to the attainment of the full enlightenment of a Buddha.

## PROMISE TO EXPLAIN THE PROFOUND EMPTINESS

The Mādhyamika explanation that phenomena are empty of inherent existence is wholly compatible with its assertion that all phenomena, including emptinesses, are dependent arisings. Thus, it is possible to see phenomena as dependent arisings and, at the same time, to understand them as empty. The consciousness that understands emptiness, therefore, does not eliminate perception of phenomena but causes them to be seen more clearly.

Not understanding this, someone might ask how a sixth-ground Bodhisattva can see suchness—emptiness—and at the same time perceive dependent arisings. The questioner thinks that someone seeing reality would not perceive dependent arisings, that the two are incompatible. He or she mistakenly considers that to say phenomena or dependent arisings lack inherent existence is to maintain that they do not exist at all.

This is completely at odds with the Mādhyamika position. As Tsong-kha-pa emphasizes, if something [that exists] is empty of inherent existence, it must be dependently arisen. If something is dependently arisen, it must be empty of inherent existence. Thus, one who comprehends emptiness comprehends dependent arising. The wisdom understanding emptiness does not remove the consciousness that knows dependent arisings; it removes the ignorance that misconceives dependent arisings to inherently exist.

Like an eye covered by cataracts, a consciousness covered by ignorance is obscured. When medicine is applied to the eye, it is the cataracts and not the eye itself that is removed; the eye becomes clearer. Similarly, when the antidote of wisdom is applied, ignorance—but not consciousness—is removed, and one is able to understand phenomena—dependent arisings—more clearly than before.

Is the perfection of wisdom completed at this time? Some say it is, some that it is not. However, there is really not so great a difference between these positions as might appear. [The Tibetan term for perfection of wisdom can be interpreted to mean either "gone" or "going" beyond]. Whether or not the term "perfection of wisdom" signifies the wisdom attained on the sixth ground depends on whether the verb is read as "gone" or "going." [Those who maintain that] the verbal *phyin* signifies *phyin zin pa*, meaning that the perfection of wisdom is completed, say that such a completed perfection is not achieved [on the sixth ground.] Those who take the verb to be a continuative meaning "going along a path" maintain that [a significant movement toward the] perfection of wisdom is achieved at this time [but not the final and complete one]. Thus, they contend that the perfection of wisdom does exist while one is a trainee. There is something to reflect on regarding each of these positions. [Both agree, however] that the perfection of wisdom has not *been* perfected but is *being* perfected.

To gain the perfection of wisdom, one must first cognize emptiness conceptually, and later directly. What realizes emptiness directly? The consciousness of a Superior in meditative equipose. As a result of this realization, the consciousness becomes clearer: it improves. Anything capable of improvement [or deterioration] is a dependent arising. Thus, the wisdom cognizing emptiness is a dependent arising, and the emptiness—the lack of inherent existence—which is its object is also a dependent arising. [The Bodhisattva therefore sees the reality of dependent arising] in the sense that reality or emptiness is a quality of phenomena which are dependent arisings, and in the sense that the emptiness itself is a dependently arisen phenomenon.

To whom is emptiness taught? The following section discusses how to identify persons who are "vessels for an explanation of the profound emptiness."

# 3

# THE STUDENTS OF EMPTINESS

## QUALIFICATIONS

An actual vessel, or suitable recipient, for the explanation of emptiness is a student already familiar with the topic through having heard it explained in a previous life and reflected upon it in this one. [In the strictest interpretation] emptiness should not be taught to anyone else, even though they are willing to listen, because they will develop [harmful] misconceptions.

There are external signs by which one can tell with confidence that someone is an actual vessel of the teachings on emptiness. We know that, in ordinary experience, tears often come to the eyes on happy or other occasions. If tears arise when a student hears about emptiness, or if the hairs on his or her body stand on end, one can have confidence that this person is a suitable vessel.[1]

If no such external signs appear, it would [in general] be better to leave aside this explanation until later. [However] because there is benefit in establishing predispositions for correct understanding of emptiness, it is also suitable to explain emptiness to someone who, even though he or she is not an actual vessel of the teaching [in the sense just described], will not go beyond the teaching of emptiness. A suitable vessel or recipient of such teaching [in this interpretation] has a strong interest in emptiness; she or he feels that unless and until they realize emptiness, there will be no way [of escaping suffering]. Impelled by a sense that continuous wandering in cyclic existence is insanity, such persons will ascertain emptiness very carefully when it is explained to them. Such a person is a vessel for the new depositing of potencies for understanding it. They will not go beyond the advice of an excellent teacher.

"Not going beyond" the precepts of the teacher means that even though tears and hairs standing on end do not occur when emptiness is taught, this person listens very carefully to what is said, likes it and understands it. Such a disciple need not be a Superior but must be capable of reflecting on emptiness and should be attracted to the topic; otherwise, it will make no difference whether the meaning is understood or not. The appropriate disciple is also unbiased. One should not think, for example, that one will favor only Tsong-kha-pa's writings and not other worthwhile discussions of this subject. If emptiness is explained well by anyone, one should listen with confidence.

The teacher must be qualified also, of course. As with other things, someone who does not know what they are doing can do more harm than good. There are people who, even though they do not understand much, have great pride in their intelligence. Explanations by such persons can be very misleading. If someone who does not understand the workings of tape recorders nonetheless tries to mend one, the machine degenerates, whereas someone skilled with such machines can repair it so that it will work well for a long time to come. Similarly, those who do not have the capacity to understand emptiness but who think they understand it and teach it to others, harm both others and themselves. Such discourse does not cause liberation for students or teachers, but results in unfortunate rebirths.

The teaching is *not* helpful to persons who, on hearing it, would veer to an extreme of nonexistence, thinking that since phenomena do not inherently exist, they do not exist at all, even conventionally. Forms, and so forth, exist, do they not? The *[Heart] Sutra*, which says, "Forms do not exist, sounds do not exist," and so forth [does not mean such things are utterly nonexistent]. It is a mistake to think that persons, and so forth, do not exist at all. You exist; I exist. There are foods to eat, liquids to drink.

Lo-sang-dam-chö (*blo bzang dam chos*) writes :

> Suppose someone asks, "If, with respect to that [phenomenon], there is no inherent existence, what exists?" The answer is given that the entities of those [things] fabricated by either the thoroughly afflicted or utterly pure causes do exist, and are dependently arisen.[2]

And that text [(Candrakīrti's) *Commentary on (Āryadeva's) "Four Hundred" (byang chub sems dpa'i rnal 'byor spyod pa bzhi brgya pa'i rgya cher 'grel pa, bodhisattvayogacāryācatuḥśatakaṭīkā)*] says:

> When the dependently arisen are seen as they are,
> They are [existent] like magical illusions, not [nonexistent] like the
> child of a barren woman.

Certain students, upon hearing that all phenomena do not exist inherently, [incorrectly] conclude that inherent existence does exist, and therefore despise the teacher as worthless. Having no confidence [in what is said], such persons imagine that a mind divested of the conception of inherent existence would become not clearer but nonexistent. They do not believe phenomena are without true or inherent existence but, like the Vaibhāṣikas and Sautrāntikas, conceive forms, and so forth, to be truly established.

However, just as in Tsong-kha-pa's example given above—"When medicine is placed in the eye, the eye becomes clearer, not nonexistent"—so it is that when the mind's eye of wisdom becomes cleared of the obscuration of ignorance, it too becomes clearer, not nonexistent.[3]

The erroneous view that considers as nonexistent something that does in fact exist is an underestimation or deprecation *(skur 'debs, apavāda)*. This should be distinguished from the type of error known as imputation by thought *(rtogs pas btags pa, *kalpanāprajñāpti)*, in which one conceives as existent what actually does not exist at all—for example, the horns of a rabbit.

It would only be harmful to teach such persons the view of emptiness. Just as, in Tsong-kha-pa's example, the mistake of a snake-handler can be fatal, so developing wrong views regarding emptiness can be very harmful. Those who fall to extreme [views] of annihilation or nonexistence proceed to an unfortunate rebirth; those who fall to extremes of existence or permanence enter a fortunate birth [but both inevitably involve suffering]. Thus, whether one thinks that things exist inherently— the extreme of permanence—or that they do not exist [at all], even conventionally—the extreme of annihilation—one has created a cause for birth in cyclic existence. More specifically, those who fall to an extreme of annihilation maintain that karma—the cause and effect of actions—does not exist. Because virtue and nonvirtue seem equally appropriate, they accumulate much nonvirtue and hence the causes for an unfortunate rebirth.

To accumulate merit by doing prostrations, making offerings, circumambulating [temples or other holy places], or having faith in Buddha's teaching—these are means for realizing emptiness. If, in addition [to the study or practice of virtue] one has a Bodhisattva motivation, this is excellent. One must also understand the texts that teach emptiness. Some people cannot do this; others think it is unnecessary. This is true among monks also. When told to study definitions [a crucial part of the monk's scholarly training], they decide, "I cannot understand these," and many do not study the texts. Feeling they cannot understand, they make prayers to have this capacity in the future.

Tsong-kha-pa also states (120.13) that one goes to a bad rebirth if one "abandons emptiness." What does this mean? In my opinion it means to exaggerate the meaning *(don, artha)* of emptiness. Emptiness is a term that negates. To negate more than is appropriate means that one has an overly broad concept of the object [to be negated]. If one overextends the object to be negated, one [erroneously] negates the subject [which, qualified by emptiness, does exist conventionally]. The mind refutes too extensive an object of negation *('gag bya khyab ches ba).* Thus, in reflecting on the nonexistence of inherent existence, one [mistakenly] concludes that the subject *(chos can, dharmin)* itself does not exist. However, it is imperative that the [conventionally existent] subject not be undermined in refuting the object of negation. If it is undermined, then it appears nonexistent to that mind, whereby one comes to devalue it as nonexistent. It then seems suitable that tables, chairs, and so forth, do not exist, so that virtue and sin also do not exist. In that case, too, there is neither liberation nor omniscience. One refutes the inherent existence of these and therefore concludes that these too do not exist. Thus one abandons emptiness—one thinks that emptiness itself does not exist. Such deprecation leads to [bad ethics and hence to] bad rebirth. It is essential to assert virtue and nonvirtue. Tsong-kha-pa's *Stages of the Path (lam rim)* refers to this [denial] as "too extensive."

If the extent [of what is negated by emptiness] is too limited, one is unable to refute the inherent existence of conventionalities. Thus [from the viewpoint of Prāsaṅgika] the object negated by Ha-shang (see below, pages 67-68) was too broad, whereas that negated by the Svātantrika system and so forth [Cittamātra, Sautrāntika, and Vaibhāṣika] is too narrow. All proponents of tenets must understand valid cognition, and these latter systems do not deny it. They [like Prāsaṅgika] maintain that things are established by valid cognition and therefore that valid cognition is correct, not deceived. The object [observed by valid cognition] exists and thus [they conclude] it exists by way of its own nature or inherently. However, they are unable to make a distinction between "existent" and "inherently existent."

Ha-shang [by contrast] has no confidence in valid cognition, which, in his view signifies the conception of true existence. Thus he finds it necessary to refute all valid cognizers (see below, page 68).[4] There is some expedience [in this position]. Beginners who cannot distinguish [conventional] existence from inherent existence but who need provisionally to diminish anger, and so forth, can simply reflect that self and others do not exist. If you think that the object of your anger does not exist, that anger diminishes. To distance yourself from the object of anger is also helpful, either physically, by moving away, or mentally, by not bringing it to mind. If one does not understand emptiness, it is appropriate at such times to think, "I do not exist," "They do not exist," and the like. But these are only temporary measures that cannot overcome the deeply internalized *(phugs)* seed of these [afflictions]. This is like using meditation on ugliness as an antidote to desire, or dependent arising as an antidote to obscuration, or the breath when [too many] thoughts arise, or love as an antidote to anger, or the divisions of constituents *(khams, dhātu)* as an antidote to pride.[5]

Such practices will diminish afflictions for a time but will not eradicate them. [They do not involve knowledge of] how to determine whether [for example] the substantially existent *(rdzas su yod pa, dravyasat)* self-sufficient *(rang rkya ba)* self of persons exists or not. The texts discuss both a self that does and a self that does not exist. One who takes rebirth has a self. There is also the [hypothetical] substantially existent, self-sufficient self which, since beginningless time, has been a referent object for ignorance. This should be refuted.

Thus, to "abandon emptiness" (119.15) means not to understand, or to be unskilled regarding, emptiness. More specifically, it means not to accept the emptiness which is a lack of inherent existence. This has to do with an inability to posit dependent arising and with the mistaken idea that if something lacks inherent existence the thing itself does not exist, or that if things are empty there can be no cause and effect of actions and that ethics, therefore, are unnecessary.

## ACHIEVING BUDDHAHOOD

[As indicated above] it is difficult but imperative for a teacher to discriminate between those to whom it is suitable and unsuitable to teach emptiness. Because the mind is empty of inherent existence [and thus is empty of being inherently mistaken], everyone can achieve a Buddha's wisdom eventually. Yet, there is the difference that in some persons this capacity is small and in others it is great.

From another [viewpoint], it is said that [there is no time when] all living beings will achieve Buddhahood, because [their number] does not decrease. Living beings are beyond limit *(dbe mtha' las 'das pa).* If one or two [achieve Buddhahood, the number decreases and so [one might argue], their number [eventually] would be exhausted. But it would not be so. Why? To have them decrease, one would first need to have their measure. If there are a thousand, a hundred thousand, or a million, they would incrementally decrease. Some say that living beings do not decrease in this way and this is probably true since there is no measure to the number of beings, just as there is no limit to space. If we limit consideration to sentient beings in our world, these probably could be counted; individual countries take a census of their own populations; animal life too could be or is enumerated. There is a measure to them, but not to the space populated by sentient beings. No matter how far you count—one, two, and so forth—[the total] will never be completed.[6]

Although beings are limitless, Bodhisattvas have strong minds. They reflect that, intimate or not, "all these limitless beings need me, and there are no exceptions." Bodhisattvas take vows [to practice] for the sake of these beings and accordingly accumulate the collections [of merit and wisdom], purify obstructions, and achieve Buddhahood. This itself does not yet fulfill their vow to offer help to everyone; such help becomes possible because a Buddha's exalted wisdom is immeasurable, enabling Bodhisattvas to accomplish the welfare [of others]. In this way the great purpose [of the vow] is completed.

All living beings can become Buddhas because the mind is empty of true existence and its defilements are ephemeral. The nature of the mind is thus clear and undefiled. If defilements were its nature, they could not be removed, and the mind would never be purified.

Although no stains *(dri ma, mala)* exist in the nature of the clear mind itself,[7] the mind does become [temporarily] obscured by defilements such as desire, hatred, and ignorance. When one's mind is purified of one's nature, the naturally abiding lineage *(rang bzhin gnas rigs, *svabhāvasthānagôtra)* proceeds to Buddhahood. I will not discuss this extensively, except to say that [such characterizes] the consciousness of every living being. Even a bug's mind is said to have a nature of clarity; the same is true of other animals, of deities, and of humans. To say that beings possessed of such a nature thereby possess a cause of Buddhahood is like categorizing all wood under the rubric *(rigs, gotra)* of what can be burned by fire.[8]

The wisdom that realizes emptiness is called fire [metaphorically] because, just as fire consumes wood, so wisdom consumes all mental defilements. When this occurs, the mind's own nature emerges; mental defilements such as hatred vanish through being burned by the fire of exalted wisdom, but the mind does not then become nonexistent. Nāgārjuna himself speaks of this in *Praising the Element of Reality (chos kyi dbyings su bstod pa, dharmadhātustôtra):*

> When a [stone, i.e., asbestos] garment stained with contaminations
> Is to be cleansed by fire
> Once placed in that fire, its stains
> Are burned, but it is not.[9]
>
> As for the mind of clear light,
> Which has the stains of desire, and so forth,
> Its stains are burned by wisdom's fire
> But not clear light, its suchness.[10]

The opening verses of Nāgārjuna's *Praising the Element of Reality* are also relevant here:

> I bow in homage to the element of reality
> Present in all sentient beings.
> When not thoroughly understood
> One wanders among the three [states of] existence.
>
> Just this is also the Actual Body (*chos sku, dharmakāya),*
> [And] nirvana, just that purity

Of having purified what serves
As the cause of cyclic existence.[11]

The first verse discusses the naturally abiding lineage, which is an ultimate truth. [Nāgārjuna] refers to the naturally abiding lineage when he says, "I bow down to this element of actuality." Those who do not understand it are those who do not understand emptiness. A distinction is made between true cessation and the naturally abiding lineage, though both are ultimates and both are permanent, in that the naturally abiding lineage is not a mind. Some say that it is emptiness and, thus, that it has no afflictions, whereas some say that it is not emptiness. But no one contends it is a mind.

The second verse [refers to] true cessation itself. It says, "This is also the Actual Body." The Nature Body *(ngo bo nyid sku, svabhāvikakāya)* can be divided into (1) the factor which is a purification of adventitious defilements *(blo bur dri ma'i rnam dag gyi cha).* [This is a subtype within the category of the Actual Body described as the ultimate true cessation][12] and (2) the factor which is the [beginningless] purification [or absence] of an inherent nature *(rang bzhin rnam dag gi cha).* These differ in terms of what is negated: the factor of purification of adventitious defilements is the negation of the mental defilements of desire, hatred, and ignorance, including the conception of true existence, for this form of ignorance is also an adventitious defilement. The factor of beginningless purification is the negation of inherent existence itself.

As beginners we are deceived by the appearance of things as good or bad, whereupon we engage in the virtues or nonvirtues that are causes of cyclic existence. To a Superior who has understood the lack of inherent existence, all is equal. If all such [mis]conceptions are abandoned, one need go neither to a good nor a bad rebirth.

However, it is not enough just [to say that Buddhahood can be achieved because] the mind is empty of inherent existence. A table is also empty of inherent existence but a mind, in addition to being empty of inherent existence, has the nature of clear light. Mind (1) is empty of inherent existence, (2) has a nature of clear light, and (3) has defilements, which are adventitious. These factors must all be considered together. The mind's emptiness of true existence is the naturally abiding lineage.

Regarding the mind's having a nature of undefiled clear light,[13] Asaṅga has written:

Because the body of the complete Buddha emanates
And because [it is] inseparable from reality
And because it is a lineage, all who have bodies
Always possess the Buddha essence.[14]

[This] is the Buddha lineage because it propels *('jug)* the exalted deeds of a perfect Buddha. The actuality *(chos nyid, dharmatā)* of the mind conjoined with defilements, the reality of the mind separate *(bral)* from defilements are not divisions of the nature [of mind]. For this reason, it is established that Buddhahood can be attained. All persons have two lineages: the naturally abiding lineage of the Buddhas and the lineage of change *(rkyen 'gyur gyi rigs).*

To speak of the nature of the mind, which is clear light, or the final meaning of "clarity" in the definition of mind as clear and knowing, [is not a reference to] all minds [but to the] fundamental mind, [which is a type of] mental consciousness *(yid kyi rnam shes, manovijñāna).* This fundamental mind, which exists in the continuum of us all, is said to be the nature of the mind. It is the most subtle of all minds.[15] This is not elaborated on in the Perfection Vehicle but in Tantric literature.

The Chinese Ha-shang came to Tibet and taught that all phenomena are neither existent nor nonexistent. Nevertheless, Ha-shang or his followers made this [false] distinction, saying that all phenomena are nonexistent like the horns of a rabbit, that they are merely conceptually imputed mental appearances. Tibetans who follow Ha-shang take the position refuted by Tsong-kha-pa when the latter quotes Candrakīrti's statement that "one who considers compositional phenomena to be nonexistent has a wrong view."[16] Ha-shang himself probably had the view that things are neither existent nor nonexistent but something in between.[17] This last is [for Ha-shang] a third alternative: although pot is neither an existent nor a nonexistent, these proponents speak of not being pot *(bum pa ma yin),* not being a pillar, not being yellow, and so forth. Thus, there is for them a category [of phenomena] that are neither existent nor nonexistent.

There is a verbal difference between "not being existent" *(yod pa ma yin)* and "being nonexistent" *(med pa yin),* but no difference in the meaning that appears to the mind. "Nonexistence" refutes "existence" in that it negates "existence" as a mental object. "Not being existent" also refutes "existence" as a mental object. It does not refute anything else.[18] The meanings these bring to mind are the same; the verbal difference is not of much account. To say something is nonexistent is to say it does not exist. If everything did not exist then there could be no cause and effect of actions, no liberation or omniscience. This does not just mean something which does not exist for a mind directly realizing emptiness, but something which does not exist in general.[19] In this way, in accordance with Ha-shang, some maintain that [phenomena] are nonexistent *(yod pa ma yin).* Does this mean they do not exist? They cannot assert such, because many texts [contradict this position]. Distinctions are made between illusory [phenomena] and [nonexistent phenomena] such as the horns of a rabbit. Illusions are used as examples of dependently arisen phenomena; Candrakīrti's own commentary to the *Entrance* and Āryadeva's *Four Hundred* state many times that illusory phenomena are not [nonexistent] as the horns of a rabbit are nonexistent.

These points were not discussed in Ha-shang's time. Later, some followers of his put forward this third category of neither existent nor nonexistent, and responses to this were considered.

*Question:* Is Ha-shang's view not clearly explained in texts?

*Answer:* Probably it is in his own books. There are Nyingmas and Gagyus nowadays who think well of Ha-shang's view. Mi-la-re-pa and others also were favorable regarding it. Those who followed Ha-shang understood his views; nonetheless, after becoming acquainted with certain books they developed some assertions of their own. This is not the talk of someone with a reasoned approach *(rigs lam);* it is unsuitable for [existent and nonexistent] not to be explicitly contradictory. Ha-shang himself had a very well reasoned approach. Indeed, when Kamalaśīla considered whether to debate with Ha-shang, he did a great deal of analysis as to whether or not the approach of his potential opponent was suitably reasoned. He concluded it was and so debated with him. One does not attempt to debate with one who has no reasoned approach.[20]

[In our view], to maintain that phenomena do not exist undermines the [conventional] existence of things, and is therefore unsuitable. The master Kamalaśīla denies that there is a third rubric other than existent and nonexistent. [As noted above,] such is claimed to have been Ha-shang's position; however, his own views were not clearly stated in [his own] time. They are known to us primarily through the refutations offered by, for example, Kamalaśīla in *Stages of Meditation (sgom pa'i rim pa, bhāvanākrama).* Kamalaśīla maintains that these two are explicitly contradictory *(dngos 'gal),*[21] meaning that when one is refuted, the other [is necessarily implied as] an object of mind. Moreover, with pairs that are explicitly mutually exclusive *(dngos su phan tshuns mi gnas pa, dngos su phan tshuns 'pangs 'gel),* unless something excluded from one [member of the set] occurs in the other, it does not exist at all. [For example, "existent" and "nonexistent" are explicitly contradictory; anything which is not included in one must be included in the other.] When two things are contradictory—whether explicitly or implicitly—there is no third category that is a combination of both, nor can there exist something which is neither.

According to Ha-shang, when a Bodhisattva achieves a Mahāyāna path of seeing, there is no consciousness which is a realizer [of emptiness],[22] no consciousness at the time of directly realizing emptiness. Why? Because "the ultimate is not an object of activity of the mind" *(don dam blo yi spyod yul min).* This is a line from sutra.[23]

In light of such statements, these proponents consider it unsuitable to assert that a consciousness [realizes emptiness] because emptiness is an ultimate. In our own view, this statement does not mean that emptiness is not an object of any mind because emptiness is an object of the nonconceptual wisdom directly realizing emptiness. There are, however, two types of minds. The first is a mind of dualistic appearance, to which conventional objects appear. Emptiness is not an object of such a mind. The term [emptiness] points to this ultimate [truth], but not in the manner of a consciousness that directly cognizes it. Thought *(rtog pa, kalpanā)* realizes emptiness, but not as the wisdom of meditative equipoise does. All proponents of emptiness agree on this [difference between thought and direct perception].[24] They differ in terms of the subtlety of their emptiness, the subtlety of the object negated, but the approach through reasoning is the same.

For Ha-shang there is no valid cognition because he takes this to be synonymous with the conception of signs *(mtshan mar 'dzin pa, nimittagrāha)*—that is, of inherent existence. According to Ha-shang, all [conceptions of existence] are conceptions of signs.[25] Thus, all are conceptions of inherent existence—that is, of phenomena as existing from their own side. For Ha-shang, phenomena do not exist; for him valid cognition and the conception of inherent existence *(bden 'dzin, satyagrāha)* are identical. Thus, "valid cognition," any thought of existence, is a consciousness that is wrong *(log shes, viparyayajñāna)* and in this way contradictory with the middle. [In general] "the middle" means that all phenomena are without inherent existence (*rang bzhin med pa)*; Ha-shang equates this with nonexistence, meaning that things do not really exist—they are like appearances in a dream, which vanish when you awake.[26] In his view, the nonexistent [i.e. inherent existence] exists; the actual Prāsaṅgika system does not say this, but maintains that inherent existence does not exist.

[Our understanding of] Prāsaṅgika follows Nāgārjuna and three others: Śāntideva, Candrakīrti, and Buddhapālita. Ha-shang considered himself a Prāsaṅgika. From among the four schools of tenets, he was a Mādhyamika, and between the two types of Mādhyamikas, a Prāsaṅgika. But he is not a true Mādhyamika because he maintains that "middle" and "valid cognition" are contradictory.[27] In [our understanding of ] Prāsaṅgika, the lack of inherent existence is emptiness; [direct] realization of this is the uninterrupted path of the Mahāyāna path of seeing, a yogic direct perception, a valid cognition, a convention[al consciousness]. For Ha-shang there is no conventional valid cognition *(tha snyad pa'i tshad ma, vyavahārapramāṇa)* and no consciousness that [validly] realizes the middle. This is an ultimate truth and as such, in accordance with Śāntideva's statement in *Engaging in the Bodhisattva Deeds*, does not appear to the mind. Śāntideva writes there (IX.2d), "The ultimate is not an object of activity of the mind."

[It is said that Ha-shang would argue that] if one has a conception [of existence], then whether one acts virtuously or nonvirtuously, one is reborn in cyclic existence;[28] whether a black dog or a white dog bites you [it is the same]; similarly, whether you do virtue or nonvirtue, you wander in cyclic existence.[29] Whether or not he actually said this is uncertain.[30]

Our own position concurs in that so long as one acts within a conception that things exist from their own side, one does not escape cyclic existence. But this has to do with conceiving of things as existing from their own side [not as merely existent]. According to Ha-shang, by contrast, existence is identical with existence from a thing's own side. No inherent existence means there are no existents. In that case, this table before us is not an existent. Is it then a nonexistent *(med pa)*? Not precisely that either.

Kamalaśīla, who directly disputed Ha-shang's position, refuted this particular point extensively, [discussing it in] his first, middling, and final texts on the *Stages of Meditation (sgom pa'i rim pa, bhāvanākrama)*. These were most likely written subsequent to his debate with Ha-shang.

Tsong-kha-pa discusses the categories of existents and nonexistents very clearly.[31] Two "nonexistents" to be discredited and two "existents" which are actual are discussed. Regarding the "nonexistents," one is [hypothetically] nonexistent from its own side, the other is nonexistent conventionally. [The former does not occur, the latter does.] For the mind directly realizing emptiness, the object [qualified by emptiness] appears to have become nonexistent. For example, if you directly cognize the emptiness of a table, the table which appears to exist from its own side vanishes for that mind. Not even the [mere] table itself remains as an object of that mind. However, this mind does not realize the nonexistence of the [conventionally existent] table. It realizes the nonexistence of [a table] which exists from its own side. This is a necessary distinction.

Similarly, there are two categories of existence: existence from its own side *(rang ngos nas grub pa, svarūpasiddhi)* and conventional existence *(tha snyad du yod pa, *vyavahārasat)*. The former does not occur; the latter does. Whatever is an established base *(gzhi grub)* must conventionally exist. The conception of true existence apprehends [things as] existing from their own side rather than as conventionally existent. There is [also] a mind that understands conventional existence, and although existence from its own side appears to such a mind, that mind does not conceive of things this way. For a Buddha Superior, there is not even a [mistaken] appearance. In the example Tsong-kha-pa uses, an illusionist projects the appearance of a horse and an elephant. [To him] these [simply] appear; there are also those [the audience] who adhere to this appearance, and those [who arrive after the spell was cast] who neither see an appearance of inherent existence nor adhere to it. In the same way, there are those to whom existence from its own side appears, those who conceive of such, and those who have neither appearance nor adherence. However, there are many proponents of [Buddhist] tenets who assert these two types of existence as identical. For example, Svātantrikas and below [Cittamātra, Sautrāntika, Vaibhāṣika] maintain that existence and existence from a thing's own side are the same. This is a point of some difficulty. If something conventionally exists, it must [according to them] exist from its own side. Prāsaṅgikas however speak of [phenomena as] being established by valid cognition and imputed by thought.

# 4

# How Good Qualities Arise When Emptiness is Explained

## EMPTINESS AND ETHICS

Like gold or treasure placed in the hands of one who will care for it well, an explanation of emptiness to one who listens correctly has far-reaching effects. A person such as the one described earlier, having heard about emptiness in this life, will [wish to] reflect on it even in future lives. Recognizing that if one is born into an unfortunate situation, it is impossible to analyze the meaning of emptiness, a person concerned with realizing the meaning of emptiness makes effort to achieve a good future rebirth. He or she does this by practicing good ethics. This person regards the teaching of emptiness as a treasure that must not be lost: just as a person with gold would make arrangements to keep it safely, so this person engages in ethics, practicing the ten virtues as a way of preserving contact with the teachings on emptiness.

Even if one has heard the view of emptiness [and subsequently attains a human rebirth], if one is then so poor as to be deprived of food or clothing, all one's efforts must be for acquiring the bare necessities of life, with no opportunity to hear about or reflect on emptiness. It is thus necessary to engage in giving [the first of the six perfections] so that one will possess resources in the future.

Regarding this, it is essential to understand the theory of karma, the cause and effect of actions. For example, by killing and eating an animal, one satisfies the stomach for the time being, but in the future will be killed oneself. This effect is similar in type to its cause, having killed. Those who understand [the doctrine of karma] are able to purify their activities a little bit.

It is, of course, important to accomplish certain things in this life; if, in addition to this, one can for the greater purpose of one's future life practice the teaching somewhat, it will be helpful to oneself and others. This does not mean to give up all work and meditate. The first is important for this life, the second for future lives. Neither should be discarded. Such accords with the circumstances in your country. In Tibet there are many who bring donations to a solitary meditator, and so one could more or less forget about working for this life and concentrate on practice. In the United States this would be shameful—and besides, one would have no money and nothing to eat.

Virtue is a cause of future resources. If one gives to others, or abandons harming them, this makes them happy and brings about one's own future happiness. This is a case of the effect, happiness, being similar in type to the cause, the giving of happiness. If one abandons killing others, then one's own life will not be cut off; even if one is reborn as an animal, one will have a long life. If one tells the truth, one will not be deceived by others. To speak harsh or angry words to others is harmful to them; if one abandons these and speaks gently, others will not address harsh words to oneself in the future. Each of these is an instance of an effect similar in type to its cause.

[Moreover] if in this life we realize emptiness, it becomes necessary to empower that wisdom over many lifetimes. One who cannot achieve Buddhahood in a single lifetime[1] needs the ability [to continue this process] in future lives. Thus, one needs to be a human being in the future, for if one is an animal or hell-being, it will be impossible to further empower the wisdom realizing emptiness. Since one needs to be a human, the causes for human [birth] are required—namely, the three [forms of] ethics [i.e., of body, speech, and mind. As a result one can attain] the seven good qualities of exalted status *(mtho ris kyi yon tan bdun)*:

1. a good physical form
2. good family or lineage
3. resources
4. power
5. wisdom
6. long life, and
7. freedom from illness.

The final purpose of realizing emptiness [in terms of one's own welfare] is to gain an antidote to the conception of inherent existence and its latencies (*bag chags, vāsanā).* To this end, one engages in giving, practices ethics, and cultivates patience. [As Śāntideva says in opening the ninth chapter of] *Engaging in the Bodhisattva Deeds,* "All these branches *(yan lag, aṅga)* are practiced for the sake of wisdom" *(yan lag di dag thams cad ni thub pas shes rab don du gsungs).* The branches alluded to here in "all these branches" are: giving, ethics, patience, effort, and concentration. Some scholars apply this statement only to the perfection of concentration,[2] but many books take the [common] purpose of all the first five Bodhisattva deeds to be the increase of wisdom. In the final analysis, these enhance wisdom so that it can act as an antidote to the obstructions to omniscience. Without this wisdom one cannot abandon the afflictions that prevent liberation or omniscience *(nyon sgrib, kleśāvaraṇa).*

Scientists today understand dependent arising well; they can identify what comes from which causes. They know that things depend on the amassing of their constituent parts and on their causes, but they do not recognize that phenomena are also dependent arisings in the sense of being imputed by thought. Their expertise lies with the temporary, immediate causes, not with the more distant [and deeper] causes of things. Buddhists, however, recognize that present circumstances depend not only on the completion of immediate causes but on the indirect causes consisting of past actions. If, for example, we engage in business and profit, our profit is an indirect effect of previous giving; it is also an effect of doing the work that is its immediate or direct cause *(dngos rgyu, sākṣātkāraṇa).*

It is the same with other things. When a farmer plows for the sake of a harvest, the harvest is not the result of that work only; there is also a prior cause. Scientists would mock this. [Yet we know that] even though [many persons] study a great deal, some achieve their purpose and others do not. Such differences occur even among children of the same father and mother, or students of the same teacher. The reason for this has to do with many causes we do not understand.[3] It is beneficial to reflect that such causes must have been accumulated in a previous lifetime and that our consciousness existed at that time. If this occurred in the past, one can reflect that it will be that way in the future. Just as, while young, one makes effort to ensure comfort later in life, so one should have concern for one's future life. It is the same continuum.[4] There are [also] many actions that have no effect; if only an indirect cause [a prior action] but not the direct cause is present, the effect will not arise.

Actions *(las, karma)* have three types of effects: (1) those which, as illustrated above, accord with their cause; (2) the ripened effect—[a more general type of concordance between cause and effect] signifying that if one does good, happiness results, and if one creates suffering for others through committing some nonvirtue, suffering will result for oneself; and finally, (3) environmental effects, which are results not included in one's own mental continuum—the mountains, houses, and so forth.[5]

Suppose one is miserly. For the time being, one's possessions remain for one's own use, but in the future one will have few resources. Similarly, if one kills animals, there is meat to eat for the present, but in the future will come those who eat oneself, and even in a "good" rebirth one tends to encounter unhappy situations, and life will be short. [Such nonvirtue and consequent suffering arises] because, until one attains Buddhahood, it is impossible to eradicate anger and the other afflictions [completely]. Unless the merit of one's ethics is dedicated to attaining enlightenment, its beneficial efficacy is lost when hatred or other nonvirtues arise.[6] Unless one realizes emptiness, anger can destroy the roots of virtue even if merit is dedicated. Bodhisattvas up to the seventh ground can have anger, but this anger does no harm insofar as its effect does not come to pass [in that the suffering ordinary persons would experience as a result of anger does not occur; however the Bodhisattva's progress toward Buddhahood is greatly obstructed].[7]

There are those who, like the Chinese Communists, do not believe [in the cause and effect of actions], thinking that charity merely depletes your resources. However, persons interested in emptiness reflect that giving leads to a good support-system for future contemplation [on emptiness], and so take pleasure in giving.[8] It also behooves such persons to cultivate compassion, since only when conjoined with compassion does the view of emptiness function as a cause of Buddhahood.

A pleasant complexion is also important so that spiritual friends, as well as teachers who are still limited by appearances, will like one. Anger causes the skin to be coarse instead of smooth, and gives rise to bad coloring.[9] Through cultivating patience, one acquires the cause for a pleasing physique and complexion, which acts as a cause for people liking you. It is customary among people to require [pleasant appearance], whether in the workplace or elsewhere. Without this, even if one is a kindly person, [it is difficult]. Without this, the Superiors are not pleased; rather, they feel there is no purpose in teaching emptiness to such a person [who bears the sign of a lack of virtue]. It is not a question of Superiors' liking one or not because of one's appearance, but there is a difference in whether one is able to fit well with a great number of people. This is not an issue of desire or attachment; Superiors have no sense that some people are close and others are distant. But if one has a pleasing appearance, there is more cause to rejoice in that person's merit. [Although] there is no difference in how such persons are regarded by Superiors, in discussing the benefits of patience [it is said that] if one has an ugly appearance, one will not find one's place in the larger compass of society, and people will not listen to one. Whether one's appearance is good or bad, Buddha finds one pleasing. Yet, because others are inclined toward those who have good appearance, it is good to have it.

Even though they articulate the same ideas, some people inspire confidence and others do not. Some have a lovely appearance but no strength, or are sick; this is due to not having cultivated patience. Others have physical strength for any kind of work, good hands, good appearance, and this is also an effect of patience. Even more to the point, if one has a disease and cannot meditate, no progress can be made. One needs an excellent body and sufficient resources. All these are effects of previous patience, ethics, and effort. This is explained by the texts and is probably so. Thus, patience gives one great capacity, power.

Through cultivating patience, the body comes to have brilliance and vibrant color, and is free from illness.

Even with faith, if one does not have these [qualities of appearance, and so forth] it is hard to accomplish a great purpose, since many causes are necessary. Otherwise, it is as if there is a seed but no water or fertilizer. Unless Superiors like you [in the sense qualified above] and you have sufficient resources and good health, you cannot practice the view.

It is good to reflect on the cause and effect of actions that are less easily observable than the cause-and-effect relationships between a seed and its sprout. Confidence increases little by little, and one comes to like those causes [such as the Bodhisattva deeds] that establish [positive effects]; one abandons [actions] that are not causes of these.

It seems suitable to consider the prior [Bodhisattva deeds] as the causes of the latter.[10] It can probably be said that giving is a cause of ethics, for example, since the enhanced perfection of giving is attained on the first Bodhisattva ground, ethics on the second, and so forth. Giving is a way of helping others by alleviating the suffering associated with poverty or fear, and thus can be considered a branch of ethics. If one can, one helps, but in any case one does not harm. As the mind to help others increases, one's own ethics improve. When ethical behavior occurs, one does not develop anger toward others; in this way ethics becomes a branch of patience.

If one cultivates patience, effort arises such that one can persevere regardless of suffering. Effort is necessary to achieve the perfection of concentration; effort itself is thus a branch of concentration—[in fact] it is included in all the other perfections.[11]

One who has the wisdom that understands emptiness knows that the cause and effect of actions exist; indeed, if understanding of the cause and effect of actions decreases, this is not a realization of emptiness. Such a person understands the causes for lower forms of rebirth, and thus practices method [especially compassion] also. This [ability to recognize the complementarity of causal functioning and emptiness] is "more marvelous than the marvelous."[12] The negation of inherent existence cannot refute cause and effect. Whereas inherent existence is refuted, cause and effect, liberation and the attainment of liberation or of omniscience are set forth. A person who does not understand that a lack of inherent existence is fully compatible with [conventional] existence will think that the meditator, the meditation, and so forth, do not exist.

## EMPTINESS AND VALIDLY EXISTENT PHENOMENA

There are two kinds of conceptual thought, that which does and does not [apprehend inherent existence]. Objects of the latter are not refuted by the reasoning that refutes inherent existence, and thus it is unsuitable to consider that the reasonings refuting inherent existence refute all phenomena [see discussion of Ha-shang above]. Moreover, unless some objects are posited [as valid—that is, as conventionally existent], the thought apprehending the view [of emptiness] would undermine the thought apprehending activities and vice versa. Having understood that phenomena are without inherent existence, the Bodhisattva [accepts the existence of] giving, and so forth. [Emptiness and conventional existence] do not undermine or weaken each other; it is not like heat becoming nonexistent due to the presence of cold. Rather, through understanding emptiness, understanding of the cause and effect of actions increases; consequently, one does not commit bad deeds, and thus does not go to bad rebirths, but practices ethics, and so forth, and eventually attains liberation. Thus, for one who understands, there is great fruit in hearing about emptiness.

In the same way, if no distinction were made between [conventional and inherent existence], the view of the emptiness of inherent existence would undermine presentations of cause and effect. It would, for example, undermine the principle that giving, and so forth, causes one to possess sufficient resources in the future; maintaining the lack of inherent existence would make it impossible to posit resources, or any other phenomena, and positing the existence of resources, and so forth, would make it impossible to posit a lack of inherent existence.

Such a view [of the two truths] has been taught by Buddhists. The Chinese Ha-shang asserted the two truths; he was a Buddhist and had faith in Buddha. However, according to his explanation of the two truths, conventional truths do not exist at all, but are just mistaken appearances. For Ha-shang [as for Prāsaṅgika, these mistaken appearances or conventional truths] exist for conventionally obscured *(kun rdzob du yod pa)* minds, but [for Ha-shang, unlike for Prāsaṅgika], this did not require that they exist *except* as mistaken appearances for our mistaken minds, whereas this other [truth—that is, emptiness—was said to] exist ultimately. It is necessary, therefore, to reduce the extent of what is negated here. In this view, phenomena are merely mistaken appearances, not ultimates [and there is no category of valid conventional existence as in Prāsaṅgika]. Since they do not exist ultimately [here meaning they do not exist at all], whether you give or do not amounts to the same in that no benefit accrues. If one misconstrues a realization of emptiness as signifying that phenomena do not exist, confidence in establishing [the cause and effect of actions] will not develop. In that case, one who realizes emptiness need have no concern for future lives.

There is nothing more marvelous or amazing than, having understood that all phenomena are empty of inherent existence, being able to present well the cause and effect of actions. For a person who [mistakenly] feels that the absence of inherent existence [means nonexistence] and that, therefore, there are no ethics, the view of emptiness does not become a cause of highest enlightenment [or even a cause of cultivating virtue].

Some say that presentations of cause and effect are only for those who do not understand the view.[13] They liken the discussion of cause and effect to counting the creases on a rabbit's horn—since there is no such horn, there are no creases. Persons with such a wrong view consider phenomena to be nonexistent except for being posited by thought. In this view, which is most likely that of Ha-shang or his followers, everything is considered [nonexistent] like the horns of a rabbit, and it is explained that at present we have mistaken appearances. None of these [conventional phenomena] appear during the spacelike meditative exalted wisdom, which is a Superior's direct realization of emptiness, just as, when we awaken from a dream, the dream is no longer there. All mistaken appearances will be extinguished when one realizes that all phenomena lack inherent existence [but conventional phenomena will still be valid]. The texts state that even a Buddha's Form Body *(gzugs sku, rūpakāya)* is a mistaken appearance, as is the Truth Body.

When emptiness is [correctly] realized, and merely the object of negation—true or inherent existence—is refuted, one very much values what remains—namely, conventionally existent phenomena, the objects of conventional valid cognition. One cherishes these. The view [of the emptiness of inherent existence] must be realized; however, as Mañjusrī exhorted Tsong-kha-pa, conventionalities are to be valued. If one thinks that these do not exist, that they are like the horns of a rabbit, one feels a need neither for ethical discourse nor for activities such as giving. So, without setting aside conventionalities, but refuting that which is to be negated, one realizes emptiness.

Through realizing emptiness, one develops an excellent understanding of how conventionalities exist. If the self-isolate *(rang ldog)* of emptiness arises [that is, is realized], other virtues concordant with it come to pass. These are the "good qualities that follow after emptiness." Virtues are false, and the happiness which is the effect of virtue is also false, but to say these are false is not to say they do not exist. Nonvirtue is also false, as is its effect, suffering. False arises from the false. If the cause is false, so will be the effect. If the cause, true paths, is false, so is its effect, liberation. They are perhaps like a dream, like an illusion, but they are not, as Āryadeva observes (see page 60) like the horns of a rabbit, a flower in the sky, or the son of a barren woman. Dreams and illusions are examples of dependent arisings; these latter are not. Illusions and reflections exist; they are instances of falsities and of dependent arisings. These exist, but the horns of a rabbit, and so forth, do not and so cannot instance dependent arisings; rather, they exemplify a lack of [any inherent] nature *(rang bzhin med ba'i dpe)*. One has to understand the dividing line between what does and does not exist. Everything that exists is established by valid cognition *(tshad mas grub pa, pramāṇasiddha)*.[14] Even though phenomena exist, they do not exist by way of their own nature. This difficult distinction is one which, among Buddhist proponents of tenets, only Prāsaṅgikas succeed in making.

Candrakīrti, Śāntideva, and Buddhapālita are the Prāsaṅgika scholars of India. Buddhapālita did not write a great deal and was not exceedingly clear, whereas Candrakīrti, who did write a great deal, clearly explained the Prāsaṅgika system. [Still, Buddhapālita] is renowned as an uncommon paver of the way for the chariot of the Prāsaṅgika system, since it was he who forged a great path for it. His followers in India were not numerous, and [his position] did not have great fame there [in his own day]. Later, many disciples of his [works] arose; thus, many became his students in this way.

The master Bhāvaviveka, and so forth, were more famous [than Buddhapālita], as was discussed by Tāranātha in *The Arising of the Dharma (chos 'byung).*[15] Nāgārjuna was very famous; followers of his thought included both Svātantrika commentators such as Bhāvaviveka and Prāsaṅgika commentators such as Buddhapālita and Śāntideva, all of whom explained Nāgārjuna's view [in their own way]. Although Śāntideva discusses the view, he is better known for his more expansive elaboration of behavior; for this reason trainees in the Bodhisattva deeds are very fond of him. He was a highly developed practitioner who studied with many teachers but did not have many students.[16] He spent much time meditating and composed texts that are very famous.

In order to overcome the ignorance that conceives of [an inherently existent] self, one must understand that this conception has no referent object *(zhen yul, *adhyavasāyaviṣaya)*. This comes about through understanding the coarse and then the subtle of the sixteen aspects of the four noble truths. Such is the order of realization. One must learn the alphabet before one can read, but once skilled in reading, one need no longer think about the alphabet. Similarly, once skilled in the subtle form of the sixteen aspects, one need no longer go back over the coarse ones.

*Question:* How does one distinguish between the coarse and subtle sixteen aspects of the four noble truths?

*Answer:* The impermanence, and so forth,[17] which are the sixteen aspects of the four noble truths spoken of by Svātantrikas on down [Cittamātra, Sautrāntika, and Vaibhāṣika] are coarse. The Prāsaṅgikas assert, in addition, an uncommon impermanence, and so forth, which are the sixteen aspects of the four noble truths; these are subtle because in the Prāsaṅgika system the emptiness of inherent existence is included with the sixteen aspects. Only Prāsaṅgikas can set forth this type of emptiness; Svātantrikas do not discuss the sixteen aspects in which there is an emptiness of inherent existence.

*Question:* You have said that one who understands emptiness on the basis of reasoning understands cause and effect better than before. Would it ever occur that someone understands emptiness on some basis other than reasoning, such as through some sign, or blessing, or great faith?

*Answer (laughs):* For the initial realization, one definitely needs reasoning; beginners need to hear and reflect about emptiness. Through such reasoning one develops an inferential valid cognition of emptiness. This inference is the beginning of an understanding arisen from reflection *(bsam 'byung, cintāmayī).* However, without extensive collections of merit one will not be able to realize emptiness.

*Question:* So long as one has not attained inference is it necessary to rely on reasoning?

*Answer:* Yes. This has to do with the initial realization. Once inference *(rjes dpag, anumāna)* is completed and well cultivated, one will remember it [emptiness] again and again without needing to depend on reasoning. If, in this life, one has manifold realization of emptiness, one need not use reasoning to realize it again in a future life. It will be like remembering something; it is re-cognition *(bcad shes, *pariccinnajñāna),* not inference. If, however, one has forgotten or cast away previous understanding, re-cognition is impossible. But if one has studied well and reflected a great deal, one will not forget. In that case, one does not need reasoning very much; if one meditates again and again, the experience arising from meditation *(sgom byung, bhāvanāmayī)* will emerge.[18] Then the levels of the path of preparation—heat, peak, forbearance, and highest mundane phenomena—are achieved. Then one need not depend on reasoning.

[In short] if understanding is cultivated upon completion of inference, one will remember without needing to depend on reasoning. For example, one uses the following syllogistic statement: "The subject [of the syllogism], a jewel, lacks true existence because of being a dependent arising." To say that this jewel is a dependent arising establishes that it lacks true existence; dependent arisings cannot be inherently existent [because these are mutually exclusive].

We do not generally recognize the dependent nature of our existence. We feel we exist without depending on anyone or anything; yet, no matter who we are, nothing comes without assistance. Kings and presidents are no exception. [In terms of objects,] a pot depends on causes and conditions such as the gathering together of various particles. If this did not occur, there would be no pot. A pot also depends on its own valid basis of designation, and on a valid mind which imputes it *('dogs byed gyi blo tshad ma la brten pa).* A pot is not *produced* in dependence on terms and mind, but it *exists* in dependence on these.[19] A pot is produced in dependence on its own causes and conditions.

*Question:* The pot is said to depends on terms and thought; in what sense are terms and thought themselves dependent arisings?

*Answer:* Both the thought realizing a pot and the term expressing a pot are produced in dependence on pot. Thus, this thought apprehending a pot is an effect of the pot. However, the pot itself is known to us through either terms or thought. In other words, a pot is a cause of the thought apprehending pot and the term expressing pot; and it is through these signs that a pot becomes an object of a [conceptual] mind.[20]

Similarly, in dependence on smoke we understand fire. Smoke arises from fire, and is an effect of fire. In dependence on this smoke, fire can appear to the mind. Without terms and thought, one does not understand pot, just as without smoke, one does not [conceptually] understand [the presence of] fire.

"The term which expresses" and "the mind which imputes" are different. One is a term; the other is a mind, a consciousness. First, there is the mind [which imputes the thing]; then one becomes able to apply the term. A term thus depends on the mind that imputes it; this is the most subtle form of dependent arising.

*Question:* Unconditioned space is a dependent arising which is permanent in that it does not change from one moment to the next. Do ordinary persons see unconditioned space? If not, in what sense is unconditioned space said to depend on a valid cognizer?

*Answer:* A valid mind can be either conceptual or nonconceptual, but a valid imputing mind must be conceptual. Inferential valid cognizers are conceptual; the thought that thinks "pillar" on hearing the term "pillar" is also conceptual. Thus, it is not necessary for the eye consciousness to see [unconditioned space directly for it to be realized by valid cognition]. The mind of one who sees this [empty atmosphere] implicitly realizes [the presence of unconditioned space].[21]

A consciousness realizing an object *(yul rtogs mkhyen)* is a valid cognizer; it can be an inferential consciousness or a direct perceiver. According to Prāsaṅgika, a direct valid cognizer generally does not have to be a *new* valid cognizer, it can also be a re-cognizer. A re-cognizer can establish by valid cognition but is not [necessarily] a valid cognizer. The [implicit] realizer of this [unconditioned space] is the eye consciousness itself. Unconditioned space is a nonaffirming negative. It cannot be realized explicitly *(dngos su, sākṣāt)* by the eye consciousness, though the eye consciousness does realize it directly *(dngos sum du)*. Thus, direct perceivers have both explicit and implicit realization.

This is not a tenet of Prāsaṅgika alone. For example, Signs and Reasonings *(rtags rigs)* texts [written from the perspective of Sautrāntikas Following Reason] discuss the nonobservation of a pot by valid cognition *(bum pa tshad mas ma dmigs pa)*. One sees with one's eyes the place that is without a pot. Although an eye consciousness can see neither the unobserved pot nor the absence of a pot, the implicit realization [that a pot is absent] comes to the mind through the eye consciousness. The eyes explicitly realize this [empty atmosphere or absence of pot]; they implicitly realize unconditioned space [or the absence of a pot if the proper context exists.] Someone who reflects on whether or not the atmosphere is obstructive implicitly realizes unconditioned space, whereas someone who does not think about this at all cannot. What the eyes have implicitly known the mind can recall. If the eyes had not first seen this area [from which a pot is absent], this mind [realizing the absence of a pot] would not be there.

[To summarize:] the eyes implicitly and directly realize [the absence of a pot]. They cannot realize this [absence] explicitly because it is a nonaffirming negative.[22] This nonaffirming negative, the absence of a pot [like unconditioned space] does not [explicitly] appear to the thought apprehending a pot; it is realized implicitly.

The self also depends on names and signs *(ming dang brda')*. Imputation occurs when an imputing valid mind or a mind arises from terms. There is a basis [or referent] of that term *('jug sa'i gzhi);* this is the object. This object is merely posited or set out *(bzhag tsam)* by terms and thought. Except for depending on causes and conditions such as a valid basis of imputation and a valid imputing mind, the object does not exist from its own side.

When we think "tape recorder," a certain type of machine appears to our mind. We press the button, and it is able to function. However, if we analyze or investigate this entity, we do not find it there; it is merely posited by the conventional mind, which neither analyzes nor investigates.

[We have said that] in Prāsaṅgika a valid cognizer of the direct *(mngon sum tshad ma, pratyakṣa pramāṇa)* can be either conceptual or nonconceptual. The word "direct" in the phrase "valid cognizer of the direct," refers to the object *(yul, viṣaya)*; in the phrase "direct valid cognition" the same word refers to a consciousness.[23] The thought apprehending sound as impermanent, or the thought apprehending a pot, is not a direct valid cognition *(mngon sum kyi tshad ma),* but it is a valid conceptual cognizer *(rtog pa tshad ma).*[24]

Sautrāntika interprets the *pra* of the Sanskrit word *pramāṇa* as "new"; hence, for them, a valid cognizer is necessarily a new mind [and cannot be a re-cognizer].[25] According to Prāsaṅgika, a direct valid cognizer does not have to be a new cognizer; it can also be a re-cognizer. A re-cognizer can establish [an object] validly. Prāsaṅgika, however, interprets the *pra* of *pramāṇa* to mean "main"; hence, for them, valid cognition is a main or prime cognizer. There is no valid direct perception in Prāsaṅgika; there is only the valid cognition of the direct [because, except for cognizing emptiness, direct perception is always mistaken regarding the appearance of inherent existence].[26]

Prāsaṅgika holds that conceptual thought may or may not realize an object, and [conceptual] realizers of objects may or may not be inferential consciousnesses. This is not true in Sautrāntika insofar as a noninferential [conceptual] realizer of an object *(rjes dpag ma yin pa'i yul rtogs mkhyen)* is not a valid cognizer.[27]

Since [in Prāsaṅgika] conceptual and nonconceptual valid cognizers of the direct are both realizers of their objects *(yul rtogs mkhyen)*, a consciousness realizing an object is a valid cognizer even if it is not an inferential consciousness. Inference, also conceptual, is a more circumscribed category than that of conceptual thought.

In the movies, various things seem to exist on the screen when actually they are projected there from the other end of the theater. Similarly, phenomena do not exist from their own side and [in this sense] do not really exist. Just as, in the movies, if the projector, film, and so forth, are of high quality, the images are very clear; similarly, with a good imputing mind, we see things very well. Or, to take an example famous in India, if a magician casts a mantra into the eyes of his audience, they will see a magically created horse or elephant. No such animal is actually present; its appearance occurs in dependence on the mantra and a special substance. Although there is no horse whatever, the appearance of a horse does exist *(snang ba la rta yod red)*. Seeing these apparent animals, people are pleased; some want to touch them, ride them, and so forth.[28]

*Question:* Since Buddhas have no conceptual thought, what sort of "imputing minds" can be ascribed to them?

*Answer:* In the case of a Buddha, the imputing mind is the omniscient mind *(rnam mkhen, sarvākārajñāna),* which knows all phenomena. Our valid mind imputing a tape recorder does not know anything except this tape recorder.[29]

*Question:* I have heard it said that when one attains Buddhahood, one sees endless purity *(dag pa rab 'byams)*. But a tape recorder is not exactly an endless purity.[30]

*Answer:* A tape recorder is not an uncommon dominant effect of karma *(thun mong ma yin pa'i bdag 'bras)* [for Buddhas as it is for us], nor an uncommon object of expression. It is something only enjoyable for them; it is not a true suffering, as it is for us. A Buddha may share food with us that we do not find tasty, but for an enlightened mind the same food is an object of enjoyment; it has the aspect of a stainless entity. As we are all humans, a particular food may be equally unsavory for each of us, but Buddhas enjoy it.

At the same time, Buddhas understand how it tastes for us, although we do not understand the good taste that they enjoy. Food not tasty for us will be extremely delicious for them, and this deliciousness is not established by our valid cognition. What we establish by valid cognition is established by a Buddha's valid cognition, yet what they enjoy is their own uncommon dominant effect *(thun mong ma yin pa'i bdag 'bras).* We do not understand their uncommon dominant effects, but they understand ours.

*Question:* Does this mean there are two types of valid cognition?

*Answer:* It is not said that Buddhas have two modes of valid establishment, but that whatever is established by [our] valid cognition is also established by theirs. If it were otherwise, then [our] valid cognition could be undermined by [their] valid cognition, but one valid cognizer does not undermine another. Nor does [our valid cognition] undermine the endless purity in which Buddhas remain; we simply do not realize it yet.

*Question:* Although Buddhas are said to have only direct perception, the assertion that they see things in dependence on the experience of others seems to describe something conceptual, or at least indirect.

*Answer:* Buddhas see such objects continually. It is not that a Buddha enters the illusionist's display and only then sees the illusory horse, or that, upon going elsewhere, the Buddha does not see it. Wherever they are, they see it. Even if far in the future there will be such a magician, a Buddha sees this now.

It is not that there are two objects—one for the enlightened and one for the unenlightened. Any one object is known by a Buddha in just the way that you know it. Even though the mode of knowing is the same, Buddhas have, in relation to their food, for example, many features unique to their perception.

Both [Buddhas and non-Buddhas] have valid cognition which operates in the same way *(tshad ma grub stangs gcig pa red)* but things are not established by their valid cognition in the same way. Buddhas' cognition is itself validating. Our valid cognition is established as valid by Buddhas *and* by valid cognition. [In eating, for example,] Buddhas experience an uncommon, undefiled bliss, but we do not know how delicious their food is. Yet, when food is served to an ordinary person and a Buddha, the Buddha knows exactly how it tastes [to the ordinary person]. This is established by a Buddha's valid cognition. If, for example, a Buddha walked into this room, that Buddha would have a mode of valid establishment like our own. However, their establishment comes about by the power of their uncommon actions. All humans probably establish [objects in] the same [way]. You and I see pretty much the same tape recorder; there is not very much that is unique. Humans see that which is damp and moistening as water, but those who have acquired the appropriate actions see it differently, in accordance with their actions. A hungry ghost, who has very little merit, sees blood and pus. When gods see it, they see nectar. When they drink it, they are drinking nectar.

The power of these beings' respective actions is the same, and all three have great potency. One is not able to demolish another, even though some actions are better or worse. For this reason, under the simultaneous gaze of these three types of beings, water is there, pus and blood are there, and nectar is also there. All three are there, but all three do not appear [together to any given ordinary observer; that is, except for a Buddha.][31]

# 5

# Exhortation to the Students of Emptiness

To know the two truths, ultimate and conventional, is to be skilled in knowledge of the profound meaning of emptiness and in conventional phenomena. With such skill arise the excellent qualities concomitant with achieving the first Bodhisattva ground.

For those wishing to attain this ground, it is essential to contemplate emptiness. Despite the difficulty, one must absolutely persevere, for even if one engages in the five perfections of giving, ethics, patience, [effort, and concentration], the first ground cannot be attained without an understanding of emptiness. Moreover, not to understand emptiness is to continue wandering in cyclic existence; understanding it gives hope of gradually attaining liberation.

Yet, unless one assists the view of emptiness by cultivating the other five perfections, it alone will not cause Buddhahood. Therefore, students engage, for example, in giving what is difficult to give. Bodhisattvas [who understand emptiness] can give away their own limbs and even their lives [without regret]. At the same time, a Bodhisattva who practices the [other five] perfections for hundreds of eons, but does not understand emptiness, gains less merit than one who simply listens without doubt to instruction on this. Further, those who understand emptiness will not enter a bad rebirth even though they have committed the ten nonvirtues, which, though normally causes for an unfortunate rebirth, are purified and demolished [through reflection on emptiness].

Meditating even once on emptiness is helpful. To whatever extent one contemplates it, so much are nonvirtues purified. Even having a suspicion that objects are empty of inherent existence can reduce the power of lesser misdeeds such as telling lies. Understanding emptiness by way of a mental image or meaning generality *(don spyi, arthasāmānya)* will suppress bad actions and help to prevent an unfortunate rebirth. This type of [conceptual] understanding, however, cannot annihilate misdeeds from the root, cannot make them utterly nonexistent. For this, one must abandon the [acquired conception of inherent existence] targeted by the path of seeing [the initial path of directly cognizing emptiness]. To actually purify, and not merely suppress, even powerful nonvirtues such as the murder of one's own parents or other of the five heinous actions, as well as other types of murder or the killing of animals, direct cognition is necessary. Practicing once or twice does not accomplish this.

The root of all nonvirtuous actions is ignorance. Meditation on emptiness obliterates that ignorance. It is like assassinating a country's king: the entire region then comes under one's power. A student who has faith in emptiness but does not understand it begins by studying the Vaibhāṣika system, then Sautrāntika, Cittamātra, Svātantrika, and finally Prāsaṅgika. This method guards against undermining students' understanding of dependent arising, so that they will not [wrongly] conclude that validly established phenomena do not exist at all. If one takes Buddha's denial of true existence to mean that phenomena do not exist at all, one falls away from the view of emptiness to an extreme of annihilation.

A Bodhisattva who has understood emptiness [and its benefits] is struck by the importance of others' understanding it also and, therefore, undertakes to instruct them: "Once I have attained Buddhahood, I will sustain as much effort as necessary to help others by giving them this teaching in order to help them." This means that as a Buddha he or she will engage in the four means of gathering students: (1) giving gifts; (2) speaking; (3) conducting oneself with purpose, and (4) practicing in accordance with one's own teaching.

If one reflects on the immense kindness shown by Buddha in teaching about emptiness, it follows that one must respond with kindness in return, just as in thinking of the kindness of our parents we reflect how we must do well by them in return. I now exist and function through the kindness of my parents; likewise, if the teachings are put into practice, liberation can be attained through Buddha's kindness. Indeed, correct motivation requires one to have great compassion. If this does not develop, at the very least one needs an intention to help others rather than only to do something for oneself. Beyond this, one's explanation must be correct.

## EMPTINESS AND THE BODHISATTVA PATH

When, on the sixth ground, a Bodhisattva gains the uncommon absorption of cessation, his or her object is the actuality *(chos nyid, dharmatā)* that itself accords with the doctrine of nonproduction [to be discussed below in the context of the ten samenesses]. On the eighth ground one may also attain the sign of being irreversible from [this] doctrine *(chos mi ldog pa'i rtags)*. [A sharper person would have achieved this sign earlier, and therefore] the sign attained at this stage is associated with persons of dull faculties. Those with middling faculties achieve the sign of not reversing from this doctrine at the path of seeing, and those with sharp faculties on the path of preparation. However, despite a sign or indication that one's progress will not come undone, some thought remains that this might happen. Such a delay is a great enemy for the Bodhisattva, and after attaining the eighth ground, this enemy is no longer feared.

On attaining the eighth ground, one also gains forbearance with respect to the nonproduction that is the meaning of emptiness.[1] At this point one is an Arhat. According to Prāsaṅgika and the Sautrāntika-Svātantrika system of Bhāvaviveka, the obstructions to liberation *(nyon mongs pa'i sgrib pa, kleśāvaraṇa)* have now been abandoned, and relinquishment of the obstructions to omniscience *(shes bya'i sgrib pa, jñeyāvaraṇa)* begins.[2] These obstructions to omniscience consist of latencies *(bag chags, vāsanā)* left by the conception of self *(bdag 'dzin kyi bag chags)*, and by afflictions *(nyon mongs kyi bag chags)* such as hatred, desire, and so forth. Latencies may or may not also be seeds *(sa bon, bīja)*. Seeds act as causes, but by the eighth ground, afflictions are no longer caused to arise; one no longer has seeds for the afflictions, but only latencies left by former afflictions.[3] Latencies that are also seeds *(sa bon yin mkhyen gyi bag chags)* are not obstructions to omniscience; only latencies that are not seeds are so designated.

Purification of these takes place over the eighth, ninth, and tenth Bodhisattva grounds. During this period, the Bodhisattva takes rebirth [through the] subtle cause and effect of actions. That is, rebirth depends on the latencies of ignorance that comprise the obstructions to omniscience [not on the afflicted obstructions to liberation]. Buddhas, having abandoned all obstructions whatsoever, have only uncontaminated actions and their effects. They take rebirth on the basis of these. Whereas Arhats [and pure-ground Bodhisattvas who have already overcome the afflictive obstructions to liberation] necessarily take rebirth through a wish or thought such as, "I will show the aspect of a human," Buddhas need no such deliberation. They reappear in accordance with the wishes of others, just as the moon shines in many pools without having to think, "I will reflect in this one, in that one."

On the eighth ground the Bodhisattva abandons all stains of [the conception of] true existence and gains a guarantee of never having an unfortunate rebirth or falling to a lower vehicle. This comes about through attainment of a true cessation of the conception of self *(bdag 'dzin gyi 'gog bden)* On the paths of accumulation and preparation, or even before entering any path, one realizes true cessations in dependence on a sign, but not directly. Even during the uninterrupted path of seeing, one does not realize [true cessations] directly because a true cessation of afflictions does not yet exist; this will be achieved on the liberation path of seeing. It is not that afflictions return after the uninterrupted path, but there is no stability in their absence. It is like the difference between simply kicking a thief out and shutting the door against him.

*Question:* The Grounds and Paths *(sa lam)* texts say that already from the forbearance level of the path of preparation one is assured against an unfortunate rebirth.[4] What is different about the eighth ground in this respect?

*Answer:* There is a saying, "Peak attained, virtuous roots are not severed"[5] and "Forbearance attained, no need for bad rebirths."[6] With attainment of the peak level of the path of preparation, one's roots of virtue can no longer be severed. "To sever virtuous roots" means to destroy the fruitional possibility of specific virtuous activities such as [an act of] giving; it does not mean that virtue is destroyed altogether. At this level, too, one probably does not again have a bad rebirth, but one does not yet have a true cessation of bad rebirths. With the forbearance level of the path of preparation, one gains a nonanalytical cessation of bad rebirths that guarantees against their recurrence. With the path of seeing, one gains an analytical cessation of bad rebirths. From the initial determination to leave cyclic existence until Arhatship, one sees the peak of cyclic existence as desirable and the lower rebirths as undesirable. However, once one attains a path of seeing, whether as a Hearer, Solitary Realizer, or Bodhisattva, no importance is attached to whether one goes to a fortunate or unfortunate rebirth within cyclic existence. This is different from not seeing any difference between worldly existence *(srid pa, bhāva)* and peace *(zhi ba, śānti),* a perception occurring only from the eighth ground. At that time, [the peace of] liberation seems [if anything] less desirable than cyclic existence because [it appears that such peace] makes it difficult to take rebirth, whereas, by entering cyclic existence [to help others], one can proceed on the Mahāyāna path.[7] If one goes to peace, one remains there for many eons; while in this state, no one but a Buddha can lead one to the Mahāyāna path, and even then it is difficult. Such a peaceful state is, therefore, [seen as] an obstruction to achieving the Mahāyāna. On the eighth ground, however, one no longer makes this discrimination.[8] Prior to the eighth ground there is some slight fear of falling from the Mahāyāna through turning only toward one's own interest. Such appears to the mind in consequence of the practitioner's reflection that cyclic existence is inferior to liberation from it, which is superior.[9]

Having achieved the eighth ground, one reflects that whether one enters cyclic existence or liberation, it is utterly the same. One has accomplished the nonabiding sameness *(mi gnas pa mnyam pa)* [in which worldly] existence and peace are experienced as equal *(srid zhi mnyam nyid).* No longer discriminating between them, one achieves a guarantee of not falling from the Mahāyāna.

*Question:* Does one remain under the influence of the cause and effect of actions after the eighth ground?

*Answer:* No, insofar as one no longer *need* remain in cyclic existence, one does not [as ordinary people do] take rebirth due to the defiled motivation of beginningless ignorance. One does, however, take rebirth due to the latencies of ignorance and uncontaminated actions *(ma rig pa'i bag chags dang zag med kyi las)* which empower the intention to take rebirth. The Bodhisattva takes up a mental body *(yid lus)*, whereby he or she can display various emanations in the form of coarse bodies. Despite the karmic process here being called "uncontaminated actions" *(zag med kyi las)*, this karma is not uncontaminated because the body itself results from contaminated actions. However, it is not contaminated by the obstructions to liberation, only by the obstructions to omniscience [the aforementioned latencies]. Thus, after the eighth ground, one does not take rebirth powerlessly, as we do. It is in one's own power to determine whether one will live a long or short time. One is not under the power of compounded actions motivated by the beginningless ignorance [which is the first of the twelve links of the dependent arising of a lifetime in cyclic existence] since such karma no longer exists for them.

# PART II

## Kensur Yeshey Tupden on The Meaning of Emptiness

# 6

# THE SAMENESS OF THINGS: DEPENDENT ARISING AND REALITY

## HOW REALITY IS TAUGHT IN SCRIPTURE

Scripture explains the meaning of emptiness through a discussion of the ten samenesses. In his discussion, Tsong-kha-pa quotes *The Sutra on the Ten Grounds (mdo sde sa bcu pa, daśabhūmikasūtra)*:[1]

> All phenomena are the same in being (1) signless, (2) characterless, likewise in being (3) productionless, (4) nonproduced—that is, void [of inherent existence], (5) pure from the very beginning, (6) without the elaborations [of inherent existence], (7) neither adopted nor discarded, and the same in being (8) like illusions, dreams, mirages, echoes, moon-images in water, reflections and (9) emanations; and all phenomena are the same in being (10) without the duality of things and non-things.

This passage differs from Asaṅga's *Bodhisattva Grounds (byang chub sems pa'i sa, bodhisattvabhūmi)*, which discusses the ten samenesses in terms of the Cittamātra system [rather than Prāsaṅgika]. Prāsaṅgika's assertion that all existent phenomena are identical in lacking inherent existence, or in lacking any signs of such existence, is to be distinguished from the Cittamātra position, which considers emptinesses, or thoroughly established phenomena *(yongs grub, pariniṣpanna)*, and impermanent or other-powered phenomena *(gzhan dbang, paratantra)*, to be truly existent. Imputational objects *(kun btags, parikalpita)* are not considered truly existent; hence, the existential status of all phenomena is not the same according to them [Cittamātra, whereas it is in Prāsaṅgika].

## THE TEN SAMENESSES

Śākyamuni did not cause things to be the same in lacking inherent existence, and so forth. They have always been this way. Since it would be unsuitable if this point could not also be established through reasoning [in addition to being described in sutra], Tsong-kha-pa, following Candrakīrti, discusses reasons that establish the meaning of emptiness.

All phenomena are identical in being signless. All lack signs or reasons that would establish them as existing from their own side or, to put this another way, would prove them to inherently exist. Being without inherent existence signifies that things lack their own character in the sense of lacking a nature that exists from its own side. Thus, all phenomena are the same in being characterless; that is, all are empty of having their own inherent nature. [Such sameness] does not mean that phenomena are empty in general. A pillar, for example, is not empty in the sense of being nonexistent. Pillars exist. However, pillars and other objects are empty, or devoid, of inherent existence. What type of phenomena exist, then? Whatever exists is just a mere imputation, a conventionality. We conceive of objects as inherently pleasant or unpleasant, but there are no such things. Pleasantness and so forth are qualities just imputed by the mind.

Phenomena are also the same in being productionless and nonproduced because all are without inherent production. Although products—impermanent phenomena—are produced, they are not inherently produced, not produced from their own side or by their own power. Tsong-kha-pa explains that "productionless" *(skye ba med pa)* refers to future [production] and "nonproduced" *(ma skyes pa)* refers to [the lack of inherent production] in the past and present.

It is not that phenomena are empty in general; the point is that they are empty or void of inherent existence. Everything that exists is identical in being from the very beginning free or void *of inherent existence*. This inherent existence is negated by all ten statements of sameness. Thus phenomena are said to be purified of the signs of inherent existence and in this sense have the sameness of being *pure from the very beginning*. This is not a circumstantial purification, not something that occurs after they are produced.

Phenomena are free of the *elaborations* of inherent existence. The objects of desire, hatred, and ignorance, which do not inherently exist, are simply elaborations of [apparent] true existence. They are analogous to the many objects that appear on a movie screen but do not exist [as they appear].

What is the sameness here? Despite a variety of elaborations, all are the same in merely being posited by convention *(tha snyad pas bzhag tsam gyi mnyam pa nyid)* and the same in not being inherently established. Good, bad, Superior, and ordinary persons, fortunate and unfortunate rebirths—all are the same in this way. There are many variegated elaborations of true existence, but no such variety in how the samenesses abide. All elaborations of true existence are pacified, which is to say they do not exist. Conventional phenomena, as well as emptinesses, are merely posited out there by the conventional mind. Products and nonproducts do not truly exist, are not truly existent elaborations; if they were, their appearance as truly existent would be valid.

Even the superiority of liberation to cyclic existence is merely posited by the mind. Thus "elaboration" [also] refers to what is placed there by the mind. The meaning here is very similar, but not identical, to [what is meant by saying that an object] "casts its aspect" [to the consciousness, which directly perceives it by way of mirroring that aspect].[2] It can probably be said that when an aspect is cast, elaborations occur, and when elaborations occur, an aspect is cast. An aspect "being cast" means that something appears to the mind in dependence on a given object and the mind apprehends that. In the case of inherent existence, it is due to the predispositions for [conceiving of] inherent existence that such an aspect appears.[3]

To say that there are no elaborations of true existence [also] means that the varieties of phenomena do not appear in meditative equipoise. The sameness of no elaborations must be applied to the second sameness, that of being characterless, which signifies that phenomena have no inherently existent character *(mtshan ma, nimitta)*, for such a character would be a sign of inherent existence *(rang bzhin yod pa'i rtags)*. [Thus,] phenomena have no inherently existent character, nor does their nature *(rang bzhin, svabhāva)* possess inherently existent defining characteristics *(mtshan nyid, lakṣaṇa)*.[4]

"Inherent" or "true" existence refers [in part] to an appearance of duality. "To elaborate" means "to make" or "engender," like someone elaborating or embellishing a painting. The true existence that appears does not exist and, therefore, is without elaborations. The consciousness itself [which conceives of inherent existence] exists, but does not inherently exist. This lack of elaborations applies to the first sameness, the lack of elaborations of dualistic appearance, where it means that phenomena do not appear in all their variety to a consciousness in meditative equipoise. The sameness of no elaborations must also be applied to the second sameness, that of being characterless. This [as noted above] signifies that phenomena have no inherently existent character, for such a character would be a sign of inherent existence.

[When phenomena are described as] being without the "elaborations of dualistic appearances" *(gnyis snang gi spros pa med)*, "dualistic appearance" signifies the conception of true existence. All appearances of true existence, and hence all dualistic appearances, vanish in meditative equipoise. Only emptiness, the lack of inherent existence, is an object for such a mind. In general, "dualistic appearances" refers to conventional appearances and themselves are a sign *(rtags, liṅga)* of inherent existence. Dualistic appearance, however, is not a correct sign of inherent existence but a fabrication *(sgro 'dogs, samāropa),* something that gives the appearance of existing. This aspect is displayed because of predispositions established from beginningless time. These appearances are called dualistic because they appear to have an existence not posited by the force of the mind [and, thus, to be separate from it, or dualistic. Such appearances] arise because of the mind's beginningless predispositions for conceiving of true existence. Thus, here "dualistic appearance" signifies a style of existence that is not posited by the force of the mind. As in the Cittamātra system this indicates that appearances arise due to latencies in the mind; however, unlike Cittamātra, it does not say that the [perceiving consciousness and object which results] are one entity.[5]

To elaborate also means mentally to desire or arrive at, whereby things come to be objects of desire. Once desire has developed, the mind moves toward its object. It is not, however, due to desire that phenomena appear truly existent. No matter how desirous, the mind cannot make truly existent phenomena; terminology and thought cannot cause phenomena to be elaborated in this sense. Rather, desire develops with respect to objects [mistakenly] apprehended as truly existent. In terms of what, or toward what, is true existence elaborated? To the mind. The aspect of true existence comes toward or is engendered in the mind. This is what is meant by "elaboration" here.

Phenomena have no inherently existent character, and they have no inherently existent defining characteristics *(mtshan nyid, lakṣaṇa).* In general, defining characteristics have to do with a thing's nature; for example, a pot [has the defining characteristic] of being able to hold water, and so forth, but its entity is not its mode of abiding *(gnas lugs).* Its nature is only posited by the mind, [meaning that] if with analytical reasoning you search for something that exists from its own side, it is not there. This is the case with all phenomena, and so all are the same in lacking such defining characteristics. Their nature or character does not exist inherently but is merely posited by thought. Even though it is a falsity, it exists, it can function. Cows give milk.

How are phenomena the same in being *nonadopted and nondiscarded*? The things to be adopted, such as liberation and the state of Buddhahood, are not established from their own side. They lack a naturally characterized entity *(rang gi mtshan nyid kyi ngo bo med pa).* They arise in dependence on causes and conditions, which would be unnecessary if they existed from their own side. If such were the status of things, we could never attain liberation, no matter how much effort we made. Similarly, the things we are to abandon, such as cyclic existence and the afflictions of desire, hatred, and ignorance, do not come about except through depending on other things. Thus, the things to be adopted have no inherent existence, and the things to be discarded have none either. Because neither category alone includes all existent phenomena, these paired aspects of not being inherently adopted or discarded are included as a single sameness. [Similarly, the tenth sameness refers to the sameness of products in not inherently being things and of nonproducts in not inherently being nonthings.][6]

Further, it is said that all phenomena are the same in being like illusions, meaning that they exist merely conventionally, not inherently. The simile of the magician's illusion is used to facilitate understanding of this. A magician or illusionist causes a stone to appear as a horse or elephant. If these animals really existed, there would have to be some [corresponding] basis of designation, but there is none. Such a horse or elephant does not exist from its own side; it is an illusion as well as an emanation. It is seen because the mind is made faulty due to a mantric spell. This is probably a type of energy *(rlung, prāṇa)* which enters the eye, though our books do not describe it exactly. There were magicians in India who used mantras to affect the eye sense, [but] very few such in Tibet. What a magician creates is a magical emanation. He himself is separate from it. Emanations can also be created in meditative stabilization: what is big is made small, the small is made large, or a bad mind is made good.

There are other ways to be affected by appearances which we can soon recognize as mistaken. While I was at Drebung in Lhasa, I rode in a car for the first time. I saw the ground move and wondered how it could be, where was the earth moving to? It also seemed to me that the trees were moving backward. This mistaken conception was due to the car's movement. Once one is accustomed to cars, one does not make this type of error.

The sameness which describes phenomena as like illusions also characterizes them as like dreams, shadows,[7] echoes, the moon in water, or reflections. These various examples are given because some people will find certain of them easier than others. When the moon is reflected in water below it, it seems to ripple; other reflections, as in a mirror, do not. Rippling can be understood to signify the impermanence of objects; moreover, we are to understand that the moon does not exist inherently.[8] Phenomena are like dreams in that something seems to be present which really is not. Dreams are certainly amazing. Whether I am in India or America I dream that I am in Tibet. I have a sense of seeing Tibet with my eyes, though, of course, I have not actually gone there.

All ten samenesses are essentially one. Nevertheless, [their meaning] can appear in various ways to our minds. By meditating on [any one instance of] this mode of being of phenomena, you can abandon all conceptions of inherent existence and attain liberation. Nevertheless, the Great Vehicle explains different varieties of this [realization], giving many synonyms for the same meaning—hence, the ten samenesses. Just as a sharp knife can cut where a dull one cannot, a sharp wisdom can understand the mode of abiding of phenomena. A duller wisdom cannot fathom that Buddha taught that phenomena neither exist inherently nor not-exist inherently.

Yet, there is no need to negate the *appearance* of true existence. This exists and appears. It is something like a meaning generality or mental image. Can there not exist an image of the horns of a rabbit? The appearance of true existence exists, and, therefore, it appears to and is realized by Buddhas also. However, it is a mistaken appearance, not truly established, and [does not lead] Buddhas to conceive of true existence. Moreover, it appears to them because of its appearing to us, not from the Buddhas' own side.[9] The appearance of true existence and endless purity *(dag pa rab 'byams)* do not impair one another; both appear directly.[10]

## UNDERSTANDING EMPTINESS

A single reasoning can overcome the subtle conception of inherent existence. Nevertheless, many types of reasonings and numerous methods of analysis are set forth—for example, in Nāgārjuna's *Fundamental Text Called "Wisdom" (rtsa ba shes rab, mūlamadhyamakakārikā).* If one becomes skilled in all of these, then as a Buddha one will be able to explain them all as necessary. When one uses reasoning to discover whether or not a pillar exists inherently, that pillar itself ceases to be an object of this analytical mind. Does this mean you find the pillar to be nonexistent? No. The pillar simply ceases to be an object of that particular mind; similarly, if you look for the mode of abiding of the selflessness of persons, that selflessness ceases to be an object for the mind which observes that selflessness' mode of abiding.

The special trainees of Nāgārjuna's *Fundamental Text* and Maitreya's *Ornament for Clear Realization (mngon rtogs rgyan, abhisamayālaṃkāra)* have the Mahāyāna lineage. Because they wish to achieve Buddhahood they must from the beginning practice limitless forms of reasonings in order to understand fully the paths of Hearers, Solitary Realizers, and Bodhisattvas. Unless one studies these from the beginning, one is not able to teach them as a Buddha.

*Question:* At Buddhahood one is said to become omniscient, so what does it matter if particular reasonings were cultivated previously or not?

*Answer:* It is not quite like that. If it were, you could say that one does not need to realize emptiness because at Buddhahood one will realize it! It is true that a Buddha is clairvoyant, but without prior practice [realization] does not come. If clairvoyance were sufficient, the Hearer Arhat ought to be able to achieve Buddhahood even without the great compassion [and other training] of Bodhisattvas, since an Arhat has clairvoyance—though not the clairvoyance knowing that all defilements have been extinguished *(zag zad kyi mngon shes).* But if you do not first meditate on emptiness, you will not realize it. One needs to engage in skillful means to teach these to others, and this comes from having first studied it oneself. To teach English, you must know it well yourself. If at the beginning, having heard [the teaching], one accumulates a great collection [of merit and wisdom], in the future one will be capable of great work. If one only reflects a little bit [on, for example, the meaning of emptiness], then in the future one will be capable of only lesser activity. Unless one studies all [the reasonings involved in this endeavor] one will not know them. Buddhas are persons who have understood that because they hold living beings dear, Buddhahood is necessary. These [reasonings] are means for achieving Buddhahood, and since they are crucial, Buddhahood will not be achieved without them. It is *because* would-be Buddhas practice in this way that they gain a clairvoyance which understands everything. One who has not become accustomed to such practices in this manner does not suddenly come to understand, as in turning on a light.[11]

Emptiness is called a highest or ultimate truth because it is an object of the highest type of consciousness. The emptiness of products and the emptiness of nonproducts are not different for the Superior's meditative equipoise. A Superior's wisdom of meditative equipoise does have a [conventional] object; the emptiness or selflessness of persons and of phenomena is the object of this mind.[12] A pot itself is not the mode of abiding *(gnas lugs)* of a pot; the mode of abiding of a non-truly existent pot has to be its absence of true existence. Thus, a pot is not an object of the wisdom which sees the mode of abiding of a pot. Similarly, selflessness is not its own mode of abiding: the mode of abiding of any selflessness is its own selflessness. Only selflessness—meaning the lack of inherent existence that characterizes, pots, pillars, and other phenomena—is an object of the consciousness that cognizes the way of abiding of those phenomena.

Further, although emptiness is both permanent and an object of knowledge, it does not appear to a consciousness of meditative equipoise *as* a permanent phenomenon or *as* an object of knowledge; these [aspects] are related to emptiness but are not objects of the wisdom of meditative equipoise. Object of knowledge, existent, established base, and so forth, are all conventional phenomena; emptiness is an ultimate object, and therefore emptiness [alone] has to be the object of a wisdom cognizing the manner of existence. Further, the object of knowledge emptiness, the established base emptiness, and so forth, are all permanent; this is why Sautrāntikas Following Reasoning do not consider them ultimate objects.[13] If they were, then the direct cognizer which realizes emptiness [being, by definition, a consciousness that engages every aspect of its object] would have to realize "object of knowledge" directly. This would make emptiness an affirming negative instead of a nonaffirming negative. However, emptiness is a nonaffirming negative, and so, except for negating inherent existence, [the term "emptiness"] does not suggest any other positive phenomenon at all.

Thus, the object of knowledge pot, the established base pot, and so forth, do not appear to the direct perceiver apprehending a pot because they have a different mode of abiding [than the pot] in that a pot is a specifically characterized phenomenon *(rang mtshan, svalakṣaṇa)*, and "object of knowledge pot" is a generally characterized phenomenon *(spyi mtshan, sāmānyalakṣaṇa)*.[14]

The lack of inherent existence is how such objects abide. Emptiness can be asserted to exist, despite some who [mistakenly] claim it does not, that it is made up by thought.[15] However, selflessness is not its own way of abiding. In order to cognize selflessness' or emptiness' mode of abiding, the consciousness must realize the emptiness of that emptiness, the selflessness of selflessness. Just as pots are qualified by emptiness, emptiness itself is so qualified.

The way a thing exists *(yod lugs)* and the style of its existence *(yod stangs)* are different. The existence of objects is styled or expressed in different ways—some are round, some square, and so forth. Such variations, however, are not perceived during a Superior's meditative equipoise on emptiness. All that appears is the empty place which is a nonaffirming negative. Just clear emptiness. Thus, one sees both true cessations and emptinesses in the manner of dualistic appearances having vanished. This is an appearance like water poured into water, with no difference in how emptinesses and true cessations appear. These are not conventionalities but ultimate truths, and so the mind seeing them directly must do so by way of a vanishing of dualistic appearances.

## True Cessations and Emptiness

Tsong-kha-pa writes, "In Candrakīrti's own system direct knowledge of cessation is established within the context of cognizing the meaning of suchness by way of a wisdom consciousness of uncontaminated meditative equipoise. Therefore, if true cessations were conventional truths, this presentation would be impossible . . . those who propound that [according to Candrakīrti] true cessations are conventional truths have not come to the right decision."[16]

One cognizes emptiness directly on both the uninterrupted and liberation paths of seeing.[17] On the liberation path, true cessations [previously] attained are also seen directly.[18] The true cessations already attained on the first through fifth grounds are objects of a sixth-ground Bodhisattva's meditative equipoise. The true cessation of the sixth ground first becomes an object on the seventh ground. This true cessation is not an emptiness; yet, it is an object of the mind in meditative equipoise on the uninterrupted path and is also considered an ultimate truth by those who maintain that whatever is an ultimate truth need not be an emptiness.

All Prāsaṅgikas agree that true cessations are ultimate truths; some scholars maintain that Svātantrikas also posit such, though I do not see it that way. Furthermore, some texts maintain that true cessations are emptinesses; some, that they are not. Scriptures having to do with the nature of mind are quoted in this regard. In my opinion, it is better to think of emptinesses and true cessations as separate because their objects of negation are different. They relate to different mental defilements. Such defilements are of two types, natural and adventitious *(rang bzhin gyi dri ma* and *blo bur ba'i dri ma).* Although there are no "natural" [or inherently existent] defilements, there is a mind which conceives of these. A true cessation is the negative or absence of [a certain type of mistaken] mind. This mind is to be ceased, and its absence, or negative, is a true cessation—that is, there occurs a nonaffirming negative which is a true cessation. That nonaffirming negative which exits in relation to the mind that conceives of inherent existence *is* the true cessation. The agent of this cessation is emptiness; [an understanding of] emptiness ceases the object of that [mistaken] mind[19] in that when this mind [which conceives of inherent existence] becomes nonexistent, the consciousness which refutes inherent existence [through realizing emptiness] brings about this cessation. The capacity of the consciousness improves and increases until it extinguishes defilements, whereupon the extinguishment itself becomes an object of the mind directly realizing emptiness.

Both emptiness and true cessations are nonaffirming negatives and appear simultaneously [in meditative equipoise]. A true cessation negates the adventitious defilements [associated with] the conception of inherent existence, and a true cessation is an ultimate truth because the mind that directly realizes emptiness realizes it. The emptiness [or reality] which ceases the natural defilements (*rang bzhin gyi dri ma 'gags pa'i stong nyid)* exists in relation to all minds, as well as in relation to the uninterrupted path. The actuality of the liberating path *(rnam 'grol lam gyi chos nyid)* ceases the natural defilements. The natural state of the mind *(sems kyi chos nyid)* ceases the adventitious defilements. This [mind which has a true cessation as its object] does not occur on the uninterrupted Mahāyāna path of seeing but on the path of liberation. The emptiness due to which the adventitious defilements are ceased is not present until the liberating path; [however] the emptiness [or reality] by which the natural defilements (*rang bzhin gyi dri ma 'gags pa'i stong nyid)* are ceased exists in relation to all minds, as well as in relation to the uninterrupted path. Emptiness negates the [natural] defilements of [holding to] inherent existence; a true cessation negates the adventitious defilements [associated with] the conception of inherent existence.

# 7

# VALID EXISTENCE AND ANALYSIS

Everyone has an innate conception of inherent existence, whether or not one has studied systems of tenets.[1] This innate misconception must be identified in order to access the referent object of this beginningless ignorance. Every tenet system designates specific "imaginaries" that it refutes. However, mere identification of the referent objects of such imaginaries does not mean one has successfully identified the referent object of the conception of inherent existence. Thus, Tsong-kha-pa emphasizes the essential of identifying the object to be negated; merely identifying "a true existence which is superficially designated by proponents of tenets and the conception of such true existence" is not sufficient. The reasoning which refutes inherent existence does not itself make this identification. Once one has identified this, one can understand that its referent object does not exist at all.

True or inherent existence can be refuted only if one clearly understands what it is. Thus, it is essential to identify well the true existence to be negated, just as you must know where an enemy is in order to go after him. Or, to give another example, if there is a thief about, you must know exactly who it is, otherwise, even as you assure yourself that no thief is present, or perhaps even before you begin to wonder whether your belongings are there or not, he will have carried off your things.

Even if you come to negate something, unless you have identified true existence well, it will be something other than true existence that you deny. Let us say that a table is the subject, and the true existence of that table is to be negated; without a proper identification you would conclude that the table itself does not exist. But it does exist; only the truly existent table does not.

Without meditation that pertains to the referent object of the conception of true existence, you will not annihilate that conception; it will only increase further. However, just to analyze a view other than your own is of little benefit. [Hence, the emphasis on identifying the object of negation as you yourself innately conceive it.]

One must analyze the valid cognition of form, sounds, smells, tastes, and tangibles. The apprehender *('dzin mkhyen)* of form is a valid cognizer. Adherence *(zhen pa)* to the [true existence of] form is a conception of true existence. It is difficult but necessary to distinguish between these. There is not as much variation in the force with which we apprehend form as there is an enormous great spectrum of possibility [in apprehending self]. For example, when one is harmed, enormous anger arises so that the "I" which was harmed comes to mind very strongly: "So-and-so harmed me, this absolutely should not be." Or, conversely, one may think, "How my mother and father have helped me; how excellent they are; I do so adore them," and at that time also the "I" which received such help comes [clearly to mind.] Usually, when there is no recollection of great help or harm, when the mind is just relaxed, the conception of true existence is also relaxed and it is difficult to observe the [difference between] the thinker that conceives of [the mere] "I" and the one that conceives of an inherently existent "I." Such identification is a bit easier when the conceiving mind is strong. One can observe this [conceiving mind] with another "small mind" without decreasing the force of the mind being observed.[2] [This is preferable, since] if the latter decreases in force one will not understand how it apprehends. Such are the instructions for identifying [the conception of the inherently existent I.] Following this, one investigates how the mere "I," which proceeds from [one] life to another, and so forth, exists.

In general "I" refers to the possessor or controller *(bdag po)* of the aggregates. This I is neither the substantially existent, self-sufficient person, nor the single, independent self, nor, in the context of Prāsaṅgika, the truly existent self. The mere I, uninvestigated and unanalyzed, serves as the basis for the cause and effect of actions and moves from life to life. A subtle consciousness travels to the next life, and the I that is the possessor of this also goes. The subtle consciousness is like the baggage for an I, which has power over it. How is this? You have hands. These hands are not you. You are the user of these. The hands do not think "I," but when the hands are hurt, one thinks, "I have been hurt."

This "mere I" [is an object of the] nonanalytical mind that thinks, "I come," and, "I go," "I eat," "I drink," and so forth. This I goes to work, goes to shows, reads texts. It exists. When, thinking of this, one reflects, "I saw a show," there exists a great "I" which exceeds the existential measure *(yod tshad)* of the conventionally existent I. The mind conceiving of this does so under its own power, without reflecting on reasons. This mind is a conceiver of true existence whose referent is "I, I." This is not something [purposely] made up by the mind; it is not acquired but innate, and [its object is] the inherently existent I. This I does not go to shows [that is, it does not exist].[3] One needs to identify the measure of apprehension *('dzin tshad)* of this mind.

At the peak of cyclic existence, which is the highest level of cyclic existence in which one can take rebirth, there is nothing except consciousness, and, with this, nonassociated compositional factors such as the impermanence of consciousness, as well as its production, abiding, and disintegration. Predispositions or latencies are also nonassociated compositional factors. They have the power to produce consciousness, just as a small seed has the power to produce a great tree. They themselves are not consciousness, though they are one entity with it. The predispositions associated with a person of the formless realm have the power to produce form [in a subsequent rebirth in the desire or form realms], but they themselves are not form. They are also not conjoined with consciousness, since in their present state they are of no help or harm to us. This is one meaning of the term "conjoined with consciousness" *(sems kyi zin pa).*[4] Another meaning has to do with whether or not a thing is included in the continuum [of mind and body, like hair or nails]. The "I" is also one entity with consciousness, which consciousness is included in the person's continuum.

The valid cognizer that apprehends the conventional I is innate. The mind that apprehends a self who watches, reads, eats, and drinks but which is not this mere conventional I is also innate. This is a mistaken consciousness, the conceiver of true existence. It is doubtful that they are actually simultaneous, though they come so quickly that they seem simultaneous to us.[5] One [consciousness] apprehends the mere I; the other apprehends what is to be negated—namely, the inherently existent I.

*Question:* Are the apprehension of a truly existent table and the apprehension of a conventionally existent table two consciousnesses or two aspects of a single consciousness?

*Answer:* If these were two aspects of a single consciousness, there would be only the one appearance *(snang ba, pratibhāsa)* [of the conventionally existent table] and hence not the [mistaken] apprehension *('dzin pa, grāhaka).* If one apprehended a [mere] pillar, therefore, one would not apprehend it as true [that is, inherently existent]. Thus, there must be two consciousnesses, for the true existence of the pillar appears to one, but [the consciousness] apprehending the [mere] pillar does not apprehend true existence.

The apprehension of a truly existent pillar is a conception of true existence. True existence is what [the mind] adheres to. The consciousness apprehending the [conventionally existent] pillar [actually] apprehends the pillar. First one apprehends *('dzin)* the pillar, then the truly existent pillar. The two apprehensions are not simultaneous because they are different substantial entities *(rdzas, dravya)*; they are two different thoughts *(rtog pa gnyis)* and, generally speaking, two thoughts are not produced simultaneously.[6] These apprehensions occur not in a single moment but serially; nonetheless, the appearances are simultaneous.

When one apprehends the [actual, conventionally existent] pillar, one does not apprehend the truly existent pillar; when one apprehends the truly existent pillar, one does not apprehend the [conventionally existent] pillar.

Nevertheless, the [actual] pillar *appears* to the consciousness apprehending the truly existent pillar. The two appearances can exist simultaneously; the two [types of apprehension] cannot.

It is necessary to recognize that the mind conceiving of true existence apprehends something beyond what the [valid] consciousness apprehending the [mere] table perceives. The mind that thinks "I" apprehends the I as a true existent, whereas an apprehender of the mere I [has as its object] the one that just exists [conventionally]. We may feel that we just exist without depending on anything and develop a conception of "I" as if we were wholly autonomous. In that case, we would not depend on any of our mental or physical aggregates—not on our hands feet, feelings, and so forth. The referent object *(zhen yul, *adhyavasāyaviṣaya)* of the mind that apprehends the I as truly existent does not exist. The referent object of a mind apprehending the mere I, also known as the imputedly existent I, does exist. It exists in dependence on the aggregates [of mind and body] which are its basis of designation. This difference with respect to referent objects can be understood even without necessarily understanding their different modes of apprehension.

In the *Sacred Word of Mañjuśrī*, the Fifth Dalai Lama describes how to identify what is negated.[7] [One must ascertain what is] merely posited by the uninvestigating, unanalytical mind and what is not. The positing mind that neither investigates nor analyzes is a valid cognizer. Indeed, it would seem that a valid cognizer is necessarily nonanalytical *(tshad ma yin na ma brtags ma dpyod pa'i tshad ma yin pas khyab)*. Being posited by such a mind to exist on its own *(yul kho rang gi thog la yod pa)* is the status of the object to be negated. One needs to understand [conventionally existent phenomena] as dependently arisen. When all its parts are gathered together, a thing comes to be; when there are only one or two, it does not. Because they must be so gathered for it to exist, that thing is a dependent arising; in addition to its parts, it requires causes and conditions, [and] a mind designating a convention. These are [the three ways in which an impermanent thing] is a dependent arising.

When uninvestigated and unanalyzed, the thing does exist [but cannot be found to exist under analysis]. If it could [be found under analysis], it would necessarily exist on its own and so would have to truly exist. If it existed that way, one would find it as either the same as or different from its parts [but when one analyzes, one cannot find it thus]. If it were one with its parts, then all the [multiplicity of] parts would be singular; or just as there are many parts, it itself would be many. This is the reasoning of the one and the many.[8]

Certain mistakes obtain here. There are those who would say, "Unanalyzed and uninvestigated, it exists; if one analyzes and investigates, it does not exist. Because it exists only in the absence of analysis and investigation, it does not exist, or the horns of a rabbit would also exist." However, even though it exists unanalyzed and uninvestigated, it is not like the horns of a rabbit, and [it does not follow that] the horns of a rabbit must exist. The horns of a rabbit do not come to be, even if they are apprehended. They can never function like the horns of a rabbit, whereas this tape recorder, unanalyzed and uninvestigated, exists, because it can carry out its own appropriate function. It is something that is *apprehended* without investigation or analysis. There is, thus, the difference that one functions and the other does not.

There are those who would say that such functioning is only a mistaken appearance. Beginners like ourselves tend to believe whatever is said and might well be convinced by such a statement. Unanalyzed and uninvestigated, this object must exist; yet if [there were something] beyond this existence, then, when one analyzed and investigated, one would get at that object. If something exists as apprehended by the mind that analyzes and investigates, it must truly exist; if it exists for the mind that neither investigates nor analyzes, then it conventionally exists, it does not utterly not exist. The manner of valid establishment must be posited by a nonanalytical, noninvestigating mind. Such a mind does analyze, but this is not the analysis of the phrase "nonanalytical, noninvestigating mind." This latter occurs after an object has been established by valid cognition. For example, once impermanence is established by valid cognition, one does not analyze its entity but investigates whether impermanence truly exists or not—that is, one analyzes its way of being. However, so long as its impermanence is not established, there is [need for] analysis: "The subject, sound, is impermanent because of being a product." Until one has analyzed whether sound is permanent or impermanent, impermanence is not established by [one's own] valid cognition. Once it has been analyzed, inferential valid cognition establishes it. When it is so established, one does not [further] analyze whether or not sound is impermanent but investigates its [hypothetical] true existence, its way of being. These are two [different] analytical procedures.

Prior to understanding selflessness, one sets out many correct signs, or reasonings, and extensively analyzes whether the thing in question truly exists or not. Once selflessness is validly established, that analysis is complete. When one analyzes a pillar, for example, one finds its lack of true existence. However, having this lack of true existence as an object is not what is intended by the phrase "coming to be an object for the analytical, investigative mind." [The point is that] having completed analysis and investigation in searching for a truly existent pillar, the truly existent pillar should be there. However, the analyzer finds the pillar's lack of true existence, not the pillar. It is the same with all phenomena.

As for the mind realizing the emptiness or selflessness of emptiness, one analyzes the entity of emptiness, which is one's object and which is established by valid cognition. If an emptiness were something made by analysis and investigation, it ought to stand up [under such analysis], but instead it becomes nonexistent for the analytical mind. When one analyzes the lack of true existence, one does not find *that* lack of true existence, one finds *its* lack of true existence. Once you investigate and analyze, emptiness itself has no way of abiding. That is what it means, to say that a thing does not exist under analysis or investigation.[9]

Emptiness, too, is merely posited by a nonanalytical mind. It exists conventionally. All established bases, all phenomena, are conventionally existent, and are not ultimately existent. They are not found by an analytical investigative mind but are merely posited as existent by a nonanalytical mind. Thus, they are nonexistent for an analytical, investigative mind. All are necessarily nominally and imputedly existent.

# 8

# THE SVĀTANTRIKA SCHOOL ON TRUE EXISTENCE

Because conventional existence is the opposite of ultimate existence, an explanation of the conventional existence of phenomena must be connected with a discussion of how things do not exist ultimately. According to Svātantrika, anything that exists without being posited by a valid mind would ultimately or truly exist. "To exist because of being posited by a valid cognizer" means, to exist conventionally.

Svātantrika states that, though things have a way of being which is posited by the mind, they are not *merely* posited by the mind. Being posited by the mind is not what the Svātantrika School means by being conventionally existent. Nor does it hold that phenomena posited by thought exist conventionally for the conceiver of true existence. Why not? That which is conventionally existent for the conception of true existence does not have its own mode of subsistence; it is a mere appearance *(snang ba, pratibhāsa).*

Even though there are no truly existent phenomena, there is a mistaken consciousness that apprehends true existence. This conceiver of true existence is called "obscure" *(kun rdzob, saṃvṛti).* Although objects of the senses—forms, sounds, odors, tastes, and objects of touch—as well as the five mental and physical aggregates—forms, feelings, discrimination, compositional factors, and consciousesses—are ultimately without a truly existent entity, these and all phenomena are apprehended as having this. A mind that apprehends this is a superimposing consciousness. It is an obscurer. What does it obscure? Its own perception of reality. This becomes as if veiled.

The word "reality" in the phrase "obscurer of reality" *(yang dag kun rdzob, samyaksaṃvṛti)* refers to the emptiness that is [veiled by] this obscuring consciousness, which is the agent of this obscuration: the conception of true existence. "Reality" *(yang dag, samyak)* refers to emptiness, and "conventional" *(kun rdzob, saṃvṛti),* to its obscurer—namely, to the conception of true existence that obscures or covers over the real [that is, emptiness]. Whatever is true for this obscurer is called a truth-for-a-concealer. Thus, that which sees conventionalities gets the name "mind that obscures."[1]

All objects such as forms are conventional objects, otherwise known as conventional or concealing truths. There are both real and unreal concealing truths. Sutra, in asserting the existence of a concealer of reality *(yang dag kun rdzob)* [takes] a consciousness conceiving true existence itself to be the concealer of reality although that is not the point here [since this is not the meaning of this term when it is used in the division of concealing truths into the categories of the real and the unreal].[2]

[According to a passage from the *Descent into Laṅkā Sutrā (lang kar gshegs pa'i mdo, laṅkāvatārasūtra),*] the mind itself is the concealer because it is a mind which apprehends true existence that is obscured from unmistaken seeing.[3] Here "concealer" and "conventional" (*kun rdzob, saṃvṛti*) have the same meaning, although the two terms are not synonymous in general. Such a mind is obscured or mistaken because, due to superimpositions, it conceives this conventionality [that is to say, phenomena in general] to truly exist. Thus, we perceive true existence because of predispositions for conceiving things this way. That which apprehends true existence due to these predispositions obscures and is obscured from seeing reality.

All other living beings, not just humans, apprehend what does not actually exist, a mode of abiding, true existence. Whether or not persons have trained in systems of tenets, all living beings have had such conceptions and the latencies for these since beginningless time. The conception of true existence does not exist in the continuum of a Buddha Superior. Because this type of existence is false, persons and all other phenomena [seen to] exist this way are like illusions. All phenomena, which [can also be called] falsities, only exist conventionally, not ultimately.

The mind apprehends as real that which is not real, and as ultimate that which is not ultimate. However, the *appearance* of a truly existent table does exist. It is not what *appears to* a consciousness conceiving true existence which is the object of negation; rather, the referent object *(zhen yul, *adhyavasāyaviṣaya)*, the object of engagement *('jug yul, *pravṛttiviṣaya)*—that is, the truly existent table itself—is to be negated.

When the eye consciousness apprehends a pillar, the pillar itself, its impermanence, and everything that is one entity of establishment and abiding *(grub bde rdzas gcig)* with the pillar appears. The true existence of the pillar appears together with these due to previous predispositions for the view of self *(snga ma nas bdag lta'i bag chags)*. The truly existent pillar appears to thought, but the impermanence of the pillar does not. [The pillar as a] basis of engagement *('jug gzhi)* appears because of predispositions for explicit verbalization *(mngon brjod gyi bag chags)*. [In the Yogācāra-Svātantrika

Mādhyamika system] the pillar itself [appears because of] predispositions for seeing [pillars as] similar in type *(rigs mthun gyi bag chags)*.[4] The first two types of predisposition [for the view of self and for explicit verbalization] exist with respect to thought. Appearances due to predispositions for seeing similarity of type seem not to exist for thought insofar as all the parts of a thing—shape, color, and so forth—do not appear to thought.

Impermanence, and so forth, [appear] because of the predispositions for [perceiving] similarity of type. The appearance of the table as existing from its own side, or the appearance of the truly existent table, occur because of predispositions for such a view of the self. Factors that exist in relation to table, such as its being an object of knowledge, an established base, and so forth, and which are merely imputed by thought, are probably [perceived because of] the latencies for explicit verbalization, as is its appearing to be a referent of the term "table" *(lcog tse zhes pa'i sgra 'jug sa'i gzhi)*. When we speak of something, the mind goes to the object of engagement; predispositions are deposited in relation to this mind, and in the future these appear to direct perception.

This general discussion of the three [types of] predispositions also exists in the Mind Only (Cittamātra) system; all these occur with respect to the sense consciousnesses [and for thought], but not in the same way. The eye consciousness is a mind of complete engagement and therefore no mental image or meaning generality appears to it. It has no appearances mixed with other appearances. The meaning generality that appears to thought is, by contrast, mixed with other appearances. It is a bit different in Prāsaṅgika, where one speaks of the valid cognition *of* what is manifest *(mngon sum gyi tshad ma)* and not of valid direct perception *(mngon sum tshad ma)*. Here "direct" *(mngon sum)* signifies the manifest object; valid cognition of the manifest is cognition of such objects. Such cognition need not be free of conceptuality because there is conceptual [valid cognition of manifest objects], in that a realization which depends on reasoning can realize manifest objects.

If you look through a small hole in, for example, a film container, you can only see a very small area. Even though light is there, you cannot see anything more because the object obstructs it. Remove the object so there is no obstruction, and you can see it all. In the same way, a conceptual image, or meaning generality, obstructs perception of other things; its appearance negates other appearances.[5]

Predispositions for the conception of true existence—that is, for conceiving that there is a way of being not posited by the force of the mind—have been with us beginninglessly.[6] But such can appear only to thought, not to nonconceptual consciousnesses. However, because the mistaken appearance is permanent, it is not produced from predispositions; it is said, however, that the mistaken appearance occurs *('byung, udaya)* through the power of the predispositions.

According to the Prāsaṅgika system, the appearance of objects as existing from their own side appears to both sense and mental consciousnesses. One does not need an articulate [conceptual] consciousness to discern it. In Prāsaṅgika the object negated is very, very subtle. [In their view, the true existence] discussed in Svātantrika does not appear [to the sense consciousnesses] because it is coarse and derived from systems of tenets, [whereas Prāsaṅgika negates a conception of inherent existence which is innate, not learned].

According to Prāsaṅgika [and Tsong-kha-pa is discussing Svātantrika here specifically in order to clarify the Prāsaṅgika position], when one sees a table, the truly existent table appears to the eye consciousness but this appearance of the truly existent table does not obstruct seeing the conventional table, nor seeing other parts of the table. It does obstruct seeing the emptiness of the table's true existence. One cannot see ultimate truths because the appearance of true existence obstructs this. However, this obscurer [the meaning generality of true existence] does not appear to direct perception. The inherent or true existence that appears to the eye consciousness is not a meaning generality because [a sense consciousness is] a mind of complete engagement [and thus, by definition, does not observe meaning generalities].[7] The true existence which [according to Prāsaṅgika, but not Svātantrika] appears to the eye consciousness does not obstruct seeing other [conventional] things, but the mind that *conceives* of true existence, the mind to which a meaning generality appears, does. [Similarly] the appearance of pillar to thought [is a mental image which] obstructs seeing other [individual] parts of a pillar. A consciousness conceiving true existence can see nothing except this [appearance of] true existence because it is obstructed from doing so. Objects cannot come to it, just as when a door is shut, one cannot come in.

[In short, the appearance of true existence to direct perception] obstructs emptiness, but not other things. It is not the appearing object of the conception of true existence that obscures, but the conception of true existence itself. Any mind which apprehends as real what is not real is an obscurer. The conceiver of true existence cannot be a sense consciousness and, at the same time, a sense consciousness is necessarily not a conceiver of true existence [because all sense perception is nonconceptual].[8]

*Question:* How then can the Svātantrika system explain the beginninglessness of the conception of true existence? If it does not appear to the senses, as Prāsaṅgika maintains, what gives rise to it?

*Answer:* It is indeed difficult for Svātantrika to uphold this point. The source Tsong-kha-pa quotes on this matter, Jñānagarbha's *Commmentary on the "Differentiation of the Two Truths,"*[9] does not set forth reasons for it; other texts do not discuss it, and in general in this system it would be difficult to do so.

[It is, however, said that] this comes about because of the predispositions related to the mind. This [conceiver of true existence] is an innate mind, not made through artifice but natural. It is not a mind that is sharp or intent. The sense consciousnesses are relaxed *(hlod hlod)*, not intent, not ready to get to work right away.[10]

Svātantrika [unlike Prāsaṅgika] does not posit existence from its own side as true existence. Svātantrikas hold that there is something to be identified after analysis and investigation [into whether something from among the bases of interpretation is the object imputed].[11] The true existence that can appear only to thought and not to sense perception is [from Prāsaṅgika's viewpoint] a coarse type of true existence. Existence from its own side, which is not negated in Svātantrika, appears to both sense consciousness and to thought. It cannot appear [merely by] the power of latencies, for these cannot present themselves to the sense consciousnesses—that is, the defilements that are latencies cannot impress or affect the sense consciousness, whereas the appearance of existence from its own side can. The appearance of true existence requires an intent mind [and can only appear to such]. Such would seem to be [Jñānagarbha's meaning]; however, this is not much discussed other texts.

*Question:* When one sees a pot, the eye consciousness takes on the aspect of that pot's impermanence. In contending that true existence appears to the eye consciousness, does Prāsaṅgika maintain that the way in which consciousness takes on the aspect of true existence is analogous to its taking on or being generated in the aspect of impermanence?

*Answer:* When true existence [that is, existence from its own side,] appears to the eye consciousness, the eye consciousness takes on, or is generated in the aspect of, true existence. Although the eye consciousness can be said to take on the aspect of true existence, the cause of [its doing so] is not the appearance of true existence. A table, for example, acts as an object condition *(dmigs rkyen, ālambanapratyaya)*, whereas the appearance of true existence does not. The table produces the consciousness perceiving it, but the appearance of true existence does not. It is only said that its appearance comes to be. This appearance is permanent; it cannot perform functions and so does not cause a consciousness.

*Question:* Since according to Prāsaṅgika true existence appears to the sense consciousnesses, why are these considered valid cognizers? Why are they not erroneous consciousnesses?

*Answer:* To be erroneous means to be mistaken regarding one's main object, otherwise known as the object of engagement. Of course, some sense consciousnesses are mistaken in this way, such as that observing a blue snow mountain. An eye consciousness apprehending pots, pillars, and so forth, is not erroneous in this way, although all eye and other sense consciousnesses in the continuums of living beings are mistaken regarding their appearing object—namely, the appearance of true existence. The appearance of true existence is permanent and is a generally characterized phenomenon. It appears to the eye [and other sense] consciousnesses of ordinary beings, and to all minds which realize conventionalities, that is, to all minds except that directly realizing emptiness. It appears because all such minds are contaminated by the obstructions to omniscience.[12] Conceptual thought has coarse and subtle error; the coarse is its mistaking the meaning generality for the actual object, subtle error is its mistake regarding the appearance of true existence. The eye consciousness apprehending form has only one place of error; thought has two.

According to Sautrāntika, the basis which is the place of engagement *('jug sa'i gzhi)* is realized; the appearance cannot be realized [by sensory direct perception]. It is realized by a self-knower *(rang rig, svasaṃvedanā).* Even in the Prāsaṅgika system, the conceptual appearance [of true existence] is a meaning generality. It exists conventionally but is not the main object of this thought; it is the appearing object. The main object [also known as the engaged object *('jug yul)* is not said to be merely the conventionally existent table. The place which is a basis of naming is the main object, the object of engagement. The basis of engagement *('jug gzhi)* and the basis which is the place of engagement *('jug sa'i gzhi)* are the same, in my opinion. To give an instance of the basis which is the place of engagement with respect to the table, one must posit a table. Similarly, in the *Collected Topics*, when asked to instance a pot's isolate [or opposite of being one with pot], one can only offer "pot." However, the place which is the basis of the term is not concordant with the object. One is permanent and the other, impermanent. That is, the place which is a basis of a term *(sgra'i 'jug sa'i gzhi)* is permanent; the pot itself is impermanent. A term is a partial engager; it operates only with respect to certain aspects, not all. The way of being of the place which is a basis of a term, and [the way of being of] the table are different.

This place which is a basis of a term is not exactly a meaning generality. The place which is a basis of the term for an eye consciousness is multiple [in that multiple aspects related to the object appear], whereas the meaning generality [that is the appearing object of] thought is much less complex. For this reason the table and the basis to which a thought places a term *(rtog pa'i 'jug sa'i gzhi)* are different. With respect to a basis of engagement such as a pot, there are many things such as its handle, mouth, and so forth, that are not the basis of engagement. The eye consciousness, unlike thought, operates with respect to all of them.

[We have observed that] according to Prāsaṅgika, true existence appears to the eye consciousness, but that this is not so for Svātantrika. The mind comes to be mistaken because of predispositions arising from its past habituation.[13] This appearance of true existence shows itself to all minds except that directly cognizing emptiness. For the mind directly realizing emptiness, there is no appearance of either true existence or conventional objects. Predispositions for true existence cannot meet with such a mind, as they can with all other consciousnesses in the continuums of sentient beings [non-Buddhas].

The aspect of true existence exists. It is a deceptive appearance *(slu snang)*. The thought realizing pot, for example, implicitly realizes the exclusion which is the nonaffirming negative of pot *(bum pa'i med dgag gi gzhan sel)*. This is similar to how a direct perceiver [such as an eye consciousness], observing the place where there is no pot, implicitly realizes the absence of pot. Implicit realizers do not take on the aspect of an image.

The mind that posits phenomena is a valid cognizer, and valid cognizers can be either conceptual or nonconceptual. Form can be posited by the eye consciousness or by the mental consciousness; sounds by the ear consciousness or the mental consciousness. And so forth. Although such positing minds can be either conceptual or nonconceptual, the mind that conceives of phenomena as the opposite of this [that is, as ultimately existent] is necessarily conceptual. Thought's error in conceiving of true existence does not *depend* on a mistake of the sense consciousness.

Svātantrika is unable to refute a mode of existence posited by the force of the mind and finds it necessary to examine whether there is a mode of existence *not* posited by the force of the mind to which it appears. Prāsaṅgika, without distinguishing between a mode of existence posited by such a mind and one not so posited, just denies that there is any mode of existence that either is or is not posited by the force of the mind to which it appears. [In their view,] either involves existing from its own side [and thus is refuted].

In this school, the conception of true existence refers to an apprehension of phenomena as if established ultimately from their own side, as if they were not [in any way] posited through the force of appearing to a nondefective consciousness. However, [when Svātantrika maintains that] all things *(dngos po, bhāva)* are posited by the power of thought, the positing mind is valid, having no superimpositions. Thus, being "posited by thought" is different from being a mistaken superimposition of a mode of existence opposite to the lack of entityness of all phenomena. According to Svātantrika, a valid cognizer is the mind by whose power [an object's] mode of subsistence is posited. According to Prāsaṅgika, this [mode of subsistence] is a superimposition by thought [and the mind apprehending it is] a conceiver of true existence. What Prāsaṅgika labels as an erroneous consciousness, however, Svātantrika considers a valid cognizer, because in Svātantrika existence from its own side does exist—it must, in their view, or the phenomenon itself would not exist. The mind apprehending a table as existing from its own side is identical with the mind apprehending the table. Both are valid.[14]

## THE MEANINGS OF "ULTIMATE"

[In discussing the Svātantrika understanding of true existence,] Tsong-kha-pa entertains a question regarding the statement in Kamalaśīla's

*Illumination of the Middle Way (dbu ma snang ba, madhyamakālokā),* "Ultimately there is no production."[15] The issue has to do with the different meanings of the term "ultimate."[16]

What does it mean when we say, "Ultimately there is no production"? Kamalaśīla indicates that it means that [production] of these other-powered phenomena *(gzhan dbang, paratantra)* is not established by [an ultimate mind—that is,] a reasoning consciousness that cognizes reality. However, Tsong-kha-pa himself has just identified "ultimate" as indicating a particular type of existence, one that is established by way of its own objective mode of subsistence without being established through the force of the mind. [The potential objection is that these two readings of "ultimate" are incongruous.]

Kamalaśīla here uses "ultimate" to refer to a reasoning consciousness. However, "ultimate" can also signify a nonexistent category—those phenomena whose mode of subsistence is not posited by the force of the mind. Such a way of existence does not exist; the mode of subsistence of phenomena is [merely] a conventionality posited by the power of appearance. But it is not posited by a conceiver of true existence—if it were, it would have to truly exist; rather, it is posited by ordinary valid consciousnesses.

Production, therefore, is not established for the consciousness of reality *(yang dag pa'i shes pa)*, the exalted wisdom of meditative equipoise realizing reality, or the uninterrupted Mahāyāna path of seeing. However, validly established production is posited by a correct consciousness.

Only that which has a mode of subsistence not posited by the power of the mind can be said to exist for a concealing consciousness—that is, to be a referent object or object of engagement for the conceiver of true existence. [But no such phenomena exist.]

Kamalaśīla's statement implicitly suggests that a consciousness of reality has an object. It would then follow that such a consciousness, being an ultimate consciousness, would have an ultimate object. This is one usage of the word "ultimate." However, Kamalaśīla says that the reasoning consciousness that analyzes reality *refutes* production; thus, production cannot be its object. An ultimate consciousness realizes emptiness; it does not realize the phenomenon—in this case, production—being qualified as empty.[17] When it examines whether production, or any other phenomenon such as a sprout, truly exists, it comes to know their lack of true existence. It does not know those phenomena themselves. If it did, then production of a sprout would have to be truly existent.

How can it be said that the analytical consciousness establishes production as existing? Or that production is established for such a consciousness? There are phenomena which are established ultimately for [reasoning] consciousnesses of hearing, thinking, or meditating. Production does not exist ultimately, but it is established for an ultimate because it is established for an "ultimate" consciousness of hearing, thinking, or meditating. However, if we take "ultimate" to mean "an ultimate consciousness analyzing reality," then, of course, production does not exist for such a consciousness. Thus, most succinctly, the point of the debate is to make the reader of aware of the very different applications of the term "ultimate."

[To put this another way,] it is established that production is not ultimately produced *(don dam par skye pa med pa)* for a consciousness of hearing, thinking, or meditating. Such consciousnesses are in general called reasoning consciousnesses or analyzers of the ultimate *(don dam dpyod byed)*. There are also nonanalytical consciousnesses of hearing, thinking, or meditating, but these are not reasoning consciousnesses; they are conventional consciousnesses [not ultimate]. It is [only] the *analytical* minds of hearing, thinking, or meditating that are ultimate.[18] Does it follow that any object of hearing, thinking, or meditating is an ultimate truth? An "ultimate truth" is the object of a reasoning consciousness that is the nonconceptual exalted wisdom of the Mahāyāna uninterrupted path of seeing.[19] "Ultimate" can mean to be established for such a consciousness. It also has the meaning, discussed above, of being ultimately established from its own side. Thus, there are phenomena that are ultimates themselves [such as emptiness]; there are also things that are [hypothetically] established ultimately.

The discussion of whether or not things exist ultimately has to do with "ultimate" as signifying "ultimately established." That which exists for a consciousness of reality, or ultimate consciousness—such as minds of hearing, thinking, or mediating—does not exist ultimately. Similarly, ultimate truths—the emptinesses that are objects of an ultimate consciousness—[do not exist ultimately].

The term "ultimate" can also refer to that which has its own mode of subsistence without being posited through the force of the mind. This type of ultimate does not exist. It is negated; it is [what Svātantrika calls] true existence. "Not having its own mode of subsistence" means that the thing itself is not its own essential mode, that something else is. For example, the essential mode of production, or of a pillar, is not the production or pillar itself, but the emptiness of these. Emptiness is the final essential mode of all objects. Thus, there is no contradiction in maintaining that, although nothing exists ultimately, there are ultimate objects.

To apprehend the [lack of the] second type of ultimate is to apprehend an ultimate truth. This ultimate truth exists. If, however, an apprehension of this were an apprehension of true existence, the referent object would have to be nonexistent conventionally. The apprehension of true existence necessarily involves apprehension of the second type of ultimate—that is, of a mode of subsistence not posited by the force of appearing to a healthy *(gnos med)* mind such as the innate apprehender of true, or ultimate existence. Such are not established for a consciousness of reality.

This is a difficult area; the texts contain many debates on this topic, especially regarding Tsong-kha-pa's statement (132.1) that apprehending the existence of the first type of "ultimate" [a reasoning consciousness of hearing, thinking, or meditating] does not constitute an innate apprehension of true existence.

Because a mere explanation of true existence and of the conception of true existence is insufficient to convey their full meaning, an example easily understood in the world is given, that of an illusion.

# 9

# THE MAGICIAN'S ILLUSION: TRUTH AND FALSITY FOR WORLDLY PERSONS

The Svātantrika School[1] maintains that an object which is established from its own side—that is, by its own uncommon mode of subsistence, without being posited by the power of appearing to the mind—is what must be negated. Therefore, one must understand the difference between being posited by the mind and not being posited by the mind. The example of a magician's illusion is praised as facilitating understanding of this point.

Illusions, as well as the other analogous instances cited in the discussion of the seventh sameness, such as reflections, dreams, shadows, echos, and a moon in water, are all examples well established in the world. The main example used here [in Tsong-kha-pa's discussion] is that of a magician's illusion; once it has been set out, its connection with the meaning [of the emptiness of true existence] is explained.

We have mentioned this example before. In brief, it has to do with a magician causing an audience to see an elephant and a horse, although actually only a stick and a stone are present. Three types of perception occur. The audience thinks, "There it is, a horse, oh, wonderful!" These people are unaware that their eyes are affected by a mantra; they do not think the magician has caused something to appear which actually does not exist. They have the impression that a horse or elephant has been led onto the stage. The magician also clearly perceives a horse, but at the same time recognizes that no such animal is present. Then a late-comer enters, unaffected by the spell, and has no sense at all that any animal is present, but sees only the stick and the stone.

All phenomena are like the illusory horse and elephant of the example. Ordinary persons like ourselves [are analogous to the audience]; we see true existence and believe in it. Persons who consider that the true existence which appears is nonexistent are like the magician. Those who have neither a perception nor a conception of true existence are like the late-comer unaffected by the magician's spell.

When one mistakes a rope for a snake, a snake exists for one's mistaken consciousness although no snake is present. Similarly, a horse and elephant exist for the mistaken consciousnesses [of the persons affected by the mantra and the magician himself]. The stick and stone now appear as a horse and elephant even though they do not appear this way in general. Despite this appearance, it is inappropriate to maintain that the stone or stick is a horse or elephant. At the same time, if the stone or stick did not appear so, there would be no basis for conjecturing the existence of horses and elephants.

How is this example used to indicate the difference between a thing's being and not being posited through the force of appearing to a mind? The illusionist apprehends what is posited through the force of the mind and knows that the mode of subsistence of the horse or elephant does not accord with its appearance. The audience thinks that an elephant which covers its own spot is actually present from its own side and is not posited by the mind. The stick and stone that are the bases of conjuring do in general exist, as does the appearance [of the animals]. These are established bases *(gzhi grub).* Although the stick and stone are not an elephant or horse, the perceiving consciousness [correctly] posits this appearance as existing and [incorrectly] posits the existence of a horse or elephant. Thus, [the horse and elephant] which exists [for this mind] are posited by the force of appearing to a mistaken consciousness. The stone or stick are not actually, from their own mode of abiding, a horse or elephant, but are posited that way through the force of appearing to a mistaken consciousness. Other than this, the objects do not exist on their own. The illusionist or magician knows what the situation is, but the audience has no thought whatever that these are merely posited through the force of appearing to the mind; they believe that real animals are present.

*Question:* When the horse and elephant are said to be "posited by the force of appearing to the mind," does "mind" refer to the eye consciousness or to thought?

*Answer:* The question of what sort of mind posits objects leads to a discussion of the self-knower *(rang rig, svasaṃvedanā).* According to Svātantrika, nonconceptual erroneous consciousnesses do not realize their object, whereas according to Prāsaṅgika, even erroneous consciousnesses realize appearances. According to Prāsaṅgika, the sense consciousness that apprehends the horse and elephant is erroneous [and thus not a valid cognizer]; it cannot realize their appearance [and therefore cannot posit it]. What realizes it? The self-knower [which is part of the system of the Yogacara-Svātantrikas founded by Śāntarakṣita but not asserted in the system of the Sautrāntika-Svātantrikas, founded by Bhāvaviveka] is said to experience [that sense consciousness].

Therefore, one can say that it is posited by the self-knower even though it does not appear to the self-knower. The self-knower [explicitly] realizes the consciousness and implicitly realizes the appearance to that consciousness. The self-knower is thus a direct cognizer with respect to that consciousness [but this does not contradict its having implicit realization]. Similarly, through seeing one's face in a mirror one can understand its condition; one is not looking at the [actual] face, but the face is implicitly realized.

We can speak of objects as posited by the power of the valid cognizers that impute them. Direct perception knows manifest objects; inferential valid cognizers can understand hidden objects. In Svātantrika, being realized by valid cognition *(tshad mas rtogs pa)* and being established by way of the object's own nature *(rang gi mtshan nyid kyis grub pa, svalakṣaṇasiddhi)* are mutually inclusive. Prāsaṅgika, however, maintains the necessity of differentiating between these [because in their view] if something is established by [ordinary] valid cognition, it necessarily has a mode of abiding which does not accord with its appearance to that valid cognizer. It is a bit more difficult to understand what "to be posited by the power of a valid cognizer" means than to understand what "to be established by a valid cognizer" means. Vaibāṣikas and Sautrāntikas recognize that tables, and so forth, are established by valid cognition, but do not see these as posited by the power of valid cognition. Why? Because they assert a mode of subsistence that is not just posited by the power of appearing to a valid cognizer. Although they refute that there is a mode of subsistence from its own side that is not *established* by valid cognition, they do accept a mode of subsistence which is not *posited* through the force of appearing to valid cognition.

Valid cognizers are minds; therefore, something posited by the force of a valid cognizer is posited by the force of the mind. [In Mādhyamika], any object of comprehension is posited by the power of a valid cognizer. To say that an object of comprehension is posited by the force of a valid cognizer means that the valid cognizer functions to realize or remove superimpositions with respect to that object. This is not the same as the object's being posited by the power of *appearing* to a valid cognizer.

If one understands how something is posited by the force of direct perception in dependence on a basis of designation, one understands that, even if something has a mode of subsistence, its appearance may or may not accord with it.

What is the difference between being and not being posited through the force of appearing to a mistaken mind? The illusionist apprehends that the horse and elephant are posited through the force of the mind and knows that the mode of subsistence of the horse or elephant does not accord with its appearance. The audience thinks that an elephant which covers its own spot is actually present from its own side, not posited in the face of a conventional or obscuring mind.

In the example, appearance and emptiness are established only for the magician. The horse and elephant do not exist the way they appear even to his eye consciousness. If they did, they could be seen by eyes unaffected [by the mantra]. This establishes both that (1) there is an appearance as a horse or an elephant *and* that (2) these do not exist as they appear. These are false even for a conventional mind that has not been affected by the study of tenets—for the magician is not someone who has studied tenets.

The emptiness of phenomena is like that appearance established for members of the audience whose eyes have not been affected [by the mantra]. Emptiness is also established for those whose eyes [or thought] have not been contaminated, like the magician, for whom both emptiness and appearance are established.

## APPLYING THE EXAMPLE TO THE MEANING

Just as a magician's audience whose eyes are affected by a mantra confidently assume that a horse or elephant is present and do not suspect in the slightest that these are posited through the force of appearing to their own minds, so we apprehend phenomena—pots, pillars, arms, legs, and the like—as truly existent. Just as the audience, on the basis of appearances, conceives of a horse or elephant when these are in fact absent, so we feel that things are truly established, as they appear to be. Svātantrikas consider this to be the innate conception of true existence. According to Prāsaṅgika, however, this is not the most subtle misconception, but a rather coarse one.[2]

In the example, the magician knows that the stick and stone are not a horse and elephant but are posited through the force of appearing to the mind. In the same way, through the application of reasons one can understand that an object of negation [a truly existent pillar or other object] does not exist. Once this is understood, one recalls that there is a mode of existence which is posited by the force of appearing to the mind *(blo la snang ba'i dbang gis bzhag pa'i sdod lugs)*. Svātantrika considers existence not posited by the force of appearing to the mind to be the most subtle object of negation. Through reflecting on the many reasons refuting true existence, one may come to think, "Well, probably there is no true existence," [meaning that] there is no mode of subsistence which is not posited by the internal mind. Then one understands that [these objects] have an existence that is just posited by the power of the mind.

If the mind that posits an object is not undermined by valid cognition, that [object] is said to conventionally exist. Valid cognition realizes a mode of being posited through the force of appearing to valid cognition. In the example of the magician, although the appearance of the stick and stone as a horse or elephant exists, that object does not necessarily exist. There are two types of phenomena that are posited through the force of appearing to the mind—those that are and are not undermined by valid cognition. Therefore, the criterion of whether or not an object is undermined by a valid cognizer is essential. If it is not, the object conventionally exists; if it is undermined by valid cognition, the object does not exist.

Does a seed produce a sprout? Yes. Is this production posited by the force of the mind? Yes. Nevertheless, the seed does from its own side produce the sprout. For example, the appearance of the stone or stick as a horse or an elephant is posited by the mind. Still, the basis of emanation abides from its own side as an appearance like a horse or an elephant.

If the basis of emanation did not appear as a horse or an elephant, there would be no basis, no ground, of appearance *(snang sa)*. To say the basis of emanation appears as the horse or an elephant is to maintain that it appears as a horse or elephant from its own side.

That appearance itself is posited by the force of the mind. This way of being, namely its being so posited, exists in relation to that appearance, but not in relation to the basis of emanation, the stick and stone. Thus, in relation to the stick and stone, there is a way of being that exists and one that does not. That which is the way of being of the stick and stone pertain to the stick and stone themselves. The appearance of horse and elephant to the eye consciousness are not the way of being of the stick and stone.

If the stick and stone had their own uncommon way of being *(thun mong ma yin pa'i gnas lugs),* they would have something not posited through the force of the mind to which they appear, [but they do not]. The appearance [as horse and elephant] is posited by the force of the mind to which they appear and, therefore, this is not the way of being of stick and stone but the way of being of the appearance itself. Similarly, pillar and pot are posited through the force of appearing to a conventional consciousness. When they are posited thus, they are realized by a conventional valid cognizer.

Just as the appearance itself has a way of subsistence *(sdod lugs)* [as appearance], pillar and pot have a way of being of pillar and pot. Such objects appear from their own side. The mind to which they appear realizes their way of being, which is posited by the force of the mind [to which they appear], and does not realize a way of being not so posited. If such a way of being existed, it would have to be the pillar or pot's own way of being, but it is not. If one investigates their final nature, one understands the lack of such a way of being. Thus, it is necessary to distinguish between something such as a pot or pillar and the true existence which pertains to these. One is established and the other is negated. The pot itself is posited through the force of its appearance; this is its way of subsistence, just as the illusionist's horse and elephant has a way of subsistence posited by the force of its appearance *(snang ba'i dbang gis bzhag)*. These [phenomena] are established from their own side and established by their own nature, but they are not truly existent.

In Svātantrika, the innate conception of true existence is the conception that phenomena exist without being posited through the force of the mind. Thus, Svantantrika teaches that one must understand phenomena to exist merely through being posited through the force of the mind. This pertains to all internal and external phenomena. Those phenomena which are not undermined by valid cognition are said to conventionally exist. For something to truly exist, it must itself be its own mode of subsistence, and these phenomena, as we have said, are not, for that would mean they had a mode of subsistence not posited by the force of their appearance. To be posited by the force of the mind [to which it appears] does not require that a thing have its own mode of subsistence, for no conventionalities [or ultimates either] have this.

A "mode of subsistence" simply means that which subsists within an object *(kho rang gi thog nas yod bsdad mkhyen).* An object itself is not its own basis of abiding. Thus, if something exists, its mode of abiding must be something other than itself. In general, emptiness or a lack of true [existence] is called the mode of abiding of phenomena. Emptiness itself, however, is not its own mode of abiding; the emptiness of that emptiness—an emptiness' own lack of true existence—is its mode of abiding. Similarly, a pillar is not the mode of subsistence of a pillar.

Prāsaṅgika maintains that there is a mode of subsistence which is merely nominally imputed. Thus, both Prāsaṅgika and Svātantrika are similar in speaking of nominal positing, but the object of negation that they are getting at is vastly different, for Svātantrika says that even though [a thing] is posited by a convention[al mind], it has a mode of subsistence posited by convention that is *not* just nominally imputed. In Prāsaṅgika, by contrast, there is *no* mode of subsistence that is not nominally imputed.[3]

Phenomena are not their own modes of subsistence. Their mode of subsistence in each case is emptiness, which must be established as permanent and as a nonaffirming negative. A pot or pillar is, by contrast, a positive phenomenon and something that is not an object of the exalted wisdom directly cognizing emptiness. Just as these phenomena are not objects of a direct realization of emptiness, so these appearances [of horse and elephant] are not of the entity of stick and stone. Just so, pots and pillars exist, but they are not their own final mode of existence. When one realizes a pot or pillar, one realizes a mode of subsistence posited through the force of appearance. Merely in dependence on having this, such things are said to exist from their own side. Thus, to say that something exists from its own side is not a very strong statement; it is not as strong as saying that something truly exists.

[Whereas Svātantrika is willing to accept that objects have a way of subsistence which, however, is posited by the force of the mind to which it appears,] Prāsaṅgika maintains that there is *no* such way of subsistence, [not even one] posited [by the force of appearing to the mind]. For them, a mode of subsistence posited through the force of appearing to the mind would mean that a thing was its own mode of subsistence. Like Svātantrika, they do not find this to be the case. The Svātantrikas' handling of this tenet brings them into difficulties when it gets down to subtle debate; nevertheless, they maintain that if there were no mode of subsistence posited by the force of the mind, then the thing in question would completely disappear.

Prāsaṅgikas, not accepting this, say rather that things are merely posited without a way of subsistence. Even so, they can function; they are neither undermined by other valid cognition, nor by a consciousness realizing the ultimate. They exist and are like illusions.[4] [However,] phenomena are not *just* mistaken appearances, and even mistaken appearances like those of the horse and elephant can exist. Such appearances inspire feelings. They are causes; they exist. Dreams also exist and are both liked and disliked. Our texts deny that an elephant exists in a dream, but they do affirm the existence of a dream elephant. [Similarly], when we say that the illusionists' horse and elephant are empty, we mean they are empty of being a horse or an elephant. In applying this [example] to pillars and the like, are we to understand that these are empty of being pillars, and so forth? No. The point is that these appear [to be pillars] but are not actual pillars.

Do the stick and stone, from their own side, appear as horse and elephant? They do. Why? Because the stick and stone *cast the aspect* of horse and elephant. The stone and the stick are the bases of emanation to the eye consciousness. If the stick and stone did not exist, then there would be no basis for the appearance of elephant and horse. For Bhāvaviveka, this appearance is form, an external object.

*Question:* How, if the existence as horse or elephant is posited by the mind, can there can be an aspect out there whose likeness is taken on by the eye consciousness?

*Answer:* This aspect is a cause of error *('khrul rgyu, *bhrāntihetu)* through which the eye consciousness takes on the image of its object. It is not that the stick and stone *exist* from their own side as horse and elephant. However, they *appear* as such from their own side. In fact, they do not exist as horse or elephant from their own side because they exist [as such] from the side of the mind. Thus, that they appear from their own side this way does not mean that they necessarily exist as horse and elephant.

Nevertheless, [even though objects, like this horse and elephant exist from the side of the mind] they depend a little bit on the stick and stone. They are not *made* by the force of the mind. If the stick and stone did not exist, the appearance as horse or elephant would not exist. In this sense, the appearance, posited by the mind, depends on the stick and stone, which are bases of emanation.

This slight dependence on the stick and stone means that the stick and stone appear from their own side as a horse and elephant. In the same way, the production of a sprout is produced by the seed from its own side, yet this production is posited by the great force of the mind. The mind has great power with respect to such production but the mind itself—without the seed—could not produce the sprout. Therefore, its production does to a smaller extent depend on the seed.

The relationship between a great leader and his servants or followers is similar. For example, a president of the United States has a great deal of power but depends on lesser people to a certain extent. Even the most ordinary citizen has a little bit of power with respect to the president because he or she has the power of one vote. In the same way, it is not contradictory for a seed to produce a sprout from its own side, even though that production is posited by the force of the mind.

Svātantrika says that phenomena do not have a mode of subsistence which is not posited by the mind [but do have a mode of subsistence which is so posited]; Prāsaṅgika says that the mode of subsistence of things is merely nominally designated, whereas for the Svātantrikas it is not. According to the Svātantrikas, [such phenomena] are not merely imputedly existent. Thus, there is a great difference in coarseness and subtlety with resect to what is being negated by Svātantrikas and Prāsaṅgikas. Through first explaining the Svāntatrika system, it becomes easier to understand the more subtle position of Prāsaṅgika.

Svātantrika asserts a mode of being that is just posited by the mind, but *not* a mode of subsistence that is merely designatedly existent—that is, not one just nominally imputed *(ming du btags pa tsam med)*. Prāsaṅgikas accept phenomena as just nominally imputed, meaning that phenomena are not established as their own basic disposition *(gshis su ma grub pa)*. In Svātantrika, however, phenomena both are established as bases and have a mode of subsistence. In Prāsaṅgika, the "mode of subsistence" of phenomena is merely imputed nominally, and designated nominally, but it is not called a mode of subsistence. It is just said that phenomena themselves are so designated. Thus, Prāsaṅgika maintains that except for being posited by the mind, phenomena do not exist. Nevertheless, they are not like the horns of a rabbit. Although the horns of a rabbit are also posited by the mind, they are undermined by valid cognition and incapable of performing functions as [conventionally existent] things are able to do.

*Question:* What is the difference between being posited by the force of appearing to a mind and being nominally imputed?

*Answer:* This is a difficult distinction. Existence from its own side, inherent existence, and existence by way of [a thing's] own entity have to do with the relative weight or power assigned to subject and object. When such power resides with mind, it is in dependence on mind that desire, harmfulness, and so forth [are seen to] arise. If the mind had no power, all its effects would not be there, and there would be no desire, anger, and so forth. [All] this comes about through the mind that thinks, "I, I." This I itself is merely imputed, as are the objects it covets. To understand that phenomena are posited by the force of appearing to the mind will cause desire, and so forth, to be somewhat reduced. Prāsaṅgika agrees with Svātantrika on this. However, there is another [more subtle] form of the apprehension of true existence; thus, from the Prāsaṅgika viewpoint, the Svātantrika position is itself ignorant and thus lends itself to the development of hatred, and so forth. According to Svātantrika, however, the conception of things as not posited by the force of the mind is an obstruction to omniscience, not an obstruction to liberation [as Prāsaṅgika maintains], and thus desire, and so forth, will not arise because of it.

The phrase "posited by the force of the mind" is mainly from Prāsaṅgika. One understands from it that there is no mode of subsistence, whereas the phrase [used in Svātantrika,] "posited by the force of the mind to which it appears," indicates a particular mode of subsistence. In general, the Svātantrikas do not assert mere nominal imputation but say that things are established by way of their own nature *(rang gi mtshan nyid kyis grub pa)*. This also obtains in their understanding of the mode of subsistence of phenomena.

Nāgārjuna's *Fundamental Text Called "Wisdom"* says that all phenomena are mere names, merely imputed. What, according to Svātantrika, is eliminated by asserting this "mere imputation"? A mode of subsistence that is not posited by the force of the mind to which it appears is eliminated. Svātantrikas consider "mere imputation by thought" to eliminate being posited by the force of a consciousness to which a thing appears; because this mode exists, mere imputation by thought does not. The "mere nominality" mentioned in the *Perfection of Wisdom Sutra* eliminates a mode of subsistence not posited by the force of the mind to which it appears; thus, Svātantrikas accept this statement. Svātantrikas, therefore, use the term "imputed by thought" to eliminate a mode of subsistence posited by the force of appearing to the mind. Since they need to assert a mode of subsistence posited by the force of the mind, they maintain that there is no "*mere* imputation by thought." No one except Prāsaṅgika is able to refute this. In this way, the [non-Prāsaṅgika] systems give more power to the object and less to the mind. Cittamātrins give about seventy percent to the mind, and in Sautrāntika and Vaibhāṣika, the object has a great deal of power. They maintain [phenomena are not] merely imputed by thought and, therefore, cannot use the term "mere." This has to do with the second meaning of "merely imputed by thought." In their view, the quoted lines from the *Perfection of Wisdom Sutra* eliminate something else.

Thus, according to Svātantrika, the mode of subsistence posited by the force of the mind to which it appears is not merely imputed by thought. Our

[Prāsaṅgika] system asserts a way of being posited by the mind that is more subtle than what is asserted by worldly persons in relation to a magician's illusions or by Svātantrikas in relation to pots, and so forth. Prāsaṅgika does not assert merely the worldly understanding of being posited by the mind but something more subtle, which pertains to objects such as pots. In their view, it is necessary to refute, even with respect to reflections, a mode of subsistence that is posited by the force of the mind. There is a type of falsity well known in the world, and there is another not known in the world. These [both] also exist in relation to a reflection. Prāsaṅgika both refutes a reflection's true existence and refutes that it is a face. The [reflection's] mode of subsistence as being posited by the force of the mind is well known to ordinary people. Merely this is not a mode of subsistence [posited by the mind] in our own system.

The Svātantrikas assert the lack of being merely nominally designated; Prāsaṅgikas say that something which is not merely nominally designated does not exist [because everything which does exist is so designated]. This is the difference in the two Mādhyamika schools' objects of negation.

Svātantrika and Prāsaṅgika do not use the concepts of being posited by the force of [appearing to] the mind and of being nominally imputed in the same sense. In Svātantrika there is a mode of subsistence posited by the force of the mind; in Prāsaṅgika such a mode of subsistence does not exist.

Svātantrika says that, in terms of its mode of subsistence, [an object] exists by way of its own entity. In Prāsaṅgika, the entity exists but is not established by way of its own entity. Thus, according to Svātantrika, there is a mode of subsistence, posited by the mind, which is not nominally imputed. Such is necessarily established by way of its own entity.

An object posited by the force of the mind [to which it appears] exists from its own side. If it did not, then, according to Svātantrika, it would be [nonexistent] like the horn of a rabbit. Thus, Svātantrika maintains that phenomena are not just posited by thought, as are the horns of a rabbit. Prāsaṅgika, by contrast, maintains that phenomena have an entity and are thus unlike the horns of a rabbit; however, that entity, which does exist, need not have a mode of subsistence other than one which is nominally imputed.

To be posited by the force of the mind means that a thing is elaborated or emanated by the mind; that is, the mind has power with respect to it. [In Svātantrika] the mind has a little power; the object also has a little power, about half and half to each. In Prāsaṅgika, the mind has more power, one hundred percent, and the object has none. In Cittamātra, too, more than half of the power is with the mind. That is my thought. The books do not say this, but if we make a new convention and do it well, this is fine. We are talking [sometimes] in ways that are and [sometimes] in ways that are not in the [traditional] texts. Still, if one can explain as the books in the past have done, that is good.

Prāsaṅgika maintains that when a seed and other appropriate causes are gathered together, the sprout, a dependent arising, will be produced. Many causes and conditions are required. When these are present and the sprout comes to be, the mind has posited its entity. First the seed was separate; then causes accrued, the sprout emerged and the mind apprehending it was formed. When the mind realizes it, it comes to be; if there were no such mind, it would not. Its coming to be and the mind's existence are simultaneous. Thus, the sprout itself depends on the mind. If the sprout had its own power, it would not need to depend on these things. The mind would not have to apprehend it; yet, there are three [ways in which it is] a dependent arising: through its dependence on causes and conditions, its dependence on its own parts, and its dependence on a mind. Finally, it is the mind that imputes its existence; when this mind exists, it can exist. Otherwise, not. Such are the assertions of Prāsaṅgika.

In Svātantrika, the thing must be posited by the force of a mind to exist.[5] If it did not require this, it would not need to depend on being posited by a mind, nor on the constellation of its parts. But it does not depend only on the mind; it also requires its parts, as well as causes and conditions. The mind is an assister. The object is not an assister [to its own existence but] exists from its own side.[6]

*Question:* In an unpeopled forest there are also sprouts being produced from seeds. By the power of whose mind is that production posited?

*Answer:* We have a ground *(sa)* of understanding what production is. It is not absolutely necessary to have a mind [present in order for production to be posited by the power of a mind].

You do not even have to speak of a forest. While we sleep, there are many phenomena [we do not see and which are still posited by the mind]. Whether phenomena are seen or unseen, they can fulfill the measure of being posited by the mind. It is not essential that a mind be present. For example, a thousand grams make a kilo of butter. I may have a one-kilo stone by which, on a balance scale, I can ascertain that a particular lump of butter weighs one kilo. Even if the stone is not present, the measure [of the amount of butter as one kilo] is there. In the same way, even if the mind which is the positer is not present, the measure of positing is still there, and it is sufficient that the measure of being posited is fulfilled. Thus, even if no one sees the production of a sprout directly, it is still posited by the mind.

In general, one can [also] say that all things are posited by a Buddha's exalted knower.[7] In fact, most [scholars] would say that these cognizers are those of a Buddha. But one does not have to resort to this because it is not essential that such a consciousness be directly present [in order to fulfill the measure of being posited by the mind], just as the kilo-weight need not be present for something to fulfill the measure of being a kilo. Since its mode of existence is the same as that of a phenomenon which is directly observed by some mind, so even phenomena that are not directly observed by some consciousnesses are posited through the force of the mind. Such positing occurs through the force of beginningless predispositions. Thus, in order to make the distinction that beginner [practitioners] must make between being and not being posited by the force of appearing to a mind, it is not necessary to understand exalted knowers. To understand valid cognition is sufficient—namely, to understand that something posited by valid cognition exists, and that something not so posited does not. If one objects that no mind is present to do the positing, as in the unpeopled forest, one can still claim the object is posited by an exalted knower. Still, [I emphasize again,] it is not necessary to understand exalted knowers, which are difficult to comprehend, in order to recognize how things are posited by our minds. It is not necessary to speak of phenomena unknown to me [as posited through the force of the mind]; one does not have a conception of true existence with respect to them. [Nonetheless, as explained above, they are technically posited in this way.]

Is emptiness posited through the force of the mind? Yes, because it is posited as existent by the power of the mind to which it appears. In general, in Svātantrika, being posited by the force of the mind means being posited as [conventionally] existent. [To put this another way,] a realizer such as the meditative equipoise of a Superior, or an inferential valid cognizer realizing emptiness, is the mind by the power of appearing to which emptiness is posited. There are no phenomena except phenomena that exist conventionally; to know that emptiness exists conventionally is a very important essential. Some might feel that because reality [or emptiness] is an ultimate truth, it does not exist conventionally. The point here is that existing conventionally does not make it a conventional truth: likewise, whatever is an ultimate truth does not necessarily exist ultimately. [In Prāsaṅgika,] to be imputed by thought *(rtog pas btags pa)* is the same as to be posited by the force of the mind. Thought and mind [here] are the same. However, in Svātantrika, to say something is "posited by the force of the mind" is, in Svātantrika, to speak of [the object's] mode of subsistence. This signifies also that its way of subsistence is valid.

It is we who [mistakenly] apprehend phenomena as not posited through the force of the mind. It is necessary that the consciousness which apprehends thus be ceased. It is necessary to establish that phenomena are posited through the force of appearing to the mind. This being so, it is necessary to acknowledge that phenomena are posited through the force of appearance in relation to a Buddha's exalted knower, and in order for something to arise for an exalted knower, it must appear.

# 10

# THE PRĀSAṄGIKA SCHOOL ON TRUE EXISTENCE

## HOW THOUGHT PARTICIPATES IN DEPENDENT ARISING

All that we enjoy—houses, airplanes, the entire world around us—is posited by thought. However, these would not exist except for their necessary causes and conditions. Imputation alone does not create functioning things. A thing exists if it is imputed by the mind in dependence on a valid basis of imputation and causes and conditions. All phenomena are posited by the power of thought; in Prāsaṅgika, this is the same as being nominally existent. When a sutra such as the *Questions of Upāli (nye bar 'khor gyis zhus pa, upālipariprcchā)* says that all phenomena are imputed by thought, this does not refer to the horns of a rabbit because these are not phenomena. Whatever is imputed by thought does not necessarily exist, since nonexistents are also imputed. The horns of a rabbit and flowers in the sky are imputed by thought, but they cannot exist. For something to exist, it must have a valid basis of imputation. This is true of both permanent and impermanent phenomena; impermanent phenomena also require the appropriate causes and conditions.

If one understands the sense in which this system considers phenomena to be (1) posited by thought and (2) only imputed by thought, it becomes easy to identify the conception of inherent existence, which conceives the opposite of this, [because] their being posited by the power of thought is the opposite of inherent existence. To understand this [latter is to reveal] what it means for something to be established by its own nature or from its own side. These [three phrases] have the same meaning. The own-nature *(rang bzhin, svabhāva)* of phenomena exists, but a thing's being established *by* its own nature does not *(rang bzhin gyis min 'dug)*. [Similarly], entities *(ngo bo, vastu)* exist, but there is no [establishment] by that entity itself.[1] [This signifies that] phenomena are only posited by the force of thought, not by their own power. They neither stand nor are set up by their own power. They have no power.

According to Prāsaṅgika, all phenomena are nominally or imputedly existent and posited by the force of convention. "Convention" here can refer either to [conventional] minds or to the conventions of names, though to understand it as mind has more force. When a thing is established by terms and minds, then this object, for example, is called a "radio" and is thought of as "radio" by the mind. This thought is not simultaneous with the thing but occurs after its existence is established.[2] Such things, being established by the force of the mind, do not exist from their own side, as they are conceived to do by the conception of true existence. To understand them as posited by convention is to understand that they do not exist this way. According to Prāsaṅgika, unlike Svātantrika and the lower systems, a cause depends on its effect [for its designation as a cause]. Nevertheless, the thing has power, even though it is an effect [of being posited].

The term "conventional" in the phrases "conventionally exists" and "conventionally does not exist" *(kun rdzob tu yod med ces pa'i kun rdzob)*, and the term "convention" in the phrase "conventional truths" *(kun rdzob bden pa zhes pa'i kun rdzob)* are different. There are more instances of the former. Truths of conventions *(tha snyad bden pa)* include only conventional or concealer-truths *(kun rdzob bden pa)*. The minds that realize ultimate truths—that is, which realize emptinesses—are not truths of conventions. They are conventions in the phrases "conventionally exists" and "conventionally does not exist." An inferential consciousness or a direct perceiver which realizes emptiness can posit it as existing conventionally. A conventional valid cognizer, also known as a truth of convention or conventional truth, probably cannot posit it. Since it exists, it exists conventionally, but [the object of such a mind] is not a truth of convention; it is an ultimate truth. Thus, to say that an ultimate truth is a truth of convention does not indicate it is a conventional truth.

In Mysore there are beautiful gardens, very famous, visited by many people. In the evenings the light shows also attract great crowds. All this, however splendid, is posited through the force of the mind. Other than this, it does not stand up by itself. The causes and conditions that precede a thing exist, as do the bases of designation and imputing minds that are coterminous with that thing. Even houses made of jewels such as occur in the godly realms and are depicted on our *thankas* are posited by the force of the mind. Does such a thing have a maker?

[The *Questions of Upāli Sutra*, which Tsong-kha-pa quotes on this matter] says that [flowers, and so forth] have no [inherently existent] maker. This does not mean such things do not exist. They do. They are conventionally realized, and they exist in dependence on their bases of imputation. [They exist] when the appropriate conditions are fulfilled—that is, when there are (1) causes and conditions, (2) a valid basis, and (3) a valid realizer.

We tend not to reflect on the many factors required for [valid] designation of phenomena. We do not reflect that phenomena [in general] and we ourselves depend on causes and conditions. We feel, "I myself exist," "I have done it" "I can do without depending on anyone or anything"—we have this sort of pride. But it is not like that; we and other phenomena exist in dependence on others.

*Question:* It would seem that dependence on causes and dependence on parts are sufficient to explain the existence of things. What is the necessity for the third form of dependent arising, being dependent on imputation by thought?

*Answer:* It is this that enables beings to understand how to use things. This is crucial, as the [mere] existence of things is of no benefit. One needs to realize the use of things and to be able to employ them in accordance with their particular capacities. The ability to use things is called the "valid cognition's effect" *(tshad 'bras)*. "Valid cognition" is a cause. Thus, an effect is posited for a consciousness which is a valid cognizer.

A subtopic here is the division into contiguous *(bar du ma chad pa)* and noncontiguous *(bar du chad pa)*[3] valid effects. In general a valid cognizer is a new and undeceived awareness. The valid cognizer is the object defined, and "new and undeceived awareness" is its definition. This definiendum is the contiguous effect [of its own definition]. This is a tenet particular to the definition of valid cognizer and not a general statement about definitions and definiendums. The definition of valid cognition is the contiguous cause, and the valid cognizer itself is the contiguous effect. ["Cause" and "effect" here do not signify sequence, since definition and definiendum] are simultaneous. An example of a noncontiguous valid cognition is knowing what to take up and what to cast aside in terms of the path. This is discussed in the second and third chapters of Dharmakīrti's *Commentary on (Dignāga's) "Compendium on Valid Cognition" (tshad ma rnam 'grel, pramāṇavārttika)* and their commentaries.

Things do not exist as we think they do but are posited by the force of the mind. This [as mentioned in chapter 9] refers to both thought and direct perception. The eye consciousness realizing a pillar realizes a pillar, as does the thought apprehending a pillar. Both posit pillar. Moreover, their way of positing things are the same, although each has its own qualities insofar as direct perception does not realize [its object] by way of a generic image, as conceptual thought does. All valid cognizers are the same in realizing their objects; however, each mind has its own qualities, and there is a variability among them, just as your pronunciation of the English alphabet is better than mine, although we can both recite it.

Both sentient beings and their environments, and thus all the phenomena of cyclic existence, arise owing to the beginningless ignorance by which afflicted actions are accumulated. Beings are referred to as the essence and their environments as the vessel. The impure essence and vessel are formed by the power of our own actions and afflictions. Thus, the world is said to be an effect of ignorance and as such, except for being posited by thought, it does not exist from its own side. If there is a world not formed by actions and afflictions, then it is not an impure essence and vessel, and not a true suffering.

*Question:* Is this world a true suffering from the viewpoint of a Buddha?

*Answer:* Since Buddha's emanation came to our world, the world which is his uncommon dominant effect is for him a pure land, a Buddha field. The things we use are of the impure essence and vessel; those that Buddha utilizes, of the pure one.

*Question:* Even when I do not observe a particular table, it is presumably an effect of some past ignorance. When I do look at it, it would seem to be an effect not only of past ignorance, but also of present ignorance? Can one consider it an effect of these "two" ignorances?

*Answer:* No matter how many pieces of wood are burned in a particular fire, the fire itself remains. The light of a particular piece of fuel increases the size of the fire [just as objects of cyclic existence increase on the basis of ignorance]. Similarly, if one is born in this world as a human being, then, as in adding wood to a fire, the light of the fire appears. When you are born, the world is newly established [for you]. Just *what* is established cannot be [fully] explained.

Things do not make themselves. They depend on (1) their causes and conditions, (2) a valid basis of designation, and (3) an imputing consciousness. Without exception, the mode of subsistence of phenomena is nominally imputed. If phenomena were not posited by thought, there could be no attachment because desire cannot exist under [other] circumstances. Therefore, no one can say that there is a correct object that is not posited by the force of thought. If there is a thought that is a positer of it, a thing exists. Without that, it cannot. It is necessary to analyze this and have no doubt about it. If one understands the three factors of valid existence with respect to a particular thing, one will understand them with respect to others.

In general, when a snake is imputed to a rope, neither (1) the entity of the snake nor (2) an establishment by its own entity exists. Like the imputed snake, all phenomena lack being established by way of their own entity; they lack their own [truly existent or self-established] entity. They are imputed [in dependence on their parts] just as the snake is imputed [in dependence on a rope]. However, they are not to be understood as not existing at all in the way that the snake does not at all exist in the example. They do exist. If they did not, then all the things we eat, our homes—the enjoyer and the enjoyed—would not exist at all. The meditator, the person who attains liberation, the wanderers in cyclic existence, would none of them exist. They would be like the horns of a rabbit. There would be no mistaken persons. Thus, the first part of the example, that things have no entity, does not apply; only that they are not established by way of their own entity. They and all things, including desire, hatred, pride, and the like, are just imputed by thought.

The example of the snake indicates how phenomena are imputed. If, at dusk, one happens to see a mottled rope coiled up on the ground, one might think that it is a snake. This thought would not occur in full daylight, but now the object is unclear. Seeing it this way, one thinks that there is a snake, but that snake is just imputed by thought. Only that. In no way are the parts of the rope a snake, nor is any snake whatever established in connection with the individual or collected parts or entity of the rope.[4] Whereas the snake imputed to the rope does not exist at all, the person [imputed in dependence upon the aggregates] is not completely nonexistent; it can perform functions, whereas the snake cannot. In this respect the snake and the person are not similar.

There is also a difference in the definiteness of ascertaining [the object]. The rope will be mistaken for a snake only in fading light, but a person or a blue thermos will be apprehended whether the light is bright or dim. The designation "person" or "thermos" will always be applied, whereas the "snake" designation will not always be applied to the rope. This means there is a difference regarding whether or not the designation will or will not be undermined by another valid cognizer. Someone might come and say, "This is not a snake" but no one will suggest, "This is not a thermos." In general, the point of the example is that there is no object established from its own side *(rang dngos nas yul med pa'i dpe red)*, but it does not mean that [the status of] person and snake are similar in all ways.

We need no effort to have a mind that thinks, "I"; it comes up naturally without our trying to remember it. If someone criticizes you, you become angry; if someone praises you, you like it. There is no need to force or urge it on. [However,] once someone reflects on selflessness, the conception of [such an inherently existent self] does not arise, since these are antithetical.

We conceive of an "I" in connection with the five aggregates. If you search, however, you will not find the "I" as either the entity, collection, continuum, or parts of the aggregates. The collection of aggregates includes earth, water, fire, wind and space.[5] None of these is the person, nor is consciousness the person, nor are discrimination and feeling the person.

If the person is none of these six constituents, is it something separate from them? No. These are all compounded aggregates *('dus byas kyi phung po)*, and all exist within the continuum of the person. All of them together are not the person, nor, as we have said, is the person other than these. [Many] non-Buddhists will agree with this latter. The Buddhists [in addition] refute a self which is the same entity as the aggregates. There is thus no [findable or truly existent] self that is either the same as or different from the aggregates.[6] The "I" or self is merely posited; it is posited by thought in dependence on the five aggregates; it is not established by way of its own entity.

A person is formed when the six constituents—earth, water, fire, wind, consciousness and space—come together. Therefore, the person is not real *(yang dag, samyak),* is not an actual [or inherently existent] object. Similarly, each of the constituents—earth, water, and so forth—are formed through the coming together of the various particles. Therefore, they also do not have their own nature. They, like the person, exist through the aggregation of their parts. There are similar arguments regarding, for example, pots. Even though the parts of a pot are not the pot, that pot itself exists. The Vaiśeṣikas and Carvākas, and perhaps all the non-Buddhists [of ancient India] maintain that something can have extension and yet be partless *(yan lag can cha med).*

Again, the person does exist. There is a person, which is merely imputed by the mind. Although one needs to identify a person on the basis of some aggregate, there is no definiteness as to which aggregate this will be. A person can merely be imputed "there." Similarly, if I ask you to bring me a thermos, it is not necessary to conceive of its extended parts *(yan lag, aṅga).* You simply bring it; you do not inspect each of the different parts and ask, "Is this the thermos?" If I say, "Pour tea into the thermos," you pour it in. Nevertheless, even though we perform actions and even though such actions are effective, it becomes confusing to think of them in terms of tenets insofar as we are confused about the entity [of things].

If you understand the emptiness of true existence in terms of living beings, it is suitable to apply this to nonliving things also: forms, sounds, nonassociated compositional factors, consciousnesses—all products and nonproducts. The elements and all [other] products are mere nominalities. In the same way, space is also a name. Forms and the like cannot be their own reality.[7] Nominal existence itself is not its own reality; it is a term. Feelings, discrimination, and so forth, are merely nominalities, not their own actuality. Except for being merely imputed, the things of the world are not established as their own reality *(yang dag par grub pa yod ma red).*

## THE IMPORTANCE OF KNOWING WHAT TO NEGATE

Whereas the conception of true existence identifies an object existing from its own side, the actual mode of existence of things is the opposite of this: phenomena are merely imputed by thought. Prāsaṅgika takes true, ultimate, or real establishment to be synonymous. Svātantrika agrees that there is no true, ultimate, or real establishment, but, unlike Prāsaṅgika, finds that there is establishment by way of own entity, by way of own characteristics, and by own nature. For Prāsaṅgika these latter conceptions [are identical with the former set] and are all innate misconceptions. Thus, Svātantrika assertions on true, real, and ultimate existence are a little different from Prāsaṅgika's understanding of these. According to the latter, these are synonymous with existence from [the object's] own side. For Svātantrika, they signify that the object has its own uncommon mode of existence which is not posited by the force of appearing to a nondefective awareness. This [as we have seen in chapters 8 and 9] is the Svātantrika object of negation. For Prāsaṅgika, the object of negation involves reflecting on [and refuting] the existence of an object from its own side. Thus, although both use the same phrases, their thought is different.

To identify the object negated, it is not sufficient to identify merely the appearing object; it is necessary to identify, as Tsong-kha-pa does, the referent object of the conception of true existence. One must understand how this object is apprehended. Such identification is a skill that initially leads one to [understand] the coarse and then the subtle [forms of selflessness]. The selflessness of persons and of phenomena are equally subtle [in Prāsaṅgika]; they are distinguished only in terms of their bases. A refutation made with respect to persons pertains to the selflessness of persons; if made in connection with other phenomena, to a selflessness of phenomena.

The referent objects [of these misconceptions] do not exist; they are imputed by the conception of true existence. The same mind both apprehends and imputes true existence. Such a consciousness has confidence in its object, just as persons whose eyes have been affected by a mantra are confident about the horse and elephant which the magician causes to appear to them. What is the measure of something truly existing? If the referent object of the conception of true existence existed, then [true existence, or a truly existent object] would exist. Otherwise, it does not.

Even though true existence does not exist, it is imputed there by the conception of true existence. That conception of true existence apprehends and adheres to it and thinks that it does exist. Nothing, however, exists in accordance with how it is thought to exist. If it did, it would have to exist by way of its own entity, by way of its own character, by way of its nature. In Prāsaṅgika, except for being posited by the mind, the object itself has no capacity *(nus pa)*. It exists because of the three forms of dependency: dependence on causes and conditions, on parts, and on being posited by the mind. In itself, it has no potency at all. Thus, the measure of existence is something left over from [the denial of existence from] an object's own side. In Svātantrika, however, this existing from an object's own side is itself the measure of existence, so that, for them, the thing exists if this exists. In Prāsaṅgika, except for necessarily being posited by the power of a mental convention *(blo'i tha snyad),* [phenomena] are not established by way of their own entity.

*Question:* What is the relationship between a valid consciousnesses *(shes pa tshad ma),* a valid convention *(tha snyad tshad ma)*, and a valid basis of imputation *(bdags gzhi tshad grub)*?

*Answer:* A valid consciousness is a mind, a valid convention is [either] an expressive term *(rjod byed kyi sgra)* or a mind. All valid cognizers are conventions. I do not believe the phrase "ultimate valid cognizers" *(don dam pa'i tshad ma, *paramārthapramāṇa)* is ever used, and this is probably because there are none.[8] A valid basis of designation is the basis which is the place of designation, its extended parts. The horn of a rabbit does not have a valid basis of designation, nor a valid cognizer that imputes it *('dogs byed kyi tshad ma)*, nor a valid convention.

A convention [also refers to a consciousness which] imputes. For example, the thought apprehending a pot understands the convention "pot," and the thought apprehending a pillar understands the convention "pillar." Just as there are thoughts apprehending the various kinds of products, so there are also realizers of more subtle things such as impermanence, the lack of true existence, and so forth. Reality *(chos nyid, dharmatā)* itself is posited by the force of convention and is conventionally existent, these two [terms] being coextensive. If reality were not posited by the force of convention, it would exist from its own side. Being so posited, it is conventionally, not ultimately, existent. It is, however, an ultimate truth.

Previously, we mentioned that the "convention" of "truth of convention" *(tha snyad bden pa)* is not a reasoning consciousness. In general, we speak of "convention" in the context of being or not being conventionally existent. However, "truth of convention" has to do [only] with conventional truth *(kun rdzob bden pa)*. On the other hand, that which is conventionally existent *(kun rdzob du yod pa)* is not necessarily a conventional truth; as we have seen, emptiness exists conventionally and is an ultimate truth.[9]

Having analyzed whether a particular subject does or does not truly exist, one understands that it does not. This [which understands] is a consciousness that observes the subject's way of being. One sees that true existence is not its way of being. The consciousness realizing its way of being realizes an absence of true existence *(bden par ma grub pa)*. The thing in question is not an object of this consciousness; it is, therefore, a conventional truth. Because [an object] is not its own way of being, it is a conventional truth and a truth of convention *(tha snyad bden pa)*.

The consciousness that realizes a thing's way of being, that understands its lack of true existence, is not [described as] conventional in the sense of conventional truth. Previously, we said that an ultimate consciousness was one of hearing, thinking, or meditating. However, such a consciousness is not an ultimate truth, since being a consciousness necessarily precludes being an ultimate truth. But such a consciousness can realize an ultimate truth; it is a valid realization consciousness [and] a valid convention *(tha snyad tshad ma)*. [This assertion is required by the previous series of reflections.]

At the same time, a conventional valid cognizer is not necessarily a valid reasoning consciousness. The consciousness which realizes a subject [such as a pot], for example, is not a valid reasoning consciousness. A valid reasoning consciousness is an analyzer of the way of being of any particular phenomenon. All minds realizing emptiness are included here, but even a mind that does not realize emptiness but analyzes with respect to emptiness can probably be categorized as a valid reasoning consciousness—for example, the minds of hearing or thinking about emptiness. Those [minds] investigating impermanence are not included here: impermanence, suffering, and [the coarse selflessness] are not emptiness. "Reasoning consciousness" has to do with realizing the way of being of a thing. Direct perception [in general] is not a valid reasoning consciousness, although yogic direct perception is, for it observes how things exist [that is, as lacking true existence]. Whatever is a valid cognizer is not necessarily a valid reasoning consciousness, since there are valid cognizers that neither investigate nor analyze [the ultimate].

Thus, reality conventionally exists because it is posited by the mind that imputes it. It is important to understand well [the meaning of] "not being posited by the power of convention." If something existed without depending on some convention,[10] it would ultimately exist.

That which is not posited by the power of [such a mind] is the object negated. It is called "self." When this self is seen as nonexistent in relation to the person, it is a selflessness of persons; when in relation to other phenomena such as eyes, and so forth, it is a selflessness of phenomena.

## MISCONCEPTIONS PERTAINING TO ONESELF: UNDERSTANDING THE DISINTEGRATING AGGREGATES OF MIND AND BODY AS A REAL I OR MINE

The conception of a self of persons is of two types: the conceiver of the I as truly existent and the conceiver of the mine *(nga yi ba, mama)* as truly existent. There are also two types of conceivers of the disintegrating aggregates *('jigs tshogs la lta ba, satkāyadṛṣṭi)*. A conceiver of the disintegrating aggregates is also necessarily a conceiver of the self of persons, but a conceiver of a self of persons is not necessarily a conceiver of the disintegrating aggregates.

To innately conceive another person as inherently existent is an innate conception of a self of persons, but it is not an innate conception of the disintegrating aggregates as a real self. To be the latter, it must have the aspect of [apprehending] one's own individual "I."

The conception of the disintegrating aggregates [the transitory collection of mind and body] observes the mere I and mine, but it observes them as having the aspect of inherent existence. Moreover, it is not the eye, nose, and so forth, which are objects of the conception of "mine"; rather it is "my eyes," and so forth, that are its objects. Tsong-kha-pa therefore quotes Candrakīrti's

*Commentary on the "Entrance"* to indicate that "nose" itself is not an instance of "mine." Otherwise, the conception of the disintegrating aggregates and the conception of a self of phenomena would not be mutually exclusive. The objects of the innate conception of a self of phenomena are the form aggregates, and so forth, in one's own and others' continuums, and also all those things not included in [anyone's] continuum.

The root of the conception of a self of persons is the conception of a self of phenomena, [especially with respect to] the aggregates included in one's own continuum. For example, the form aggregate is not the I, but is a basis of designating I. If the form aggregate were the I, then the hands also must be the I. There would be many I's; for feet, head, and so forth, would also have to be the self. But there is only one.

We conceive of animals and other persons as established by their own character also, but we do not think, "I," with respect to them; we think, "you" [or "them," and so forth]. This is a conception of the inherent existence of persons, but it is not a conception of the disintegrating aggregates [as a real I or mine.]

The conception of the disintegrating aggregates as a real I and mine observes only the person, not the aggregates. Thus it does not observe forms, feelings, discrimination, or any consciousness, for these aggregates are not the person but the person's basis of designation. This is mentioned in the root text, where observation of the aggregates [by the conception of the disintegrating aggregates] is refuted.[11] The commentary explains that such [a mind] observes a self which is imputed in dependence on these aggregates. Another way to put this is that the conception of the disintegrating aggregates observes the mere I, the mere person *(gang zag tsam).*

*Question:* Yet the mere I cannot, by definition, appear unless one observes the aggregates?

*Answer:* True. However, on the basis of [seeing] the aggregates, one thinks, "I." This I which one thinks of at that time is the person. You may first see the hands or feet or [experience] the aggregates of consciousness, such as discrimination or feelings. These are the bases of designation, the places of imputation.

Since these are the bases of imputation, they themselves are not the thing imputed; this means that they themselves are not the mere I. The mind that apprehends the phenomenon imputed is called the conceiver of a self of persons; the mind that conceives of the bases of imputation [the mind and body] as truly existent is the conceiver of a self of phenomena. When these are conceived of as inherently existent, the aspect apprehended is not the referent object [because this does not exist], but is made up by conceptual superimpositions.

The conceiver of the mine as inherently existent also observes the I. In this way, the mine, which is not the I, tends a bit toward [being included in] the category of the aggregates. Thus, while the conception of the disintegrating aggregates as a truly existent I observes the I, its scope of observation is not limited to this [as is true of the conception of the self of persons]. However, the *Entrance* refutes that the conception of the disintegrating aggregates observes the aggregates; it observes, as we have said, the mere I.

Observing that I, which is merely imputed, it [erroneously] conceives of an I which exists by way of its own nature. The mere I is imputed; the hands, head, legs, and so forth, are all [its] bases of imputation. There is an extraordinary amount of debate on this topic; I have seen such debates continue on for days and still not be decided.

The conception of the disintegrating aggregates, the mind and body, as an inherently existent I has to do with the apprehension of an I that does not exist, the inherently existent or substantially existent self-sufficient self. The conception of I *(ngar 'dzin)* has to do with the conventionally existent I. In our continuums, these two apprehensions [alternate] very quickly.

The conception of an inherently existent I is the same as the conception of the I as inherently existent, except the [relationship] between qualified and qualifier is reversed.

The conceiver of a self of persons does not conceive of the aggregates as truly existent, and the conceiver of the aggregates as truly existent does not conceive of the person as truly existent.

*Question:* Then at the time of thinking, "I," one is not observing the aggregates?

*Answer:* While observing the aggregates, one does not observe the I, and in observing the I, one does not observe the aggregates. That is what the books say. But one should think about this. It may be that you have the conception of a self of persons and [of an aggregate such as] consciousness simultaneously. [In general, however] the conception of the aggregates as truly existent comes first; then the self imputed in dependence on them is conceived to truly exist. As Nāgārjuna states in the *Precious Garland* (v. 35):

> There is misconception of an 'I' as long
> As the aggregates are misconceived
> When this conception of an 'I' exists,
> There is action which results in birth.[12]

The conception of true existence which conceives of the aggregates as truly existent produces the root of the conception of true existence pertinent to the self. [In this view,] the two probably do not come about at the same moment but serially. In experiential terms, however, they seem simultaneous.

*Question:* Do both the merely nominally existent I and the truly existent I appear to direct perception?

*Answer:* According to Prāsaṅgika, yes, but not in Svātantrika.

*Question:* Since the conventionally or nominally existent I appears to ordinary direct perception, can you say that such direct perception is a consciousness to which something appears without being ascertained *(snang la ma nges pa, *aniyatapratibhāsa)*?

*Answer:* Such a direct perceiver does ascertain the appearance [of the conventionally existent self]; it is a valid cognizer. The eye consciousness that observes this ascertains the conventionally existent I. Thus, it is not like a consciousness to which something appears without being ascertained. In general, direct perception is not a nonascertaining consciousness. In observing a person or an animal from a distance, one sees the [nominally existent] self; however, this is not the eye consciousness' object of apprehension *(mig shes kyi bzung bya).* Only form [color and shape] can be objects of apprehension of the eye consciousness;[13] whereas form becomes a visual object without depending on any other object, it is in dependence on seeing the form aggregate [that the eye consciousness] sees the I.

*Question:* Yet an ordinary person is described as unable to distinguish the appearance of the nominally existent self from the appearance of the truly existent one.[14] Therefore, it would seem that the conventionally existent self is not being noticed by that consciousness.

*Answer:* When I say, "This is Annie," I am not making a distinction between the conventionally and truly existent selves. But I do speak of a person, and this suffices to conclude that I understand a person, or pillar, or whatever the object might be. If one goes on to ask whether this exists conventionally or ultimately, that is different. Even though the eye consciousness ascertains the [conventionally or] nominally existent self, it does not ascertain it to *be* conventionally existent rather than ultimately existent. This is difficult to realize.

In conceiving the truly existent I, there comes the conception of [a truly existent] mine. This thought of "mine" does not [necessarily] observe the aggregates; there are many other things, such as houses, that we regard as "mine." However, the aggregates are instances *(mtshan gzhi)* of what is "mine." The aggregates [conceived as] "mine" are seen as inherently existent; observing them, one apprehends the "mine" as inherently existent. This apprehension of "mine" as inherently existent is a conception of a self of persons.

It is not that the aggregates are apprehended as inherently existent; rather, "my aggregates" are so construed. Therefore, both "mine" and "I" are necessarily observed. Thus, one first observes the aggregates, then adheres to these as "mine," and then to the "mine" as inherently existent. This is an erroneous consciousness. It is also probably the case that the mind apprehending an inherently existent "mine" observes an inherently existent "I." At that time, except for observing "mine," one does not observe the [inherently existent] "I." This point is a little difficult [to hold, and will in fact be undermined below]. The mind apprehending a truly existent "mine" does not observe an I that inherently exists; it apprehends the [nominally existent] I. Having observed the I, it apprehends [or conceives of] the aspect *(rnam pa, ākāra)* of inherent existence. Although its referent object [the inherently existent I] does not exist, its object of operation and its appearing object [the nominally existent I] do exist.

The point is not simply that the view of the disintegrating aggregates observes the mere I and mine, but that it observes these as having the aspect of inherent existence. The "mine" is not the person; even so, it is the object observed by the conception of the disintegrating aggregates as a real I and mine. Whatever is the object of the conception of a self of persons, therefore, is not necessarily a person [since "mine" is not a person].[15]

The conceiver of the "mine" as inherently existent also conceives of the inherent existence of the I, and it observes the I. There is no way to apprehend the "mine" without also observing the I. The object [actually apprehended] here is the [nominally existent] I; the aspect [one seems to apprehend] is an inherently existent I. Regarding the mind that realizes the absence of the inherent existence [of persons], its object is also the [nominally existent] I, but its aspect is the lack of inherent existence. The aspect is a quality *(khyad chos)*, and the object the basis of those qualities *(khyad gzhi)*. For example, although there is no disagreement regarding the stewardship of your country, there is debate regarding Tibet. We Tibetans say that Tibet is independent; the Chinese say it is not. We both have the same object of observation, the land of Tibet, but the aspects are very different. Similarly, when [Indian] non-Buddhists and Buddhists debate about sound, the former consider it permanent, whereas the latter take it to be impermanent; also, when the various schools debate the self, non-Buddhists as well as Svātantrikas and the lower Buddhist systems maintain it is established by way of its own entity, whereas Prāsaṅgikas say it is not. The basis of debate, the nominally existent self, is the same [but the aspect or feature attributed to it is different]. Similarly, I and mine both exist and are the bases of debate.

Eyes, and so forth, are not examples of "mine"; however, "the eye which is mine" *(mig nga'i ba)* is an example of "mine". If it were otherwise, the conception of the disintegrating aggregates as a real I or mine and the conception of a self of phenomena would not be mutually exclusive.

*Question:* What would the fault be there?

*Answer:* They are mutually exclusive. Why? Because the first has to do with observing persons, and the second with observing [other] phenomena. Thus, the conception of the eyes as inherently existent is not a conception of an inherently existent "mine," and thus not a form of the conception of the disintegrating aggregates.

This topic comes up because Candrakīrti's *Entrance*[16] might be [misinterpreted to indicate] that "my nose" or "my eye" [are instances of the conception of "mine"]." That is why Tsong-kha-pa entertains a question on this topic (see pages 180-181). Further, whereas "my eye" *(nga'i mig)* signifies "eye," to say "the eye which is mine" makes "mine" a qualifier of "eye." In that case, the eye itself is observed and "mine" is its aspect. In other words, something is understood in addition to eye.The "mine" is not a person; it is instantiated by the aggregates.

Candrakīrti's *Entrance* presents two categories of selflessness—the selflessness of persons and of phenomena [other than persons]. In Prāsaṅgika, no distinction in coarseness or subtlety is made in terms of these categories. Svātantrika does not distinguish between the selflesnesses of persons and phenomena in terms of the object qualified but in terms of the coarseness and subtlety of the object of negation. The selflessness of persons is coarse, and that of phenomena is subtle, but both apply to all types of phenomena.[17] In Svātantrika, the selflessness of phenomena is said to be the lack of an uncommon mode of existence that is not posited by the force of appearing to a nondefective awareness. Persons as well as other phenomena are qualified by this type of selflessness.[18] The conception of a substantially existent self-sufficient person also pertains to aggregates that are employed or used by such a self. Thus, there is a conception of a self of persons in relation to [other] phenomena, but this does not require the [personal] aggregates, or [external aggregates] such as [those of] pillars and pots, to be apprehended as substantially existent or self-sufficient. Further, both substantial existence and imputed existence are posited with respect to form.

The various senses know different aspects [related with] a person. The eye sense knows the color and shape, the ear sense hears speech, and nose sense knows its scent, and so forth. *The person itself is an object of all six sense consciousnesses.* Thus, the person [also] becomes an object [of consciousness].

According to Prāsaṅgika, valid cognition is erroneous. It may be valid regarding the entity of, for example, a pillar, but is not valid with respect to the nature of its object. Things do not exist as they appear. They are merely posited [though they appear truly existent]. Thus, the perceiver is deceived.

All the twelve links of dependent arising cease with the development of wisdom. The ignorance that spawns them is the conception of a self of persons, and the conception of the self of phenomena is the root of this. Still, realization of the selflessness of phenomena must be preceded by realization of the selflessness of persons. Without realizing the selflessness of persons, you cannot realize the selflessness of other phenomena. Nevertheless, so long as the aggregates are conceived to truly exist, the person is necessarily conceived to truly exist.

Just as gold and jewels are precious, so our own minds are invaluable. With good effort,the mind can improve more and more until finally

Buddhahood is attained. Thus, it is good to undertake methods for realizing emptiness, prostrations, making offerings, engaging in giving, holding to good ethics, becoming accustomed to patience. All these, it should be remembered, are methods for understanding emptiness.

Desire, hatred, and ignorance are poisons requiring a medicinal antidote. It is important, for example, to think about what will prevent anger from arising. If its object [for example, an inherently existent person] is seen as nonexistent, anger [toward it] will evaporate. It is the same with desire. Thus, it is not sufficient merely to curtail the coming and going of the mind with respect to a certain object; it is necessary to realize that its referent object does not exist.

There is also a type of mind which neither conceives of true existence nor realizes the lack of true existence.[19] For example, the thought apprehending a pillar does not conceive it to be truly existent, but also does not realize that it lacks true existence. It apprehends the mere pillar [without ascertaining it as such]. Thus, not apprehending something as truly existent does not mean that you realize its lack of inherent existence. For this it is necessary to understand how the referent object of the conception of true existence is *conceived* to exist. Then, after inquiring whether or not such does exist, one realizes that it does not. [Without this initial identification] it is as if one is searching for a thief in one place when the thief has gone elsewhere. Unless you analyze [regarding the status of the referent object of the conception of true existence], you will never undermine the conception of self.

By understanding the conception of true existence, one can understand that there are many minds which are not conceivers of true existence. [Indeed] to say that all minds are conceivers of true existence is a sign of not understanding [this conception], as is thinking that phenomena do not exist. Understanding the conception of true existence well means that you understand its referent object [and thus understand the object to be negated]. The method for understanding these is the same. Tsong-kha-pa brings this up by way of thoroughly refuting that the negation of true existence also negates the existence of phenomena. Phenomena do exist, though not by way of their own entity.

# PART III

Tsong-kha-pa's *Illumination of the Thought, Extensive Explanation of (Candrakīrti's) "Entrance to (Nāgārjuna's) 'Treatise on the Middle Way'"*

Commenting on Chapter Six, stanzas 1-7
of Candrakīrti's text

Peking edition vol. 154, 27.4.6 to 27.4.8
Sarnath edition p. 114.11-16
Dharamsala edition p. 62.9-12

Translated by Jeffrey Hopkins and Anne Klein
Annotated by Jeffrey Hopkins

# CONTENTS

# 1

# Introduction to the Profound Meaning

The explanation[1] of the sixth ground,[2] the Manifest, has four parts: (1) etymology of the ground and indication that the perfection of wisdom is surpassing, (2) praise of the perfection of wisdom, (3) explanation of suchness in which the profound dependent arising is seen, and (4) conclusion by way of expressing the features of this ground.[3]

## ETYMOLOGY OF "THE MANIFEST" AND INDICATION THAT THE PERFECTION OF WISDOM IS SURPASSING

Candrakīrti's *Entrance to (Nāgārjuna's) "Treatise on the Middle"* says:[4]

*1* *Approaching the qualities of a perfect Buddha*
*And seeing the suchness of arising-dependent-upon-this*[5]
*Due to which they abide in wisdom, [Bodhisattvas]*
*On the Manifest,*[6] *abiding in equipoise, attain cessation.*

Because [Bodhisattvas] attained the thoroughly pure perfection of concentration on the fifth ground, they abide in a fully developed mind of meditative equipoise [on emptiness] on the sixth ground, the Approaching, or the Manifest. Based on this, they abide on the sixth Bodhisattva ground seeing the profound suchness of mere conditionality—dependent arising. Because of this, they abide in the fully developed perfection of wisdom, whereby they attain [an uncommon absorption of][7] cessation. Prior to this, on the fifth ground and below, they did not attain [an uncommon absorption of] cessation because of not having the surpassing form of the fully developed perfection of wisdom. One cannot attain [an uncommon absorption of] cessation merely through the five fully developed perfections of giving, and so forth [that is, ethics, patience, effort, and concentration].

This ground[8] is called "The Manifest" or "The Approaching" (*mngon du gyur pa, abhimukhī*) because (1) the reflection-like nature of phenomena has become *manifest* by way of their wisdom, which is surpassing in the way [just described]; (2) on the fifth ground they *observed* true paths [and thus have newly gained complete wisdom with respect to the four truths],[9] and (3) they are *approaching* attainment of a perfect Buddha's qualities [in that they now have the surpassing form of the perfection of wisdom].[10]

With respect to the meaning of the second reason [why the sixth ground is called "The Manifest," Jayānanda's] *Commentarial Explanation*[11] [incorrectly] explains this [second reason] to be that [Bodhisattvas] manifest a path in which knower and known are not observed. However, that on the fifth ground true paths are observed is a case of [referring to the four truths by way of] mentioning the last of the four truths. Hence, since on that [fifth ground, Bodhisattvas] attain skill with regard to the coarse and subtle four truths, on the sixth the wisdom that is comprised of skill with regard to the four truths is complete. This is what is meant [by Candrakīrti's referring to the fact that fifth ground Bodhisattvas "observe true paths." This skill is attained on the fifth ground, but on the sixth one has such skill by way of a fully developed perfection of wisdom.][12]

The first reason [above, which states that the reflection-like nature of phenomena—the emptiness of inherent existence which is *itself* like a reflection in that it exists but is not truly established—has become manifest] indicates that they have completed the training in wisdom which consists of skill in the forward procedure [of entry into cyclic existence when there is ignorance][13] and the reverse procedure [of liberation from cyclic existence[14] when ignorance is overcome, these being in terms of the twelve links of] dependent arising. Hence, [the name, the Manifest] means that the truths and dependent arising have become manifest by way of [Bodhisattvas'] completing these two trainings in wisdom [regarding the four truths and regarding the twelve links of dependent arising].[15]

Thus, on this ground they complete the three trainings in wisdom [that is, skill regarding emptiness, the four truths, and dependent arising].[16] Further, as much as calm abiding (*zhi gnas, śamatha*) is enhanced, so much is their special insight (*lhag mthong, vipaśyanā*) enhanced, and on the fifth ground they attained full development of the perfection of concentration whereby, in dependence on it, here [on the sixth ground] their perfection of wisdom is fully developed. Therefore, an uncommon absorption in cessation [that is, a wisdom consciousness directly realizing emptiness within the context of the cessation of coarse discrimination and feeling][17] is attained from this [ground].

Moreover, Nāgārjuna's *Precious Garland* (*rgyal po la gtam bya ba rin po che'i phreng ba, rājaparikathāratnāvalī*, stanza 451) says:

The sixth is called the Approaching because
They are approaching the qualities of a Buddha.
Through familiarity with calm abiding and special insight
They attain cessation[18] and hence are advanced [in wisdom].

Through the maturation of these [qualities] they become
A king of the gods [in the land of Enjoying] Emanation.
Since Hearers cannot surpass them, they pacify
Those having the pride of superiority.

[In that] "Emanation" (*rab 'phrul*) means "Enjoying Emanation" (*'phrul dga,' nirmāṇarati*).[19]

## PRAISE OF THE PERFECTION OF WISDOM

To indicate that the collections of giving, and so forth—which are other than wisdom—progress to the ground that is the fruit [namely, Buddhahood] in dependence on the perfection of wisdom, Candrakīrti's *Entrance to (Nāgārjuna's) "Treatise on the Middle Way"* says:

2 *Just as a person having eyes easily leads*
*All in a blind group to their desired destination,*
*So here also the mind [of wisdom], taking hold of virtues*
*That lack the eye [of wisdom], goes to the state of a Conqueror.*

Just as one sighted person easily leads all of—that is, an entire—group of blind persons to a place where they wish to go, so also at this point on the path awareness—the perfection of wisdom—fully taking hold of the good qualities of giving, and so forth, which themselves lack the eye seeing suchness, goes to the state of a Conqueror, the fruit [namely, Buddhahood]. For, the perfection of wisdom unerringly perceives correct and incorrect paths. Moreover, the *Superior Sutra of the Condensed Perfection of Wisdom* (*'phags pa sdud pa, sañcayagāthāprajñāpāramitāsūtra*) says:[20]

How could billions of blind and guideless persons,
Not even knowing the path, enter the city?
Without the perfection of wisdom, these five sightless perfections
Lack a guide and thus cannot reach enlightenment.

Also, the *Diamond Cutter Sutra* (*rdo rje gcod pa, vajracchedikāsūtra*) says:

A Bodhisattva who gives gifts upon falling into [misapprehending] things [such as gift, giver, and recipient, as inherently existent] should, for

> example, be viewed as like a person with eyes who sees nothing upon having entered into darkness.
>
> Subhūti, it is this way: A Bodhisattva who, not having fallen into [such misapprehension of] things, gives gifts should be viewed as like a person with eyes who, when the sun shines at dawn, sees varieties of forms.

The same is so also for ethics and so forth.

## EXPLANATION OF SUCHNESS IN WHICH THE PROFOUND DEPENDENT ARISING IS SEEN

This section has five parts: [Candrakīrti's] promise to explain the meaning of the profound [emptiness], identification of those who are vessels for an explanation of the profound meaning, [description of] how good qualities arise when it is explained to them, exhortation to those who are vessels to listen, and [description of] how the suchness of dependent arising is explained.[21]

### Promise to Explain the Profound Emptiness

[First, Candrakīrti indicates that he cannot, on his own, explain emptiness, the profound suchness of dependent arising. He further points out that since scriptures on this topic are so difficult, he cannot give an explanation based solely on scripture either; rather, he will base his explanation on the more accessible writings of Nāgārjuna.]

*Question:* [You said] before [in the first stanza of this chapter] that when sixth-ground Bodhisattvas see dependent arising, they see the suchness of the arising of this [particular phenomenon] in dependence on that [particular phenomenon]. How is this?

In answer to this, Candrakīrti's [*Auto*]*Commentary* states that:[22]

> The entity of that [suchness of dependent arising—namely, the emptiness of inherent existence,][23] is not an object for us whose mental eye is completely covered by the thick cataracts of ignorance; it is an object for those who dwell on the higher grounds—the sixth, and so forth. Therefore, this question should not be put to us. You should speak with just Buddhas and Bodhisattvas whose mental eye is free from the dimming cataracts of ignorance because they have applied the eye-medicine of the good perception of emptiness that overcomes the cataracts of ignorance.

This indicates that one who would ask about making manifest the meaning of suchness should ask them.

[Since Candrakīrti is indicating that one should definitely ask such beings about *perceiving* suchness, it would be a mistake to conclude that in Candrakīrti's system there is no mind perceiving suchness in meditative equipoise.] Hence, just as, when eye-medicine is applied, one's eyes become clearer but the eyes are not extracted, so, by applying the eye-medicine which is perception of emptiness, the mental eye becomes clearer—the eye of exalted wisdom is not extracted. If you understand this, you will not be polluted by the bad view consisting of the deprecation (*skur 'debs, apavāda)* that there is no exalted wisdom consciousness in a Superior's[24] meditative equipoise.[25]

*Question:* Does it not say in sutras such as the Mother Sutras [that is, the Perfection of Wisdom Sutras], the *Sutra on the Ten Grounds* (*mdo sde sa bcu pa, daśabhūmikasūtra*), and so forth, that Bodhisattvas coursing in the perfection of wisdom see the suchness of dependent arising? Therefore, give an explanation following scripture [rather than Nāgārjuna's *Treatise*].

*Answer:* Because it is difficult even to ascertain the thought of scripture, someone like myself [that is, Candrakīrti] is unable to teach suchness even through scripture. This is said in terms of [being unable to give] an independent explanation; however, the thought of scripture can be ascertained through seeing a treatise teaching suchness that was written by a valid being [that is, Nāgārjuna] and that unerringly explains scripture.

To indicate this, Candrakīrti's *Entrance to (Nāgārjuna's) "Treatise on the Middle Way"* says:

3 *Since with scripture as well as reasoning*
*[Nāgārjuna taught] how those [sixth-ground Bodhisattvas] realize*
*The very profound doctrine, I [Candrakīrti] will speak*
*In accordance with the system of the Superior Nāgārjuna.*[26]

In his *Treatise on the Middle Way* (*dbu ma'i bstan bcos, madhyamakaśāstra*) the Superior Nāgārjuna, with unerring knowledge of the scriptures, taught very clearly the suchness of phenomena[27] in accordance with how sixth grounders realize the very profound doctrine [of emptiness]. He did so through scriptures from the sets of discourses (*mdo sde, sūtrānta*)[28] and, beyond that, in addition to scriptures, through the use of reasoning. Therefore, the honorable Candrakīrti will relate how suchness is taught in the textual system of the Superior Nāgārjuna, just as it is in the system that Nāgārjuna taught.

*Question:* How is it [determined] that the Superior Nāgārjuna errorlessly ascertained the meaning of the definitive scriptures [that is, those explaining the emptiness of inherent existence]?

*Answer:* This is known from scripture. The *Descent into Laṅkā Sutra* (*lang kar gshegs pa, laṅkāvatāra*) says:[29]

In the south, in the area of Vidarbha[30]
Will be a monk known widely as Śrīmān
Who will [also] be called Nāga.
Destroying the [extreme] positions of existence and nonexistence,

He will thoroughly teach in the world
The unsurpassed Great Vehicle *(theg pa chen po, mahāyāna)*—my vehicle.
Having done this, he will achieve the Very Joyous[31] ground
And then go to the Blissful[32] [Pure Land upon passing away].

Thus [Buddha] said that Nāgārjuna would comment on the definitive vehicle, free from the extremes of existence and nonexistence.

He is a rebirth of a Licchavi[33] youth, known as Liked-When-Seen-By-All-The-World,[34] during the time of the Teacher [Buddha] who is mentioned in the *Excellent Golden Light Sutra* (*gser 'od dam pa, suvarṇaprabhāsottama*).[35] The *Great Cloud Sutra*[36] says:

> Four hundred years after I [Śākyamuni Buddha] pass from sorrow [that is, die], this youth [Liked-When-Seen-By-All-The-World][37] will become a monk known as Nāga and will disseminate my teaching. Finally, in the land called Very Pure Light[38] he will become a Conqueror named Light-Which-Is-A-Source-Of-All-Wisdom.[39]

Hence it is established that [Nāgārjuna] had unmistaken ascertainment of the definitive scriptures [because such ascertainment is necessary to attain the first ground].[40] Also, in the *Mañjuśrī Root Tantra* (*'jam dpal rtsa ba'i rtog pa, mañjuśrīmūlakalpa*) the time of Nāgārjuna's appearance and his name are the same, and it is explained that he will live for six hundred years.[41]

The *Great Drum Sutra* (*'phags pa rnga bo che chen po'i le'u zhes bya ba theg pa chen po'i mdo, āryamahābherīharakaparivartanāmamahāyānasūtra*)[42] says:

1. that after the Teacher's passing away, when the [average] lifespan is eighty years[43] and the teaching [of the Mahāyāna] has degenerated, this Licchavi youth Liked-When-Seen-By-All-The-World, having become a monk bearing the Teacher's name [in the sense of being of the Śākya clan],[44] will disseminate the teaching, and
2. that, after one hundred years, he will die and be born in the Blissful [Pure Land].[45]

That this scripture also prophesies the master [Nāgārjuna, even though it does not explicitly mention his name] is asserted by Sthavira Bodhibhadra and the

Great Elder [Atīśa]; they are relying on the explanation that the Licchavi Liked-When-Seen and Nāgārjuna are of one continuum [that is to say, earlier and later births in a single stream of rebirth].[46]

The *Great Drum Sutra* states that this monk [Nāgārjuna] is a seventh-ground [Bodhisattva].[47] It cannot be established that such an explanation contradicts the former [statement in the *Descent into Laṅkā Sutra* that Nāgārjuna was a first-ground Bodhisattva], for variations among scriptures do occur [because some scriptures describe how great beings appeared to ordinary sight, and others describe their actual attainment].[48] In some scriptures, for instance, certain great kings are said to be Stream Enterers, whereas in other scriptures they are said to be Buddhas.[49]

### Identification of Those Who Are Vessels for an Explanation of the Profound Emptiness

Furthermore,[50] [Nāgārjuna's] *Treatise* (*bstan bcos, śāstra*)[51] on the definitive meaning [that is, emptiness] should be taught just to those who through[52] prior cultivation have established seeds in their [mental] continuums for the realization of emptiness. It should not be taught to others, for, even if they have heard texts that teach emptiness, they have thoughts wrongly oriented with respect to emptiness, and hence [teaching it to them] is disastrous.

With respect to how such disaster comes about, some through lack of skill abandon emptiness and thereby go to a bad transmigration [upon rebirth]. Others, erroneously apprehending the meaning of emptiness, which is the non-establishment of inherent existence, think that these phenomena [due to lacking inherent existence] simply do not exist (*med pa nyid*) or are nonexistent (*yod pa ma yin*). First they generate the wrong view deprecating all things—causes and effects—and then, since they do not give it up, this view increases more and more.

[Nāgārjuna's *Treatise* (XXIV.11) says:][53]

> Those of little wisdom are harmed
> When their view of emptiness is faulty,
> Just as [harm comes to] those who faultily hold a snake
> Or faultily use a knowledge-mantra.

Furthermore, Candrakīrti's *Clear Words* (*tshig gsal, prasannapadā*), commenting on this, says that (1) in order not to fall to the extreme of deprecating conventionalities, it is necessary not to undermine [the validity of nominally existent] actions and their effects which are like reflections and (2) in order not to fall to the extreme of superimposing ultimate existence [onto phenomena, which only nominally exist], it is necessary to see that actions and their effects pertain only to things that lack inherent existence. Candrakīrti describes the opposite of these two [that is, undermining the validity of nominally existent phenomena and misconstruing that actions and their effects pertain only to inherently existent phenomena] as falling to the extremes of annihilation and permanence [respectively].

[Candrakīrti] says that one who considers compositional phenomena (*'du byed, saṃskāra*) to be nonexistent has a wrong view; hence, even though there is a verbal difference between "not existent" (*med pa*) and "not being existent" (*yod pa ma yin pa*), the appearance to the mind of the aspect of "not existent" (*med pa*) does not differ at all [from the appearance to the mind of the aspect of "not being existent" (*yod pa ma yin pa*)] even though one looks into it in detail.[54]

[Candrakīrti,] in commenting on Āryadeva's *Four Hundred* (*bzhi rgya pa, catuḥśataka*) where it states:[55]

> The one goes just to a bad transmigration [upon rebirth]
> Whereas the nonordinary[56] goes to peace,

says:

> On hearing the teaching of selflessness, the unwise abandon it or realize it incorrectly, whereby they go just to a bad transmigration [upon rebirth].

Thus [Candrakīrti] explains that both [those who abandon the teaching of emptiness and those who realize it incorrectly] go to a bad transmigration [upon rebirth].

To realize [emptiness] erroneously is to apprehend the meaning of emptiness as signifying nonexistence. Therefore, when prideful persons—who lack the mental capacity to discriminate the very subtle meaning [of emptiness] and yet fancy that they have [such capacity]—develop a strong facsimile of belief in the mere words of the profound meaning which [actually] is unsuited to their faculties, this leads to disaster. Consequently, you should take care regarding these points.

*Question:* How can one ascertain what is difficult to ascertain—that it is suitable to teach emptiness to this person and not to that person?

*Answer:* To indicate that one can ascertain this through external signs, Candrakīrti's *Entrance to (Nāgārjuna's) "Treatise on the Middle Way"* says:

4 *Even while an ordinary being,*
*On hearing about emptiness inner joy arises again and again,*
*Tears arising from this happiness moisten the eyes,*
*And the hairs of the body stand on end.*

5 *Such [persons] have the seed of the awareness of a perfect Buddha.*
*They are vessels for the teaching of suchness.*
*The ultimate truth is to be taught to them.*

Even while they are ordinary beings and beginners, when they hear nonerroneous discourse about emptiness, from hearing it strong joy arises again and again internally with regard to that discourse; tears arising from that strong joy moisten the eyes, and the hairs of the body stand on end. Such [persons] have the seed of realizing emptiness, called the seed of the awareness of a perfect Buddha, the nonconceptual exalted wisdom. Those persons are vessels for the teaching of suchness by a skilled master. The ultimate truth, having the characteristics about to be explained, should be taught to them.

If these physical marks are seen to arise when [a person] has the composite of (1) having heard nonerroneous discourse on emptiness and (2) not having misunderstood it, this is an unambiguous sign. If the meaning is not understood or, even if understood, these marks do not arise, one cannot determine that [such persons] are vessels for the profound for the time being; still, if they will not depart from what is set out by an excellent lama [that is, will not merely follow their own conjecture], they are suitable vessels for newly infusing many potencies [that will serve as] a causal lineage for [developing] realization of emptiness.[57]

## How Good Qualities Arise When the Profound Emptiness is Explained to Proper Vessels

Teaching emptiness to listeners such as are described above will not be fruitless.[58] Why? Candrakīrti's *Entrance to (Nāgārjuna's) "Treatise on the Middle Way"* says:

5d *The good qualities that follow [hearing this teaching]*
*will arise for them.*

Not only will such listeners not incur the disaster generated by erroneous conception of emptiness, but also the good qualities that follow as effects upon [hearing] about the view of emptiness will arise for them.

*Question:* How do these good qualities arise?

*Answer:* Candrakīrti's *Entrance to (Nāgārjuna's) "Treatise on the Middle Way"* says:

6 *Having adopted ethics, they always abide in ethics.*
*They give gifts, sustain compassion, meditate patience,*
*And fully dedicate the virtue of these toward enlightenment*
*For the sake of releasing transmigrating beings.*

7a *They respect the perfect Bodhisattvas.*

Those who are vessels [of the teaching of emptiness] consider hearing about the view of emptiness to be like finding a treasure. To prevent that view from deteriorating even in other rebirths, they adopt ethics and always abide in ethics. Concerning this, they think, "If through the circumstance of faulty ethics I fall into a bad transmigration, the continuum of [my] view of emptiness will be severed." Thus, they adopt proper ethics and guard against degeneration.

One need not have sworn to [a code of] ethics previously in order to have faulty ethics. For, *naturally* unseemly [behavior] which is discordant with proper ethics also constitutes faulty ethics.[59]

[Persons who are vessels of the teaching of emptiness also] think, "Through maintaining proper ethics I will be born in a happy transmigration; yet, if I am poor, I will be bereft of necessities such as food, drink, medicine, and clothing. Due to my being preoccupied with seeking these, the continuum of hearing about the view, meditating on its meaning, and so forth, will be severed." Thus, as explained above [in the section on the perfection of giving],[60] they give gifts to high and low fields [of merit, for such giving acts as a cause of possessing resources in future lives].

Thinking, "The view of emptiness induces Buddhahood when conjoined with the great compassion explained earlier [in the section on compassion][61] and not otherwise," they sustain familiarization with great compassion, the root. Thinking, "Through anger one goes to a bad transmigration [upon rebirth]; virtue is destroyed, and one acquires a very ugly complexion, and because of this, Superiors are displeased [and do not teach the view of emptiness to such a person],"[62] they meditatively cultivate patience.

Ethics, and so forth, that are not dedicated again and again toward [attainment of] omniscience will not become causes of attaining Buddhahood and will not uninterruptedly give rise to the immeasurable effects of [a healthy, nondefective][63] body, resources, and so forth. Therefore, they also fully dedicate the virtue of these ethics, and so forth, toward enlightenment for the sake of releasing transmigrating beings from cyclic existence.

They see that, except for Bodhisattvas, others—that is, Hearers, Solitary Realizers, and so forth—cannot teach the profound dependent arising as a Bodhisattva does. Thus, they greatly respect the perfect Bodhisattvas.

Once pure understandings, such as these explained above, are generated in beings of the Mahāyāna whose understanding of the view of emptiness has arrived at the essential points, they have great respect for achieving the class of extensive [compassionate deeds of giving, and so forth].[64] That [combination of the wisdom of emptiness and practice of compassionate deeds] is a source of great praise, for Nāgārjuna's *Essay on the Mind of Enlightenment* (*byang chub sems 'grel, bodhicittavivaraṇa*) says:

Resorting to actions and their effects
Upon understanding this emptiness of phenomena
Is more wonderful than the wonderful,
More marvelous than the marvelous.

Such [a combination] comes to those who:

1. have abandoned the two faults of the two types of non-vessel—(1) forsaking the view because of disbelief or (2) although having a facsimile of belief, [mistakenly] understanding that cause and effect are refuted by the reasoning [establishing emptiness]—and
2. in addition realize, in dependence on the view of the emptiness of inherent existence itself, the great feasibility of all actions and agents.

Otherwise, if something else is taken as the manner of having found the view, all presentations of actions and their effects such as ethics [erroneously] come to be [seen as] like counting the creases in the horn of a rabbit. This being so, one [mistakenly] thinks that such [teachings on ethics, and so forth] are for the sake of those who have not understood the definitive meaning [that is, emptiness] but are unnecessary for those who have understood it. For, [one mistakenly thinks that] all these [phenomena of cause and effect] are created by conceptuality and that all conceptual consciousnesses apprehend signs—that is, [wrongly] adhere to true existence—and, like the Chinese Ha-shang,[65] one destroys all virtue.

Some say that adopting [virtue] and discarding [nonvirtue] are done for the time being in the perspective of a mistaken [awareness]. However, if conceptual consciousnesses are [rightly] taken to be of two types—those that do and do not conceive of true existence—it is prattle to say that the reasoning refuting inherent existence refutes all objects. If conceptual consciousnesses are [wrongly] not treated as having those two types, then the two—the conceptual consciousnesses of the view and of the class of [ethical] behavior—[absurdly] would mutually damage each other, like hot and cold [which are such that the one cannot exist unaltered in the presence of the other]; also, there would be no ground for positing (1) the mistaken perspective in which [adopting virtue and discarding nonvirtue] are posited, (2) the positer, and (3) those which are posited as such [since all thought would be mistaken]. Hence, such talk is a creation of darkness. Therefore, [those who put forth these notions] are holding the position of the opponents in the above passages [cited from Nāgārjuna and Candrakīrti, for they misunderstand the reasonings proving emptiness to be negating cause and effect].

## Exhortation to Vessels to Listen [to This Explanation of the Profound Emptiness]

Candrakīrti's *Entrance to (Nāgārjuna's) "Treatise on the Middle Way"* says:[66]

*7bcd Beings skilled in the modes of the profound [meaning of emptiness] and the vast [compassionate deeds]*
*Will gradually attain the Very Joyous ground.*
*Hence, those seeking that [ground] should listen to this path.*

Beings skilled in the modes of the profound and the vast as explained above will definitely accumulate for a long time, without interstice, while on the level of a common being, the collections of virtues in [both] the profound and the vast classes. Thereby, they will attain the Very Joyous ground in stages. Therefore, those seeking the Very Joyous ground should listen to the profound path about to be explained. In this way [Candrakīrti] exhorts one to listen.

Furthermore, Candrakīrti's *Commentary on (Āryadeva's) Four Hundred* (*bzhi rgya pa'i 'grel pa, bodhisattvayogacaryācatuḥśatakaṭīkā*, chapter 12), says:[67]

> When [persons] develop an interest in discourse on the emptiness of inherent existence, they establish conditions concordant with it so as to increase clarity with respect to emptiness. They are very compassionate and grateful to the Supramundane Victors—the Ones Gone Thus. Due to wishing to abandon completely the causes for [falling into] the great abyss [of bad rebirths],[68] a circumstance that interrupts their [practice of] excellent doctrine, they resort to repentance and give even what is difficult to give [that is, even their own flesh].[69] They also gather [students] through the four modes of gathering.[70] They teach this excellent doctrine with all endeavor to beings who have become vessels for the excellent doctrine.

Accordingly, this doctrine must be taught with great endeavor to those free of the two faults of non-vessels [that is, forsaking the view due to disbelief and, although having a facsimile of belief, mistakenly understanding that cause and effect are refuted by the reasoning establishing emptiness]. Through use of a technique that does not undermine ascertainment of dependent arising,[71] explanations should be given even to those who, though having belief, do not understand [the view] just as it is.

For those who know how to explain [this topic] well, there is great merit in explaining it to those listeners who are suitable vessels, from the minimally qualified on up. Nāgārjuna's *Compendium of Sutra* (*mdo kun las btus pa, sūtrasamuccaya*) says:[72]

> Belief in the profound doctrine gathers all virtues. Until the achievement of Buddhahood it accomplishes all mundane and supramundane marvels. The *Given by the Precious Child*[73] *Sutra* (*khye'u rin po ches byin pa'i mdo*) says:
>
>> Mañjuśrī, whoever listens [even] with doubt to this rendition of the teaching generates much greater merit than a Bodhisattva who, lacking skill in means,[74] practices the six perfections for a hundred thousand eons. This being so, what need is there to say anything about a person who listens without doubt! What need is there to say anything about a person who imparts the scripture in writing, memorizes it, and also teaches it thoroughly and extensively to others!
>
> Also, the *Diamond Cutter Sutra* says:
>
>> The Supramundane Victor said, "What do you think, Subhūti? If the banks of the river Ganges themselves became as numerous as the grains of sand on the banks of the Ganges, would their grains of sand be many?"
>>
>> Subhūti replied, "Supramundane Victor, since even [the banks] which would be as numerous as the grains of sand of the Ganges would be many, what is there to say about the grains of sand on those [banks]!"
>>
>> The Supramundane Victor said, "Subhūti, I will instruct you; you will understand. If a certain man or a woman completely filled worldly realms as numerous as the grains of sand on those banks of the Ganges with the seven varieties of precious objects and gave these to the One Gone Thus, would that man or woman thereby develop much merit or not?"
>>
>> Subhūti replied, "Supramundane Victor, it would be much; it would be much, One Gone to Bliss."
>>
>> The Supramundane Victor said, "If someone retains [in memory][75] merely a stanza of four lines from this rendition of the teaching and also teaches it to others, much more merit than that is generated."

Also the *Treasury of the One Gone Thus Sutra* (*de bzhin gshegs pa'i mdzod kyi mdo*) lists the ten great nonvirtues and then says that:[76]

> A living being—who, possessing all these, enters into the doctrine of selflessness and has faith and belief that all phenomena are from the beginning pure—does not go to a bad rebirth.

Also, the *Chapter on Taming Demons* (*bdud 'dul ba'i le'u*) says that:[77]

> A monk—who knows all phenomena as utterly subdued [of inherent existence] and knows that the extremes, which are the origin of faults, are also devoid of inherent existence—is free of contrition for faults that have occurred and consistently does not commit them. Therefore, if even deeds of immediate retribution [that is, those most vile actions causing one to take rebirth in a hell immediately after death][78] are overwhelmed [through knowledge of emptiness], what is there to say about [its overwhelming] the trifling [faults] of wrongly engaging in rites and ethics?

And the *Sutra of Ajātaśatru* (*ma skyes dgra'i mdo, ajātaśatrusūtra*) says:[79]

> When someone, who has committed a deed of immediate retribution, enters into and has belief in this excellent doctrine upon hearing it, I do not call that deed a karmic obstruction.

Thus, these are benefits of having belief in and thinking about the profound meaning [of emptiness] on the occasions of hearing and explaining, as well as on other occasions.

There are two requirements for obtaining well the benefits of [giving such] an explanation: (1) a pure motivation—not looking for goods, services, fame, and so forth—and (2) nonerroneous explanation of the meaning of the doctrine to be explained without misapprehending it. For, it is said that an explanation within having either or both of these faults will serve to interrupt [the fruition of] a great deal of merit. In this vein, the master Vasubandhu says:

> Therefore, persons who explain the doctrine erroneously or who—having an afflicted mind—explain it out of desire for goods, services, or fame, cause a large amount of their own merit to degenerate.

It is important that the listener also have a pure motivation for listening and not misapprehend the meaning. Therefore, both [teacher and student] should have the minimum qualifications at the time of explaining and listening.

# 2

# Dependent Arising and Reality

The presentation of how the suchness of dependent arising is explained[1] has three parts: how the meaning of reality is explained through scripture, establishing the meaning of scripture through reasoning, and explaining the divisions of the emptiness so established.[2]

## HOW REALITY IS EXPLAINED IN SCRIPTURE

This section has two parts: stating how reality is set out in scripture and identifying what is discordant with knowing suchness.

### How Reality is Set Out in Scripture

The *Sutra on the Ten Grounds* says:

> When fifth-ground Bodhisattvas enter the sixth ground, they do so by way of the ten samenesses of phenomena. What are the ten? All phenomena are the same in being signless; all phenomena are the same in being characterless, likewise in being productionless, nonproduced, void, pure from the very beginning, without the elaborations [of inherent existence], and nonadopted and nondiscarded; and all phenomena are the same in being like a magician's illusions, dreams, optical illusions, echoes, moons in water, reflections, and emanations; and all phenomena are the same in being without the duality of [functioning] things and non[functioning] things. When in that way they thoroughly realize the nature of all phenomena, through sharp and concordant forbearance they attain the sixth Bodhisattva ground, the Manifest.[3]

The word "likewise" [means that] "all phenomena" is to be applied up to [the eighth which is the sameness in being] nonadopted and nondiscarded. [With regard to how the list is taken as ten samenesses] those two samenesses [of being non-adopted and nondiscarded] are taken as one, and the seven samenesses of being like an illusion, and so forth, are taken as one sameness, and the last two [the sameness of being without the duality of things and nonthings] are taken as one.

With respect to the identification of the ten samenesses, even [Vasubandhu's] *Commentary on the "Sutra on the Ten Grounds"* and Asaṅga's *Bodhisattva Grounds* (*byang chub sems dpa'i sa, bodhisattvabhūmi*) do not appear to agree. Because these two [texts] do not accord with the mode of commenting on emptiness in this [Prāsaṅgika-Mādhyamika] system, [the ten samenesses] are explained differently here [in the context of Candrakīrti's Prāsaṅgika text].

Concerning that, the first sameness is that all phenomena are similar in that appearance of [their] dissimilar characteristics does not exist in the perspective of a Superior's meditative equipoise. The second is that all phenomena are the same in being without establishment by way of their own character. These two are the general teaching; the other eight are taught in the context of making differentiations within the meaning of the general teaching itself.

"Productionless" (*skye ba med pa*) refers to future [production], and "nonproduced" (*ma skyes pa*) refers to the other times [past and present]. That these are the same, or similar, *with respect to all phenomena* also should be understood with respect to the other [samenesses]. Voidness is an emptiness of the produced and the to-be-produced, i.e., void of [these as] qualified by being established by way of their character as in the context of the second sameness. That such is not created adventitiously by scripture or reasoning but [that phenomena] abide in such purity from the very beginning is the sixth [sameness].

The seventh [sameness, that all phenomena are the same in] lacking the elaboration of dualistic appearance, applies to the first [sameness in the sense of being that way in meditative equipoise on suchness], whereas [that all phenomena are] the same in being unelaborated by terms and thoughts should be affixed with the qualification of the second [sameness in the sense that all phenomena are the same in that their being elaborated by terms and thoughts is not established by way of its own character]. Such qualification should also be applied to the eighth sameness [that all phenomena are the same in not involving adopting and discarding *that exist by way of their own character*]. The ninth [sameness] is many forms of examples for ascertaining the meanings explained earlier. The tenth [sameness] is the similarity of all phenomena in not being inherently existent as things or nonthings [that is, as inherently existent impermanent functioning phenomena or inherently existent permanent nonfunctioning phenomena].

*Sharp* refers to quickness of wisdom. *Concordant* means concordant with an eighth-ground Bodhisattva's forbearance with respect to the doctrine of nonproduction. There appear to be many different [interpretations] of "concordant forbearance" due to [different] contexts [that is, due to its being explained in the context of the different Bodhisattva grounds].

Although there are many scriptures that teach the suchness of phenomena, [the explanation] here is in the context of describing how suchness is realized by a sixth-ground Bodhisattva's wisdom; hence [Candrakīrti] cited a scripture that describes entry into the sixth ground by way of the ten samenesses.

### Identifying What is Discordant with Knowing Suchness

With regard to settling the absence of true existence in phenomena,[4] if you do not understand well just what true establishment is, as well as how [phenomena] are conceived as truly existent, the view of suchness will definitely go astray. Śāntideva's *Engaging in the Bodhisattva Deeds* (*byang chub sems dpa'i spyod pa la 'jug pa, bodhi[sattva]caryāvatāra*: IX.140) says:[5]

> Without making contact with the thing imputed
> [by the mind—that is, true existence,]
> The nonexistence of that thing is not apprehended.

He says that if the thing imputed—the generality [or image] of the object of negation—does not appear to the mind well, it is impossible to apprehend well the nonexistence of the object of negation. Therefore, unless true establishment, which is what does not exist, and the aspect of the object of negation, which is that of which [phenomena] are empty, do not appear, just as they are, as objects of the mind, good ascertainment of the lack of true establishment and of the entity of emptiness cannot occur.

Furthermore, the mere identification of a true existence that is superficially imputed by proponents of tenets and of the consciousness conceiving such true existence is not sufficient. Because of this, it is a very important essential to identify well the innate conception of true existence that has operated beginninglessly and exists both in those whose awarenesses have been affected through [study of philosophical] tenets and in those whose awarenesses have not been affected in this way, and to identify the true existence that is conceived by that mind. For, if you have not identified this, even if you refute an object of negation through reasoning, the adherence to true existence that has operated beginninglessly is not harmed at all; therefore, the meaning at this point would be lost.

Furthermore, having initially identified the conception of inherent existence in your own [mental] continuum, you should know[6] how the reasonings serve to disprove the object of that [conception] directly and indirectly. For, the refutation and proof of one who is only directed outside is of very little benefit.

If you know well the identification of this [conception of true existence and true existence itself] by both the Svātantrika-Mādhyamika and Prāsaṅgika-Mādhyamika systems, you will discriminate them well. Hence, the explanation of these has two parts: identification of the conception of true existence in the Svātantrika-Mādhyamika School and in the Prāsaṅgika-Mādhyamika School.

# 3

# THE SVĀTANTRIKA SCHOOL ON TRUE EXISTENCE

## IDENTIFICATION OF THE CONCEPTION OF TRUE EXISTENCE IN THE SVĀTANTRIKA SCHOOL

This section has three parts: identifying true existence and its conception, indicating truth and falsity relative to worldly persons through the example of an illusion, and applying the example to the meaning.[1]

### Identifying True Existence and the Conception of True Existence

Other reliable sourcebooks of the Svātantrika School do not have a clear identification of the object of negation, but the existence that is the opposite of the mode of conventional existence explained in Kamalaśīla's *Illumination of the Middle Way* (*dbu ma snang ba, madhyamakāloka*) is to be known as ultimate or true existence, and, therefore, let us explain that. Kamalaśīla's *Illumination of the Middle Way* says:[2]

> The mistaken awareness that superimposes—on things which in reality [or ultimately] are without their own entityness—an aspect opposite to that [absence of ultimate entityness] is called the "concealer" (*kun rdzob, saṃvṛti*) because it obstructs [itself] from [perception of] suchness or because it veils [other awarenesses] from perception of suchness. [The *Descent into Laṅkā] Sutra* also says:
>
>> Things are produced conventionally (*kun rdzob tu, saṃvṛtitas*).
>> Ultimately they are without inherent existence.
>> That which is mistaken about the lack of inherent existence
>> Is asserted as the concealer (*kun rdzob, saṃvṛti*) of reality.
>
> Since [an artificial awareness in the continuum of a Proponent of True Existence] arises from that [conception of true existence], all false things

> which [such an artificial awareness] sees displayed by that [conception of true existence as if they are truly established] are called "mere conventionalities." Moreover, that [conception of true existence] arises through the maturation of beginningless predispositions for error, whereby all living beings see [phenomena] displayed as if [they had] an [inherently established] nature in reality. Therefore, all entities of false things [which exist] through the power of those [sentient beings' nondefective] thoughts [that is to say, conceptual and nonconceptual consciousnesses unaffected by the conception of true existence] are said "only to exist conventionally."

"The mistaken awareness that superimposes—on things which in reality [or ultimately] are without their own entityness—an aspect opposite to that" refers to [a consciousness that] mistakes what does not ultimately exist inherently to exist ultimately. ". . . is called a 'concealer' (*kun rdzob, saṃvṛti*) because it obstructs [itself] from [perception of] suchness or because it veils [other awarenesses] from perception of suchness" is the meaning of "the concealer (*kun rdzob, saṃvṛti*) of reality" [in the citation from the *Descent into Laṅkā Sutra*]. *Saṃvṛti* [here] is taken as [meaning] "obstructor" (*sgrib byed*), concealing reality.

Since [an artificial awareness in the continuum of a Proponent of True Existence] arises from that [conception of true existence], that which sees the display by the conception of true existence as if [objects] are truly established is a conceptual consciousness, not a sense consciousness. For, Jñānagarbha's *[Auto]Commentary on "Distinguishing the Two Truths"* (*bden pa gnyis rnam par 'byed pa'i 'grel pa, satyadvayavibhaṅgavṛtti*) explains that true [existence]—the object of negation—does not appear to sense consciousnesses, and it is the same here [in the Yogācāra-Svātantrika-Mādhyamika School.

"Moreover, that [conception of true existence] arises through the maturation of beginningless predispositions for error" indicates that this conception of true existence [from which the artificial conception of true existence arises] is innate. Therefore, [Kamalaśīla] speaks of "all living beings."

The "thoughts" of those living beings are not just conceptual consciousnesses but also refer to nonconceptual consciousnesses. False things which do not exist ultimately but are posited as existing through the force of those two [that is, conceptual and nonconceptual consciousnesses] exist only conventionally. This is the meaning of the statement in the *Descent into Laṅkā Sutra,* "Things are produced conventionally (*kun rdzob tu, saṃvṛtitas*)." Moreover, this does not mean that [such falsities] exist conventionally in the sense of existing for that [sort of invalid] conventional [awareness], which is a consciousness conceiving of true existence. [Rather, they exist for conventional valid consciousnesses.]

Thus, [in the Svātantrika School] to exist in the manner of an objective mode of subsistence without being posited through appearing to an awareness—or through the force of an awareness—is to exist truly, to exist ultimately, and to exist as [the object's own] reality. Also, conceiving such is an innate conception of true existence.

*Objection:* Kamalaśīla's *Illumination of the Middle Way* says:

> That "ultimately there is no production" is to be explained as [meaning] that "the production of these is not established by a consciousness of reality [that is, a reasoning consciousness]."

Implicitly, [Kamalaśīla] is explaining that [to be] ultimately existent and ultimately produced [means, to be] established by a reasoning consciousness understanding suchness as existent and as produced. [Since, just above, you have explained the meaning of being ultimately existent and ultimately produced differently] how [do you take Kamalaśīla's explanation]?

*Answer:* That is true. You need to understand that the qualification "ultimately" is affixed in two [senses] to the object of negation:

1. The reasoning consciousnesses of hearing, thinking, and meditating are taken as the ultimate, [and thus what is established by them is ultimately existent, and] what is not established by them, as [the objector just] mentioned above, [is not ultimately established].
2. Being existent in an objective mode of subsistence without being posited by the force of an awareness is posited as being ultimately existent [and not existing this way is called not being ultimately established].

The first of these two ultimates [that is, a reasoning consciousness of hearing, thinking, or meditating], as well as something that is established in its perspective [namely, emptiness], exists. However, both the latter ultimate [that is, existence in an objective mode of subsistence without being posited by the force of an awareness] and something that exists that way do not occur.

Therefore, although whatever exists ultimately in the latter sense would [hypothetically] exist ultimately in the former sense, the conception of the former type of existence [that is, of an object established for a reasoning consciousness] is not an innate conception of true existence [since, indeed, emptiness exists this way and even it is not truly established, and since conceiving any other phenomenon to be established for such a reasoning consciousness would be an *artificial* conception of true existence]. To have such an [innate] conception of true existence, one must conceive of the latter type of existence [that is, of an objective mode of subsistence not posited through the force of the mind].

Not differentiating these [two meanings of "ultimate"], many have held that the measure of the object of negation is something able to bear reasoned analysis or something able to bear analysis. In dependence upon this, many appear to have made the mistake of asserting that ultimate truths are not established bases [that is, do not exist] or that they are truly established. If you understand this well, you will understand the essential points that the statements that "nothing exists as [its own] basic disposition" and that "nothing exists ultimately" do not contradict the assertion that the real nature (*chos nyid, dharmatā*) exists and the proposition that it is the basic disposition [of phenomena] and is the ultimate.

**Indicating Truth and Falsity Relative to Worldly Persons Through the Example of Illusion**

Since using the example of a [magician's] illusion[3] is praised for understanding the status of existence that is posited through the force of an awareness and of existence that is not posited through the force of an awareness, let us explain it. When a magician causes a pebble, twig, or the like to appear as a horse or elephant, there are three [types of persons present]:

1. the magician
2. the audience whose eyes have been affected [by the mantra the magician has cast]
3. a person [who comes later and thus] whose eyes have not been affected [by the mantra].

For the first [that is, the magician] there is the mere appearance as a horse or elephant, but he/she does not adhere to such [as being true]. The second [the audience whose eyes have been affected] have both the appearance [as horse or elephant] and adherence to that appearance. The third [a person whose eyes have not been affected] has neither the appearance as a horse or elephant nor adherence to it.

When, for example, a rope is mistaken for a snake, it is said that the rope is a snake in the perspective of that consciousness but in general is not a snake. However, it is not suitable to say that similarly, when a basis of conjuring appears as a horse or elephant, the appearance as a horse or elephant is only in the perspective of a mistaken consciousness but in general the basis of conjuring *does not appear* as a horse or elephant [because it does]. Even though that qualification [that is, "in general"] is not affixed, it must be asserted that the basis of conjuring does appear as a horse or elephant [even though it only appears so for a mistaken consciousness]. For, if this were not the case, mistake regarding appearances would not occur.

Therefore, that the basis of conjuring can be posited as appearing as a horse or elephant is, according to the magician, through the force of appearing that way to a mistaken awareness; it is not posited otherwise through the force of the mode of subsistence of the basis of conjuring itself. As for the audience, the appearance as a horse or elephant does not seem to be posited through the force of an internal awareness; rather, they conceive that there is a fully qualified horse or elephant dwelling on that place where the appearance is, covering that spot.

In terms of an example, those are how something is conceived to be posited by the force of an awareness and is conceived not to be posited by the force of an awareness. When a basis [that is, an object] appears in a certain way, there are two [types]—those that do and do not correspond with the mode of subsistence as it appears.

When you understand well this [presentation of how phenomena are posited through the force of the mind according to the Svātantrika School], you will come to differentiate the two positions [of the Svātantrika School and the Proponents of True Existence which some] confuse. They think:

> Objects of comprehension [that is, all objects] are posited through the force of valid cognitions, and since valid cognitions are awarenesses, the positing of objects of comprehension through them is a case of positing [objects] through the force of an awareness. Hence, even the systems of the Proponents of True Existence refute true establishment.

[However,] that objects of comprehension are posited [that is, certified] through the force of valid cognitions means that valid cognitions realize the mode of subsistence of the two [types of] objects of comprehension [specifically and generally characterized objects or impermanent and permanent objects or manifest and hidden objects]. Therefore, the two—this [meaning of positing, or certifying, objects of comprehension according to the Proponents of True Existence] and the former [meaning of positing objects through the force of an awareness according to the Svātantrika School] are utterly dissimilar.

According to the Yogācāra-Svātantrika-Mādhyamika School [which does not assert external objects], the appearance of such an illusion is established [or certified] by a self-knowing direct perception, and according to the Sautrāntika-Svātantrika-Mādhyamika School, which asserts external objects, the appearance of such an illusion is established [or certified] by a sense direct perception apprehending the basis—for instance, the area [on which the illusion appears] or intermediate space [in which it appears].

With respect to its not existing in accordance with how it appears, [that the illusory horse or elephant exist as they appear] is refuted with signs [that is, reasons] such as, "If it did exist that way, it would be seen by those whose eyes are not affected [by the mantra], but they do not see it." At this time, a combination of the two—appearing that way and an emptiness of that—is established, whereby [the illusion] is established as a falsity relative to an ordinary conventional awareness which is not involved in [philosophical] tenets. Hence, the awarenesses that establish [or certify] this [composite of appearance and emptiness] and a reflection's emptiness of what it appears to be are not asserted to be either coarse or subtle reasoning consciousnesses.

Even with respect to what is truly established in terms of a conventional ordinary awareness,[4] if [an object] appears as something, it could not be empty of that, and also if it is empty of something, it could not appear that way. Hence, if a combination of those two [that is, appearing one way and existing another] occurs, it is only a falsity in terms of an ordinary awareness.

**Applying the Example to the Meaning**

When external and internal phenomena appear as truly existent, sentient beings, like the audience of magic whose eyes are affected [by the mantra cast by the magician], conceive that a mode of subsistence of those phenomena that is not posited by the force of an awareness exists.[5] This conception is the innate conception of true existence, which has operated beginninglessly.

What the Svātantrikas posit this way is very coarse relative to the Prāsaṅgikas' apprehension of the object of negation; hence, it is not the innate subtle conception of true existence [according to the Prāsaṅgikas].

When the true existence apprehended by the conception of true existence is refuted through reasoning, one—like the magician—does not conceive of external and internal phenomena as having a mode of subsistence that is not posited through the force of an internal awareness; rather, one understands [phenomena] as mere existents posited through the force of an awareness. Moreover, those [phenomena] posited through the force an awareness not damaged by valid cognition are asserted as conventionally existent; however, everything posited through the force of an awareness is not asserted as existing conventionally.

Although the production of a sprout from a seed is posited through the force of an awareness, it is not contradictory that the sprout also is produced from the seed from its own side. This is like the fact that there is an appearance as a horse or elephant even from the side of the basis of conjuring [that is, a pebble or twig]. Through that, all conventionally existent phenomena are to be understood.

Even reality is posited as existing through the force of the awareness to which it appears. Hence, it is not an exception to being posited as conventionally existent.

Therefore, the significance of applying the example—a magician's illusion—to the meaning—other phenomena—is not at all that just as a magician's illusion appears to be a horse or elephant but is empty of being such, so all phenomena such as pots appear to be pots, and so forth, but are empty of being pots, and so forth. For, if that were the case, being that phenomenon [for example, being a pot] would not occur, and the application of the example to the meaning would be that [phenomena] appear to be such-and-such but are not the actual thing.

When the nonconceptual exalted wisdom of meditative equipoise is generated, in its perspective all dualistic appearances are extinguished. This is like one whose eyes, not having been affected [by the magician's mantra], have neither the illusory appearance nor adherence to it.

There is no indication later [in Candrakīrti's text] of the Svātantrikas' uncommon mode of refutation [of true existence] by reasoning; therefore, let us express briefly and [in words] easy to understand how in this system all phenomena are caused to appear as like illusions.

Objects of knowledge are inclusively divided into the two: [functioning] things and non[functioning] things [or impermanent and permanent phenomena]. Let us explain [emptiness] with respect to [functioning] things first. [Functioning] things are inclusively divided into the physical and nonphysical. Applying the refutation, as explained elsewhere, of physical things that are directionally partless—eastern direction, and so forth—and of consciousnesses that are temporally partless, [the Svātantrikas] prove that [functioning] things necessarily have parts. Then, if parts and whole were different entities, they would be unrelated; thereby [such] is refuted, and [parts and whole] are shown to be one entity.

At that time, no matter how the mind looks into it, it is undeniable that, although the mode of being [of parts and whole] is to be one entity, in their mode of appearance [to thought] they appear to be different entities. Thereby, it is settled that [functioning things] are, like a magician's illusions, a combination of the two—appearing one way and being empty of [existing] that way.

Then, although such is not contradictory in the context of the mode of subsistence of a falsity posited through the force of appearing to an awareness, if a certain base [that is, a certain phenomenon] had a mode of subsistence not posited through the force of appearing to an awareness, [such a combination of appearance and emptiness] would not at all be suitable because discordant modes of abiding and of appearance cannot occur in what is truly established such as was explained earlier. For, if something is truly established, it must abide in a manner devoid of falsity in all respects, and [since appearance and being would necessarily be concordant] the awareness to which [parts and whole] appear as different entities would have to be unmistaken, thereby damaging their being one entity.

Once this is established, in dependence on that reasoning it can be refuted that non[functioning] things are truly established. For, even with respect to uncompounded space, it must be asserted that it pervades certain physical objects, and it must be further asserted that it has a part pervading the east and parts pervading the other directions. Likewise, reality [or emptiness] also has many parts pervading [phenomena], as well as many different parts realized by different earlier and later awarenesses. Also, other uncompounded [phenomena] are similar. Therefore, since the two, the many parts and the whole—are not fit to be different entities, they are one entity. Also, that [same discrepancy between modes of being and of appearance] is suitable in a falsity but not suitable in what is truly established. Hence, [the true establishment of uncompounded phenomena] is refuted as before [with compounded phenomena], whereby all objects of knowledge are established to be without true existence. Since this treatment is the assertion of the father Śāntarakṣita and his spiritual son Kamalaśīla, reckoning part and whole only for [functioning] things is a flaw of those with small intelligence.

The falsity renowned among those whose minds have not been affected by tenets is not the same in meaning as the falsity asserted by the Mādhyamika School. Although [a falsity such as a magician's illusion, which is renowned as false among those whose minds have not been affected by tenets], is posited by an awareness, [the status of being posited by an awareness] is in accordance with how that is renowned to those [whose minds have not been affected by tenets]. In the [Svātantrikas'] own system it is not merely that status which is asserted as [the meaning of being] posited by an awareness.

Thus, even though there is no mode of subsistence not posited by the force of appearing to an awareness, in this system it is not contradictory for there to be a mode of subsistence posited by the force of that but which is not merely nominally imputed. Hence, the objects of negation in the two Middle Way Schools come to differ greatly for the mind.

Having seen that contemporary persons—who have been briefly instructed well in [the Svātantrikas'] identification of true [existence] and [their estimation of] the conception of true existence, as well as [their] reasonings refuting those—discern the Prāsaṅgikas' view well when, afterwards, that system is taught, [I] have explained it here.

# 4

# The Prāsaṅgika School on True Existence

## IDENTIFICATION OF THE CONCEPTION OF TRUE EXISTENCE IN THE PRĀSAṄGIKA-MĀDHYAMIKA SCHOOL

With respect to this, if you understand how in this system phenomena are assigned as merely posited through the force of conceptuality, you will easily understand the conception of true existence that conceives the opposite of this. Therefore, the presentation of the identification of the conception of true existence in the Prāsaṅgika School has two parts: how phenomena are posited through the force of conceptuality and the conception of true existence that conceives the opposite of this.

### How Phenomena are Posited through the Force of Conceptuality

The *Questions of Upāli Sutra* (*nye bar 'khor gyis zhus pa, upāliparipṛcchā*) says that phenomena are posited through the force of conceptuality:

> Here the various mind-pleasing blossoming flowers
> And attractive, shining, supreme golden houses
> Have no [inherently existent] maker at all.
> They are posited through the power of conceptuality.
> Through the power of conceptuality the world is imputed.

There are also many other statements that all phenomena are merely imputed by conceptuality or that they are posited through the force of conceptuality.

Furthermore, Nāgārjuna's *Sixty Stanzas of Reasoning* (*rigs pa drug cu pa, yuktiṣaṣṭikā*) says:

> The perfect Buddha stated that the world
> Has the condition of ignorance.
> Therefore, how could it not be feasible
> That this world is [imputed by] conceptuality?

The meaning of this statement is explained in Candrakīrti's commentary as being that the worlds [that is, beings and environments] are imputed by conceptuality, not established by way of their own entities.

Also, Āryadeva's *Four Hundred* (VIII.3) says:[1]

> Since desire, and so forth,
> Do not exist without conceptuality,
> Who with intelligence would hold
> That these are real objects and are [also] conceptual?

Also, Candrakīrti's *Commentary on (Āryadeva's) "Four Hundred"* says:[2]

> Those that exist only when conceptuality exists and do not exist when conceptuality does not exist are undoubtedly ascertained as not established by way of their own entity, like a snake imputed to a coiled rope.

"Real objects" are those established by way of their own entity. "Conceptual" [means] "produced in dependence upon that [conceptuality]."

The statement in the commentary that *desire, and so forth* are [imputed] like the imputation of a snake to a rope is just an illustration; all other phenomena are also explained to be posited by conceptuality like the imputation of a snake to a rope. [The rope's] speckled color and mode of coiling are similar to those of a snake, and when the rope is perceived in a dim area, the thought arises, "This is a snake." As for the rope, at that time [when it is imputed to be a snake], the collection and parts of the rope are not even in the slightest way positable as an illustration of a snake [that is, as a snake]. Therefore, that snake is merely imputed by conceptuality.

In the same way, when the thought, "I," arises in dependence upon the [mental and physical] aggregates, nothing in terms of the aggregates—neither the collection which is the continuum of the earlier and later [moments], nor the collection [of the parts] at one time, nor the parts of those [mental and physical aggregates]—is even in the slightest way positable as an illustration of that I [that is, as I]. This will be explained at length below.

Because of this and because there is not even the slightest something that is an entity different from the parts of the aggregates or the whole and that is apprehendable as an illustration[3] of that [I], the I is merely posited by conceptuality in dependence upon the aggregates; it is not established by way of its own entity. This is also said in Nāgārjuna's *Precious Garland* (stanza 80):

A being is not earth, water,
Fire, wind, nor space,
Not consciousness and not all of them;
What being is there other than these?

In that, a "being" (*skyes bu, puruṣa*) is a person (*gang zag, pudgala*), sentient being (*sems can, sattva*), I (*nga, ahaṃ*), and self (*bdag, ātman*). ". . . not earth, water, fire, wind, nor space, not consciousness" refutes positing the parts—which are the six constituents of a sentient being—as a person, and ". . . not all of them" refutes positing the collection of the constituents as a person. "What person is there other than these?" refutes positing something that is a different entity from the constituents as a person.

Nevertheless, it is not that persons are not asserted [to exist]. Also, a mind-basis-of-all,[4] and so forth, are not asserted to be persons. Therefore, in accordance with the commentary by the commentator [Candrakīrti], Superiors are also asserted.[5]

When the mode of positing persons through conceptuality is understood in this way, the mode of positing all other phenomena through conceptuality is also similar to that. The *King of Meditative Stabilizations Sutra* (*ting nge 'dzin rgyal po'i mdo, samādhirājasūtra*) says:[6]

Just as you have known the discrimination of self,
Apply this mentally to all [phenomena].

Also, the *Superior Sutra of the Condensed Perfection of Wisdom* says:

Understand all sentient beings as like the self,
Understand all phenomena as like all sentient beings.

Also, Nāgārjuna's *Precious Garland* (stanza 81) clearly says:[7]

Just as the person is not [established as its own reality]
Because of being [only imputed in dependence upon]
  an aggregation of the six constituents,
So each of the constituents also
Is not [established as its own] reality because of being
  [imputed in dependence upon] an aggregation.

The meaning of the second line [that is, "because a person is an aggregation of the six constituents"] is "because a person is imputed in dependence upon an aggregation of the six constituents."[8] The meaning of the third and fourth lines is that, because there is no occurrence of [a phenomenon] devoid of parts and a whole, each of the constituents is also imputed in dependence upon an aggregation of its own many parts and, therefore, is not established as [its own] reality—that is to say, is not established by way of its own entity.

Furthermore, with regard to whatever is imputed in dependence upon an aggregation of parts, the parts or the whole are not suitable to be posited as an illustration of it [that is, as something that is it], and anything that is a different entity from those two also could not be an illustration of it either.

The mere factor of how a pot, and so forth, are posited by conceptuality is similar to the imputation of a rope as a snake. However, whether those two—a pot, and so forth, and a rope-snake—exist or do not exist, are able or unable to perform functions, and so forth, are not at all similar. This is because they are in all ways not equivalent in terms of whether or not the designations of those two must be made, whether or not making those designations is invalidated [by conventional valid cognition], and so forth.

The feasibility of [an object's] respective functionality within the context of being posited by conceptuality is an uncommon mode of commentary by Buddhapālita, Śāntideva, and this master [Candrakīrti] from among the commentators on the words and meaning [of the works] of the two—the father, the Superior [Nāgārjuna], and his spiritual son [Āryadeva]. Just this is also the final difficult point in the view of the Mādhyamika School.

This being the case, Nāgārjuna's *Precious Garland* (stanzas 99-100) says that even mere nominality does not exist ultimately and that nothing exists except for only being posited conventionally through the force of nominal conventions:[9]

> Because the phenomena of forms are only names,
> [Uncompounded] space too is only a name.
> Without the elements how could forms exist?
> Therefore, even name-only-ness does not [inherently] exist.
>
> Feelings, discriminations, compositional factors,
> And consciousnesses are to be considered
> As like the elements and the self.
> Hence the six constituents are selfless.

And (114bcd):

> Except for being a convention designated,
> What world exists in fact [that is, ultimately]
> Which would be "is" or "is not"?

As Nāgārjuna says, [phenomena] abide as mere nominal imputations.

If you understand those [points] well, you will understand well:

1. that all phenomena must be posited dependently,
2. that because they are just dependently imputed and dependently produced, they are not established by way of their own entity and do not have a self-powered entity which is not posited through the force of conventions which are other [than themselves], and
3. that no matter what phenomenon is posited as existing, it is posited in the context of not seeking the object imputed.

## The Conception of True Existence That Conceives the Opposite of This

The conception of existence not posited merely through the force of nominal conventions explained above is the innate conception of true establishment, ultimate establishment, or establishment as [the object's own] reality, as well as the innate conception of existing by way of [the object's] own entity, existing by way of [the object's] own character, and existing inherently. The referent object conceived by that [consciousness] is the hypothetical measure of true [establishment].

The need to know the two modes of the ultimate in the qualification of the object of negation with [the term] "ultimately" is also the same here [in the Prāsaṅgika School as in the Svātantrika School, explained in the previous chapter]. However, although the Svātantrika-Mādhyamikas assert that true, ultimate, and real establishment do not occur in objects of knowledge, they assert that the three—establishment by way of [the object's] own entity, establishment by way of [the object's] own character, and inherent establishment—exist conventionally. This is seen as a very skillful means for leading those who are temporarily unable to realize easily the very subtle suchness to that [realization of suchness].

In this way, just that inherent existence (*rang bzhin*, *svabhāva*) which is an entity of phenomena not depending on or not posited through the force of another—that is, a subjective terminological conceptual consciousness—is called the self that is the object of negation. The nonexistence of just this with a person as the substratum is said to be a selflessness of persons, and the nonexistence of it with a phenomenon such as an eye or ear [as the substratum] is said to be a selflessness of phenomena.

Thereby, it is implicitly understood that the conceptions of that inherent existence as existing in persons and in phenomena are the conceptions of the two selves [of persons and other phenomena]. It is as Candrakīrti's *Commentary on (Āryadeva's) "Four Hundred"* says:[10]

> Here "self" is inherent existence, an entity of things that does not depend on another. Its nonexistence is selflessness. This [selflessness] is under-

> stood as twofold through a division into persons and [other] phenomena—a selflessness of persons and a selflessness of phenomena.

Also, just this [*Entrance* VI.179bc] says, "Through a division of persons and [other] phenomena, it is said to be of two aspects." [Candrakīrti] speaks of the two selflessnesses as divided not by way of the object negated but by way of the subject that is the substratum [of selflessness—persons and other phenomena].

With respect to the innate view of the transitory collection which is a conception of [an inherently existent] self, in the root text [Candrakīrti's *Entrance to (Nāgārjuna's) "Treatise on the Middle Way"*][11] it is refuted that the object of observation is the [mental and physical] aggregates, and in the commentary[12] [Candrakīrti] says that the self imputed in dependence [upon the aggregates] is the object of observation. Therefore, the mere I or mere person, which is the object of observation generating the mere thought "I," is to be taken as the object of observation.

With respect to the subjective aspect [of a consciousness misconceiving the inherent existence of the I], Candrakīrti's *Autocommentary on the "Entrance to (Nāgārjuna's) 'Treatise on the Middle Way'"* says:

> Having imputed that a self which is [actually] nonexistent exists, a [consciousness] conceiving I adheres to just this as true.

Hence, it conceives the I to be truly established. Moreover, Candrakīrti's [*Auto*]*commentary* says:[13]

> With respect to that, the view of the transitory collection is an afflicted intelligence (*shes rab nyon mongs pa can*, **kliṣṭaprajñā*) which is engaged in such thoughts of [inherently existent] I and mine.

Thus, the object of observation of an innate view of the transitory collection must be something that naturally generates an awareness thinking "I"; therefore, the innate conception of persons—who are of a different continuum [from your own continuum]—as established by way of their own character is an innate conception of a self of persons but not an innate view of the transitory collection [as an inherently existent I].

[In the citation, just above, from Candrakīrti] ". . . engaged in such thoughts of I and mine" does not indicate that mere I and mere mine are the objects of the subjective aspect of the mode of apprehension. Rather, it indicates that [a view of the transitory collection] has the aspect of conceiving those two to be established by way of their own character.

The object of observation of an innate view of the transitory collection conceiving [inherently existent] mine is just the mine; it should not be held that one's own eyes, and so forth, are the object of observation. The subjective aspect is, upon observing that object of observation, to conceive the mine to be established by way of its own character.

*Objection:* In Candrakīrti's own commentary on "This is mine," [which is the last line of stanza 3:[14]

> Homage to that compassion for transmigrators who are
> Powerless like a bucket traveling in a well
> Through initially adhering to a self, an "I,"
> And then generating attachment for things, "This is mine."]

he says, "Thinking, 'This is mine,' one adheres to all aspects of things other than the object of the conception of an [inherently existent] I." [Given your explanation above that the object of observation of a false view of the transitory collection as inherently existent mine is not eyes, and so forth, but the mine itself,] how can you take [Candrakīrti's] explanation that upon observing a base such as an eye adherence to it thinking, "This is mine," is a conception of [inherently existent] mine?

*Answer:* This refers to adherence to the mine as truly established *upon perceiving eyes, and so forth, as mine*; it does not indicate that eyes, and so forth, which are illustrations of the mine are the object of observation. For, if that were not the case, the two—the view of the transitory collection and the conception of a self of phenomena—would not be mutually exclusive [whereas they are].

The objects of observation of an innate conception of a self of phenomena are the form aggregate, and so forth, and eyes, ears, and so forth, in your own and others' continuums, as well as the environment that is not included in the [personal] continuum. Its subjective aspect is as explained before [to conceive these to be established by way of their own character].

In this way, the conception of the two selves [of persons and other phenomena] is the ignorance binding one in cyclic existence. Nāgārjuna's *Seventy Stanzas on Emptiness* (*stong pa nyid bdun cu pa, śūnyatāsaptati*) says:

> That which conceives things produced
> From causes and conditions to be real
> Was said by the Teacher to be ignorance.
> From it the twelve links arise.

The conception that a thing that is a phenomenon [other than a person] is established as [its own] reality is said to be the ignorance that is the root of cyclic existence. Since the ignorance that is the conception of a self of persons arises from the conception of a self of phenomena, the twelve [links of dependent arising] are described as arising from it.

In order to overcome this ignorance, it must be seen that [phenomena] are empty of how they are conceived by that [conception of inherent existence], and it must be seen that self [that is, inherent existence] conceived in this way does not exist. Nāgārjuna's *Seventy Stanzas on Emptiness* says:

> If through seeing reality one knows well
> That things are empty, ignorance does not arise.
> That is the cessation of ignorance,
> Whereby the twelve links cease.

Also, Nāgārjuna's *Praise of the Element of Reality* (*chos dbyings bstod pa, dharmadhātustotra*) says:

> Through the conception of "I" and "mine"
> All external [phenomena] whatsoever are imputed
>   [to inherently exist].
> When the two aspects of selflessness are seen,
> The seeds of cyclic existence are ceased.

Also:

> The supreme doctrine purifying the mind
> Is the absence of inherent existence.

Furthermore, Āryadeva's *Four Hundred* (XIV.25cd) says:[15]

> When selflessness is seen in objects,
> The seeds of cyclic existence are ceased.

Also (VI.10c-11):[16]

> Therefore, all afflictions are destroyed
> By destroying obscuration.
>
> When dependent arising is seen,
> Obscuration does not arise.
> Therefore, with all endeavor here
> Just discourse on this should be proclaimed.

Since the obscuration mentioned [in that stanza] is on the occasion of identifying the obscuration that is one of the three poisons [desire, hatred, and obscuration], it is afflictive ignorance. Also, it is stated that in order to overcome this ignorance one must realize the meaning of profound dependent arising in which emptiness appears as the meaning of dependent arising.

Furthermore, the commentator [Candrakīrti] says that [when his *Entrance* (VI.120d) says,] "The yogi refutes self," [this means] that selflessness must be realized in the manner of eradicating the object of the conception of self [that is, inherent existence]. Therefore, although, without eradicating the object of the conception of self, you merely withdraw the mind here from going there to objects, through this it cannot be posited that you are engaged in selflessness. The reason is this: When the mind operates on an object, there are three [modes of conception]:

1. conceiving that the object of observation is truly established
2. conceiving that it is not truly established
3. conceiving it without qualifying it as either of these two.

Hence, although [the object] is not conceived to be without true establishment, it is not necessarily conceived to be truly established. Similarly, although [when merely withdrawing the mind in meditation] you are not engaged in [conceiving] the two selves, you are not necessarily engaged in the two selflessnesses. For, there are limitless [ways of] abiding in a third category of awareness.

Having identified the two conceptions of self in your own continuum, you need to settle that the bases with respect to which you make the mistake [of apprehending the two selves] do not exist as they are apprehended. Otherwise, refutation and proof that are directed outward are like searching for a robber on the plain after he has gone to the woods and hence are not to the point.

When, in that way, you have identified well the conception of true existence, you will understand that there are many conceptions that are not the two conceptions of self. Consequently, all wrong ideas of asserting that the reasoning analyzing suchness refutes all objects apprehended by conceptuality will be overcome.

Although there are many [points] stemming from these [topics] that should be explained, I will not elaborate on them here as some have already been explained at length elsewhere [in my *Great Exposition of the Stages of the Path to Enlightenment*, *The Essence of the Good Explanations*, and *Explanation of (Nāgārjuna's) "Treatise on the Middle Way"*] and some will be discussed below.

# GLOSSARY

## *English-Tibetan-Sanskrit*

*Note:* Sanskrit terms preceded by an asterisk are probable reconstructions and have not been found in Sanskrit texts.

| *English* | *Tibetan* | *Sanskrit* |
|---|---|---|
| absorption | snyoms 'jug | samāpatti |
| absorption of cessation | 'gog snyoms | nirodhasamāpatti |
| accompanies | dang tshung ldan | |
| action | las | karma |
| Actual Body | chos kyi sku | dharmakāya |
| actuality/reality/nature | chos nyid | dharmatā |
| adherence | zhen pa | |
| adventitious defilements | blo bur ba'i dri ma | |
| advisory speech | gdams ngag | upadeśa |
| affirming negative | ma yin dgag | paryudāsapratiṣedha |
| afflicted contaminations | nyon mong pa'i zag pa | *kleśāsrava |
| afflicted intelligence | shes rab nyon mongs pa can | *kliṣṭaprajñā |
| afflictive obstructions | nyon sgrib | kleśāvaraṇa |
| analysis | dpyod pa | vicāra |
| analytical meditation | dpyad sgom | |
| analyzers of the ultimate | don dam dpyod byed | |
| appearance | snang ba | pratibhāsa |
| appearing object | snang yul | *pratibhāsaviṣaya |
| apprehend | 'dzin | grāha |
| apprehender | 'dzin mkhan | |
| apprehension of signs/ conception of signs | mtshan mar 'dzin pa | nimittagrāha |
| approaching | mngon du phyogs pa | abhimukhī |
| Approaching/Manifest | mngon du gyur pa | abhimukhī |
| Arhat/Foe Destroyer | dgra bcom pa | arhan |
| arising | 'byung ba | samutpāda/udaya |
| Asaṅga | thogs med | asaṅga |

| *English* | *Tibetan* | *Sanskrit* |
|---|---|---|
| aspect | rnam pa | ākāra |
| aspirational prayer | smon lam | praṇidhāna |
| attain | thob | |
| | | |
| basis | gzhi | |
| basis of designation | gdags gzhi | |
| basis of engagement | 'jug gzhi | |
| basis of the qualities | khyad gzhi | |
| basis of the term | sgra'i gzhi | |
| basis on which thought places a term | rtog pa'i 'jug sa'i gzhi | |
| basis which is the place of engagement | 'jug sa'i gzhi | |
| being | skyes bu | puruṣa |
| benefit | phan yon | anuśaṃsa |
| bliss | bde ba | sukha |
| Buddhapālita | sangs rgyas bskyangs | buddhapālita |
| | | |
| calm abiding | zhi gnas | śamatha |
| Candrakīrti | zla ba grags pa | candrakīrti |
| capacity | nus pa | śakti |
| cause of error | 'khrul rgyu | *bhrāntihetu |
| cessation of discrimination and feeling | 'dus shes dang tshor ba 'gog pa | saṃjñāveditanirodha |
| cessation/stopping | gog pa | nirodha |
| changeable mental factor | sems byung gzhan 'gyur | *anyathābhāva-caitta |
| character/sign | mtshan ma | nimitta |
| Cittamātra | sems tsam pa | cittamātra |
| clairvoyance | mngon par shes pa | abhijñā |
| clairvoyance knowing that all defilements have been extinguished | zag zad kyi mngon shes | |
| clear appearance of emptiness | stong nyid kyi gsal snang | |
| Collected Topics | bsdus grva | |
| compositional phenomena | 'du byed | saṃskāra |
| compounded aggregates | 'dus byas kyi phung po | |
| concealer/conventional | kun rdzob | saṃvṛti |
| concentration | bsam gtan | dhyāna |
| conception of [an inherently existent] I | ngar 'dzin | |
| conception of inherent existence | bden 'dzin | *satyagrāha |

| *English* | *Tibetan* | *Sanskrit* |
|---|---|---|
| conception of self | bdag 'dzin | ātmagrāha |
| conceptual thought | rtog pa/rnam rtog | kalpanā |
| concordant | mthun pa | anukūla |
| condition | rkyen | pratyaya |
| conjoined with consciousness | sems kyis zin pa | |
| connectives | 'brel ba | |
| consciousness | shes pa/rnam par shes pa | jñāna/vijñāna |
| consciousness analyzing the conventional | tha snyad spyod byed kyi shes pa | |
| consciousness of reality | yang dag pa'i shes pa | |
| consciousness realizing an object | yul rtogs mkhyen | |
| constituent | khams | dhātu |
| contaminated | zag bcas | sāsrava |
| contamination | zag pa | āsrava |
| contamination which is an obstruction to omniscience | shes sgrib kyi zag pa | |
| contamination of cyclic existence | 'khor ba'i zag pa | |
| contiguous | bar du ma chad pa | |
| contradictory | 'gal ba | virodha |
| conventional consciousness | tha snyad pa'i shes pa | *vyavahārajñāna |
| conventional phenomena | tha snyad pa'i chos | *vyavahāradharma |
| conventional subjects | kun rdzob pa'i chos can | |
| conventional truth | kun rdzob bden pa | saṃvṛtisatya |
| conventional valid cognition | tha snyad pa'i tshad ma | *vyavahārapramāṇa |
| conventionality | tha snyad/kun rdzob | vyavahāra/saṃvṛti |
| conventionally existent | tha snyad du yod pa/kun rdzob du yod pa | vyavahārasat/saṃvṛtisat |
| correct assumption | yid spyod | *manaḥ parīkṣā |
| cyclic existence | 'khor ba | saṃsāra |
| deceptive appearance | slu snang | |
| deep | phugs | |
| defining characteristics/ definition | mtshan nyid | lakṣaṇa |
| dependent arising | rten 'brel/rten 'byung | pratītyasamutpāda |
| deprecation | skur 'debs | apavāda |
| determining mental factor | sems byung yul nges | *viśayapratiniyama-caitta |
| different isolates | ldog pa tha dad | |

| *English* | *Tibetan* | *Sanskrit* |
|---|---|---|
| direct cause | dngos rgyu | sākṣātkāraṇa |
| direct perceiver/direct perception | mngon sum | pratyakṣa |
| direct speech | man ngag | upadeśa |
| direct valid cognition | mngon sum gyi tshad ma | |
| disintegrating collection | 'jig tshogs | satkāya |
| disintegration | 'jig pa | vināśa |
| doctrine | chos | dharma |
| dualistic appearance | gnyis snang | |
| effort | brtson 'grus | vīrya |
| elaborations | spros pa | prapañca |
| elaborations of dualistic appearances | gnyis snang gi spros pa | |
| emanation | sprul pa | nirmāṇa |
| emptiness | stong pa nyid | śūnyatā |
| endless purity | dag pa rab 'byams | |
| energy | rlung | prāṇa/vāyu |
| engaged object | 'jug yul | |
| engages | 'jug | |
| enjoying emanation | 'phrul dga' | nirmāṇarati |
| entity | ngo bo | vastu |
| erroneous consciousnesses/ wrong consciousnesses | log shes | mithyājñāna |
| established as [its own] reality | yang dag par grub pa | |
| established base | gzhi grub | |
| established by valid cognition | tshad mas grub pa | pramāṇasiddha |
| established by way of [the object's] own nature | rang gi mtshan nyid kyis grub pa | |
| established from [the object's] own side | rang ngos nas grub pa | svarūpasiddha |
| establishment | grub pa | siddhi |
| ethics | tshul khrims | śīla |
| exalted wisdom | ye shes | jñāna |
| exclusion | sel ba | apoha |
| exertion | rtsol ba | vyāyāma |
| existent | yod pa/srid pa | bhāva/sattva/bhava |
| experience | myong ba | |
| [experience] arisen from meditation | sgom byung | bhāvanāmayī |
| explicitly | dngos su | sākṣāt |

| *English* | *Tibetan* | *Sanskrit* |
|---|---|---|
| explicitly contradictory | dngos 'gal | |
| explicitly mutually exclusive | dngos su phan tshun mi gnas/phan tshun spangs 'gal | |
| expressive term | rjod byed kyi sgra | |
| eye consciousness | mig gi rnam shes | cakṣurvijñāna |
| eye sense power | mig gi dbang po | cakṣurindriya |
| | | |
| fabrication/superimposition | sgro 'dogs | samāropa |
| factor | cha | amṣa |
| feeling | tshor ba | vedanā |
| Foe Destroyer | dgra bcom pa | arhan |
| Form Body | gzugs sku | rūpakāya |
| | | |
| generally characterized phenomenon | spyi mtshan | sāmānyalakṣaṇa |
| giving | spyin pa | dāna |
| grasp/apprehend | 'dzin pa | grāha |
| great emulation | bsgrub chen | |
| Great Vehicle/Mahāyāna | theg pa chen po | mahāyāna |
| ground/earth | sa | bhūmi |
| grounds and paths | sa lam | *bhūmimārga |
| | | |
| healthy/unharmed | gnod med | |
| herdswomen | rdzi mo | |
| Highest Yoga Tantra | rnal 'byor bla med kyi rgyud | anuttarayogatantra |
| horn of a rabbit | ri bong rva | |
| | | |
| I | nga | ahaṃ |
| ignorance | ma rig pa | avidyā |
| impelling action | phen byed kyi las | |
| impermanent | mi rtag pa | anitya |
| impress/affect | 'kos | |
| imputation | kun btags | parikalpita |
| imputation by thought | rtogs pas btags pa | |
| impute | rtog | prekṣate |
| imputed dependently | brten nas btags pa | |
| imputed existent | btags yod | prajñaptisat |
| imputed ultimate | don dam btags pa ba | |
| imputing mind | rtogs byed gyi blo | |
| inference | rjes dpag | anumāna |

| *English* | *Tibetan* | *Sanskrit* |
|---|---|---|
| inherent existence | rang bzhin | svabhāva/svarūpa |
| inherent existence/inherent establishment | rang bzhin gyis grub pa | svabhāvasiddhi |
| initiation | dbang | abhiṣeka |
| innate | lhan skyes | sahaja |
| inner currents, wind | rlung | prāṇa/vāyu |
| instance | mtshan gzhi | |
| instruction | khrid | |
| instruction from experience | myong khrid | |
| Jam-yang-shay-ba | 'jam dbyangs bzhad pa | |
| Joyous | dga' ldan | tuṣita |
| just nominally imputed | ming du btags pa tsam | |
| Kamalaśīla | padma'i ngang tshul | kamalaśīla |
| lacking a naturally characterized entity | rang gi mtshan nyid kyi ngo bo med pa | |
| latencies | bag chags | vāsanā |
| latencies of afflictions | nyon mongs kyi bag chags | |
| latencies of the conception of self | bdag 'dzin kyi bag chags | |
| latencies that are also seeds | sa bon yin mkhan gyi bag chags | |
| lay practitioner | dge bsnyen | upāsaka |
| limb | yan lag | aṅga |
| lineage of change | rkyen 'gyur gyi rigs | |
| lineage/type | rigs | gotra |
| Mādhyamika | bdu ma pa | mādhyamika |
| Mahayana/Great Vehicle | theg pa chen po | mahāyāna |
| Maitreya | byams pa | maitreya |
| Manifest/Approaching | mngon du gyur pa | *abhimukhī |
| Mañjuśrī | 'jam dpal | mañjuśrī |
| meaning | don | artha |
| meaning generality/ mental image | don spyi | arthasāmānya |
| measure of apprehension | 'dzin tshad | |
| medicine | sman | |
| meditative absorption | snyoms 'jug | samāpatti |
| meditative equipose | mnyam bzhag | samāhita |
| meditative stabilization | ting nge 'dzin | samādhi |
| memorize | blo la 'dzin | |
| mental body | yid lus | |

| *English* | *Tibetan* | *Sanskrit* |
|---|---|---|
| mental consciousness | yid kyi rnam par shes pa | manovijñāna |
| mental contemplation which is knowledge of the individual character | mtshan nyid so sor rig pa'i yid byed | lakṣaṇapratisaṃvedī-manaskāra |
| mental continuum | sems rgyud | cittasaṃtāna |
| mental convention | blo'i tha snyad | |
| mere person | gang zag tsam | |
| merely posited | bzhags tsam | |
| mind | sems | citta |
| mind of complete engagement | sgrub 'jug gi blo | *viddhipravṛttibuddhi |
| mind of enlightenment | byang chub kyi sems | bodhicitta |
| mind of parital engagement | sel 'jug gi blo | *apohapravṛttibuddhi |
| mind-basis-of-all | kun gzhi rnam par shes pa | ālayavijñāna |
| Mindful | blo 'chang | śrīmān |
| mine | nga yi ba | mama |
| mistaken | 'khrul ba | bhrānta |
| mistaken regarding the appearance [of its object] | 'khrul snang yod mkhan | |
| mode of abiding, way of being | gnas lugs | |
| mode of subsistence | sdod lugs | |
| momentary | skad cig ma | kṣaṇika |
| movement | rgyu ba | cāraṇa |
| my eye | nga'i mig | |
| Nāgārjuna | klu grub | nāgārjuna |
| naked instruction | dmar khrid | |
| natural defilements | rang bzhin gyi dri ma | |
| natural state of mind | sems kyi chos nyid | |
| naturally abiding lineage | rang bzhin gnas rigs | *svabhāvasthānagotra |
| nature | rang bzhin | svabhāva/prākṛti |
| nature/actuality/reality | chos nyid | dharmatā |
| Nature Body | ngo bo nyid sku | svabhāvikakāya |
| negative phenomenon | dgag pa | pratiṣedha |
| nonabiding nirvana | mi gnas pa'i myang 'das | apratiṣṭhitanirvāṇa |
| nonaffirming negative | med dgag | prasajyapratiṣedha |
| nonassociated compositional factor | ldan min 'du byed | viprayuktasaṃskāra |
| nonconceptual | rtog pa med pa | nirvikalpaka |
| nonconceptual wisdom | rnam par mi rtog pa'i ye shes | nirvikalpajñāna |
| nonconceptuality | mi rtog pa | avikalpa |
| nonexistent | med pa | asat |

| *English* | *Tibetan* | *Sanskrit* |
|---|---|---|
| nonobservation of a pot by valid cognition | bum pa tshad mas ma dmigs pa | |
| nonproduced | ma skyes pa | |
| noncontiguous | bar du chad pa | |
| not existent | med pa | asat |
| nothing whatever exists | ci yang med pa | |
| | | |
| object | dmigs pa | ālambana |
| object condition | dmigs rkyen | ālambanapratyaya |
| object expressed by a term | sgra'i brjod bya | |
| object of engagement | 'jug yul | *pravṛttiviṣaya |
| object of knowledge | shes bya | jñeya |
| object of negation | dgag bya | pratiṣedhya |
| object of observation/ observed object | dmigs pa/dmigs yul | ālambana |
| object of the conception of a [truly existent] I | ngar 'dzin gyi yul | |
| obscurer of reality/ concealer of reality | yang dag kun rdzob | samyaksaṃvṛti |
| obstructions to omniscience | shes bya'i sgrib pa/shes sgrib | jñeyāvaraṇa |
| obstructions to liberation | nyon mongs pa'i sgrib pa/ nyon sgrib | kleśāvaraṇa |
| obstructor | sgrib byed | |
| omnipresent mental factor | sems byung kun 'gro | sarvatragacaitta |
| omniscience | rnam mkhyen | sarvākārajñāna |
| one entity | ngo bo gcig | *ekavastu |
| one substantiality of establishment and abiding | grub bde rdzas gcig | |
| other-powered phenomenon | gzhan dbang | paratantra |
| | | |
| path of meditation | sgom lam | bhāvanāmārga |
| path of preparation | sbyor lam | prayogamārga |
| path of seeing | mthong lam | darśanamārga |
| patience | bzod pa | kṣānti |
| perfection | pha rol tu phyin pa | pāramitā |
| person | gang zag | pudgala |
| posited by the force of appearing to the mind | blo la snang ba'i dbang gis bzhag pa | |
| power | stobs | bala |
| practice | nyams len | |
| | | |
| quality | khyad chos | |

| *English* | *Tibetan* | *Sanskrit* |
|---|---|---|
| re-cognition | bcad shes | *pariccinnajñāna |
| real | yang dag | samyak |
| reality/actuality/nature | chos nyid | dharmatā |
| realization | rtogs pa | pratipad/adhigama |
| realize by valid cognition | tshad mas rtogs pa | |
| realizers of their objects | yul rtogs mkhan | |
| reason/sign | rtags | liṅga |
| recitation of mantra | dzab dbyangs | jāpa |
| referent object | zhen yul | *adhyavasāyaviṣaya |
| relaxed | hlod hlod | |
| root | rtsa ba | mūla |
| | | |
| sameness | mnyam pa nyid | samatā |
| Śāntideva | zhi ba lha | śāntideva |
| Sautrāntika | mdo sde pa | sautrāntika |
| scriptural collection of knowledge | mngon pa'i sde snod | abhidharmapiṭaka |
| scriptural collection of sets of discourses | mdo sde'i sde snod | sūtrāntapiṭaka |
| scripture | lung | āgama |
| seed | sa bon | bīja |
| self | bdag | ātman |
| self-isolate | rang ldog | vivartana |
| self-knower | rang rig | svasaṃvedana |
| self-sufficient | rang rkya ba | |
| selflessness | bdag med | nairātmya |
| sense power | dbang po | indriya |
| sentient being | sems can | sattva |
| separate from | bral | |
| sets of discourses | mdo sde | sūtrānta |
| seven good qualities of exalted status | mtho ris kyi yon tan bdun | |
| sign of not reversing from the doctrine | chos mi ldog pa'i rtags | |
| sign/character | mtshan ma | nimitta |
| sign/reason | rtags | liṅga |
| skillful means | thabs | upāya |
| Song of the Vajra | rdo rje glu | |
| sound | sgra | śabda |
| special insight | lhag mthong | vipaśyanā |
| specifically characterized phenomenon | rang mtshan | svalakṣaṇa |
| speech | ngag | vāc |

| *English* | *Tibetan* | *Sanskrit* |
|---|---|---|
| stabilizing meditation | 'jog sgom | |
| stage of completion | rdzogs rim | niṣpannakrama |
| stage of the path | lam rim | *mārgakrama |
| stain | dri ma | mala |
| style of existence | yod stangs | |
| subject | chos can | dharmin |
| substantial entity | rdzas | dravya |
| substantially existent | rdzas su yod pa | dravyasat |
| suchness | de nyid/de kho na nyid | tattva |
| superimposition | sgro 'dogs | samāropa |
| Superior | 'phags pa | ārya |
| support | rten | āśraya |
| supreme qualities | chos mchog | agryadharma |
| Svātantrika | rang rgyud pa | svātantrika |
| | | |
| tenet system | grub mtha' | siddhānta |
| term/sound | sgra | śabda |
| textual instruction | dpe khrid | |
| that which hold its own entity | rang gi ngo bo 'dzin pa | |
| thing/functioning thing | dngos po | bhāva/vastu/padārtha |
| thoroughly established phenomenon | yongs grub | pariniṣpanna |
| thought/conceptual thought | rtog pa | kalpanā |
| too extensive an object of negation | dgag bya khyab ches pa | |
| treatise | bstan bcos | śāstra |
| Tri-song-day-tsen | khri srong lde btsan | |
| true cessation | 'gog bden | nirodhasatya |
| true cessation of the conception of selflessness | bdag 'dzin gyi 'gog bden | |
| | | |
| ultimate attainment | thob pa don dam | |
| ultimate truth | don dam bden pa | paramārthasatya |
| ultimate valid cognizers/ ultimate valid cognition | don dam pa'i tshad ma | *paramārthapramāṇa |
| uncommon absorption of cessation | thun mong ma yin pa'i 'gog snyoms | *asādhārananiro-dhasamāpatti |
| uncommon dominant effect of karma | thun mong ma yin pa'i bdag 'bras | |
| uncontaminated | zag med | anāsrava |

| *English* | *Tibetan* | *Sanskrit* |
|---|---|---|
| uncontaminated actions | zag med kyi las | |
| underestimation/ deprecation | skur 'debs | apavāda |
| understanding arisen from thinking | bsam 'byung | cintāmayī |
| uninterrupted path | bar chad med lam | ānantaryamārga |
| uninterrupted path of seeing | mthong lam bar chad med lam | |
| unsurpassed | bla na med pa | anuttara |
| | | |
| Vaibhāṣika | bye brag smar ba | vaibhāṣika |
| valid cognition | tshad ma | pramāṇa |
| valid direct perception | mngon sum tshad ma | pratyakṣapramāṇa |
| valid cognition's effect | tshad 'bras | |
| valid cognition that imputes | 'dogs byed kyi tshad ma | |
| Very Joyous | rab tu dga' ba | pramuditā |
| view of the disintegrating aggregates | 'jig tshogs la lta ba | satkāyadṛṣṭi |
| virtuous mental factor | sems byung dge ba | kuśalacaitta |
| | | |
| way of being | gnas lugs | |
| way of existence | yod lugs | |
| way of subsistence | sdod lugs | |
| wind/inner current | rlung | prāṇa/vāyu |
| wisdom | shes rab | prajñā |
| wisdom realizing emptiness | stong nyid rtogs pa'i shes rab | |
| worldly existence/ existence/mundane existence/occurs | srid pa | bhava/prabhavati |
| wrong consciousness | log shes | viparyayajñāna |
| | | |
| yogic direct perceiver/ yogic direct perception | rnal 'byor mngon sum | yogipratyakṣa |

# Glossary

## *Tibetan-Sanskrit-English*

| *Tibetan* | *Sanskrit* | *English* |
|---|---|---|
| kun btags | parikalpita | imputation |
| kun rdzob | saṃvṛti | concealer/conventional |
| kun rdzob bden pa | saṃvṛtisatya | conventional truth |
| kun rdzob pa'i chos can | | conventional subjects |
| kun gzhi rnam par shes pa | ālayavijñāna | mind-basis-of-all |
| klu grub | nāgārjuna | Nāgārjuna |
| 'kos | | impress/affect |
| rkyen | pratyaya | condition |
| rkyen 'gyur gyi rigs | | lineage of change |
| skad cig ma | kṣaṇika | momentary |
| skur 'debs | apavāda | underestimation/deprecation |
| skyes bu | puruṣa | being |
| khams | dhātu | constituent |
| khyad chos | | quality |
| khyad gzhi | | basis of the qualities |
| khri srong lde btsan | | Tri-song-day-tsen |
| khrid | | instruction |
| 'khor ba | saṃsāra | cyclic existence |
| 'khor ba'i zag pa | | contamination of cyclic existence |
| 'khrul rgyu | | cause of error |
| 'khrul snang yod mkhan | | mistaken regarding the appearance [of its object] |
| 'khrul ba | bhrānta | mistaken |
| gang zag | pudgala | person |
| gang zag tsam | | mere person |
| grub 'jug gi blo | *viddhipravṛttibuddhi | mind of complete engagement |
| grub mtha' | siddhānta | tenet system |

| *Tibetan* | *Sanskrit* | *English* |
|---|---|---|
| grub bde rdzas gcig | | one substantiality of establishment and abiding |
| grub pa | siddhi | establishment |
| dgag pa | pratiṣedha | negative phenomenon |
| dgag bya | pratiṣedhya | object of negation |
| dga' ldan | tuṣita | Joyous |
| dge bsnyen | upāsaka | lay practitioner |
| dgra bcom pa | arhan | Foe Destroyer/Arhat |
| 'gog pa | nirodha | cessation/stopping |
| gag bya khyab ches pa | | too extensive an object of negation |
| 'gal ba | virodha | contradictory |
| 'gog snyoms | nirodhasamāpatti | absorption of cessation |
| 'gog bden | nirodhasatya | true cessation |
| rgyu ba | cāraṇa | movement |
| sgom byung | bhāvanāmayī | [experience] arisen from meditation |
| sgom lam | bhāvanāmārga | path of meditation |
| sgra | śabda | term/sound |
| sgra'i gzhi | | basis of the term |
| sgra'i brjod bya | | object expressed by a term |
| sgrib byed | | obstructor |
| sgro 'dogs | samāropa | fabrication/superimposition |
| bsgrub chen | | great emulation |
| | | |
| nga | ahaṃ | I |
| ngar 'dzin | | conception of [an inherently existent] I |
| nga yi ba | mama | mine |
| ngag | vāc | speech |
| nga'i mig | | my eye |
| ngar 'dzin gyi yul | | object of the conception of a [truly existent] I |
| ngo bo | vastu | entity |
| ngo bo gcig | *ekavastu | one entity |
| ngo bo nyid sku | svabhāvikakāya | Nature Body |
| dngos 'gal | | explicitly contradictory |
| dngos rgyu | sākṣātkāraṇa | direct cause |
| dngos po | bhāva/vastu/padārtha | thing/functioning thing |
| dngos su | sākṣāt | explicitly |
| dngos su phan tshun mi gnas/phan tshun spangs 'gal | | explicitly mutually exclusive |

| *Tibetan* | *Sanskrit* | *English* |
|---|---|---|
| mngon du gyur pa | abhimukhī | Approaching/Manifest |
| mngon du phyogs pa | abhimukhī | Approaching |
| mngon pa'i sde snod | abhidharmapiṭaka | scriptural collection of knowledge |
| mngon par shes pa | abhijñā | clairvoyance |
| mngon sum | pratyakṣa | direct perceiver/direct perception |
| mngon sum gyi tshad ma | | direct valid cognition |
| mngon sum tshad ma | pratyakṣapramāṇa | valid direct perception |
| ji yang med pa | | nothing whatever exists |
| bcad shes | *pariccinnajñāna | re-cognition |
| cha | amṣa | factor |
| chos | dharma | doctrine |
| chos kyi sku | dharmakāya | Actual Body |
| chos can | dharmin | subject |
| chos mchog | agryadharma | supreme qualities |
| chos nyid | dharmatā | actuality/reality/nature |
| chos mi ldog pa'i rtags | | sign of not reversing from the doctrine |
| 'jam dpal | mañjuśrī | Manjushri |
| 'jam dbyangs bzhad pa | | Jam-yang-shay-ba |
| 'jig tshogs | satkāya | disintegrating collection |
| 'jig pa | vināśa | disintegration |
| 'jig tshogs la lta ba | satkāyadṛṣṭi | view of the disintegrating aggregates |
| 'jug | | engages |
| 'jug gzhi | | basis of engagement |
| 'jug yul | *pravṛttiviṣaya | object of engagement |
| 'jug sa'i gzhi | | basis which is the place of engagement |
| 'jog sgom | | stabilizing meditation |
| rjes dpag | anumāna | inference |
| rjod byed kyi sgra | | expressive term |
| nyams len | | practice |
| nyon mong pa'i zag pa | *kleśārava | afflicted contaminations |
| nyon mongs kyi bag chags | | latencies of the afflictions |
| nyon mongs pa'i sgrib pa/ nyon sgrib | kleśāvaraṇa | obstructions to liberation/ afflictive obstructions |
| gnyis snang | | dualistic appearance |

| *Tibetan* | *Sanskrit* | *English* |
|---|---|---|
| gnyis snang gi spros pa | | elaborations of dualistic appearances |
| mnyam pa nyid | samatā | sameness |
| mnyam bzhag | samāhita | meditative equipose |
| snyoms 'jug | samāpatti | meditative absorption/ absorption |
| ting nge 'dzin | samādhi | meditative stabilization |
| btags yod | prajñaptisat | imputed existent |
| rtags | liṅga | reason/sign |
| rten | āśraya | support |
| rten 'brel/rten 'byung | pratītyasamutpāda | dependent arising |
| rtog | prekṣate | impute |
| rtog pa/rnam rtog | kalpanā | thought/conceptual thought |
| rtog pa med pa | nirvikalpaka | non-conceptual |
| rtog pa'i 'jug sa'i gzhi | | basis on which thought places a term |
| rtogs pa | pratipad/adhigama | realization |
| rtogs pas btags pa | *kalpanāprajñāpti | imputation by thought |
| rtogs byed gyi blo | | imputing mind |
| stong nyid kyi gsal snang | | clear appearance of emptiness |
| stong nyid rtogs pa'i shes rab | | wisdom realizing emptiness |
| stong pa nyid | śūnyatā | emptiness |
| stobs | bala | power |
| brten nas btags pa | | imputed dependently |
| bstan bcos | śāstra | treatise |
| tha snyad/kun rdzob | vyavahāra/saṃvṛti | conventionality |
| tha snyad du yod pa/kun rdzob du yod pa | vyavahārasat/ saṃvṛtisat | conventionally existent |
| tha snyad pa'i chos | *vyavahāradharma | conventional phenomena |
| tha snyad pa'i tshad ma | *vyavahārapramāṇa | conventional valid cognition |
| tha snyad pa'i shes pa | *vyavahārajñāna | conventional consciousness |
| tha snyad spyod byed kyi shes pa | | consciousness analyzing the conventional |
| thabs | upāya | skillful means |
| thun mong ma yin pa'i 'gog snyoms | *asādhārananirod-hasamāpatti | uncommon absorption of cessation |

| *Tibetan* | *Sanskrit* | *English* |
|---|---|---|
| thun mong ma yin pa'i bdag 'bras | | uncommon dominant effect of karma |
| theg pa chen po | mahāyāna | Great Vehicle/Mahāyāna |
| thogs med | asaṅga | Asaṅga |
| thob | | attain |
| thob pa don dam | | ultimate attainment |
| mthun pa | anukūla | concordant |
| mtho ris kyi yon tan bdun | | seven good qualities of exalted status |
| mthong lam | darśanamārga | path of seeing |
| mthong lam bar chad med lam | | uninterrupted path of seeing |
| dag pa rab 'byams | | endless purity |
| dang tshung ldan | | accompanies |
| de nyid/de kho na nyid | tattva | suchness |
| don | artha | meaning |
| don dam btags pa ba | | imputed ultimate |
| don dam bden pa | paramārthasatya | ultimate truth |
| don dam pa'i tshad ma | *paramārthapramāṇa | ultimate valid cognizers/ ultimate valid cognition |
| don dam dpyod byed | | analyzers of the ultimate |
| don spyi | arthasāmānya | meaning generality/ mental image |
| dri ma | mala | stain |
| gdags gzhi | | basis of designation |
| gdams ngag | upadeśa | advisory speech |
| bdag | ātman | self |
| bdag med | nairātmya | selflessness |
| bdag 'dzin | *ātmagrāha | conception of self |
| bdag 'dzin kyi bag chags | | latencies of the conception of self |
| bdag 'dzin gyi 'gog bden | | true cessation of the conception of selflessness |
| bdu ma pa | mādhyamika | Mādhyamika |
| bde ba | sukhā | bliss |
| bden par grub pa | | existence/true establishment |
| bden 'dzin | satyagrāha | conception of inherent existence |
| mdo sde | sūtrānta | sets of discourses |
| mdo sde pa | sautrāntika | Sautrāntika |

| *Tibetan* | *Sanskrit* | *English* |
|---|---|---|
| mdo sde'i sde snod | sūtrāntapiṭaka | scriptural collection of sets of discourses |
| 'du byed | saṃskāra | compositional phenomena |
| 'dus byas kyi phung po | | compounded aggregates |
| 'dus shes dang tshor ba 'gog pa | saṃjñāveditanirodha | cessation of discrimination and feeling |
| 'dogs byed kyi tshad ma | | valid cognition that imputes |
| rdo rje glu | | Song of the Vajra |
| ldan min 'du byed | viprayuktasaṃskāra | nonassociated compositional factor |
| ldog pa tha dad | | different isolates |
| sdod lugs | | way of subsistence |
| bsdus grva | | Collected Topics |
| nus pa | śakti | capacity |
| gnas lugs | | way of being/mode of abiding |
| gnod med | | healthy/unharmed |
| rnam mkhyen | sarvākārajñāna | omniscience |
| rnam pa | ākāra | aspect |
| rnam par mi rtog pa'i ye shes | nirvikalpajñāna | nonconceptual wisdom |
| rnal 'byor mngon sum | yogipratyakṣa | yogic direct perceiver/yogic direct perception |
| rnal 'byor bla med kyi rgyud | anuttarayogatantra | Highest Yoga Tantra |
| snang ba | pratibhāsa | appearance |
| snang yul | *pratibhāsaviṣaya | appearing object |
| dpe khrid | | textual instruction |
| dpyad sgom | | analytical meditation |
| dpyod pa | vicāra | analysis |
| spyi mtshan | sāmānyalakṣaṇa | generally characterized phenomenon |
| spyin pa | dāna | giving |
| sprul pa | nirmāṇa | emanation |
| spros pa | prapañca | elaborations |
| pha rol tu phyin pa | pāramitā | perfection |
| phan yon | anuśaṃsa | benefit |
| phugs | | deep |
| phen byed kyi las | | impelling action |
| 'phags pa | ārya | Superior |

| *Tibetan* | *Sanskrit* | *English* |
|---|---|---|
| 'phrul dga | nirmāṇarati | Enjoying Emanation |
| | | |
| bag chags | vāsanā | latencies |
| bar chad med lam | ānantaryamārga | uninterrupted path |
| bar du ma chad pa | | contiguous |
| bar du chad pa | | noncontiguous |
| bral | | separate from |
| bum pa tshad mas ma dmigs pa | | non-observation of a valid pot |
| byang chub kyi sems | bodhicitta | mind of enlightenment |
| byams pa | maitreya | Maitreya |
| bye brag smar ba | vaibhāṣika | Vaibhāṣika |
| bla na med pa | anuttara | unsurpassed |
| blo 'chang | | mindful |
| blo bur ba'i dri ma | | adventitious defilements |
| blo la snang ba'i dbang gis bzhag pa | | posited by the force of appearing to the mind |
| blo la 'dzin | | memorize |
| blo'i tha snyad | | mental convention |
| dbang | abhiṣeka | initiation |
| dbang po | indriya | sense power |
| 'byung ba | samutpāda/udaya | arising |
| 'brel ba | | connectives |
| sbyor lam | prayogamārga | path of preparation |
| | | |
| ma skyes pa | | nonproduced |
| ma yin dgag | paryudāsapratiṣedha | affirming negative |
| ma rig pa | avidyā | ignorance |
| man ngag | upadeśa | direct speech |
| mi rtag pa | anitya | impermanent |
| mi rtog pa | avikalpa | nonconceptuality |
| mi gnas pa'i myang 'das | apratiṣṭhitanirvāṇa | nonabiding nirvana |
| mig gi rnam shes | cakṣurvijñāna | eye consciousness |
| mig gi dbang po | cakṣurindriya | eye sense power |
| ming du btags pa tsam | | just nominally imputed |
| med dgag | prasajyapratiṣedha | nonaffirming negative |
| med pa | asat | nonexistent/not existent |
| myong khrid | | instruction from experience |
| myong ba | | experience |
| dmar khrid | | essential instruction |
| dmigs rkyen | ālambanapratyaya | object condition |
| dmigs pa/dmigs yul | ālambana | object of observation/ observed object |
| sman | | medicine |

| Tibetan | Sanskrit | English |
|---|---|---|
| smon lam | praṇidhāna | aspirational prayer |
| rtsa ba | mūla | root |
| rtsol ba | vyāyāma | exertion |
| brtson 'grus | vīrya | effort |
| tshad 'bras | | valid cognition's effect |
| tshad ma | pramāṇa | valid cognition |
| tshad mas grub pa | pramāṇasiddha | established by valid cognition |
| tshad mas rtogs pa | | realize by valid cognition |
| tshur byed | | take in/understand |
| tshul khrims | śīla | ethics |
| tshor ba | vedanā | feeling |
| mtshan nyid | lakṣaṇa | defining characteristics/ definition |
| mtshan nyid so sor rig pa'i yid byed | lakṣaṇapratisaṃ-vedīmanaskāra | mental contemplation which is knowledge of the individual character |
| mtshan ma | nimitta | character/sign |
| mtshan mar 'dzin pa | nimittagrāha | apprehension of signs/ conception of signs |
| mtshan gzhi | | instance |
| dzab dbyangs | jāpa | recitation of mantra |
| 'dzin mkhan | | apprehender |
| 'dzin | grāha | apprehension/grasp/ apprehend |
| 'dzin tshad | | measure of apprehension |
| rdzas | dravya | substantial entity |
| rdzas su yod pa | dravyasat | substantially existent |
| rdzi mo | | herdswomen |
| rdzogs rim | niṣpannakrama | stage of completion |
| zhi gnas | śamatha | calm abiding |
| zhi ba lha | śāntideva | Śāntideva |
| zhen pa | | adherence |
| zhen yul | *adhyavasayaviṣaya | referent object |
| gzhan dbang | paratantra | other-powered phenomenon |
| gzhi | | basis |
| gzhi grub | | established base |
| bzhags tsam | | merely posited |
| zag bcas | sāsrava | contaminated |

| *Tibetan* | *Sanskrit* | *English* |
|---|---|---|
| zag pa | āsrava | contamination |
| zag med | anāsrava | uncontaminated |
| zag med kyi las | | uncontaminated actions |
| zag zad kyi mngon shes | | clairvoyance knowing that all defilements have been extinguished |
| bzod pa | kṣānti | patience |
| zla-ba-grags-pa | candrakīrti | Candrakirti |
| gzugs sku | rūpakāya | Form Body |
| yang dag | samyak | real |
| yang dag kun rdzob | samyaksaṃvṛti | obscurer of reality/ concealer of reality |
| yang dag pa'i shes pa | | consciousness of reality |
| yang dag par grub pa | | established as [its own] reality |
| yan lag | aṅga | limb/link |
| ye shes | jñāna | exalted wisdom |
| yid kyi rnam par shes pa | manovijñāna | mental consciousness |
| yid spyod | *manaḥ parīkṣā | correct assumption |
| yid lus | | mental body |
| yul rtogs mkhan | | consciousness realizing an object/realizers of their objects |
| yongs grub | pariniṣpanna | thoroughly established phenomenon |
| yod pa/srid pa | bhāva/sattva/bhava | existent |
| yod lugs | | way of existence |
| rang rkya ba | | self-sufficient |
| rang gi ngo bo 'dzin pa | | that which hold its own entity |
| rang gi mtshan nyid kyi ngo bo med pa | | lacking a naturally characterized entity |
| rang gi mtshan nyid kyis grub pa | | established by way of [the object's] own nature |
| rang rgyud pa | svātantrika | Svatantrika |
| rang ngos nas grub pa | svarūpasiddha | established from [the object's] own side |
| rang ldog | vivartana | self-isolate |
| rang mtshan | svalakṣaṇa | specifically characterized phenomenon |
| rang bzhin | svabhāva/svarūpa/ prākṛti | inherent existence/nature/ |

| Tibetan | Sanskrit | English |
|---|---|---|
| rang bzhin gyi drima | | natural defilements |
| rang bzhin gyis grub pa | svabhāvasiddhi | inherent existence/inherent establishment |
| rang bzhin gnas rigs | *svabhāvasthāna-gotra | naturally abiding lineage |
| rang rig | svasaṃvedana | self-knower |
| rab tu dga' ba | pramuditā | Very Joyous |
| ri bong rva | | horn of a rabbit |
| rigs | gôtra | lineage/type |
| rlung | prāṇa/vāyu | inner currents/wind/energy |
| lam rim | *mārgakrama | stage of the path |
| las | karma | action |
| lung | āgama | scripture |
| log shes | mithyājñāna | erroneous consciousnesses/wrong consciousnesses |
| hlod hlod | | relaxed |
| shes sgrib kyi zag pa | | contamination which is an obstruction to omniscience |
| shes pa/rnam par shes pa | jñāna/vijñāna | consciousness |
| shes bya | jñeya | object of knowledge |
| shes bya'i sgrib pa/shes sgrib | jñeyāvaraṇa | obstructions to omniscience |
| shes rab | prajñā | wisdom |
| shes rab nyon mongs pa can | *kliṣṭaprajñā | afflicted intelligence |
| sa | bhūmi | ground/earth |
| sa bon | bīja | seed |
| sa bon yin mkhan gyi bag chags | | latencies that are also seeds |
| sa lam | *bhūmimārga | grounds and paths |
| sangs rgyas bskyangs | buddhapālita | Buddhapālita |
| sems | citta | mind |
| sems kyi chos nyid | | natural state of mind |
| sems kyis zin pa | | conjoined with consciousness |
| sems byung kun 'gro | sarvatraga-caitta | omnipresent mental factor |
| sems byung dge ba | kuśala-caitta | virtuous mental factor |
| sems byung gzhan 'gyur | *anyathābhāva-caitta | determining mental factor |
| sems byung yul nges | *viśayapratiniyama-caitta | determining mental factor |

| *Tibetan* | *Sanskrit* | *English* |
|---|---|---|
| sems rgyud | cittasaṃtāna | mental continuum |
| sems can | sattva | sentient being |
| sems tsam pa | cittamātra | Cittamātra |
| sel 'jug gi blo | *apohapravṛttbuddhi | mind of parital engagement |
| sel ba | apoha | exclusion |
| srid pa | bhava/prabhavati | worldly existence/existence/ mundane existence/ occurs |
| slu snang | | deceptive appearance |
| bsam gtan | dhyāna | concentration |
| bsam 'byung | cintāmayī | understanding arisen from thinking |
| lhag mthong | vipaśyanā | special insight |
| lhan skyes | sahaja | innate |

# GLOSSARY

*Sanskrit-English-Tibetan*

| *Sanskrit* | *English* | *Tibetan* |
|---|---|---|
| amṣa | factor | cha |
| agryadharma | supreme qualities | chos mchog |
| aṅga | limb/link | yan lag |
| adhigama/pratipad | realization | rtogs pa |
| *adhyavasāyaviṣaya | referent object | zhen yul |
| anāsrava | uncontaminated | zag med |
| anitya | impermanent | mi rtag pa |
| anukūla | concordant | mthun pa |
| anumāna | inference | rjes dpag |
| anuśaṃsa | benefit | phan yon |
| anuttara | unsurpassed | bla na med pa |
| anuttarayogatantra | Highest Yoga Tantra | rnal 'byor bla med kyi rgyud |
| *anyathābhāva-caitta | changeable mental factor | sems byung gzhan 'gyur |
| apavāda | underestimation/ deprecation | skur 'debs |
| apoha | exclusion | sel ba |
| *apohapravṛttibuddhi | mind of parital engagement | sel 'jug gi blo |
| apratiṣṭhitanirvāṇa | nonabiding nirvana | mi gnas pa'i myang 'das |
| abhidharmapiṭaka | scriptural collection of knowledge | mngon pa'i sde snod |
| abhijñā | clairvoyance | mngon par shes pa |
| *abhimukhī | Approaching/Manifest | mngon du gyur pa/mngon du phyogs pa |
| abhiṣeka | initiation | dbang |
| *asādhārananirodha-samāpatti | uncommon absorption of cessation | thun mong ma yin pa'i 'gog snyoms |
| artha | meaning | don |
| arthasāmānya | meaning generality/ mental image | don spyi |

| *Sanskrit* | *English* | *Tibetan* |
|---|---|---|
| arhan | Foe Destroyer/ Arhat | dgra bcom pa |
| avidyā | ignorance | ma rig pa |
| avikalpa | nonconceptuality | mi rtog pa |
| asaṅga | Asanga | thogs med |
| asat | nonexistent/not existent | med pa |
| ahaṃ | I | nga |
| | | |
| āgama | scripture | lung |
| ākāra | aspect | rnam pa |
| ālambana | object of observation/ observed object | dmigs pa/dmigs yul |
| ālambanapratyaya | object condition | dmigs rkyen |
| ālayavijñāna | mind-basis-of-all | kun gzhi rnam par shes pa |
| ānantaryamārga | uninterrupted path | bar chad med lam |
| ārya | Superior | 'phags pa |
| āśraya | support | rten |
| āsrava | contamination | zag pa |
| ātmagrāha | conception of self | bdag 'dzin |
| ātman | self | bdag |
| | | |
| indriya | sense power | dbang po |
| | | |
| upadeśa | direct speech | man ngag |
| upadeśa/ avadāvad ādeśa | advisory speech | gdams ngag |
| upāya | skillful means | thabs |
| upāsaka | lay practitioner | dge bsnyen |
| | | |
| *ekavastu | one entity | ngo bo gcig |
| | | |
| karma | action | las |
| kalpanā | thought/conceptual thought | rtog pa/rnam tog |
| kuśala-caitta | virtuous mental factor | sems byung yul nges |
| *kliṣṭaprajñā | afflicted intelligence | shes rab nyon mongs pa can |
| kleśāvaraṇa | obstructions to liberation/ afflictive obstructions | nyon mongs pa'i sgrib pa/ nyon sgrib |
| *kleśāsrava | afflicted contaminations | nyon mong pa'i zag pa |
| kṣaṇika | momentary | skad cig ma |
| kṣānti | patience | bzod pa |

| *Sanskrit* | *English* | *Tibetan* |
|---|---|---|
| grāha | apprehend | 'dzin |
| gotra | lineage/type | rigs |
| | | |
| cakṣurindriya | eye sense power | mig gi dbang po |
| cakṣurvijñāna | eye consciousness | mig gi rnam shes |
| candrakīrti | Candrakīrti | zla ba grags pa |
| cāraṇa | movement | rgyu ba |
| citta | mind | sems |
| cittamātra | Cittamātra | sems tsam pa |
| cittasaṃtāna | mental continuum | sems rgyud |
| cintāmayī | understanding arisen from thinking | bsam 'byung |
| | | |
| jāpa | recitation of mantra | dzab dbyangs |
| jñāna | exalted wisdom | yeshes |
| jñāna/vijñāna | consciousness | shes pa/rnam par shes pa |
| jñeya | object of knowledge | shes bya |
| jñeyāvaraṇa | obstructions to omniscience | shes bya'i sgrib pa/shes sgrib |
| | | |
| tattva | suchness | de nyid/de kho na nyid |
| tuṣita | Joyous | dga' ldan |
| | | |
| dāna | giving | spyin pa |
| dravya | substantial entity | rdzas |
| | | |
| dravyasat | substantially existent | rdzas su yod pa |
| dharma | doctrine | chos |
| dharmakāya | Actual Body | chos kyi sku |
| dharmatā | actuality/reality/nature | chos nyid |
| dharmin | subject | chos can |
| dhātu | constituent | khams |
| dhyāna | concentration | bsam gtan |
| | | |
| nāgārjuna | Nāgārjuna | klu grub |
| nairātmya | selflessness | bdag med |
| nimitta | character/sign | mtshan ma |
| nimittagrāha | apprehension of signs/ conception of signs | mtshan mar 'dzin pa |
| nirodha | cessation/stopping | 'gog pa |
| nirodhasatya | true cessation | 'gog bden |
| nirodhasamāpatti | absorption of cessation | 'gog snyoms |

| Sanskrit | English | Tibetan |
|---|---|---|
| nirmāṇa | emanation | sprul pa |
| nirmāṇarati | enjoying emanation | 'phrul dga |
| nirvikalpaka | nonconceptual | rtog pa med pa |
| nirvikalpajñāna | nonconceptual wisdom | rnam par mi rtog pa'i ye shes |
| niṣpannakrama | stage of completion | rdzogs rim |
| paratantra | other-powered phenomenon | gzhan dbang |
| *paramārthapramāṇa | ultimate valid cognizer/ ultimate valid cognition | don dam pa'i tshad ma |
| paramārthasatya | ultimate truth | don dam bden pa |
| pāramitā | perfection | pha rol tu phyin pa |
| *pariccinnajñāna | re-cognition | bcad shes |
| *pratibhāsaviṣaya | appearing object | snang yul |
| *pravṛttiviṣaya | object of engagement | 'jug yul |
| parikalpita | imputation | kun btags |
| pariniṣpanna | thoroughly established phenomenon | yongs grub |
| paryudāspratiṣedha | affirming negative | ma yin dgag |
| pudgala | person | gang zag |
| puruṣa | being | skyes bu |
| prajñaptisat | imputed existent | btags yod |
| prajñā | wisdom | shes rab |
| praṇidhāna | aspirational prayer | smon lam |
| prapañca | elaborations | spros pa |
| pramāṇa | valid cognition | tshad ma |
| pramāṇasiddha | established by valid cognition | tshad mas grub pa |
| pramuditā | Very Joyous | rab tu dga' ba |
| pratipad/adhigama | realization | rtogs pa |
| pratibhāsa | appearance | snang ba |
| pratiṣedha | negative phenomenon | dgag pa |
| pratiṣedhya | object of negation | dgag bya |
| pratītyasamutpāda | dependent arising | rten 'brel/rten 'byung |
| pratyakṣa | direct perceiver/direct perception | mngon sum |
| pratyakṣapramāṇa | valid direct perception | mngon sum tshad ma |
| pratyaya | condition | rkyen |
| prasajyapratiṣedha | nonaffirming negative | med dgag |
| prayogamārga | path of preparation | sbyor lam |
| prāṇa/vāyu | inner currents/wind/energy | rlung |
| prekṣate | impute | rtog |

| *Sanskrit* | *English* | *Tibetan* |
|---|---|---|
| bala | power | stobs |
| bīja | seed | sa bon |
| buddhapālita | Buddhapālita | sangs rgyas bskyangs |
| bodhicitta | mind of enlightenment | byang chub kyi sems |
| bhāva/sattva/bhava | existent | yod pa/srid pa |
| bhava/prabhavati | worldly existence/ existence/mundane existence/occurs | srid pa |
| bhāva/vastu/padārtha | thing/functioning thing | dngos po |
| bhāvanāmayī | [experience] arisen from meditation | sgom byung |
| bhāvanāmārga | path of meditation | sgom lam |
| bhūmi | ground/earth | sa |
| *bhūmimārga | grounds and paths | sa lam |
| bhrānta | mistaken | 'khrul ba |
| *bhrāntihetu | cause of error | 'khrul rgyu |
| mañjuśrī | Mañjuśrī | 'jam dpal |
| *manab parīkṣā | correct assumption | yid spyod |
| manovijñāna | mental consciousness | yid kyi rnam par shes pa |
| mama | mine | nga yi ba |
| mala | stain | dri ma |
| mahāyāna | Great Vehicle, Mahāyāna | theg pa chen po |
| *mārgakrama | stage of the path | lam rim |
| maitreya | Maitreya | byams pa |
| mādhyamika | Mādhyamika | bdu ma pa |
| mithyājñāna | erroneous consciousnesses/ wrong consciousnesses | log shes |
| mūla | root | rtsa ba |
| yogipratyakṣa | yogic direct perceiver/ yogic direct perception | rnal 'byor mngon sum |
| rūpakāya | Form Body | gzugs sku |
| lakṣaṇa | defining characteristics/ definition | mtshan nyid |
| lakṣaṇapratisaṃvedī-manaskāra | mental contemplation which is knowledge of the individual character | mtshan nyid so sor rig pa'i yid byed |
| liṅga | reason/sign | rtags |
| vastu | entity | ngo bo |
| vāc | speech | ngag |
| vāsanā | latencies | bag chags |

| Sanskrit | English | Tibetan |
|---|---|---|
| vedanā | feeling | tshor ba |
| vicāra | analysis | dpyod pa |
| vināśa | disintegration | 'jig pa |
| vipaśyanā | special insight | lhag mthong |
| viprayuktasaṃskāra | nonassociated compositional factor | ldan min 'du byed |
| virodha | contradictory | 'gal ba |
| vivartana | self-isolate | rang ldog |
| viśayapratiniyama-caitta | determining mental factor | sems byung yul nges |
| vīrya | effort | brtson 'grus |
| vaibhāṣika | Vaibhāṣika | bye brag smar ba |
| vyavahāra/saṃvṛti | conventionality | tha snyad/kun rdzob |
| *vyavahāradharma | conventional phenomena | tha snyad pa'i chos |
| *vyavahārapramāṇa | conventional valid cognition | tha snyad pa'i tshad ma |
| *vyavahārajñāna | conventional consciousness | tha snyad pa'i shes pa |
| vyavahārasat/saṃvṛtisat | conventionally existent | tha snyad du yod pa/kun rdzob du yod pa |
| *viddhipravṛttibuddhi | mind of complete engagement | grub 'jug gi blo |
| vyāyāma | exertion | rtsol ba |
| | | |
| śakti | capacity | nus pa |
| śabda | term/sound | sgra |
| śamatha | calm abiding | zhi gnas |
| śāntideva | Śāntideva | zhi ba lha |
| śāstra | treatise | bstan bcos |
| śīla | ethics | tshul khrims |
| śūnyatā | emptiness | stong pa nyid |
| | | |
| saṃvṛti/vyavahāra | concealer/conventional | kun rdzob |
| saṃvṛtisatya | conventional truth | kun rdzob bden pa |
| saṃsāra | cyclic existence | 'khor ba |
| saṃskāra | compositional phenomena | 'du byed |
| saṃjñāveditanirodha | cessation of discrimination and feeling | 'dus shes dang tshor ba 'gog pa |
| satkāya | disintegrating collection | 'jig tshogs |
| sattva | sentient being | sems can |
| satyagrāha | conception of inherent existence | bden 'dzin |
| satyasiddha | true establishment | bden par grub pa |
| *saṃsārasāsrava | contamination of cyclic existence | 'khor ba'i zag pa |

| *Sanskrit* | *English* | *Tibetan* |
|---|---|---|
| samatā | sameness | mnyam pa nyid |
| samādhi | meditative stabilization | ting nge 'dzin |
| samāpatti | meditative absorption/ absorption | snyoms 'jug |
| samāropa | fabrication/superimposition | sgro 'dogs |
| samāropa | superimposition | sgro 'dogs |
| samāhita | meditative equipose | mnyam bzhag |
| samutpāda/udaya | arising | 'byung ba |
| samyak | real | yang dag |
| samyaksaṃvṛti | obscurer of reality/ concealer of reality | yang dag kun rdzob |
| sarvākārajñāna | omniscience | rnam mkhyen |
| sarvatraga-caitta | omnipresent mental factor | sems byung kun 'gro |
| sahaja | innate | lhan skyes |
| sākṣāt | explicitly | dngos su |
| sākṣātkāraṇa | direct cause | dngos rgyu |
| sāmānyalakṣaṇa | generally characterized phenomenon | spyi mtshan |
| sāsrava | contaminated | zag bcas |
| siddhānta | tenet system | grub mtha' |
| siddhi | establishment | grub pa |
| sūtrānta | sets of discourses | mdo sde |
| sūtrāntapiṭaka | scriptural collection of sets of discourses | mdo sde'i sde snod |
| sukhā | bliss | bde ba |
| sautrāntika | Sautrāntika | mdo sde pa |
| *svabhāvasthānagotra | naturally abiding lineage | rang bzhin gnas rigs |
| svabhāva/prākṛti | nature | rang bzhin |
| svabhāva/svarūpa | inherent existence | rang bzhin |
| svabhāvasiddhi | inherent existence/inherent establishment | rang bzhin gyis grub pa |
| svabhāvikakāya | Nature Body | ngo bo nyid sku |
| svalakṣaṇa | specifically characterized phenomenon | rang mtshan |
| svarūpasiddha | established from [the object's] own side | rang ngos nas grub pa |
| svasaṃvedana | self-knower | rang rig |
| svātantrika | Svātantrika | rang rgyud pa |

# NOTES

## PREFACE

1. For a discussion of these five works, and especially of the *Great Exposition of the Stages of the Path*, see Napper, *Dependent-Arising and Emptiness* (London: Wisdom Publications, 1989), p. 7ff.

2. Indeed, this title can also be translated "Supplement to (Nāgārjuna's) Treatise" since the term *'jug* means both "entry" and "supplement." See Hopkins, *Meditation on Emptiness*, pp. 868-71 n. 545.

3. For different opinions on the chronological placement of this text among Tsong-kha-pa's other Mādhyamika works, see Napper, *Dependent-Arising and Emptiness*, pp. 646-47 n. 8.

4. For an excellent recent translation of this text, see Huntington and Wangchen, *The Emptiness of Emptiness* (Honolulu: University of Hawaii Press, 1989), pp. 149-96.

5. Snellgrove, *Indo-Tibetan Buddhism*, vol. II (Boston: Shambhala, 1987), pp. 444-45.

6. Ibid., p. 433. See also Bu-ston, *History of Buddhism*, Obermiller, vol. II, pp. 191ff.

7. Thurman, tr., *Tsong-kha-pa's Speech of Gold in the Essence of True Eloquence* (Princeton: Princeton University Press, 1984), pp. xiii-272.

## INTRODUCTION

1. Not to be confused with *gzhung bsgrigs*, to compile or compose texts.

2. For an example of contemporary oral commentary on the Sautrāntika chapter of Jang-gya's (lcang-skya rol-pa'i rdo-rje) *Presentation of Tenets (Grub mtha'i rnam bzhag)* text, see Klein, tr., *Knowing, Naming, and Negation.* This book also contains oral commentary, drawn from several important Gelukba scholars, on a typical debate text, in this case the *Collected Topics from a Spiritual Son of Jam-yang-shay-ba (go mang yig cha/kun mkhyen 'jam dbyangs bshad pa'i thugs sras ngag dbang bkra shis kyis mdzad pa'i bsdus grva )* by Nga-wang-dra-shi (*ngag dbang bkra shis*, 1648-1721), n.p., n.d. (available from Gomang College, Mundgod, India).

3. Gen Yeshey Thapkey, Tibetan Buddhist Learning Center, July 30, 1993.

4. How one refers to it simply depends on which aspect of its function one wishes to emphasize—that is, whether one emphasized the explanations it itself contained, or that it is an expansion of a particular text. Gen Yeshey Thabkey and Losang Tsayden (both students of Kensur Yeshey Tupden), Tibetan Buddhist Learning Center, Washington, New Jersey, July 30, 1993. All subsequent citations from Yeshey Thabkey are from this conversation.

5. The title of the meditation text discussed below also includes this term.

6. Gen Yeshey Thabkey

7. See especially Walter Ong, *Orality and Literacy: The Technologizing of the Word* (London and New York: Methuen & Co. Ltd., 1982), chapter 3.

8. Ibid., p. 33.ff.

9. Ibid., p. 38.

10. Ibid., p. 39; Ong also says oral cultures encourage "fluency, fulsomeness, volubility" (pp. 40-41).

11. Ibid., p. 42.

12. Ibid., p. 45

13. Randolph Franklin Lumpp, "Culture, Religion, and the Presence of the Word: A Study in the Thought of Walter Ong," (Ph.D Dissertation, University of Ottowa, 1976, p. 25). I would not, however, follow Ong in suggesting that oral cultures necessarily are associated with "a cyclic understanding of time" or lack a sense of historicity. For example, this long-held generalization about India (which I would place as a secondary oral culture) has been admirably reconsidered by Steven Collins, "Historiography in the Pāli Tradition," presented at the AAR annual meeting in Kansas City, November 1991.

14. Goody and Watt refer to this as the "homeostatic adjustment of past oral traditions to the present." See "The Consequences of Literacy" in Goody, J. R. ed., *Literacy in Traditional Societies* (Cambridge: Oxford University Press, 1968), p. 59ff.

15. Another difference Tibetan themselves perceive between their own and Western orientations is that "In Tibet we accept many things that cannot be seen by the eye; the West does not accept many unseen things. This is the kind of difference there is" (Denma Lochö Rinboche, private taped conversation, June. 1990, Tibetan Buddhist Learning Center, Washington, New Jersey). Lobön Tenzin Namdag made the same point during a lecture for Ligmincha Institute, July 17, 1992, Head Water, Virginia.

16. Debate thus occupies an interesting place between the written and the oral. Tibetan monastic debates can be considered a form of rhetoric. However, whereas Ong (*Orality and Literacy,* p. 110) has noted that in the West "rhetoric retained much of the

old oral feeling for thought," Tibetan stylistic debate was directly modeled on Indian forms of textual disputation, which, however, may well have had their origins in spoken debate. For examples of how these forms are related, see Klein, *Knowing, Naming, and Negation*. For detailed discussion of Tibetan debate, see Daniel E. Perdue, *Debate in Tibetan Buddhism* (Ithaca: Snow Lion, 1992).

17. In some monastic colleges older students visit younger debaters to help them develop skills.

18. For elaboration of this topic, see Klein, *Knowledge and Liberation* (Ithaca: Snow Lion, 1986), especially chapters 4 and 6.

19. However, Gelukbas will stop short of saying that, for example, Avalokiteśvara is present in the mantra associated with him, *oṃ māṇi padme hūṃ*. Saying such a mantra causes help from the deity associated with it to flow to oneself but not, as in some forms of Hinduism, because the deity is *present* in the sound, but because hearing that sound is like hearing his or her own name, and s/he will automatically respond to it (Denma Lochö Rinboche, Tibetan Buddhist Learning Center, Washington, New Jersey, June, 1990). This said, it should be noted that much of the ritual power Tibetans attribute to sound in general and mantra in particular is derived from the Indian ritual context. See, for example, Agenanda Bharati, *The Tantric Tradition* (London: Rider & Co., 1965), and Jan Gonda, "The Indian Mantra," *Oriens* 16 (1963) 244-97. For an extensive discussion of whether or not a mantra is a speech act, see Harvey P. Alper, ed., *Mantra* (Albany: State University of New York Press, 1989). For a stimulating discussion of mantra and its relation to *dhāraṇī* see Janet Gyatso, "Letter Magic," in *In the Mirror of Memory*, ed. J. Gyatso (Albany: SUNY, 1992).

20. More technically, this has to do with interactions between direct perception, which is a complete engager *(sgrub 'jug kyi blo, *vidhipravṛttibuddhi)* to its object, and to conceptual thought, which approaches and isolates its object through a negative process, and which is known as a partial engager *(sel 'jug gi blo, *apohapravṛtti)*. For further Gelukba elaborations of this distinction, see Klein, *Knowledge and Liberation*, especially chap. 3 and 4.

21. Often referred to as *dpe khrid*. According to Yeshey Thabkey, however, *gzhung khrid* is the correct term.

22. Khenbo Palden Sherab, December 1990, Houston, TX.

23. Khetsun Sangpo Rinboche, March 1991, Houston TX.

24. Long-chen-rab-jam (klong-chen-rab-'byams), *Treasure of Precious Direct Speech Instructions (man ngag rin po che'i mdzod)* published by Dodrup Chen Rinpoche in *kLong chen mdzod bdun*, sde-dge edn. from blocks commissioned by the Saraswati Block Makers, Lanaka, Varansi 5, n.d. (Gantok, Sikkhim c. 1969) Vol. 5, 56b.2.

25. Ibid.

26. Khetsun Sangpo Rinboche, Houston, Texas, March 1991.

27. *tshegs chung don che thabs mang ba/bya ba sla dpag dka' man ngag go.* From the *rdzogs chen a di bgod ba'i rgyud* in the Nyingma *rgyud 'bum;* recited by Khenbo Palden Sherab, oral commentary, December 9, 1990, Houston, Texas. A similar description occurs in *zab mo yang tig*, vol 2 p. 427.3: *tshegs chung la don che ba'i thabs dam pa'o* (Thanks to David Germano for this citation). A traditional etymology of "essential teachings" (*man ngag, upadeśa)* indicates the diverse qualities of speech around which oral genres are grouped in Tibet.

28. *Treasure of Precious Direct Speech*, rept. 1983. Gantok, Sikkhim: Sherab Gyaltsen and Khentse Labrang Palace Monastery, p. 5a.5.

29. Ibid., 56b.1-2.

30. Khetsun Sangpo, in discussion, March 1991, Houston, Texas.

31. Khetsun Sangpo noted that the terms "kindly speech" and "harmful speech" have the same meaning (etymologically) but their object of operation *('jug yul)* is different. "Object of operation" is a term associated with Tibetan discussions of *instructional* speech genres. The explanation of oral genres has to be discussed in those terms. Yet, these etymologies themselves are part of oral tradition.

32. Khetsun Sangpo Rinboche, March 1991, Houston, Texas. This is an oral etymology. Rinboche notes that he speaks of this from his own experience. Texts do not give a clear etymology of *ngag* in this way, although there are occasional statements that may accord with this one.

33. Indeed, the scriptural teaching *(lung gi chos, āgamadharma)* has, from at least the fourth century in India, been one of two major divisions of Buddhist teaching, the other being the teaching which is realized *(rtogs kyi chos, adhigamadharma).*

34. Khenbo Palden Sherab, oral commentary.

35. Khetsun Sangpo Rinboche, March 1990, Houston, Texas.

36. Khetsun Sangpo Rinboche, March 1990, Houston, Texas. Because of its association with blessings and power, sound is considered a subtle type of form.

37. Denma Lochö Rinboche, private conversation taped June 1990, Tibetan Buddhist Learning Center.

38. For a study of the physiological and psychological effects of rhythm, see Marcel Jousse, 1990. *The Oral Style,* tr. Edgard Sienaert and Richard Whitaker, The Alfred Bates Lord Studies in Oral Tradition (New York: Garland Publishing).

39. Diane Ackerman, 1991. *A Natural History of the Senses* (New York: Vintage), p. 205.

40. We generally acknowledge the ability of sound to take over our interior in another way; in the presence of very loud noise we say, "It's so loud I can't hear myself

think." See, for example, Don Ihde,1976. *Listening and Voice* (Athens, Ohio: Ohio University Press), especially pp. 133 ff.

41. From Khetsun Sangpo Rinboche's explication of the deity yoga associated with the practice of Hail Protection. According to Gen Yeshey Thabkey, Geluk engages in *bsgrub chen* and *sgrub sogs* but not *dpa' bo gcig*—that is, they do not consider recitation done alone as a formal category (a different point from saying that individuals do not do recitation in their own personal practice).

42. Gen Yeshey Thabgey.

43. For example, an important Nyingma meditational practice for evoking the Hundred Peaceful and Wrathful Deities who exist in the body involves such chanting. Simultaneous with the vocalization, one visualizes these figures at certain places in the body. A similar effect occurs when chanting, for example, a multi-line mantric poem known as the ancient "Song of the Vajra" (*rdo rje glu*) in which the sound of every syllable is said to correspond to and affect certain parts of the body. This is a genre present in Nyingma and in Geluk Tantric practices, and I believe, though I have not ascertained, that it exists in the other Tibetan religious traditions as well.

44. I use the term "vocalization" to signify oral genres in which sound is as important or more important than meaning.

45. For a classic Gelukba discussion of calm abiding *(zhi gnas, śamatha)* see Geshe Gedün Lodrö, *Walking Through Walls*. For Gelukba sources on special insight *(hlag mthong, vipaśyanā)* see Jeffrey Hopkins, *Meditation on Emptiness*.

46. Although early stages of concentration, especially the cultivation of mindfulness, can make one more aware of unique and particular aspects of one's persona or personal history, deep concentration causes these to recede from awareness. They no longer impinge on experience as they did before, because one has literally "pushed down the head" *(mgo gnon)* of one's particular desires and other distractions, thereby gaining a greater capacity to focus most explicitly on emptiness. The highest levels of concentration, technically known as the four concentrations *(bsam gtan, dhyāna)* and four absorptions (*snyoms 'jug, samāpatti)*, are increasingly expansive and unparticularized, moving from infinite space, to infinite consciousness, to nothingness, and culminating in the peak of cyclic existence. Thus, whereas Western psychology takes one to what is most specific and idiosyncratic about one's mind and self, the higher Buddhist stages of practice described here take one to what is considered universal in the human mind. Whereas psychotherapy honors the project of each person fulfilling her or his own unique and creative vision, here the goal is to leave behind the "personal" for entry into an unconditioned arena where what matters most is what is most universally available to Bodhisattvas everywhere.

47. Much of the material in this section appears in different form in Klein, "Mental Concentration and the Unconditioned: A Buddhist Case for Unmediated Experience" in Gimello and Buswell, eds., *Paths to Liberation*: *The Mārga and its Transformations in Buddhist Thought* (Honolulu: University of Hawaii Press, 1992).

48. Lati Rinbochay, Denma Lochö Rinbochay, Leah Zahler, Jeffrey Hopkins, *Meditative States in Tibetan Buddhism* (London: Wisdom Publications, 1983), p. 176; Panchen Sönam Drakba, *dbu ma'i spyi don*, 156.b3-4. See Klein, "Mental Concentration and the Unconditioned," n. 19.

49. Sarnath edition, 115.15-16.

50. Notable in this group are the *General Meaning of the Middle Way (dbu ma'i spyi don)* and *Response to Queries on the "Entrance" (dbu ma la 'jug pa'i brgal lan)* by Panchen Sönam Drakba, (*paṇ-chen bsod nams grags pa*, 1478-1554), a major author of Drebung-Loseling textbooks who studied at Sera and later became an abbot of Loseling and Ganden-Shardzay—thus enjoying a career across monastic boundaries which, Yeshey Tupden observed, would be impossible in modern times. Other important sources for discussions of the uncommon absorption of cessation are *Good Explanation of the General Meaning, Clarifying the Difficult Points of [Tsong-kha-pa's] "Illumination of the Thought" (bstan bcos dbu ma la 'jug pa'i rnam bshad dgongs pa rab gsal gyi dka' gnad gsal bar byed pa'i spyi don legs bshad skal bzang mgul rgyan)* by Jetsun Chö-gyi-gyal-tsen (*rje-bstun chos kyi rgyal mtshan*, 1469-1546) and *Great Exposition of the Middle Way (dbu ma chen mo)* by Jam-yang-shay-ba (*'jam dbyangs bzhad pa*, 1648-1721).

Tsong-kha-pa may well have been the first to use the term "uncommon absorption of cessation"; his own teacher Ren-da-wa *(red mda' ba)* does not mention it in his commentary on Candrakirti's *Entrance.*

51. Ren-da-wa (*red mda' ba gzhon nu blo gros*, 1349-1412), *Explanation of [Candrakirti's] "Entrance to the Middle Way, A Lamp Illuminating Reality (dbu ma la 'jug pa'i rnam bshad de kho na nyid gsal ba'i sgron ma)* Delhi: Ngawang Topgay, 1974, 76.2ff., comments on verse VI.1d. Other positions of Ren-da-wa are noted in Klein, "Concentration and the Unconditioned."

52. Jetsun Chös-gyi-gyal-tsen *(rje btsun chos kyi rgyal mtshan), Clarifying the Difficult Points (dka' gnad gsal bar byed pa) p.* 89a.4.

53. For a discussion of how these conjoin and the problematic involved, see Klein, *Knowing, Naming, and Negation*. For more on "mental basis," see Ladrö, *Walking Through Walls*, pp. 347-49 and 357-66.

54. Lo-sang-da-yang *(blo bzang rta mgrin)* (also known as *blo bzang rta dbyangs*, 1867-1937), *Annotations on [Panchen Sönam Drakba's] "General Meaning of Mādhyamika," A Lamp Illuminating the Profound Meaning (dbu ma'i spyi don gyi mchan 'grel)* (New Delhi: Tibet House, 1974), 96.1-2.

55. Some editions give *'thob* here, whereas a modern edition has *thob*. I doubt any difference in tense is to be construed. (See Klein, "Mental Concentration and the Unconditioned," n. 54).

56. *rang 'grel*, Sarnath 61.4-8.

57. *dbu ma dgongs pa rab gsal*, Sarnath, 114.14-115.1.

58. Ibid., 115.16. The earliest post -Tsong-kha-pa Gelukba commentator on the *Entrance*, Ge-dun-drub (*dge 'dun grub*, 1391-1475), later known as the first Dalai Lama, glosses the meditative equipoise of the sixth ground as an uncommon absorption of cessation and then, unlike slightly later commentators such as Panchen Sönam Drakba and Jetsun Chö-gyi-gyal-tsen, says no more about it. See Ge-dun-drub, *Mirror Thoroughly Clarifying the Treatise "Entrance to the Middle Way" (dbu ma la 'jug pa'i bstan bcos kyi dgongs pa rab tu gsal ba'i me long)* (n.p., n.d., block print from private collection of L. T. Doboom Tulku), 10b.3-4.

59. *rang 'grel*, 61.6-9. Also cited by Jam-yang-shay-ba *('jam dbyangs bzhad pa), Great Exposition of the Middle Way (dbu ma chen mo)* (Buxador: Gomang, 1967), trs. Jeffrey Hopkins, unpub. ms., p. 1.

60. For a discussion of how this differs from other Mahāyāna forms of absorption, see Klein, "Mental Concentration and the Unconditioned."

61. *Response*, 53.b6-54a.1. *sher phyin gyi nyams len ches lhag pas zin pa'i chos nyid la mngon sum du mnyam par gzhag pa'i mnyam gzhag ye shes de.*

62. See, for example, Panchen Sönam Drakba *(pan chen bsod nams grags pa) Response*, 51a.ff; "whatever is an absorption of cessation is not necessarily a nonassociated compositional factor" (ibid., 52b.1, 54a.4-54a.6; see also idem, *General Meaning (dbu ma'i spyi don* ), 127.6ff where he distinguishes between subject *(yul can 'gog snyoms)* and object *(yul 'gog snyoms)* cessations; and Jetsun Chö-gyi-gyal-tsen, *Clearing Away the Difficult Points (dka' gnad gsel bar byed pa),* 89a.3ff.

63. *Illumination,* Sarnath edition, 114.20.

64. Lo-sang Chö-gyi-gyal-tsen (*blo bzang chos kyi rgyal mtsan*, 1570-1661. This work has been translated, based on commentary by Denma Lochö Rinboche, by Joshua W. C. Cutler, Director of the Tibetan Buddhist Learning Center in Washington, New Jersey. The phrase *bde lam* could be translated as "path of bliss"; since, however, here *bde ba* clearly includes the sense of well-being brought about by the earlier stages of the path, as well as the special bliss unique to its higher reaches, the broader term "well-being" has been used. Cutler's translation has not yet been published.

65. The "of" used in translating this term is ambiguously multidirectional in order to suggest that the teaching comes from and is enriched by the teacher's own past experience, though he will not necessarily describe or even refer to his own practice, and is also meant to produce certain experiences for the listener-meditator in the future.

66. This discussion is based on the Denma Lochö Rinboche's teaching of the *Path of Well-Being (bde lam)* at the Tibetan Buddhist Learning Center in the summer of 1990. Along with Elizabeth Napper and Joshua Cutler, I was one of the oral translators of his lectures.

67. These include: instructions for relying on a spiritual teacher; an exhortation to utilize the special situation of leisure and opportunity which makes practice possible; training in the contemplations of impermanence and death, the suffering of the bad rebirths, going

for refuge, and developing conviction in the cause and effect of actions *(karma)*. Then one goes on to train in a desire for liberation and its associated practices; when this is complete one begins the practices unique to the Mahāyāna. These are (1) the development of the compassionate or altruistic determination to seek enlightenment in order to be in a position maximally to help and benefit all living beings; (2) having developed this intention, carrying it out by training in the Bodhisattva deeds, also known as the six perfections; (3) in particular training in the last two perfections—namely, calm abiding, described as the "essence of concentration," and special insight, described as the "essence of wisdom."

68. The seven branches are: refuge, mental or physical prostration, offering, confession or purifying of nonvirtue, rejoicing in one's own and others' virtues, requesting the Lamas to continue to teach, requesting one's teacher to have a long life, and, finally, dedication of the merit of all acts of body, speech, and mind for the benefit of living beings. One then offers a mandala, representative of the entire world, including the objects of the senses of that world, to those Lamas and Buddhas. These are described in the oral commentary of Geshe Ngawang Dhargyey in classes at the Library of Tibetan Works and Archives, July 1971. His lectures during the 1971-72 year, the first year of classes at the Library, were published in 1974 as *Tibetan Tradition of Mental Development: Oral Teachings of Tibetan Lama Geshey Ngawang Dhargyey* (Dharamsala: Library of Tibetan Works and Archives).

Physical gestures or *mudrā* are also involved; for example, the offerings that comprise the second of the branches are indicated by a flowing set of hand gestures that symbolize the traditional seven offerings. These are: water for drinking, water for washing, flowers, incense, light, perfume, and food. These are also typically symbolized on an altar by seven bowls of water. An eighth offering, sound, is not symbolized through form since sound itself has no visible form (Geshe Rabten, oral commentary and demonstrator of the *mudrās*, summer 1971, Dharamsala, India).

69. Note the interlacing and repetitiveness; one has already taken refuge and already cultivated the compassionate aspiration of a Bodhisattva when one "cultivates" it in this sequence. Such reiteration is typical of an oral/rhetorical strategy.

70. In addition, the preparatory section on calm abiding notes the importance of finding "an isolated place which you find agreeable" and reducing one's desire for objects of the senses; then sitting in the lotus posture and quieting thoughts by observing three sets of inhalation and exhalation through the left nostril, the right nostril, and both nostrils; and then observing twenty-one breaths (*Path of Well-Being*, 416.1ff.). The precise instructions on "quieting the winds" are not included in the text but were given by Denma Lochö Rinboche in teaching the text. See Cutler translation, p. 60 n. 15.

The meditative sessions focused on special insight involve a rigorously text-based but otherwise free-form analysis on the meaning of emptiness. (For extensive discussion of this analysis, see Hopkins, *Emptiness Yoga* (Ithaca: Snow Lion, 1987). See also Hopkins, *Meditation on Emptiness*.) Once conceptual understanding arises, one stabilizes one's mind on that meaning. In this way the practitioner alternates between conceptual analysis and mental concentration, technically known as analytical and stabilizing meditation. These two kinds of subjectivity are, as we have seen, crucially addressed in both the letter and media of textual and meditative engagement.

71. Similarly, the omniscient mind of a Buddha, like sound, is said to be as all-encompassing, and unlike linear writing or ordinary conceptuality it does not proceed from one point to another, from past to future, but simultaneously encompasses the past, the present, and the future. One could also say, though it would not be possible to argue this systematically, that the intertwining of aural and visual functions is an index of Tibet's situation betwixt and between powerful oral/aural *and* visual/textual orientations. Further, this interfusion of the visual and aural may be analogous to the third of Ong's cultural stages, electronic, where once again words and images can be embodied, can even surround one, as in the computerized, holistic construction of "virtual reality." (The more things change . . .).

72. Indeed, the most accomplished meditators are said to be able to cause others to see emanations from their own minds.

73. In Ong's terms, Tibet is a visual/oral or secondary oral culture, in which the oral/aural dimension of communication coalesces to a certain extent with the visual orientation of print culture (Lumpp, "Culture, Religion, and the Presence of the Word," p. 18).

74. This is a most interesting idea that probably needs further documentation. Ong, *The Presence of the Word,* discusses this (p. 69), citing J. C. Carothers, "Culture, Psychiatry, and the Written Word" in *Psychiatry* 22 (1959), 307-20.

75. The aesthetic function here is rather like that of the artist in Bakhtin's description:

> Lived experiences, when experienced outside myself in the other, possess an inner exterior, an inner countenance adverted toward me, and this inner exterior or countenance can be and should be lovingly contemplated, it can be and should be remembered the way we remember a person's face [and not the way we remember some past experience of our own], it can be and should be made secure, given a form, regarded with loving-mercy, cherished with our inner eyes, and not our physical outward eyes.

Mikhail Bakhtin, *Art and Answerability: Early Philosophical Essays* (Austin: University of Texas Press, 1990) p. 102.

76. In the act of visualization, the meditator is a bit like an artist described by Mikhail Bakhtin: "language-consciousness is no more than a constituent, a material that is totally governed by the purely artistic task." For Bakhtin, "the author's creative consciousness is not a language-consciousness (in the broadest sense of the word); language-consciousness is merely a passive constituent in creative activity—an immanently surmounted material." Bakhtin, op. cit., p. 194.

77. Roland Barthes, *S/Z*, tr. Richard Miller (New York: Hill and Wang, 1974), pp. 15-16. Discussed in Barbara Johnson, *The Critical Difference* (Baltimore: Johns Hopkins University Press, 1980), p. 5 ff. Texts not susceptible of such rewriting by a reader Barthes calls "readerly." For him a "readerly" text is a product consumed by the reader; by contrast, "writerly" texts emerge through a process in which the reader, too, becomes a producer.

78. Thanks to Janet Gyatso for stimulating this insight.

79. Obviously, not a category appropriate for most Western "readers." Although it cannot be developed here, this is another "difference that makes a difference" between modern and traditional forms of reading.

80. Barbara Johnson, 1980. *The Critical Difference,* p. 4 ff.

## CHAPTER 1. INTRODUCTION TO THE SIXTH BODHISATTVA GROUND

Peking edition, vol. 154, 27.4.6-27.4.8; Sarnath edition, 114.11-16; Dharamsala edition, 62.9-62.12; translation, pp. 149-150.

1. Such images are not altogether dispensed with, however; until the seventh ground, one must still enter direct perception by way of a meaning generality. See Jam-yang-shay-ba (*'jam dbyangs bzhad pa ngag dbang brtson grus*, 1648-1721), *Great Exposition of the Middle Way (dbu ma chen mo)* (Buxaduor: Gomang, 1967), 101b.1 ff. See also Klein, "Mental Concentration and the Unconditioned" in *Paths to Liberation*, ed. Buswell and Gimello (Honolulu: University of Hawaii Press, 1992).

2. *yul dang yul can gnyis gcig po red song bsam pa lta bu'i snang ba yod pa red.*

3. A clear semantic distinction between subject and object even during nondualistic experience of emptiness is an important feature of Tsong-kha-pa's soteriology. Compare with his teacher Ren-da-wa's commentary on Candrakīrti's text; Ren-da-wa *(red mda' ba gzhon nu blo gros,* 1349-1412) states that during direct cognition a yogi's mind becomes "of the nature of thusness." See Ren-da-wa (red mda' ba), *Explanation of [Candrakīrti's] "Entrance to the Middle Way, A Lamp Illuminating Reality" (dbu ma la 'jug pa'i rnaṃ bshad de kho na nyid gsal ba'i sgron ma)* (Delhi: Ngawang Topgay, 1974), pp. 77.6-78.1.

4. *Illumination (dbu ma dgongs pa rab gsal),* chapter 1, translated by Hopkins in *Compassion in Tibetan Buddhism* (Ithaca: Snow Lion, 1980), p. 133; Peking, 34.4-7).

5. Jeffrey Hopkins reports that, according to Geshe Gedün Lodrö, being "cast toward" the perceiving consciousness may be the meaning of inherent existence.

6. These are analogous to, but not synonymous with, special insight and calm abiding, respectively. The compass of the former pair is far broader than that of *vipaśyanā* and *śamatha*. If one were to maintain that calm abiding is stabilizing meditation and that special insight is analytical meditation, then, the texts say, [it would absurdly follow that] a Mahāyāna uninterrupted path of seeing and the uninterrupted path at the end of the continuum [of an ordinary being] would be posited in the same way [because one can have stabilization without insight]. See the *yun don gsal sa'i sgron me* by Panchen Sönam Drakba (*paṇ chen bsod nams grags pa*, 1478-1554), *Collected Works* (Mundgod, Karnataka State: Jayyed Press Ballimaran Delhi, 1983), vol. 3, p. 218.7. See also Lati Rinbochay, Denma Lochö Rinbochay, Leah Zahler, Jeffrey

Hopkins, *Meditative States in Tibetan Buddhism* (London: Wisdom publications, 1983) for a discussion of the scope of these terms.

7. Kensur used the term *dang tshung ldan*, here translated as "accompanies."

8. Among major Gelukba-affiliated commentators on the *Entrance,* Ren-da-wa is unique in taking up the issue of nonconceptual thought at this point in the discussion. See note 3 above.

9. The predispositions for the conception of inherent existence are not fully eradicated until Buddhahood; however, their ability to cause mistaken appearances is inoperative during direct cognitions of emptiness that precede Buddhahood.

10. The basic Gelukba definition of yogic direct perception is taken from Sautrāntika: "a nonconceptual *nonmistaken* exalted knower in the continuum of a Superior that is produced from a meditative stabilization which is a union of calm abiding and special insight and which has become its own uncommon empowering condition" (Pur-bu-jok, "Explanation of the Presentation of Objects and Object Possessors as Well as Awareness and Knowledge" in *Magical Key to the Path of Reasoning, Presentation of the Collected Topics Revealing the Meaning of the Treatises on Valid Cognition* [*yul yul can dang blo rig gi rnam par bshad pa* in *tshad ma'i gzhung don 'byed pa'i bsdus grva'i rnam bzhag rigs lam 'phrul gyi sde mig*); Buxa: n.p., 1965 4a.1-2]; translated and discussed in Elizabeth Napper, *Mind in Tibetan Buddhism* [Ithaca: Snow Lion, 1980), pp. 61-62 ff.]. However, in Prāsaṅgika, unlike in the lower tenet systems, direct perception must be correct only regarding its object of engagement *('jug yul, pravṛttiviṣaya);* however, all direct perception (except that of Buddhas and non-Buddhas' meditative equipoise on emptiness) is mistaken regarding its appearing object (*snang yul, pratibhāsa-viṣaya).*

11. Calm abiding is the lowest level of mental pacification that can support a direct cognition of emptiness. Calm abiding is also known as the approach to the first concentration. See Geshe Gedun Lodrö, *Walking Through Walls (*Ithaca: Snow Lion, 1992) p. 212, and *passim.* However, the path of seeing is most commonly gained in conjunction with the fourth concentration, not calm abiding. See Lati Rinbochay et. al., *Meditative States,* p. 197, and Panchen Sönam Drakba, "Concentrations and Formless Absorptions" section of his *General Meaning of (Maitreya's) "Ornament for Clear Realization" (phar phyin spyi don/shes rab kyi pha rol tu phyin pa'i man ngag gi bstan bcos mngon par rtogs pa'i rgyan 'grel pa dang bcas pa'i rnam bshad snying po rgyan gyi don legs par bshad pa yum don gsal bai sgron me)*; Buxaduor: Nang bstan shes rig 'dzin skyong slob gnyer khang, 1963), p. 162a.6.

12. See definition and discussion of direct perception as a complete engager in Napper, *Mind in Tibetan Buddhism*, pp. 141-42, and Klein, *Knowledge and Liberation* (Ithaca: Snow Lion, 1986), p. 92.

13. "To engage by the power of the object" is another way, according to Geshe Gedün Lodrö, of stating the meaning of inherent existence. (Reported by Jeffrey Hopkins.) This is, after all, another way of saying that the aspect of the object is cast toward the perceiving subject (see note 5 above).

14. *gang gis dngos gcig de bzhin nyid mthong ba/ de yis dngos kun de bzhin mngon du mthong.*

15. See Klein, *Knowledge and Liberation,* p. 100 ff., for a discussion of aspected direct perception. The implicit conclusion seems to be that the mind directly cognizing emptiness is not produced through the aspect of emptiness being cast toward it.

16. For a discussion of explicit and implicit objects of expression, see Klein, *Knowledge and Liberation*, chap. 4 and 7, especially pp. 146-47, 194-95, 209-10.

17. For an extensive discussion of the meditative absorptions of the form and formless realms based on Panchen Sönam Drakba's *General Meaning of (Maitreya's) "Ornament for Clear Realization" (phar phyin spyi don)*, see Lati Rinbochay, et. al., *Meditative States,* especially pp. 119 ff. This text, however, does not discuss absorptions of cessation *('gog snyoms, nirodhasamāpatti).* Panchen Sönam Drakba elaborates on these in the *Response to Queries/Response to Queries Regarding [Candrakīrti's] "Entrance to the Middle Way," A Lamp Fully Iluminating the Profound Meaning (rgal lan/dbu ma la 'jug ba'i brgal lan zab don yang gsal sgron me)* in *The Collected Works of Pan-chen bsod-nams-grags-pa* (Mundgod, Karnataka: Drebung Loseling Library Society, 1985), vol. 7, 256.3, where he discusses both common and uncommon absorptions of cessation. The main difference he makes between them is that the "common" variety, as asserted outside Prāsaṅgika, is a nonassociated compositional factor *(ldan min 'du byed, viprayuktasaṃskāra)*, which by definition is neither form nor consciousness, whereas the uncommon absorption of cessation is a consciousness.

Panchen Sönam Drakba defines a common absorption of cessation most briefly as "a meditative absorption of cessation included in the nine serial concentrations and absorptions" (*Response* 256.6). He offers a lengthier definition of it as "a nonassociated compositional factor included in the nine serial meditative absorptions, a category distinguished as free from desire for the peak of cyclic existence; it is attained in dependence on (1) the supramundane path which attains it and (2) a mind of the peak of cyclic existence" (*Response*, 256.5-6). See also Jetsun Cho-gyi-gyal-tsen, *Clarifying the Difficult Points of (Tsong-kha-pa's) "Illumination" (dgongs pa rab gsal dka' gnad gsal bar byed pa*; woodblock print, n.p; n.d), 89a.6-89b.1.

Panchen Sönam Drakba describes an uncommon absorption of cessation as "a Bodhisattva's wisdom of meditative equipoise which is conjoined with a surpassing practice of the perfection of wisdom" (*Response*, 255.2). This makes it clear that an uncommon absorption of cessation is a consciousness, whereas a common absorption of cessation, as indicated by the above definition, is included among nonassociated compositional factors and, thus, is not a consciousness. Panchen further observes (253.3) that an *absorption* of cessation need not be a *common* absorption of cessation because an absorption of cessation is not necessarily a nonassociated compositional factor. Similarly (253.5), an absorption of cessation is not necessarily a wisdom of meditative equipoise which is directly and evenly placed on reality *(mngon sum du mnyam par gzhag pa'i mnyam gzhag ye shes)* because uncommon absorptions are consciousnesses but common absorptions of cessation are not, since they are nonassociated compositional factors. Uncommon absorptions are also distinguished from common ones because they are not included in the nine meditative absorptions mentioned above (Panchen Sönam Drakba, *Response*, 253.2 ff.).

Also acceptable, and for Yeshey Tupden preferable, as a definition of an uncommon absorption of cessation: "a wisdom of meditative equipoise which is evenly and directly placed on reality and which is conjoined with a surpassing practice of the perfection of wisdom" (Panchen Sönam Drakba, *Response*, p. 256.3 ff.).

As Kensur Yeshey Tupden points out, only Prāsaṅgikas formulate the category of uncommon absorptions of cessation. Are the common absorptions of cessation accepted by Svātantrika and below synonymous with those accepted by Prāsaṅgikas? Panchen says no, because only Prāsaṅgika asserts the uncommon absorption of cessation *(Response,* 254.7 ff.). But although uncommon absorptions of cessation are indeed asserted only in Prāsaṅgika, Prāsaṅgikas also assert common absorptions of cessation.

Similarly, although the absorptions of cessation described in Svātantrika and the other non-Prāsaṅgika systems are common absorptions, a common absorption is not necessarily one of these because non-Prāsaṅgika systems do not include a meditative absorption of cessation which is included among the nine meditative absorptions *(snyoms 'jug, samāpatti)* abiding at the limit (*Response,* 255.5) of establishment from its own side.

Panchen Sönam Drakba, whose work on these topics is so important and whose texts form a major component of studies at Loseling College of Drebung Monastic University, was himself a Khenbo (abbot) of both Loseling and Ganden Shardzay. Prior to this, he studied at Sera, where his teacher was Dön-yo-bel-den (also known as *yongs 'dzin don yod dpal ldan*). In modern times it would be inconceivable that one man should be abbot at two different universities, especially ones other than his alma mater. At that period, however, there were not such rigid divisions among the monastic colleges as there are today. (These observations from Kensur Yeshey Tupden. )

18. Panchen Sönam Drakba makes this point by saying that a meditative equipoise on the first five grounds is not a common absorption because, being a consciousness, it is not a nonassociated compositional factor *(ldan min 'du byed, viprayuktasaṃskāra)*, and not an uncommon one because the Bodhisattva has not yet achieved the enhanced perfection of wisdom that necessarily provides the basis for this absorption. See Panchen, *Response*, 254.3-5. Panchen also makes this point in the *General Meaning of the Middle Way (dbu ma'i spyi don* New Delhi: Mādhyamika Text Series, vol. 6, Lhamkhar Yongs-'dzin Bstan-pa-Rgyal-mtshan, 1973), 127.4. Here, however, Panchen observes that this is a matter "to be analyzed."

19. See Donald S. Lopez, Jr., *A Study of Svātantrika* (Ithaca: Snow Lion, 1987), especially pp. 76-77, 116-17,149-51.

20. This term is often translated as "path of meditation" because the Tibetan word *sgom* often simply means "meditation." In the context of the five paths, however, the term more specifically signifies the cultivation or bringing to maturation of the direct cognition of emptiness initiated on the third path.

For a discussion of the peculiar tenet that "a true cessation is not necessarily an emptiness," see Guy Newland, *The Two Truths in the Mādhyamika Philosophy of the Ge-luk-ba Order of Tibetan Buddhism (*Ithaca: Snow Lion, 1992), p. 162 ff.

21. For a discussion of these and the other twenty-eight mental factors, see Napper, *Mind in Tibetan Buddhism,* 35-39, 99-101, and Hopkins, *Meditation on Emptiness* (London: Wisdom Publications, 1983), pp. 236-68.

22. Tsong-kha-pa and his two main disciples, Kay-drup *(mkhas sgrub)* and Gyaltsap *(rgyal tshab),* hold that true cessations are ultimates. See Newland, *Two Truths*, for discussion of the relationship between true cessatons and ultimates. Kay-drup maintains that Svātantrika and Cittamātra agree with this assertion, whereas Gyel-tsap and Tsong-kha-pa himself maintain that such is stated only in Prāsaṅgika.

23. Discussed, for example, in Lo-sang-da-yang (*blo bzang rta dbyangs*; also known as *blo bzang rta mgrin*, 1867-1937), *Presentation of Grounds and Paths in the Prāsaṅgika System* (*thal 'gyur pa'i sa lam*; n.p. n.d.), p. 69.

In Panchen Sönam Drakba's extensive discussion of this matter, the most compelling reason for considering a true cessation to be an ultimate truth appears to be that it is an ultimate which brings to an end the defilements to be abandoned by the power of an antidote. (See *Response*, 247.1 ff.). However, he makes clear (247.2) that in his own system a true cessation is not an actual nature *(chos nyid, dharmatā)* of phenomena. In his view, however, it is suitable to divide ultimates into (1) true cessations and (2) the emptiness which is a mere negation of true existence and which is not that [i.e., is not a true cessation]. The object negated by emptiness [true existence, and so forth] is not included among existents, whereas that negated by a cessation (i.e., an affliction) is.

Kensur Yeshey Tupden points out that, whereas Panchen states (*Response* 250.4) that among ultimate truths there are true cessations and the actual nature which is not a true cessation, the actual nature itself is not divided [into those which are and are not true cessations]. He also observes that some texts take true cessations to be ultimates because of their status as objects of the wisdom realizing emptiness on a path of liberation *(rnam 'grol lam, vimuktimārga).* See also Lati Rinbochay et. al., *Meditative States*, pp. 165-66.

24. On the basis of this, it later will be possible to proceed to the seventh ground. A common absorption of cessation has neither of these characteristics [of enabling one to pass to the sixth and then the seventh ground]. Upon developing the uncommon absorption, the Bodhisattva has a consciousness of the sixth ground and the special realizations that accompany it.

## CHAPTER 2. THREE FEATURES OF UNDERSTANDING

Peking edition, vol. 154, 27.4.8-28.4.8; Sarnath edition, 114.16-119.12; Dharamsala edition, 62.12-65.1; translation, pp. 150-155.

1. Panchen Sönam Drakba makes virtually the same points in giving reasons why the sixth ground is called *mngon du gyur pa* . See *Response* 252.5. See also translation, chapter 1, n. 6.

2. *mnyam gzhag nam mkha' lta bu.* Discussed in Tsong-kha-pa's *lam rim mnyam mgur bshugs* in *zhal 'don nyer mkho phyogs bsdebs bshugs* (Sarnath: Gelukba Students Welfare Committee, 1979), p. 72.

3. *rjes thob sgyu ma lta bu.* Ibid.

4. For further detail, see Hopkins, *Meditation on Emptiness*, p. 759, for different interpretations of the twelve-linked cycle; see ibid., p. 763 ff. and p. 705, for general discussion of the twelve links of dependent arising. See also Geshe Gedun Lodrö, *Walking Through Walls,* especially pp. 123-38.

5. For an interesting and thorough discussion of Indian Mādhyamika views on the relationship of analysis and insight, see Peter Fenner, "A Study of the Relationship between Analysis *(vicāra)* and Insight *(prañā)* Based on the Madhyamakāvatāra" in *Journal of Indian Philosophy* 12 (1984), 139-97.

6. *Illumination*, 134.16 (Sarnath edition).

7. In a work written prior to the *Illumination*, Tsong-kha-pa defined ultimate and conventional truths in connection with Nāgārjuna's *Treatise* as follows: "That which is explicitly *(dngos su)* found by a conventional valid cognizer is a conventional truth, and that explicitly found by a reasoning consciousness analyzing the ultimate is the meaning of ultimate truth" (*Explaining Eight Difficult Points in [Nāgārjuna's] "Treatise on the Middle Way"* [*rtsa ba shes rab kyi dka' gnas chen po brgyad kyi bshad pa*]; Sarnath: Pleasure of Elegant Sayings Press, 1970], pp. 11-12). See also ibid., pp. 9-13, as well as Tsong-kha-pa's discussion in *Illumination*, 464.10, where, drawing from sutra and Candrakīrti's *Clear Words* (*tshig gsal, prasannapadā)*, he describes ultimate truth as that toward which the nonconceptual mind turns.

8. This appears to be a theoretical model used for pedagogical purposes. It does not describe stages of the path, since direct realization of emptiness is not said to occur independently from realization of the emptiness of emptiness. Nonetheless, the distinction fits with Tsong-kha-pa's claim that on the sixth ground one gains a particularly strong understanding of emptiness as illusory which, by implication, did not accompany one's previous direct realizations of emptiness.

9. Three categories seem implicit in the discussion here: (1) a conventional consciousness, which includes all valid cognizers, (2) a consciousness analyzing conventionalities, which is every consciousness except those analyzing the ultimate, and (3) a non-analytical conventional consciousness. For an interesting discussion of a Nyingma presentation of valid cognition, which is both different from and explicitly critical of Geluk, see Kennard Lipman, "What is Buddhist Logic" in *Tibetan Buddhism: Reason and Revelation*, ed. Steven D. Goodman and Ronald M. Davidson (Albany: SUNY Press, 1992), pp. 25-44.

10. A consciousness analyzing conventionalities, for example, is a consciousness realizing the measure of existence of a conventional truth. A consciousness analyzing the ultimate is one that analyzes to find the final mode of existence of a conventional truth—namely, its emptiness of inherent existence.

11. To say that for phenomena to exist conventionally means that "they exist for a conventional consciousness" is key to Yeshey Tupden's way of discussing the relationship between a conventional consciousnesses and a valid cognizer. This is an unusual point to uphold.

12. Jayānanda, *Explanation of (Candrakīrti's) "Entrance to the Middle Way" (dbu ma la 'jug pa'i grel bshad)* P5271, vol. 99; quoted *Illumination* (Sarnath), 115.5 ff.

13. See Jangya's discussion of these, translated in Klein, *Knowing, Naming and Negation,* pp. 185-90.

14. Kensur Yeshey Tupden's main reference is probably to the *Collected Topics (bsdus grva)* that are the standard textbooks of monastic learning. The definition of impermanence as momentary *(skad gcig ma, kṣaṇika)* occurs in the second section of these texts, that on established bases *(gzhi grub).*

15. The discussion here is based on Panchen Sönam Drakba.

16. There appears to be some ambiguity on this point: in a subsequent discussion Yeshey Tupden suggested that thought could isolate the two but indicated they were not entirely different entities.

17. Quoted *Illumination*, (Sarnath), 116..

## CHAPTER 3. THE STUDENTS OF EMPTINESS

Peking edition, vol. 154, 28.4.8-29.2.2; Sarnath edition, 119.12.121.141; Dharamsala edition, 65.1-66.4 ; translation, pp. 155-157.

1. Robert Buswell observes that the *Abhidharmamahāvibhāṣā* [A-p'i-tan-mo ta p'i p'o-sha lun, Taisho 1546.28] takes tears and horripilation on hearing the teaching in general as a sign that virtuous roots of liberation (*mokśabhāgīyakuśalamūla)* have been planted (Buswell, "The Path to Perdition: Wholesome Roots and their Eradication" in *Paths to Liberation*, ed. Buswell and Gimello (Honolulu: University of Hawaii Press, 1992), p. 111.

2. *ten 'brel bstod pa'i tikka mkhas mang dgyes pa* by the Go-mang monk Losang-dam-chö (*blo bzang dam chos*; blockprint in possession of Kensur Yeshey Tupden, n.d.), 29.b.3. The Tibetan reads:

> *sgal te de la rang bzhin med na ci zhig yod ce na brjod par bya ste gang kun nas nyon mongs pa dang rnam par byang pa'i rgyud byas pa'i ngo bo rten cing 'brel par 'byung ba de yod lan zhes dang yang de nyid las rten cing 'brel par 'byung ba ni ji lta ba bzhin mthong ba na sgyu ma byas pa lta bur 'rgyur gyi mo gzham gyi bu lta bur ma yin no.*

Kensur Yeshey Tupden also referred in passing to the *shing rta'i blo* [by] Harchen-hla-tshon-mtho-mtho-nyi-ma. I have not succeeded in locating this text, though I understand from Kensur that it has been published by Drebung. For a listing of the classes of phenomena, see Hopkins, *Meditation on Emptiness* pp. 201-212.

3. Elsewhere, Tsong-kha-pa emphasizes that this error can result from imprecisely identifying what is negated *(dgag bya, pratiṣedhya)* by the theory of emptiness. For his

classic discussion of this topic, and subsequent Gelukba elaborations on it, see Elizabeth Napper, *Dependent-Arising and Emptiness* (London: Wisdom Publications, 1989), especially 44-49 and 87-88.

4. This refutation may derive in part from Ha-shang's emphasis on the non-necessity of thinking, which is associated with his idea that the practice of virtue will not lead to liberation (see also note 26 below). As an important source for this construction of Ha-shang's position, Kensur Yeshey Tupden points to the following passage from the final volume of Kamalaśīla's *Stages of Meditation (bsgom rim, bhāvanākrama)*

> *gang zhig ji yang mi sems par 'gyur ro. de ltar bas na ji yang mi bsam mo. sbyin pa la sogs pa sbyod pa ni skye bo blun po'i dbang du mdzad nas bstan pa. kho na yin no snyam du sems zhing de skad kyang smra ba de ni theg pa chen po mtha' dag spangs pa yin no. theg pa thams cad kyi rdza ba ni theg pa chen po yin pas de spang na theg pa thams cad spangs par 'gyur ro. 'di ltar ji yang mi bsam mi zhes smra ba ni yang dag par so sor rtog pa'i mthsan nyyid gyi shes rab spangs par 'gyur ro.* (P5312, vol. 102, 38.5.7 ff.)

Kensur Yeshey Tupden also reports that in a version of this text he saw published in Varanasi, not presently at his disposal, he saw a discussion of this issue using the example of a black or a red [*sic*] dog, either of whose bite would be equally problematic. The inference was that whether one does virtue or nonvirtue one cycles in cyclic existence. (Untaped private discussion, July 1987, Tibetan Buddhist Learning Center, Washington, New Jersey.)

5. This topic is classically elaborated in texts on calm abiding. See for example Jam-yang-shay-ba (*'jam dbyangs bzhad pa*, 1648-1721) *bsam gzugs chen mo/bsam gzugs gyi snyoms 'jug rnams kyi rnam par bzhag pa'i bstan bcos thub bstan mdzes rgyan lung dang rigs pa'i rgya mtsho skal bzang dga' byed (Great Exposition of the Concentrations and Formless Absorptions/Treatise on the Presentations of the Concentrations and Formless Absorptions, Adornment Beautifying the Subduer's Teaching, Ocean of Scripture and Delighting the Fortunate)*, folio printing in India; n.p., n.d. This and related texts are discussed in Lati Rinbochay, et. al., *Meditative States,* pp. 82-91.

For a similar discussion in the context of Theravāda see Buddhaghosa, *Path of Purification*, tr. Bhikku Ñyāṇamoli (Berkeley: Shambala, 1976), vol. 1, III.121 ff. For Buddhaghosa's related description of the locales suitable to each disposition, see III. 74-103. These sections represent one of the few places in exoteric Buddhist literature where specific consideration is given to issues of personality difference.

6. The problem of whether cyclic existence ever ends is discussed at length in Donald S. Lopez, Jr., "Paths Terminable and Interminable," in *Paths to Liberation*, ed. Robert Buswell, Jr. and Robert M. Gimello (Honolulu: University of Hawaii Press, 1992).

7. Complex permutations of this doctrine were crucial to the development of Mahāyāna in India, China, and Tibet, Tathāgathagarbha and Gotra theories being perhaps the most influential. See David Seyfort Ruegg, *La Théorie du Tathāgathagarbha et*

*du Gotra* (Paris: École Française d'Extrême-Orient, 1969). For an exemplary discussion of the relationship between the idea of the luminosity of thought and Tathāgathagarbha theory see Poussin, *Abhidharmakośa* 6, p. 299 n. (cited in Ruegg, *op. cit.*, p. 412). Probably the earliest Buddhist textual evidence of this idea occurs in the Pāli canon, *Anguttara-Nikāya* I.10. (Thanks to Robert Buswell on this point.) Unlike Mahāyāna, Theravāda never made extensive use of the concept.

As Ruegg notes (p. 31), it is impossible to say exactly when this doctrine first made its appearance in Mahāyāna texts. Ruegg also observes (p. 8) that Gelukba works on the topic are valuable because they represent a continuation of the Indian Mādhyamika tradition. For a study of the development of this theory in Tibet prior to Gelukba, see Ruegg, *La Traité sur le Tathāgatha garbha de Bu-ston* (Paris: École française d'Extrême Orient, A. Maissonneuve, 1969).

8. This is an ancient idea found in Indian tantra and elaborated upon by Tsong-kha-pa in his own major exposition of tantra, *The Great Exposition of Secret Mantra (ngags rim chen mo).* In an early section of that text, Tsong-kha-pa quotes Vīryavajra's *Commentary on the Saṃpuṭa Tantra* on its use of the metaphor "in the manner of insects" to indicate how a particular practice causes the affliction of desire to become consumed, like insects born from wood who then consume it (*Tantra in Tibet,* tr. Jeffrey Hopkins, London: George Allen & Unwin, 1977), p. 161.

9. P2010, vol. 46, 31.5.4. The same verse is quoted by Tsong-kha-pa in the opening section of *Illumination* (Peking edition, 34.4.7), tr. in Hopkins, *Compassion*, p. 133. (My translation adapted from his.)

10. Nāgārjuna's text only uses the term *gos* (garment), so that the actual material of this garment is not clearly identified, but it is almost certainly asbestos. Tsong-kha-pa in glossing this word uses the term *rdo gyas*. Kensur Yeshey Tupden thinks this should be *rdo rgyen*, though the two are very similar types of stone. Sarat Chandra Das defines *rdo rgyas* as "chalk" which according to Yeshey Tupden is not the substance intended here. In any case, *rdo rgyas* appears to be a subcategory of *rdo rgyen.*

11. P2010, vol. 46, 31.3.6. Quoted by Tsong-kha-pa, *Illuminations* (Sarnath edition) 113.10, p. 229. Translation here adapted from Hopkins tr., *Compassion*, p. 229.

12. See Hopkins, *Meditation on Emptiness*, pp. 118-20. See also Panchen Sönam Drakba, chap. 8 of *dbu ma spyi don* (*General Analysis of the Middle Way*) and chap. 2 of *dbu ma dgongs pa rab gsal*, tr. in *Compassion*, pp. 192 ff.

13. Yeshey Tupden here cited Dharmakīrti, *Commentary on Dignāga's "Compendium on Valid Cognition" (rnam 'grel pramāṇavārttikakārikā)*, chapter 2 (P5709, vol. 130, 87.1.6): *sems gyi rang bzhin 'od gsal ba 'dri ma rnams ni glo bur ba* ["Regarding the clear light which is the mind's nature, [its] stains are adventitious"].

14. This is stated in the *rgyud bla ma (uttaratantra)* by Asaṅga, quoted in *Response* by Panchen Sönam Drakba, in Pan-chen Sungbum, vol. 7 (Mundgod: Karnataka, printed at Jayyed Press, Ballimaran, Delhi, 1985, 258.1. (Panchen Sönam Drakba Literature Series, vol. 23) by Drebung Loseling Library Society). The Tibetan

reads: *rdzogs sangs sku ni 'phro phyir dang/de bzhin nyid dbyer med phyir dang. rigs yod phyir na lus can kun/rtag tu sang rgyas snying po can.*

15. This fundamental mind is not a topic of the Perfection Vehicle but is discussed in many tantric texts, especially, in Gelukba, in the context of the Stages of Completion *(rdzogs rim)*. For discussion of this subtle mind, see *Death, the Intermediate State and Rebirth* by Yang-chen-ga-way-lo-drö *(dbyangs-can-dga'-ba'i-blo-gros)*, tr. by Jeffrey Hopkins and Lati Rinbochay (Ithaca: Snow Lion, 1986); see also Daniel Cozort, *Highest Yoga Tantra* (Ithaca: Snow Lion, 1986) and Geshe Kelsang Gyatso, *Clear Light of Bliss* (London: Wisdom Publications, 1982).

16. See discussion in the special insight section of the middling of Tsong-kha-pa's *lam rim (lhag mthong 'bring)*, translated by Robert Thurman as "The Middle Transcendent Insight."

17. Daishun Ueyama suggests that the Ch'an school which contended with Indian Buddhism during this period in Tibet was unique and did not represent Northern or Southern Ch'an, nor the Pao-t'ang school. "The Study of Tibetan Ch'an Manuscripts Recovered from Tun-huang: A Review of the Field and Its Prospects," in *Early Ch'an in China and Tibet*, ed. Whalen Lai and Lewis Lancaster (Berkeley: Berkeley Buddhist Studies Series, no. 5), p. 338. Hironobu Obata concludes that this Ch'an was only superficially like the Northern Ch'an, and doctrinally affiliated with Pao t'ang while also borrowing from Shen-hui and the Dharma school. No independent Chinese writings authored by Ha-shang Mahāyāna have been located (Ueyama, "Study of Tibetan Ch'an Manuscripts," p. 330). At the same time, quotations from Ha-shang and other writings associated with Tun-huang hint of early connections between Ch'an and Tibetan Dzogchen *(rdzogs chen)*. See, for example, Jeffrey Broughton, "Early Ch'an Schools in Tibet" in *Studies in Ch'an and Hua-yen*, Robert M. Gimello and Peter N. Gregory, eds. (Honolulu: Kuroda Institute, University of Hawaii, 1983) and Herbert V. Guenther, "Meditation Trends in Early Tibet," in *Early Ch'an in China and Tibet*, and Namkhai Norbu, *Dzog Chen and Zen* ed. by Kennard Lipman (Oakland, CA: Zhang Zhung Editions, 1984).

It is not clear whether Ha-shang himself maintained that "things are neither existent nor nonexistent but something in between," but Gelukbas perceive this as a view that arose in the wake of his teachings and influence. Ha-shang speaks also of the importance of "not thinking" *(myi sems)*, or the practitioner's discovery that the mind has self-nature. (See Luis O. Gomez, "The Direct and Gradual Approaches of Zen Master Mahāyāna: Fragments of the Teachings of Mo-Ho-Yen," in *Studies in Ch'an and Hua'yen*, pp. 75-76). As Gomez and others have shown, Ha-shang's discussion was intended to address the broader concerns of sudden versus gradual technique and enlightenment.

The ninth-century Nub-chen-sang-gyey-ye-shey *(gnubs chen sangs rgyas ye shes)* used the Tibetan and Chinese terms for "sudden" and "gradual" (Guenther, "Meditation Trends in Early Tibet," p. 352), but by the time of Tsong-kha-pa and his students, this dichotomy was no longer a concern to Gelukba scholars; their discussion of the subject is made primarily in terms of conceptual thought *(rnam tog, kalpanā)* and direct perception *(mngon sum, pratyakṣa)*. These categories are related to ontological descriptions of the object. This is also the case with Kensur Yeshey Tupden's discussion at this point, which associates Ha-shang's followers with a view that products do not exist. More historical analysis is needed to substantiate the foregoing hypothesis. At the very least, however, it is notable that Kensur Yeshey Tupden, unlike some Gelukba scholarship, here does not fault "Ha-shang's followers" for a kind of quietism. This latter is probably an unwarranted criticism in any case: "If one fails to have this awareness of the arising of thoughts, or if the awareness is incorrect, one will . . . cultivate meditation in vain" (Gomez, "Direct and Gradual Approaches," p. 109). Nevertheless, this is a fault which Gelukba commentators have implied with respect to those who, like the Ha-shang of their interpretation, overestimate what is negated by the theory of emptiness. See, for example, *The Four Interwoven Annotations on (Tsong-kha-pa's) "Great Exposition of the Stages of the Path,"* in Napper, *Depending-Arising and Emptiness* (London: Wisdom Publications, 1989), pp. 237 and 669). This is a charge that, throughout Buddhist history, has often been levied against contemplatives outside one's own circle: Ha-shang himself accuses non-Buddhists of adhering to a view of a real self or of finding delight in nothingness (Gomez, "Direct and Gradual Approaches," p. 110). However, Kensur Yeshey Tupden is not here questioning the style of meditation, which is the context in which Ha-shang's remarks are primarily framed, but focuses on the faulty understanding of objects which seems to have developed from Ha-shang's own position.

In general, in Tibet, Ha-shang's view was described as "nothing whatever exists" *(ji yang med pa*; private conversation, Lama Tharchin, Aptos, CA, June 1987.) Indeed, in describing proper meditation Ha-shang notes that one "does not examine [to see] whether [thought] has arisen or not, whether they exist or not, whether they are good or bad . . . he does not examine any dharma [phenomenon—ed.] whatsoever" (Gomez, "Direct and Gradual Approaches," p. 108).

One issue pertaining to the differences in question here—an elaboration of which could could easily encompass detailed analyses of Gelukba Prāsaṅgika, Nyingma Dzogchen, and early Ch'an—may be the Gelukba emphasis on knowing not just the nature of the mind but the nature of objects which are themselves not mind. Thus, for them, "turning the light of mind on the mind" (Ha-shang, citing *The Vimalakīrti Sutra*, quoted by Gomez in "Direct and Gradual Approaches," p. 93) would by definition be an incomplete gesture.

18. This last sentence from I.590 winter series.

19. Kensur Yeshey Tupden further observes, "This discussion probably comes from Ha-shang's own works, but I have not seen a book of Ha-shang's; probably they no longer exist in Tibet. [In addition to Kamalaśīla,] books such as [Tsong-kha-pa's] works on the Stages of the Path (*lam rim)* refer to him, and our discussion is based on those texts and on material in those texts, and the *Illumination of the Thought* which contain [often oblique] references to Ha-shang. There are also many references to Ha-shang in Tsong-kha-pa's the *Essence of the Good Explanation (legs shad snying po)* and in Candrakīrti's *Clear Words,* and his commentary to *Entrance to the Middle Way."*

20. Modern scholarship questions the nature of the interaction between Ha-shang and Kamalaśīla, if any. L. O. Gomez' suggestion that their interaction be considered part

of the "Tibetan controversies of the eighth century" is well taken. (Gomez, "Direct and Gradual Approaches," p. 147 n. 9.) Gomez further elaborates his views on the nature of this "controversy," Ibid., pp. 69 ff., and in the opening segment of "Indian Materials on the Doctrine of Sudden Enlightenment," in *Early Ch'an in China and Tibet*, pp. 393 ff.

*The New Red Annals (deb t'er dmar po gsar ma)* by Panchen Sönam Drakba describes Kamalaśīla's system as *tsan min pa* and *ton min pa*, which Panchen glosses in Tibetan as "gradual" and "that of eighteen names" *(bcu brgyad pa'i ming)*, signifying "sudden." (Text reproduced and translated as *Deb T'er dmar po gsar ma: Tibetan Chronicles* by Giuseppe Tucci, Serie Orientale Roma (Roma: Istituto Italiano Per Il Medio Ed Estremo Oriente, 1971), pp. 27.6-27a.1 and p. 155).

21. This is one of the topics of *The Middling Path of Reasoning (rigs lam 'bring)*, the middle section of the "Collected Topics" (*bsdus grva*) texts which form the early part of the monastic curriculum. The oldest, largest, and most famous of the genre is the *Rva stod bsdus grva* attributed to Ra-dö *(rva stod)* and compiled by Jam-yang-chok-hla-ö-ser (*'jam dbyangs phyogs lha 'od zer*, about fifteenth century). The *Ra-dö* (Dharamsala, India: Damchoe Sangpo, Library of Tibetan Works and Archives, 1980), p. 92.4, defines "contradictory" *('gal ba)* as "a state of being mutually incompatible" *(phan tshun mi mthun par gnas pa)*; "explicit contradictories" are a sub-set of this category and defined by Ra-dö (92.6-93.1) as "a state of being explicitly mutually incompatible . . . like permanent and impermanent." See Jam-yang-chok-hla-ö-ser, *Collected Topics of Ra-dö* (*rva stod bsdus grva*; Dharamsala: India, Dhamchoe Sangpo, Library of Tibetan Works and Archives, printed at Jayyed Press, Ballimaran, Delhi, 1980); the discussion of contradictories and connectives *('gal 'brel)* begins p. 78.5.

22. There are statements attributable to Ha-shang which support this view and others which contest it. See for example Gomez, "Direct and Gradual Approaches," p. 89, quoting Ha-shang thus: "The state of saṁsāra is merely the result of deluded thoughts *(myi-bden-pa'i 'du-ses)*. Enlightenment is achieved by not grasping at these thoughts and not dwelling on them . . . by not bringing them to the mind . . . by not inspecting the mind, but by merely being aware *(tshor ba, vedanā)* of all thoughts as they arise." See also Pelliot 4646, 135a.2-4 (Gomez, p. 126). (Pelliot Tibetan numbers refer to the 2216 Tibetan manuscripts collected at Tun-huang by Paul Pelliot and catalogued in Marcelle Lalou, *Inventaire des manuscrits tibétains de Touenhouang conservés à la Bibliothèque Nationale* [Paris: Bibliothèque Nationale, 1939, 1950, 1950, and 1961].) Elsewhere Ha-shang appears less sanguine about the possibilities of "knowing," although as far as I can determine he does not actually contradict his injunction to awareness: "[. . . meditators] do not reflect on or examine anything, they do not practice anything, and do not apprehend anything. [This] immediate access is equal to the tenth state [*sa, bhūmi*]." (Gomez, "Direct and Gradual Approaches," p. 146 n. 5).

Similarly, Panchen Sönam Drakba describes Ha-shang as teaching that Buddhahood means abiding within an inactivity in which there is no need for virtuous deeds of body or speech (Tucci, *op cit.*, 26a.6-27.1).

23. Quoted by Tsong-kha-pa, *Illumination*, 177.8. This line also appears at the beginning of the ninth chapter of Śāntideva's *Engaging in the Bodhisattva Deeds.* (IX. 2c) [Yeshey Tupden referred also to *Illumination*, 176.1-8, which is a quote from

Śāntideva's *Compendium of Learning (śiksāsamuccaya, bslab btus)*; see also ibid., p. 177.15: *don dam pa kang yin pa de ni brjod du med pa ste shes par bya ba ma yin pa rnam par shes ba bya ba ma yin ma bsten pa).*] Yeshey Tupden notes that these two have the same meaning.

24. For a discussion of Gelukba delineations of the functions unique to thought and direct perception, respectively, see Klein, *Knowledge and Liberation,* chap. 2 and 3.

25. Judging from the fragments available to us (c.f. Gomez), Ha-shang, in keeping with his emphasis on nonduality, has little soteriological use for conceptualization. Though he does cede it some legitimacy, he does so in the context of "gradual" practice. In a passage highly reminiscent of the *Platform Sūtra* number 17 (tr. Yampolsky 1967, p. 137), Ha-shang is quoted as follows: "As long as one [is not capable] of practicing meditation, one has recourse to the perfection of morality, the four immeasurable states of mind, and other such practices." (See Gomez, "Direct and Gradual Approaches," p. 96.) However, in his *Short Treatise on the Six and the Ten Perfections in Nonconceptual Practice* it is clear that the actual perfections are not engaged except in the nonconceptual state. (Gomez, "Direct and Gradual Approaches," p. 121 ff.)

Somewhat parallel to this, Tsong-kha-pa, and Gelukba thought generally, emphasize that the "surpassing" form of the perfections is achieved only after the path of seeing—that is, only after and in conjunction with a nondualistic cognition of emptiness.

26. This and subsequent paragraphs on Ha-shang from discussions with Yeshey Tupden summer 1985, Tibetan Buddhist Learning Center.

27. For a discussion of "nonabiding" and other types of Mādhyamika, see Hopkins, *Meditation on Emptiness*, pp. 435-36, 567-67, n. 504 pp. 857-58. The Prāsaṅgika system was not very strong in Tibet during Ha-shang's time, and Yeshey Tupden observes that Kamalaśīla, renowned as a Svātantrika, no doubt used this perspective, rather than Prāsaṅgika, to defeat Ha-shang.

Yeshey Tupden here cited Bu-dön (*bu ston rin chen grub*, 1290-1364) as stating that in India there was no difference between Svātantrikas and Prāsaṅgikas and that this was a distinction which arose later, in Tibet. The *Word Commentary on the "Wisdom" Chapter, "The Norbu Ketaka" (she rab le'ui tshig don go sla bar rnam par bshad pa nor bu ke da ka)* by Mipham (*mi pham rnam rgyal*, [Varanasi: Tarthang Tulku, Sanskrit University, 1966)], p. 11.9) maintains that even if there were no difference in their final thought [and Mipham contends that Bhāvaviveka was actually a Prāsaṅgika who taught Svātantrika], their textual explanations differed. (In his discussion of Śāntideva at the University of Virginia, 1982, Yeshey Tupden noted that there was in any case a debate over Bhāvaviveka's contention that Buddhapālita was incorrect in not applying the epithet "ultimate" to the object of negation.)

28. I have yet to locate a statement attributable to Ha-shang which states the matter this precisely. However, Kensur Yeshey Thupden's remarks here can probably be understood as representing a Gelukba interpretation of remarks we can attribute to Ha-shang—e.g., his statement in the *Cheng-li-chueh* (a text that does not appear in Tibetan except through paraphrase and quotation, reporting that Ha-shang won the Samye

"debate"; (see Ueyama, p. 341). "As long as one [is not capable of practicing meditation, one has recourse to the perfection of morality . . ." (Gomez, "Direct and Gradual Approaches," p. 96). This leads almost to the "fatal slip" (Gomez, p. 98) of denying the necessity of method altogther, which Ha-shang subsequently qualifies.

For an overview of recent scholarship on the developments stemming from the presence of Mo-ho-yen and other Ch'an masters in Tibet, as revealed in Tibetan manuscripts from Tun-huang, see Daishun Ueyama, "The Study of Tibetan Ch'an Manuscripts Recovered from Tun-huang: A Review of the Field and Its Prospects," in *Early Ch'an in China and Tibet*, pp. 327-49. For antinomian charges against Ha-shang and criticism of him by Shen-hsiu, see Gomez, "Purifying Gold: The Metaphor of Effort and Intuition in Buddhist Thought and Practice," in *Sudden and Gradual Approaches to Enlightenment in Chinese Thought*, ed, Peter N. Gregory (Honolulu: Kuroda Institute, University of Hawaii Press, 1987).

29. Kensur Yeshey Tupden candidly notes: "Our monastic curriculum does not emphasize Kamalaśīla's texts, so I have not worked much with them. Each of our colleges studies Tsong-kha-pa's writings and its own textbooks in connection with these."

Luis Gomez gives an excerpt from Bu-dön' s *(bu ston)* summary of Ha-shang's views which support Yeshey Thupden's analysis here:

> Everything is constructed by the conceptual mind. Through the power of [our idea of] the pleasant and the unpleasant, there is karma, good and bad. One experiences its fruit in the heavens and the evil destinies and one wanders in transmigration. Whoever does not reflect, whoever does not fix the mind on anything, will be completely liberated from transmigration. Therefore do not reflect on anything. As to the practice of the ten [good] dharmas—generosity and the rest—it has been preached for those persons who are of inconstant virtue, weak minds, and dull faculties. For those who already have purified their minds and have acute faculties, sin and virtue alike veil [the mind], just as clouds whether they are white or dark, veil the sun. Consequently, do not reflect on or examine anything, do not practice anything, and do not apprehend anything. [This] immediate access is equal to the tenth state [*sa, bhūmi*]. (Gomez, "Gradual Approaches," p. 146 n.5).

This is obviously a good source for those who feel Ha-shang thinks the meditator's mind does not realize anything. Compare with the *Platform Sūtra*'s discussion of no-thought (Yampolsky, pp. 137ff.), and its claim that "the mind has nothing to do with thinking" (p. 166).

Bu-dön (p. 70) explains Ha-shang's first thesis thus: "As long as one carries out good or evil acts, one is no free from transmigration as [these acts] lead to heaven or to hell [respectively]. It is like clouds which cover the empty sky irrespective of their being white or black" (Gomez, "Gradual Approaches" p. 70). Gomez here draws from *sba bzed,* R. A. Stein, *Une chronique ancienne de bSam-yas*: *sBa bzed* (Paris: n.p., 1961), pp. 57.16-58.7).

30. Sumba Khenpo's *History of Tibet* cites an instance of Ha-shang's apparently rejecting the viability of virtuous and nonvirtuous thought. This discussion appears in the context of the debate about sudden *(gcig car)* and gradual *(rim gyis pa)* styles of meditation:

> *Ha shang na re gzhi la yod pa sna ma yin pas 'dr'am lan gtab cas dris pa la Kamalaśīla las de nyid kyi dgongs pa ltar zhags gsungs shig cas smras pas ha shang na re las dge mi dge spyod pa'i bya byed kyis mtho ris dang ngan song du 'gro shing 'khor ba las mi thar pas sangs rgyas mthong ba la sgrib pa yin te dper na sprin dkar nag gang gis kyang nyi zla dang rnam mkha' sgrib pa zhin no.*

See "Sumpakhampo's History of Tibet" (*sumbha mkhan po dpal 'byor gyi gsung rgya gar 'phags yul rgya nag chen po gangs can bod yul sogs yul rnam su dam chas rin chen byung tshul dpag bsam lcon bzang las gang can bod kyi yul du dam chos dang tshul gyi dpe deb)* [Sarnath, Varanasi, U.P.: Mongolian Lama Guru Deva, Pleasure of Elegant Sayings Press, 1985]), p. 41.17 ff.

31. See Tsong-kha-pa, *Illumination*, Sarnath edition, p. 304.5 ff. in the context of a discussion of the two truths.

## CHAPTER 4. HOW GOOD QUALITIES ARISE WHEN EMPTINESS IS EXPLAINED

Peking edition, vol. 154, 29.2.2-29.4.6, Sarnath edition, 121.14-124.1; Dharamsala edition, 66.5-67.11; translation, pp. 157-159.

1. Gelukba finds this possible only through Highest Yoga Tantra *(rnal 'byor bla med, anuttarayogatantra)*, which is outside the scope of both Tsong-kha-pa's text and Kensur Yeshey Tupden's exposition.

2. Sāntideva, *Engaging in the Bodhisattva Deeds* (*byang chub sems dpa'i dpyod pa la 'jug pa,* P5272, vol. 99; Sarnath edition, p. 99); see also Mipham, *Word Commentary on the "Wisdom" Chapter, "The Norbu Ketaka" (shes rab le'ui tshig don go sla bar rnam par bshad pa nor bu ke da ka),* 2.20 ff., arguing against unidentified proponents of the position that only the fifth perfection, and not all five, was "taught for the sake of wisdom."

3. It would be interesting to compare the structure of this problematic with current work in chaos theory, where "sensitive dependence on initial conditions" means, in part, that causal sequences are extraordinarily complex and may preclude predictability. For a modern scientific exploration of this principle, see James Gleick, *Chaos* (New York: Viking, 1987) p. 8 and *passim.*

4. For a stimulating contemporary discussion of issues of identity implicit here, see Derek Parfit, *Reasons and Persons* (Oxford: Clarendon Press, 1984), especially pp. 165-86. For the specific relevance of Parfit's book to issues in Buddhist philosophy, see Matthew Kapstein, "Collins, Parfit, and the Problem of Personal Identity in Two Philosophical Traditions—a Review of *Selfless Persons,*" in *Philosophy East and West* 36: 3 (July 1986), 289-98.

5. For a classic contemporary Tibetan discussion of karmic fruition see Geshey Ngawang Dhargyey, *Tibetan Tradition of Mental Development* (Dharamsala: Library of Tibetan Works and Archives, 1974), pp. 75-104.

6. The remainder of this paragraph and the next from discussion, summer 1985, Tibetan Buddhist Learning Center.

7. This is discussed in the third chapter of the *Illumination.* The effects are said to be especially disastrous if a Bodhisattva becomes angry at another Bodhisattva. However, Tsong-kha-pa also observes, commenting on *Entrance* III. 33, that "When anger develops, it destroys roots of virtue even if neither the object nor subject are Bodhisattvas" (see also Hopkins, *Compassion*, p. 213). As to the type of effect experienced by the Bodhisattva ". . . if, for example, one who has the capacity to pass quickly from a Bodhisattva's great path of accumulation to a path of preparation becomes angry at another [Bodhisattva] . . . he cannot pass to the path of preparation for as many aeons as the number of instants of anger and must train in the path from the beginning" (tr. Hopkins, *Compassion*, p. 212).

8. Robert Buswell, "The Path to Perdition: Wholesome Roots and Their Eradication," in *Paths to Liberation*, p. 108 and pp. 123 ff., documents the suggestion that, from its earliest period, Buddhism has found the act of giving to encompass all the important characteristics of Buddhist ethics.

9. See *The Precious Garland (rin che'i phreng ba, ratnāvalī)*, tr. Hopkins, New York: Harper & Row, 1975), I.18, "A bad colour comes through anger." For general discussion of the cause and effect of actions, see *Garland,* I.14-23.

10. Discussed by Mipham in *Word Commentary on the "Wisdom" Chapter, "The Norbu Ketaka,"* I.18-2.2. Though it is not part of the Gelukba curriculum, Kensur Yeshey Tupden chose to read and lecture on this text in a seminar on Śāntideva's *Engaging in the Bodhisattva Deeds* given at the University of Virginia, spring 1979.

11. For discussion of these, and the three types of effort made in cultivating calm abiding, see Lati Rinbochay et al., *Meditative States* pp. 52-72.

12. Yeshey Tupden here echoes Nāgārjuna's *Essay on the Mind of Enlightenment (byang chub sems 'grel, bodhicittavivarana)* verse 67 (P2665 and P2666, vol. 61). In this he follows Tsong-kha-pa, who quotes this passage (*Illumination*, p. 123.4 ff., Sarnath edition).

13. See chap. 3, n. 4.

14. See Ra-dö (*rva stod bsdus grva*, by Jam-yang-chok-hla-ö-ser), p. 8.4; see also Pur-bu-jok (phur bu lcog byams pa rgya mtsho, 1825-1901), *Collected Topics* (*bsdus grva*; Buxa: n.d., 1965), p. 8.5 ff.

15. See Tāranātha (b. 1575) *History of Buddhism in India*, tr. Obermiller (Simla: Indian Institute of Advanced Study, 1970 [mainly follows Potala edition published 1946]), p. 187: "The number of disciples of Buddhapālita was not very large while ācārya Bhāvya [Bhāvaviveka] had . . . thousands of monks [and thus] his views were more extensively spread."

16. This was not for want of reputation. Tāranātha observes that Śāntideva and Candragomin were "famed among the learned" as "the two wonderful teachers" *(History*

*of Buddhism,* p. 18). Nonetheless, as is well known, while at Nālanda Śāntideva did not reveal himself as a scholar until he recited the *Bodhisattvacaryāvatāra*, after which he disappeared from the area, subsequently founding a forest monastery with five hundred monks (Tāranātha, *History,* pp. 217-19).

17. These are elaborated in Hopkins, *Meditation on Emptiness,* pp. 292-96. See also Jang-gya (*lcang skya rol ba'i rdo rje,* 1717-86), *Presentation of Tenets (grub pa'i mtha'i rnam bzhag*; Varanasi: Pleasure of Elegant Sayings Press, 1970), 126.10-128.4 (tr. in Klein, *Knowing, Naming, and Negation*).

18. Technically, this does not occur until calm abiding *(zhi gnas, śamatha)* is accomplished. At the latest this occurs at the onset of the path of accumulation. Conceptual understanding is cultivated until the path of seeing.

19. Kensur notes: The thought apprehending a pot can probably be called a valid cognizer, though it is usually most likely a correct assumption (*yid spyod, *manaḥ pārikṣā).*

20. This could be considered an ontologically framed parallel to Lacan and to recent literary criticism's emphasis on paying attention to the "transference"—that is, the interaction between analyst and analysand, or text and reader. See, for example, Jane Gallop, *Reading Lacan* (Ithaca: Cornell University Press, 1985), pp. 25-30.

21. Summer 1985 D.037

22. For Gelukba use of this category, see Klein, *Knowledge and Liberation*, chap. 7.

23. Thus, as Panchen Sönam Drakba points out, the thought apprehending sound as impermanent is not a *mgnon sum gyi tshad ma*—not a valid direct cognizer. See *General Meaning of the Middle Way (dbu ma'i spyi don)* in the *Collected Works of Pan-chen Sö-nam-drak-ba* (Mundgod, Karnataka, Drebung Loseling Library Society 1985) vol. 7, 160.7 ff. Panchen also observes here that thought does not realize impermanent sound manifestly (161.2).

24. Untaped discussion, summer 1987. Panchen defines a valid cognizer of the direct as: "a consciousness which either is a determinative undeceived knower that depends on the path of correct reasoning which is its own foundation or is undeceived with respect to its own main object due to such manifesting of it (*Collected Works*, vol. 7, 161.6).

25. See Panchen Sönam Drakba, *Response*, *Collected Works*, vol. 7, 160.5.ff. See also his *General Meaning of the Middle Way (dbu ma mtha' dpyod)*, 307.7 ff.

26. Developing this in an ancillary discussion, Yeshey Tupden observed: In Prāsaṅgika, as in Svātantrika [and the non-Mādhyamika systems], mental direct perception is a valid cognition. However, the manner of positing mental direct perception is not the same here as in the lower systems. [See Nagatomi: 1980, "Mānasa-pratyakṣa: A Conundrum in the Buddhist Pramāṇa System."] Feelings accompany the mental con-

sciousness, and we can talk about the experience *(myong ba)* and realization *(rtogs pa)* of the sense and mental consciousnesses, and of feelings itself.

The feelings associated with the mental consciousness realize and experience happiness, suffering, and so forth. What happiness do they realize and experience? That which is the feeling associated with the sense consciousness. This realization and experience are simultaneous for the mental consciousness.

The eye sense consciousness both experiences and realizes form, but the experience of the eye consciousness and the experience of feelings are different. The eye consciousness neither experiences nor realizes the feeling of happiness. Happiness, and so forth, are experienced by the feeling which is associated with the eye consciousness. However, with respect to the eye consciousness we can speak of that which knows feelings and that which does not. The eye experiences its own feeling—as when seeing a pleasant object—but does not realize it. Feeling itself experiences happiness, and so forth, but does not realize these. We can take a different type of example: if some object comes in contact with the eye, the mind realizes and experiences it; the eye itself experiences but does not realize it.

In terms of the sense consciousness, then, that which is realized and that which is experienced are different. We do not say that the eye sense, which itself is subtle form, either realizes or experiences [only the eye consciousness can do this]. The feelings associated with the sense consciousnesses experience pleasure, and so forth, but do not realize them.

27. This paragraph from a summer 1987 untaped conversation.

28. Tape VII.068.

29. Tape blurred at this point.

30. Indeed, at V. 138, this segment was difficult to decipher completely because of blurred sound on the tape.

31. Thus, an ordinary person's valid cognition is confirmed, not undermined, by a Superior's understanding of emptiness and by a Buddha's simultaneous direct cognition of emptiness and conventional objects. The complementarity of dependently arisen, ordinary agents and objects, and the emptiness which qualifies them, grounds the compatability of virtuous activity and wisdom, making it possible for an understanding of, or even an interest in, emptiness to become a moral force in one's own life.

## CHAPTER 5. EXHORTATION TO THE STUDENTS OF EMPTINESS

Peking edition, vol. 154, 29.4.6-30.2.8; Sarnath edition, 124.14-127.2; Dharamsala edition, 67.11-69.1; translation, pp. 160-162.

1. *chos nyid stong pa nyid kyi don la skye ba med pa'i bzod pa thob pa red.*

2. Yeshey Tupden observes that in the Yogācāra-Svātantrika system, unlike Prāsaṅgika, the obstructions to liberation and omniscience are overcome gradually over

the ten grounds and then abandoned simultaneously on the final ground, making Arhatship and Buddhahood simultaneous. Thus, Yogācāra-Svātantrikas maintain that in attaining the eighth ground one does *not* abandon the obstructions to liberation and is not an Arhat. In their view, one begins to overcome the artificial form of the obstructions to liberation and omniscience on the first-ground path of seeing, and on the first-ground path of meditation one begins to abandon the innate obstructions to liberation and omniscience. The category of a first-ground path of meditation does not exist in Prāsaṅgika or Sautrāntika-Svātantrika, and even in the context of Yogācāra-Svātantrika appears to be a special feature of Loseling's discussion of the topic of Grounds and Paths.

3. See Tsong-kha-pa, *Illumination*, 195.8-196.6, which comprises the concluding section of Tsong-kha-pa's discussion of *Entrance* VI.28.

4. These texts, usually written from the viewpoint of Svātantrika, define and debate the particular characteristics of the five paths and ten grounds. See, for example, Gön-chok-jig-may-wang-bo [dkon-mchog-'jigs-med-dbang-po, known also as the second Jam-yang-shay-ba, 1728-91], *Presentation of the Grounds and Paths, Beautiful Ornament of the Three Vehicles, (sa lam gyi rnam bzhag theg gsum mdzes rgyan)*; New Delhi: Ngawang Gelek Demo, *The Collected Works of dkon-mchog-'jigs-med-dbaṅ-po*, 1972, vol. 7. There are also important *sa lam* texts by Kay-drup, Gyal-tsap, and Panchen Sönam Drakba.

5. *rtse mo thob pa rtsa mi chad.*

6. *bzod thob ngan song yong mi 'gro.*

7. This sentence from an untaped discussion with Yeshey Tupden, summer 1987, Tibetan Buddhist Learning Center.

8. On the eighth ground Bodhisattvas are said to become so fond of the uncommon absorption of cessation on emptiness that was initially gained on the sixth ground and familiarized with over the seventh ground, that a Buddha must rouse them from it. Jam-yang-shay-ba summarizes the progression from sixth to eighth ground thus:

> On the sixth ground one attains an uncommon absorption of cessation; on the seventh, one attains power over the absorption of cessation; on the eighth ground one enters absorption in the sense of manifesting it, and the Conquerors raise one from cessation. *(dbu ma chen mo*, 97b.1-3.)

For a discussion of this term in Gelukba as descriptive of a particular form of wisdom consciousness, see Klein, "Mental Concentration and the Unconditioned," in *Paths to Liberation.*

9. In the Gelukba sūtra system, such reflection is crucial for developing the concentrations and formless absorptions. The second of the mental contemplations cultivated between each level of concentration in order to reach the next is known as the "mental contemplation which is a knowledge of the individual character" (*mtshan nyid so sor rig pa'i yid byed, lakṣaṇapratisaṃvedīmanaskāra*). This is, in general, defined as a mind that views one's own realm as coarse and the higher realm, toward which the

practitioner is headed, as peaceful. For discussion of this and the other mental contemplations associated with concentration, see Lati Rinbochay, et. al., *Meditative States.*

## CHAPTER 6. THE SAMENESS OF THINGS: DEPENDENT ARISING AND REALITY

Peking edition, vol. 154, 30.2.8-30.4.1; Sarnath edition, 127.2-128.20; Dharamsala edition, 69.1-70.2; translation, pp. 163-165. Tape IX.100.

1. Cited by Tsong-kha-pa, *Illumination*, 127.5; translated by M. Honda in "An Annotated Translation of the Daśabhūmika," in *Studies in Southeast and Central Asia*, ed. D. Sinor, Satapitaka Series 74 (New Delhi: 1968), pp. 115-276; also by Johannes Rahder, *Daśabhūmikasūtra et Bodhisattvabhūmi: Chapitres Vihāra et Bhūmi* (Paris and Louvain, 1926). The sutra itself explains that realization of the ten samenesses is the means by which a fifth-ground Bodhisattva proceeds to the sixth ground (Hopkins, *Meditation on Emptiness*, p. 131), a point reiterated by Panchen Sönam Drakba in his *General Meaning (spyi don)*, 133.4. Candrakīrti lists and briefly discusses these in connection with VI.7bcd in his *[Auto]commentary to the Entrance (dbu ma'i 'jug pa'i rang 'grel)*, p. 66.17. The ten samenesses are also discussed in the *Illumination*'s description of the tenth ground.

2. For Gelukba understandings of this as it pertains to the workings of direct perception, see Klein, *Knowledge and Liberation*, pp. 100-114.

3. This paragraph from discussion with Yeshey Tupden, winter, 1984-85 at the Tibetan Buddhist Learning Center (VIII.040) regarding Tsong-kha-pa, *Illumination*, p.128.

4. From discussion in winter 1984-85 (VIII.153).

5. Ibid., winter, VIII.100.

6. See *Meditation on Emptiness* p. 132. Hopkins also points out, following Nga-wang-bel-den (*ngag dbang dpal ldan*, b. 1797), that the seventh sameness is an attribute of the first; the third, fourth, and fifth are attributes of the second, and the rest are attributes of both the first and second.

7. Yeshey Tupden suggests *mig yor* can signify anything which deceives the eyes—for example, scenery which appears to move as one observes it from a moving vehicle, or the swinging flame that appears to form a circle of light.

8. See Candrakīrti, *Entrance (dbu ma la 'jug ba, madhyamakāvatāra)* I.4abc; also, Candrakīrti, *[Auto]commentary (rang 'grel)*, p. 9.14 ff. Tsong-kha-pa's discussion of this verse is translated in Hopkins, *Compassion,* p. 120 ff.

9. See Tsong-kha-pa, *Illumination*, p. 460.3ff. Tsong-kha-pa takes up this topic in the eleventh and final chapter of *Illumination* where he explicitly relates it to an understanding of the two truths. Although Buddhas do not see consciousnesses and objects in

terms of their own appearances, they do directly see all objects of knowledge by way of their appearances to others—namely to disciples. These two styles of knowing, Tsong-kha-pa emphasizes, are not in the slightest bit contradictory. (460.10-15)

10. This paragraph from discussion with Yeshey Tupden, summer 1985, Tibetan Buddhist Learning Center.

11. In a subsequent discussion, Yeshey Tupden noted that some things are newly understood at Buddhahood: "Prior to full enlightenment one does not directly understand the subtle cause and effect of actions but realizes it on the basis of reasoning. At Buddhahood it is like being able to see everything with one's eyes. Knowledge of, for example, the subtle cause and effect of actions is newly understood at Buddhahood. This is not something practiced on the path. Even if one knew such [earlier], it would not act as an antidote to the obstructions to liberation or omniscience. A Buddha also knows data such as the number of stones in the ocean, for example, but there is no point in teaching it."

12. The question of whether the mind in meditative equipoise has an "object" (*dmigs pa/ālambana* or *yul, viṣaya*) is a considerable bone of contention between Gelukba and other Tibetan Buddhist traditions, especially Nyingma. Sometimes the argument turns on interpretation of Śāntideva's statement in the *Engaging in the Bodhisattva Deeds (spyod 'jug, bodhisattvacaryāvatāra,* IX.2d), "The ultimate is not an object acted upon by the mind" *(don dam blo yi spyod yul min).* Gelukba scholars typically understand this to mean that ultimate truths, or emptinesses, are not objects of an ordinary, conventional mind.

13. This paragraph from discussion in summer 1985.

14. This last sentence from discussion of July 1987.

15. This can be contrasted with the Indian Buddhist notion, classically stated by Ratnakīrti in reference to mistaken Mādhyamikas, that only impermanent phenomena *(dngos po, bhāva)* are "real" or "functional," and the association, in Sautrāntika, of permanent phenomena with imputed existence *(ldog chos, prajñaptisat).* See Klein, *Knowledge and Liberation, pp.* 52-58; 84 ff., 181 ff.

16. Cited by Tsong-kha-pa in the fifth chapter of *Illumination*, in commentary on verse 43.cd; translation adapted from Hopkins, *Compassion*, p. 229

17. There are three meditative equipoises on emptiness, but only two [uninterrupted and liberation paths] occur on the [Bodhisattva's] path of seeing. However, when a Hearer Arhat initially enters the Mahāyāna and arrives at the path of seeing, it is neither an uninterrupted nor a liberating path; it is a mere meditative equipoise (Yeshey Tupden).

18. Perhaps this can be considered a soteriological analogue to Western psychological injunctions to "integrate," or bring to consciousness, momentous experiences that lie outside ordinary memory.

19. Discussion with Yeshey Tupden, summer 1985 (VII.590)..

## CHAPTER 7. VALID EXISTENCE AND ANALYSIS

Peking edition, vol. 154, 30.4.1-30.5.8; Sarnath edition, 128.20-129.19; Dharmsala edition, 70.2-70.15 ; translation pp. 165-166.

1. This chapter corresponds to the section in *Illumination* entitled "Identifying What Is Discordant with Knowing Suchness." Begins on tape XI.360.

The major Mādhyamika texts give five types of reasonings that analyze the referent object of the conception of inherent existence. These are listed by Yeshey Tupden as: (1) The reasoning of one and many *(gcig du 'bral gyi rtags)*; (2) the reasoning of dependent arising *(rten 'brel gyi rtags)*; (3) the Diamond Slivers *(rdo rje'i gzegs ma)*; (4) the reasoning of the four extremes *(mtha' bzhi skye 'gog gi rtags)*; (5) the mandala of existing or nonexisting *(yod med dkyil 'khor gyi gtan tshigs).* There are many methods of reasoning, but these five are considered the most important. For (2), (3), and (4) see Hopkins, *Meditation on Emptiness*; for (1) see Lopez, *A Study of Svātantrika.*

2. Discussed in chap. 5 of the *Sacred Word of Mañjuśrī ('jam dpal shal lung)*, tr. by Hopkins as "Practice of Emptiness" (Dharamsala: Library of Tibetan Works and Archives, 1974); see especially pp. 12-13. Jam-yang-shay-ba calls this an "unprecedented good explanation" in *Great Exposition of Tenets (grub mtha' chen mo)*, p. 139; see Hopkins, *Meditation on Emptiness*, p. 685.

3. These two paragraphs from winter, IX.66.

4. In the Gelukba curriculum this term is also used in the context of categorizing sounds. See Sopa and Hopkins, *Cutting Through Appearances* 2nd ed. (Ithaca: Snow Lion, 1989), pp. 201 ff; this is a translation of Gön-chok-jik-may-wang-bo, *Precious Garland of Tenets (grub pa'i mtha'i rnam par bzhag pa rin po che'i phreng ba)*, 23-24.

5. Tsong-kha-pa discusses the difference between the existent I *(bdag yod pa)* and the object of the conception of a [truly existent] self *(ngar 'dzin gyi yul* and *'jig lta'i dmigs rnam gyi yul)* in the last quarter of the "Perfection of Wisdom" chapter; see *Illumination*, Sarnath edition, 363.17 ff. For detailed Gelukba Sautrāntika consideration of this issue, see Klein, *Knowledge and Liberation*, pp. 108-14.

6. This paragraph from summer 1985, C.119.

7. Kensur Yeshey Tupden suggests that the Fifth Dalai Lama was probably the first to describe observation of conception of self in this way, that is, via a "corner of the intellect." See note 2 above.

8. For the Indian sources of this analysis, as well as its significance for Svātantrika-Mādhyamika, see Lopez, *A Study of Svātantrika*, especially pp. 167-91.

9. Last two paragraphs from summer 1985, C.59.

# CHAPTER 8. THE SVĀTANTRIKA ON TRUE EXISTENCE

Peking edition, vol. 154, 30.5.8-31.3.5; Sarnath edition, 129.19-132.8; Dharamsala edition, 70.15-71.24; translation pp. 167-170.

1. This paragraph from winter discussion series, X.084.

2. The classic statement of the Svātantrika position on conventional truths is Jñānagarbha, *Differentiation of the Two Truths (bden pa gnyis rnam 'byed, satyadvayavibhaṇga)*, 8abc, tr. David M. Eckel, *Jñānagarbha's Commentary on the Distinction Between the Two Truths* (Albany: SUNY Press, 1986), p. 75. See also Guy Newland, *The Two Truths,* pp. 90-93 and 106 ff.

3. Important sources for this position are Kamalaśīla's *Illumination of the Middle Way (dbu ma snang ba, madhyamakāloka),* 372.3-5, P5765, and Jñānagarbha's *Differentiation of the Two Truths*, 62a.5; tr. and discussed, Lopez, *A Study of Svātantrika,* pp. 205 ff.

4. See Klein, *Knowledge and Liberation,* pp. 189-90, 201-203. Den-dar-hla-ram-ba (*bstan dar hla ram pa*, b. [759]), in the context of a discussion of Sautrāntika, gives this description of how phenomena come to be posited as similar in type: "Two phenomena are posited as one type [if] those trained in terminology *naturally* develop a mental conception of them as similar due to merely perceiving them by way of turning the mind [to them]" (*Presentation of Generally and Specifically Characterized Phenomena,* 195.2, tr. in Klein, *Knowing, Naming, and Negation*).

5. See Klein, *Knowledge and Liberation,* pp. 126-30.

6. For a discussion of the innate conception of true existence in Svātantrika, see Lopez, *A Study of Svātantrika*, p. 143 ff., based on Den-dar-hla-ram-ba, 430.4-5.

7. See Klein, *Knowledge and Liberation, pp.* 94-100.

8. A famous statement by Jñānagarbha, later quoted by Tsong-kha-pa, supports this position: "That seen even by cowherds and [herds?]women and so forth abides as conventional truths" (Jñānagarbha, *Differentiation of the Two Truths,* TOH. 3882, vol. 12, 2.3.3; tr. and discussed in Lopez, A *Study of Svātantrika,* p. 145 ff., and Eckel, *Jñānagarbha*, p. 71.

9. Quoted by Tsong-kha-pa, *Illumination*, 131.1: "The object to be negated (*dgag bya, pratiṣedhya)* does not appear to the sense consciousnesses. . . ."

10. See Lopez, A *Study of Svātantrika*, p. 72 ff. Jñānagarbha discusses this issue in the *Differentiation of the Two Truths* and its commentary. In the latter he maintains that [true existence] does not appear to the sense consciousnesses. Such is stated even in [Sautrāntika-Svātantrika], which does not accept external objects. Bhāvaviveka and Jñānagarbha are Sautrāntika-Svātantrikas who assert the existence of external objects. This is also true in the system of Yogacāra-Svātantrikas who do not assert external objects, such as Āryavimuktisena, and Haribhadra, Śāntarakṣita, and Kamalaśīla.

11. See Lopez, *A Study of Svātantrika*, pp. 76-78.

12. There are three types of contamination *(zag pa, sāsrava)*: afflicted contaminations *(nyon mong pa'i zag pa, *kliṣṭasāsrava)*, contamination of cyclic existence *('khor ba'i zag pa, *saṃsārasāsrava)*, contaminations of thought *(rtog pa'i zag pa, *kliṣṭakalpanā)*—that is, contamination due to the obstructions to omniscience *(shes sgrib gyi zag pa, *jñeyāvaraṇāsrava)*. The third occurs because all conceptual consciousnesses are necessarily conjoined with contamination through being mistaken regarding their appearing object (Kensur Yeshey Tupden, untaped discussion).

13. Last part of this paragraph from winter discussion series, X.534.

14. This paragraph from winter series, XII.002.

15. Jñānagarbha also states in his autocommentary to his *Differentiation of the Two Truths*, "Real production, and so forth, do not appear when a thing appears." Quoted and discussed in Den-dar-hla-ram-ba *(bstan dar hla ram pa)*, *Presentation of the Lack of Being One or Many (gcig du bral gyi rnam gzhags legs bshad rgya mtsho las btus pa 'khrul spong bdud rtsi'i gzegs ma)*. See Lopez, *A Study of Svātantrika*, p. 75 ff.

16. This is a crucial topic in Svātantrika. See Lopez, *A Study of Svātantrika*, pp. 134-43; 314-20.

Yeshey Tupden further observes, following Maitreya's *Discrimination of the Middle Way and the Extremes (dbus dang mtha' rnam par 'byed pa, madhyāntavibhaṅga)*, that there are three types of ultimates: ultimate consciousness, ultimate object, and ultimate attainment *(thob pa don dam)*. Ultimate consciousness and ultimate attainment are not ultimate truths. An ultimate truth is necessarily an ultimate object; Svātantrikas and Cittamātrins do not posit the ultimate attainment [i.e., a nirvana] as an ultimate truth, as does Prāsaṅgika. Accordingly, in the Stages of the Path *(lam rim)* texts liberation and true cessations [which are ultimate attainments] are ultimate truths, and the mind directly cognizing emptiness is a consciousness that is an ultimate truth. The reasoning consciousness itself is an ultimate [insofar as it is] a knower of ultimate truths *(don dam bden pa'i shes pa'i don dam)*, but that which is taken as ultimate *for* it is an ultimate [in a different sense]—namely, the ultimate truth observed on the Mahāyāna uninterrupted path of seeing. These are ultimate truths but do not exist ultimately. There are ultimate and conventional truths, but no ultimate existence. All phenomena exist conventionally; thus, there is no distinction to be made between that which does and does not exist ultimately. If it did exist, it would be something that existed without being posited through the force of appearing to a healthy mind. But there is no such thing.

17. Yeshey Tupden takes "mode of subsistence" *(sdod lugs)* and "mode of abiding" *(gnas lugs)* as synonymous with the "basic modality" (*gshis lugs)* [of an existent thing]. Whatever has a basic modality does not necessarily exist in that basic modality *(gshis lugs yin na gshis lugs la yod pas khyab kyi ma red)*. Not to exist in that basic modality is not to have its own objective mode of subsistence. (From Winter series, XII.212.)

18. Winter series, XII. 212ff.

19. For a discussion of the types of ultimate in Svātantrika, see Eckel, *Jñānagarbha*, p. 71 and Lopez, *A Study of Svātantrika,* 198ff.

## CHAPTER 9. THE MAGICIAN'S ILLUSION: TRUTH AND FALSITY FOR WORLDLY PERSONS

Peking edition, vol. 154, 31.3.5-32.3.4; Sarnath edition, 132.8-136.19; Dharamsala edition, 71.24-74.11; translation, pp. 170-174.

1. For discussion of different Svātantrika subdivisions as formulated in Tibet, see Katsumi Mimaki, *Blo gsal grub mtha* (Kyoto: Zinbun Kagaku Kenkyusyo, Université de Kyoto, 1982), pp. 27-54. Among other interesting points, Mimaki notes that the terms "Svātantrika" and "Prāsaṅgika" do not appear in the *lta ba'i khyad par* of Ye-shey-dey (*ye shes sde*, the eighth-century student of both Padmasambhava and Śāntarakṣita). It was during the second dissemination of Buddhism to Tibet, the period of translations by Rin-chen-sang-bo *(rin chen bzang po*, tenth century) that the classification of Mādhyamika into Svātantrika and Prāsaṅgika gained currency. These two terms were never used India. (Lopez, *A Study of Svātantrika*, p. 57.) For a discussion of later Tibetan definitions of Svātantrika, particularly Jang-gya and Jam-yang-shay-ba, see Lopez, *A Study of Svātantrika* p. 59 ff.

2. This section from YT 84-90d; tape XIV.300ff; TKP 134.3

3. Last two paragraphs from winter series.

4. This sentence and previous three paragraphs from discussion, winter, XII. 344 ff.

5. Mipham observes that both Svātantrika and Prāsaṅgika, being Mādhyamika, consider all phenomena to be imputed by thought and to lack even a particle which is established from their own side (*brgal lan nyin byed snang ba*, [Varanasi: 1967], 7.9). However, as he subsequently observes (12.8-13), "The positing [of objects] as established through mere mental imputation can never be established without depending on prior ultimate analysis; if it could, all [tenet systems?] would from the beginning be Mādhyamika. Therefore, even in the Prāsaṅgika system, things are accepted conventionally as merely posited by the force of appearing to an unmistaken mind" (*blos phar btags tsam gyis grub par 'jog pa 'di ni don dam dpyod pa sngon du song ba la ma ltos par nam yang grub mi nus te nus na thams cad ye nas dbu ma par 'gyur ro de'i phyir na thal 'gyur pa'i lugs la'ang blo gnod med la snang ba'i dbang gis gzhag pa tsam la tha snyad du 'dod de).* Mipham then goes on to quote and reflect on the *Entrance*, VI.25.

6. Yeshey Tupden also notes that, whereas we apprehend phenomena having parts as established from their own side, there seems to be some ambivalence regarding whether we also apprehend as established from their own side the uncommon features of any given phenomenon, the qualities it does not share with any other thing.

7. A Buddha's exalted knower exists everywhere, hence the tree does fall in the apparently empty forest. I find Yeshey Tupden's own reflection on the issue considerably more subtle and illuminating than the standard reference to a pervasive omniscient consciousness in order to explain how all things are "posited by the mind."

## CHAPTER 10. PRĀSAṄGIKA ON TRUE EXISTENCE

Peking edition, vol. 154, 32.3.4-34.2.1; Sarnath edition, 136.19-144.19; Dharamsala edition, 74.11-78.24; translation, pp. 175-183.

1. The difference in Tibetan is accomplished through adding the instrumental ending.

2. See Tsong-kha-pa, *Illumination*, Sarnath edition, 140.11; tr. p. 179. [Phenomena . . .] do not have a self-powered entity [which is, for example, a "pot"] posited through the force of conventions which are other [than themselves], . . .

3. See Dharmakīrti, *Commentary on (Dignāga's) "Compendium on Valid Cognition" (tshad ma rham 'grel, pramāṇavārttika)*, III.138b.

4. Classic sources of the "snake example" are Candrakīrti's [*Auto*]*Commentary on the "Entrance"* (commenting on VI.97 (P5263, vol. 98, 136.4.7 ff., discussed in *Illumination* [P6143, vol. 154, 76.3.6 ff.; Sarnath edition, 137.19; Dharmsala edition, 74.25]) and *The Essence of the Good Explanations* (P6142, vol. 152, 204.5.3 ff.). See Hopkins, *Meditation on Emptiness, pp.* 437-38; 619-20, 626, 627. Jam-yang-shay-ba refers to all of these, and also to Bhāvaviveka's *Essence of the Middle Way (dbu ma'i shying po, madhyamakahṛdaya)* as discussed in Lopez, *A Study of Svātantrika,* p. 124).

5. Nāgārjuna analyzes the self this way in *Precious Garland*, v. 80 ff.

6. For an elaboration of Nāgārjuna's fivefold analysis and the expansion of this into the more widely used sevenfold analysis of Candrakīrti, see Hopkins, *Meditation on Emptiness,* pp. 178-92. For a classic if somewhat limited scholarly critique of this analysis, see Richard Robinson, "Did Nāgārjuna Really Refute All Views?" in *Philosophy East and West* 22 (1972), 325-31. For a discussion of Robinson's critique, see Napper, *Dependent-Arising and Emptiness,* especially pp. 74-75 and 87-88.

7. *gzugs dang rang gi dngos yul yod thub kyi ma red* is how I heard this phrase.

8. Yeshey Tupden's way of thinking brings him to this position—that is, if the conventionally existent (*tha snyad du yod pa, *vyavahārasat)* is equivalent to existing for a valid cognizer *(tshad ma'i ngor yod pa)*, then all valid cognizers, whether of conventional objects or the ultimate, are conventional (*tha snyad/vyavahāra).* Thanks to Jeffrey Hopkins on this point.

9. See Newland, *The Two Truths*, p. 40 ff.

10. I could not here ascertain whether Yeshey Tupden was saying "convention of imputation *(*'dogs byed kyi tha snyad)* or "convention of thought" *(rtog pa'i tha snyad*), though it is probably the former.

11. Yeshey Tupden is probably referring to the statement from Candrakīrti's [*Auto*]*commentary,* quoted by Tsong-kha-pa in his discussion of the selflessness of persons: "With respect to that [the conception of an I which results from having imputed a self which actually does not exist], the view of the transitory collection is an afflicted intelligence *(shes rab nyon mongs pa can, *kliṣṭaprajñā),* which is engaged in such thoughts of [inherently existent] I and mine." (pp. 180-181, tr.)

12. Tr. Hopkins, *Precious Garland*, p. 22. Tsong-kha-pa quotes this verse much later in *Illumination,* chapter 6 (p. 358, Sarnath edition).

13. See Klein, *Knowledge & Liberation*, p. 97 ff.

14. In the "Perfection of Wisdom Chapter" of the *Sacred Word of Mañjuśrī,* the Fifth Dalai Lama states, "The conventional valid cognizer which establishes the existence of "I" . . . exists in the continuums of those . . . who do not differentiate nominal imputation and inherent existence. In this case, the "I" is not qualified with being nominally imputed or inherently existent." Tr. in "Practice of Emptiness" by Jeffrey Hopkins (Dharamsala: Library of Tibetan Works and Archives, 1974), pp. 10-11.

15. Jam-yang-shay-ba, however, would say that the "mine" *is* a person.

16. See Tsong-kha-pa, *Illumination*, 142.10, Sarnath edition; Peking edition 33.4.3.

17. Yeshey Tupden points out that Gomang College considers that *rang skya grub pa* and *rang skya 'dzin grub pa* are not the same for Svātantrika.

18. Tsong-kha-pa says that the selflessness of persons is said to be easier to understand than the selflessness of phenomena (*lhag mthong 'bring* discussed by Hopkins, *Emptiness Yoga*, p. 249 and translated by him [unpublished ms.] as *"Middling Exposition of Special Insight."* See also the translation of this text as "The Middle Transcendent Insight" in *Life and Teachings of Tsong Khapa*, ed. by Robert A. F. Thurman [Dharamsala: Library of Tibetan Works and Archives, 1982], p. 129).

19. Discussed in chapter 5 of the *Sacred Word of Mañjuśrī*, tr. Hopkins, pp. 10-11. In listing three types of innate conceivers of the "I," the Fifth Dalai Lama describes the third as "the conventional valid cognizer which establishes the existence of "I." This consciousness exists [for example] in the continuums of those common beings whose mental continuums are not affected by systems of tenets and who thus do not differentiate nominal imputation and inherent existence. In this case, the "I" is not qualified by being nominally imputed *or* inherently existent."

## TRANSLATION

### 1. Introduction to the Profound Meaning

1. Four editions of Tsong-kha-pa's text (*dbu ma la 'jug pa'i rgya cher bshad pa dgongs pa rab gsal*) were used:

Dharamsala, India: Tibetan Cultural Printing Press, n.d.: 62.9-78.24.

Sarnath, India: Pleasure of Elegant Sayings Press, 1973: 114.11-144.19.

*Tibetan Tripiṭaka* (Tokyo-Kyoto: Tibetan Tripiṭaka Research Foundation, 1956; offset of the Peking edition), P6143, vol. 154, 27.4.6-34.2.1.

*The Collected Works (gsuṅ 'bum) of the Incomparable Lord Tsoṅ-kha-pa Blo-bzaṅ-grags-pa*, vol. 16 *ma*, 127.3-160.6 [photographic reprint of the "1897 old źol (*dga'-ldan-phun-tshogs-gliṅ*) blocks"]. New Delhi: Guru Deva, 1979.

Jayānanda's *Commentarial Explanation of Candrakīrti's) Entrance to (Nāgārjuna's) "Treatise on the Middle Way"* (*dbu ma la 'jug pa'i 'grel bshad, madhyamkāvatāraṭīkā*: P5271, vol. 99, 117.1.3-120.2.7) was also consulted.

2. The uncontaminated wisdom of meditative equipoise of a Bodhisattva is called a "ground" or "earth" (*sa, bhūmi*) with the sense that it serves as a *basis* (*gzhi*) of high qualities of mind just as the earth serves as the basis of myriads of activities. As Candrakīrti's commentary (Poussin, Osnabrück, 12.1) says, "When a Bodhisattva's uncontaminated wisdom, conjoined with compassion, and so forth, is divided into parts, each part is called a 'ground' because it is a base of qualities." Tsong-kha-pa comments, "A 'ground' (*bhūmi*, literally 'earth') is like the earth because it acts as a source or base of auspicious qualities." See Tsong-ka-pa, Kensur Lekden, and Jeffrey Hopkins, *Compassion in Tibetan Buddhism*, pp. 133-34. Although the term "ground" (or the French "*terre*" used by Poussin and Ruegg) seems awkward in the context of a discussion of spiritual paths in English, Tibetan oral traditions explain that it is employed because of its familiarity and ease of understanding:

> The reason why the paths of the three vehicles are called grounds is that they serve as bases of one's generating higher qualities in one's own mental continuum. If, in the designation of a name, one employs a term from common usage, then it is easily remembered and used. The term "ground" is known well, for if we are going, wandering, lying down, or sitting, our activities are involved with the ground [or earth]. Thus, through skill in means—using a term that is easy to understand—the term "ground" is used. The reason for designating the paths of the three vehicles as grounds is from the viewpoint of a similarity of function.

(From Jeffrey Hopkins, "A Tibetan Perspective on the Nature of Spiritual Experience" in *Paths to Liberation*, ed. by Robert E. Buswell, Jr., and Robert M. Gimello, pp. 248-49.)

3. The translation here includes all of the first two items and a portion of the third. Like many Tibetan commentaries, Tsong-kha-pa's provides a table of contents.

4. Tsong-kha-pa gives commentary on the stanzas of Candrakīrti's *Entrance* as well as the auto-commentary, but he does not quote the stanzas themselves; to make the translation of his text more comprehensible, the stanzas have been inserted into the translation.

5. *'di rten 'byung ba'i de nyid.* Both Tsong-kha-pa (62.13) and tr. Poussin (*Muséon* 11, 272 n. 1) gloss this term as "the suchness of conditionality," the former as

*rkyen nyid 'di pa tsam gyi zab mo'i de kho na nyid* ("the profound suchness of mere conditionality") and the latter as *rkyen nyid 'di pa'i de nyid* ("the suchness of conditionality"). Poussin gives the Sanskrit as *idampratyayatātattva*. Candrakīrti, just below (61.6), substitutes "dependent arising" (*rten cing 'brel par 'byung ba, pratītyasamutpāda*) for "arising-dependent-upon-this" in his commentary.

Conditionality here is not limited to the production of effects in dependence upon causes but also includes the establishment of objects in dependence upon their bases of designation. Therefore, conditionality applies to both impermanent and permanent phenomena. Thus, "arising" (*'byung ba, samutpāda*) is not limited to production but also refers to establishment (*grub pa, siddhi*) or existence (*yod pa, sat*). For Jam-yang-shay-ba's exposition of Candrakīrti's discussion of the formation, etymology, and meaning of *pratītyasamutpāda* in his *Clear Words*, see Hopkins, *Meditation on Emptiness*, pp. 662-76.

6. The name of the sixth ground in Tibetan is either *mngon du gyur pa* (manifested) or *mngon du phyogs pa* (approaching). The preferred term in Tsong-kha-pa's commentary is clearly the former, as is indicated by his glossing *mngon du phyogs pa* (approaching) with *mngon du gyur pa* (manifested): *mngon du phyogs pa ste gyur pa* (Tibetan Cultural Printing Press, 62.12). This accords with the predominance in Tibetan of *mngon du gyur pa* (manifested) over *mngon du phyogs pa* (approaching). In this stanza the dual meaning of *abhimukhī*, however, is emphasized when Candrakīrti explains it as *approaching* the Buddha qualities and *manifesting*, or manifestly seeing, the suchness of dependent arising.

The basic meaning of *abhimukhī*, given these two etymologies, is "thoroughly facing" in the sense that Bodhisattvas are now *faced toward* (Poussin, *Muséon* 11, 272: "*tourné vers*") or are nearing the qualities of a Buddha, such as the ten powers, owing to the fact that sixth-ground Bodhisattvas are *facing* the surpassing form of the perfection of wisdom—i.e., that wisdom is manifest to them (or its face has been made obvious). For "nearing," see Jayānanda's *Commentarial Explanation* (P5271, vol. 99, 117.1.6). See also n. 9 for an extension of this etymology.

7. See, below, Tsong-kha-pa's statement, "Therefore, an uncommon absorption of cessation is attained from this [ground]."

8. Yeshey Tupden's commentary, chapter 2; Peking edition, vol. 154, 27.4.8; Samath edition, 114.16; Dharamsala edition, pp. 62.12-65.1.

9. Jayānanda (P5271, vol. 99, 117.3.1) glosses "observed" (*dmigs pa*) with "manifested" (*mngon du gyur pa*), and thus this meaning is a variation on "manifest" in that on the sixth ground, wisdom regarding the four truths is observed, or apprehended, and thus manifest. We might conjecture that two reasons why the translators into Tibetan settled on *mngon du gyur pa* (manifest) as the main translation equivalent for *abhimukhī* are that this second etymology is also a variation of "manifest," and that in his commentary Candrakīrti makes the etymology as "manifest" the first of the three.

10. Jayānanda, P5271, vol. 99, 117.1.5. Except for the initial table of contents, up through this point Tsong-kha-pa has merely expanded slightly on Candrakīrti's commentary; the rest of this section, however, has no counterpart in Candrakīrti's commentary.

11. P5271, vol. 99, 117.2.8.

12. Yeshey Tupden, oral commentary.

13. Yeshey Tupden, oral commentary.

14. Yeshey Tupden, oral commentary.

15. Yeshey Tupden, oral commentary.

16. Yeshey Tupden (oral commentary) explained that this fully developed perfection of wisdom sees emptiness to be like a reflection in the sense that it exists but is not truly established; it also observes the coarse and subtle sixteen aspects of the four truths and the procedure of entry into and reversal from cyclic existence through the twelve links of dependent arising.

17. In his *Analysis of the Great Treatise, (Candrakīrti's) Entrance to (Nāgārjuna's) "Treatise on the Middle Way": Lamp of Scripture and Reasoning: Oral Transmission of the Omniscient Lama, Jam-yang-shay-bay-dor-jay* (*bstan gcos chen po dbu ma la 'jug pa'i mtha' dpyod lung rigs sgron me zhes bya ba kun mkhyen bla ma 'jam dbyangs bzhad pa'i rdo rje'i gsung rgyun*; The Collected Works of dkon-mchog-'jigs-med-dbaṅ-po [New Delhi: Ngawang Gelek Demo, 1972], vol. 6, 184.5), Gön-chok-jik-may-wang-bo, said to be the reincarnation of Jam-yang-shay-ba, identifies an absorption of cessation as an exalted wisdom that realizes emptiness and involves a cessation of coarse feeling and discrimination (*'tshor 'du rags pa bkag pa'i stong nyid rtogs pa'i ye shes*).

18. That is, an uncommon absorption of cessation, according to Tsong-kha-pa's interpretation given above.

19. This is one of the levels of gods of the Desire Realm.

20. This and the next citation from sutra are not in Candrakīrti's commentary.

21. The translation here includes the first four items and part of the fifth.

22. The indented material is a close paraphrase of Candrakīrti.

23. That the "suchness of dependent arising" is emptiness is clear from Candrakīrti's example of "the eye medicine of the good perception of emptiness" just below. (Candrakīrti actually speaks of "the eye-medicine of the *nonerroneous* perception of emptiness"; Tsong-kha-pa changed "nonerroneous" to "good" in his paraphrase.)

24. *'phags pa, ārya.* A Mahāyāna Superior is someone who has become elevated through attaining at least the path of seeing and, thus, the first Bodhisattva ground.

25. This material, after the paraphrase of Candrakīrti's commentary, is not found in his commentary. It is interesting that the position that Tsong-kha-pa is refuting is presented by his teacher, Ren-da-wa of the Sa-gya order, in his commentary on Candrakīrti's *Entrance to (Nāgārjuna's) "Treatise on the Middle Way,"* entitled *Lamp Illuminating Suchness* (*dbu ma la 'jug pa'i rnam bshad de kho na nyid gsal bai' sgron*

*ma*; Delhi: Ngawang Topgay, 1974), 77.6-80.1. Ren-da-wa clearly says that the nonconceptual exalted wisdom (*rnam par mi rtog pa'i ye shes*) cannot be asserted to be a consciousness (*shes pa*) because otherwise it would not be free from the fictive elaborations of subject and object. Nevertheless, he explains that this position does not entail the fault that suchness is not realized, for the nonconceptual is not the mere stoppage of conceptuality but occurs after analyzing the inherent existence of phenomena and not apprehending even a speck of inherent existence in any phenomenon, and then setting one's mind in such a real nature. He says that through becoming accustomed to this state, the mind becomes of the nature of suchness and does not observe any signs, such as of object known, and so forth. He holds that this is merely designated with the convention of the perfection of wisdom but is not an actual consciousness (which would have to be dualistic). Tsong-kha-pa, on the other hand, innovatively asserts that this totally nondual state is an actual consciousness. As he says earlier in his *Illumination of the Thought*:

> The books of the master Candrakīrti contain many references to "knowledge" and "wisdom" free from the darkness of ignorance. Therefore, it would be an extremely deprecating denial to link ignorance and the predisposing latencies of ignorance with all knowledge and propound that according to this master's system wisdom disappears when ignorance and its predispositions are extinguished. These explanations are on a par with the Forder (*tīrthika*) Mimāṃsakas' assertion that if the pollutions were extinguished, so would be the mind. Saying that there is no wisdom in a Superior's meditative equipoise is also similar. (Hopkins, *Compassion*, p. 132.)

26. Poussin (*Muséon* 11, 274) construes this stanza differently from Tsong-kha-pa (64.6). He interprets *de yis* as referring to Nāgārjuna ("*cet* [*homme*]," which refers to "*un homme qui fait autorité*," i.e., Nāgārjuna), whereas Tsong-kha-pa interprets it as referring to the sixth-ground Bodhisattva (*sa drug pa ba de yis*). Candrakīrti's commentary favors Tsong-kha-pa's reading of *de yis* since, in an apparent gloss of that line in his [*Auto*]*Commentary*, he says, ". . . in accordance with how a Bodhisattva coursing in the perfection of wisdom sees the essence of phenomena" (*shes rab kyi pha rol tu phyin pa la spyod pa'i byang chub sems dpas chos rnam kyi bdag nyid ji lta ba nyid ji ltar mthong ba de ltar*), the instrumental on *byang chub sems dpas* being the equivalent of *de yis*.

Also, Poussin does not emend *chos zab chos* (VI.3a) which he interprets as referring to the profound nature of things *("la nature profonde des choses")* and only indicates that *ches zab chos* is a variant reading which means "the very profound dharma" *("le très profond dharma")*. However, Ren-da-wa (*Lamp Illuminating Suchness*, 80.6) reads *ches zab chos* which he glosses with *ches zab pa'i chos*, and Tsong-kha-pa indicates that he accepts the same reading when he glosses it with *ches shin tu zab pa'i chos zab mo* (literally, "the profound doctrine that is extremely profound").

27. The term *dharma* (*chos*) is not limited in meaning to merely the basic categories of things but also refers to such phenomena as tables, chairs, bodies, people, and so forth, which, although they can be included in these categories called *dharma*, are also *dharmas* themselves. The definition of *dharma* when it refers, not to religious

practices, but to phenomena is, as abundantly found in the basic textbooks of the Gelukba system of education: something that holds its own entity (*rang gi ngo bo 'dzin pa*). This means that phenomena are one with themselves—that everything is not an indistinguishable mass. Tables, chairs, and so forth, fit this definition and thus are *dharmas*, phenomena.

From the point of view of Gelukba scholarship, the frequent nontraditional interpretation of *dharma* as only referring to the basic categories of phenomena, with the consequence that nothing else exists, is a case of mistakenly assessing the usage of the term. Most likely, the Gelukba usage represents a scholastic tradition from India. For more discussion on this translation, see Hopkins, *Meditation on Emptiness*, pp. 214-15.

28. "Sets of discourses" here must refer to sutras in general and not just the scriptural collection of sets of discourses (*mdo sde'i sde snod, sūtrāntapiṭaka*), since the teaching on emptiness is to be found mainly in the scriptural collection of manifest knowledge (*mngon pa'i sde snod, abhidharmapiṭaka*).

29. X.165-66. The Sanskrit, as given in *Saddharmalaṅkāvatārasūtram*, ed. by Dr. P. L. Vaidya, Buddhist Sanskrit Texts No. 3 (Darbhanga: Mithila Institute, 1963), p. 118, is:

*dakṣiṇāpathavedalyām bhikṣuḥ śrīmān mahāyaśāḥ/*
*nāgāhvayaḥ sa nāmnā tu sadasatpakṣadārakaḥ//*
*prakāśya loke madyānaṃ mahāyānamuttaram/*
*āsādya bhūmiṃ muditāṃ yāsyate 'sau sukhāvatīm//*

For an excellent bibliography of scholarship on Nāgārjuna's prophecies, see David S. Ruegg, *The Literature of the Madhyamaka School of Philosophy in India* (Wiesbaden: Otto Harrassowitz, 1981), p. 5 n. 11. For a sense of the variety of accounts of Nāgārjuna's life, see especially M. Walleser, "The Life of Nāgārjuna from Tibetan and Chinese Sources," *Asia Major*, Introductory Volume (Hirth Anniversary Volume, Leipzig, 1923), 421-55; rpt. (Delhi: Nag Publishers, 1979). For Bu-dön's account of Nāgārjuna's life, see E. Obermiller, *History of Buddhism by Bu-ston* (Heidelberg: Harrassowitz, 1931), Part 2, pp. 110-11, 122-30. Also see *Tāranātha's History of Buddhism*, tr. Lama Chimpa and Alaka Chattopadhyaya, ed. D. Chattopadhyaya (Calcutta: Bagchi, rpt. 1980), pp. 106-19 ff.

30. Poussin (Osnabrück, 76.13), the Dharamsala edition (63.14), and Tsong-kha-pa (Tibetan Cultural Printing Press, 64.12) read *be ta*, but Nga-wang-bel-den (*ngag dbang dpal ldan*) in his *Annotations for (Jam-yang-shay-ba's) "Great Exposition of Tenets," Freeing the Knots of the Difficult Points, Precious Jewel of Clear Thought* (*grub mtha' chen mo'i mchan 'grel dka' gnad mdud grol blo gsal gces nor*; Sarnath: Pleasure of Elegant Sayings Press, 1964), *dngos* 58a.3, gives *be da* (misprinted as *pe da*) and identifies the place as Vidarbha (*be dar bha*). He etymologizes the name as a place where a certain type of grass (identified in Chandra Das's *Tibetan-English Dictionary* as *Andropogon muricatus*) grows (*'jag ma skye ba'i yul*). Poussin (*Muséon* 11, 274) also identifies the place as Vidarbha. M. Walleser, in his *The Life of Nāgārjuna from Tibetan and Chinese Sources* (rpt. 6, n. 2) further identifies Vidarbha as now called Berar. E. Obermiller, in his *History of Buddhism by Bu-ston* (p. 110) identifies the place as

Vedalya, based on the Sanskrit edited by Bunyiu Nanjio (p. 286); see the Sanskrit stanza cited above. Yeshey Tupden identified the term as meaning a place of *kuśa* grass, which he said is an area near present-day Madras.

Both Poussin (*Muséon* 11, 274) and Obermiller (p. 110) take *dpal ldan* (*śrīmān*) as adjectival to "monk" (*bhikṣuḥ*), the former as "illustrious" (*illustre*) and the latter as "glorious," but Nga-wang-bel-den (*dngos* 58a.3) takes it as Nāgārjuna's name given at ordination (*dge slong du gyur ba'i ming dpal ldan zhes grags pa*), saying that he was otherwise known in the world as "Nāga" (*de'i ming gzhan 'jig rten na klu zhes 'bod pa ste*). This accords with Jam-yang-shay-ba's statement in his *Great Exposition of Tenets* (*grub mtha' chen mo/grub mtha'i rnam bshad rang gzhan grub mtha' kun dang zab don mchog tu gsal ba kun bzang zhing gi nyi ma lung rigs rgya mtsho skye dgu'i re ba kun skong*; Musoorie: Dalama, 1962), *ca* 5a.4, that the name given at ordination was *dpal ldan blo 'chang*. Bu-dön refers to Nāgārjuna early in his life as *śrīmān* (*dpal ldan*), and Obermiller (p. 123 n. 891) recognizes this but does not carry it over to his translation of this passage in the *Descent into Laṅkā Sutra (lang kar gshegs pa'i mdo, laṅkāvatārasūtra)*.

Nga-wang-bel-den (*dngos* 58a.4) takes "destroying the positions of existence and nonexistence" (*yod dang med pa'i phyogs 'jig pa*) as modifying "my vehicle":

> Having thoroughly—clearly—explained in this world the final path of the Great Vehicle *(theg pa chen po, mahāyāna)*, of which there is none higher among my vehicles, and which destroys—abandons—the two positions, or extremes, of [inherent] existence and [conventional] nonexistence which, when apprehended, bring ruination, he, having achieved the first ground, the Very Joyful, will go to the Blissful Land.

Poussin (*Muséon* 11, 274) takes "destroying the positions of existence and nonexistence" as referring to Nāgārjuna, as is justified by the Sanskrit *sad-asat-pakṣa-dārakaḥ* (given also in Obermiller, p. 110 n. 759) which is a nominative whereas the unsurpassed Great Vehicle (*mahāyānamuttaram*) is accusative. Jam-yang-shay-ba (*Great Exposition of Tenets*, *ca* 5b.8) gives a different reading of the Tibetan (*yod dang med pa'i phyogs 'jig cing*) which more accurately reflects the Sanskrit in that the particle *cing* prevents taking "destroying the positions of existence and nonexistence" as modifying "my vehicle," whereas *yod dang med pa'i phyogs 'jig pa* does not do this.

31. *rab tu dga' ba, pramuditā*. This is the first Bodhisattva ground.

32. *bde ba can, sukhāvatī*.

33. *li tsa byi*; Jayānanda's *Commentarial Explanation* (P5271, vol. 99, 118.2.5) has *litstshabi*—i.e., *licchavi*. This is the name of a people whose capital was Vaiśāli (Edgerton, *Buddhist Hybrid Sanskrit Grammar and Dictionary*, p. 462).

34. *'jig rten thams cad kyis mthong na dga' ba, sarvalokapriyadarśana*. The Sanskrit is from *Suvarṇaprabhāsottamasūtra, Das Goldglanz-Sūtra*, ed. Johannes Nobel, (Leiden: Brill, 1950), Glossary, 65.

35. *Suvarṇaprabhāsottamasūtra, Das Goldglanz-Sūtra*, Text chapter II, 12.13-17.6. Liked-When-Seen-By-All-The-World is mentioned three times in the sutra (13.2,

14.1, and 16.2). Thanks to Professor Shotaro Iida of the University of British Columbia for providing this edition. Candrakīrti does not refer to this sutra.

In this sutra, Liked-When-Seen-By-All-The-World speaks with Kauṇḍinya about whether Buddha would leave relics upon passing away. Kauṇḍinya, inspired by Buddha, answers that because a Buddha's body is not made of blood and bone, there could not be any such relics but that Buddha, out of skillful means, would nevertheless leave relics. (An almost identical conversation is also found in the *Great Cloud Sutra* [P898, vol. 35, 250.1.7-250.4.7; see n. 36 below].) Nāgārjuna is a rebirth of this illustrious youth.

The *Great Cloud Sutra* (P898, vol. 35, 251.4.3) identifies Kauṇḍinya as a previous rebirth of the great Buddhist king Aśoka:

> Goddess, the prophesied master, the Brahmin Kauṇḍinya also will be born, one hundred twenty years after I pass away, in the royal lineage of a half-universal emperor called the Maurya lineage. . . . Goddess, he will become the lay practitioner (*dge bsnyen, upāsaka*) King Aśoka. Goddess, that half-universal emperor called Aśoka will proclaim the initial great lion's roar of the treatises of doctrine and will manifestly make worship.

36. *'phags pa sprin chen po zhes bya ba theg pa chen po'i mdo, āryamahāmeghanāmamahāyānasūtra*; P898, vol. 35. As given in Poussin (*Muséon* 11, 275) the title is *āryadvādaśasahasramahāmegha* (*'phags pa sprin chen po stong phrag bcu gnyis pa*), this being how Candrakīrti cites it.

37. The identification of his name is in the sutra itself as cited by Candrakīrti:

> Ānanda, four hundred years after I [Śākyamuni Buddha] pass away, this Licchavi youth Liked-When-Seen-By-All-The-World will become a monk known as Nāga and will disseminate my teaching. Finally, in the land known as Very Pure Light he will become a One Gone Thus, a Foe Destroyer *(dgra bcom pa, arhan)*, a completely perfect Buddha named Light-Which-Is-A-Source-of-All-Wisdom.

Tsong-kha-pa's abridgment of the citation is typical; instead of Candrakīrti's "Ānanda, this Licchavi youth Liked-When-Seen-By-All-The-World" (*kun dga' bo li tsa byi gzhon nu sems can thams cad kyis mthong na dga' ba zhes bya ba 'di ni*), Tsong-kha-pa has only "this youth." Tsong-kha-pa clearly wants to get to the point; he eliminates mention of Ānanda—the person whom Buddha was addressing—and what, in his own prose, is an unnecessary repetition of the youth's name, since he has just given it in the previous sentence. He also shortens ". . . he will become a One Gone Thus, a Foe Destroyer, a completely perfect Buddha named Light-Which-Is-A-Source-of-All-Wisdom," to ". . . he will become a Conqueror [Buddha] named Light-Which-Is-A-Source-of-All-Wisdom," leaving out the verbiage unnecessary to his point.

Tsong-kha-pa's abridgment is clearly not due to his using a different translation of the sutra since this particular passage is not found in the Tibetan translation of the *Great Cloud Sutra.* It appears that Tsong-kha-pa condenses the passage in order to make his point more efficiently.

38. *rab tu dang ba'i 'od.* Poussin (*Muséon* 11, 275) gives the Sanskrit as *Suviśuddhaprabhābhūmi*, but Obermiller (*History of Buddhism by Bu-ston*, p. 129) gives *Prasannaprabhā*.

39. *ye shes 'byung gnas 'od.* Both Poussin (*Muséon* 11, 275) and Obermiller (*History of Buddhism by Bu-ston*, p. 129) give the Sanskrit as *Jñānākaraprabha*.

Poussin (*Muséon* 11, 275) has Buddha identifying the Licchavi youth as Ānanda (*"Prince Licchavi, cet Ānanda, ainsi nommé parce que toute créature se réjouit en le voyant, quatre siécles aprés le nirvāṇa, sera le bhikṣu nommé Nāga . . ."*), whereas, according to Tsong-kha-pa, Buddha is talking about the Licchavi youth who is a contemporary of Ānanda. In his condensation Tsong-kha-pa has dropped the reference to Ānanda, but it is clear that he takes it as vocative—that is to say, Buddha is addressing Ānanda and talking about the Licchavi youth. There is considerable justification for Tsong-kha-pa's reading because his additional reference to the *Great Drum Sutra* indicates that Buddha is talking to Ānanda *about* the Licchavi youth who is called Liked-When-Seen-By-All-The-World (*'jig rten thams cad kyis mthong na dga' ba, sarvalokapriyadarśana*), this phrase constituting his name and not describing Ānanda as Poussin has it. Poussin was perhaps misled into thinking that *'jig rten thams cad kyis mthong na dga' ba* refers to Ānanda because "Ānanda" means "thoroughly happy."

40. Jam-yang-shay-ba makes this point in the *Four Interwoven Annotations to (Tsong-kha-pa's) "Great Exposition of the Stages of the Path"* (*lam rim mchan bzhi sbrags ma*; New Delhi: Chophel Lekden, 1972), 153.3.

41. Candrakīrti does not mention this prophecy. The *Mañjuśrī Root Tantra* is classified as an Action Tantra, and the specific passage (P162, vol. 6, 259.3.8-259.4.2, chapter 36) is:

> When four hundred years have passed
> After I, the One Gone Thus, have passed away,
> A monk called Nāga will arise.
> Faithful in and helpful to the teaching,
> He will attain the Very Joyful ground.
> Living for six hundred years,
> That great being will also achieve
> The knowledge[-mantra] of *Mahāmayūrī* (*rma bya chen po*).
> He will know the meaning of various treatises
> And the meaning of no inherent existence (*dngos po med pa*).
> When he leaves that body,
> He will be born in the [Pure Land of] Bliss (*bde ba can, sukhāvatī*).
> Finally he will just definitely attain
> Thoroughly the state of Buddhahood.

For Obermiller's translation of this passage, see his *History of Buddhism by Bu-ston*, 111. He cites it as Kg. RGYUD. XI. 450a.5-6.

Jam-yang-shay-ba (*Tenets*, ca 4a.3, 5b.8, 6b.5) cites the relevant parts of the passage with slightly different readings:

When four hundred years have passed. After I, the One Gone Thus, have passed away,/A monk called Nāga will arise . . . /Living for six hundred years . . . /He will know many treatises teaching the basic constituent/And the suchness of the meaning of no inherent existence.//

42. The sutra (which is not mentioned by Candrakīrti here) is foretelling Nāgārjuna's third appearance in South India, this being during his third proclamation of the doctrine; see Gön-chok-jik-may-wang-bo, *Lamp of Scripture and Reasoning,* 185.4-185.6; and Jam-yang-shay-ba, *Great Exposition of the Middle Way/Analysis of (Candrakīrti's) "Entrance to (Nāgārjuna's) 'Treatise on the Middle Way,'", Treasury of Scripture and Reasoning, Thoroughly Illuminating the Profound Meaning [of Emptiness], Entrance for the Fortunate* (*dbu ma chen mo/dbu ma 'jug pa'i mtha' dpyod lung rigs gter mdzod zab don kun gsal skal bzang 'jug ngogs*; Buxaduor: Gomang, 1967), 194b.4-195a.6. Tsong-kha-pa himself says this in an earlier composition, his *Ocean of Reasoning, Explanation of (Nāgārjuna's) "Treatise on the Middle Way"* (*dbu ma rtsa ba'i tshig le'ur byas pa shes rab ces bya ba'i rnam bshad rigs pa'i rgya mtsho*; Sarnath, India: Pleasure of Elegant Sayings Printing Press, no date, 4.17):

> That prophecy in the *Great Drum Sutra* is said to [refer to] the final appearance in the south; therefore, [Nāgārjuna's] coming at four hundred years [refers] to [his] second appearance in south [India].

When Tsong-kha-pa says that such is "said," he means, as can be seen from Jam-yang-shay-ba's annotations to Tsong-kha-pa's *Great Exposition of the Stages of the Path,* that the *Great Drum Sutra* itself (P888, vol. 35, 99.4.6) says this in a verse summation of the prophecy later in the sutra:

> That is his final emergence
> In the southern direction.

For the Jam-yang-shay-ba reference, see *Four Interwoven Annotations to (Tsong-kha-pa's) "Great Exposition of the Stages of the Path"/Clear Lamp of the Mahāyāna Path, Good Explanation by Way of the Four Annotations on the Difficult Points of the "Great Exposition of the Stages of the Path to Enlightenment" Composed by the Unequalled Foremost Venerable Tsong-kha-pa* (*lam rim mchan bzhi sbrags ma/mnyam med rje btsun tsong kha pa chen pos mdzad pa'i byang chub lam rim chen mo'i dka' ba'i gnad rnams mchan bu bzhi'i sgo nas legs par bshad pa theg chen lam gyi gsal sgron*; New Delhi: Chophel Lekden, 1972), 153.6.

43. Tsong-kha-pa's text (Dharamsala edition, 64.22) reads *lo brgyad cu'i dus su,* which could mean "when eighty years [old]"; however, Jam-yang-shay-ba (*Great Exposition of the Middle Way,* 194b.4) makes it clear that the reference is to lifespan: ". . . when the [average] lifespan is eighty years" (*tshe lo brgyad cu'i dus su*).

44. See n. 46.

45. The actual passage in the sūtra (P888, vol. 35, 88.2.4 ff.) is:

> When the Protector called Śākyamuni emerges in this obdurate (*mi mjed*) world realm, you will become the Licchavi Liked-When-Seen. Then, when the [aver-

age] lifespan is eighty years at a time of the diminishment of the teaching after the Protector [Śākyamuni Buddha] has passed away in that worldly realm, you—having become the monk called Mindful (*blo 'chang*), will bring out this sutra without concern for your own life. Then, dying after a hundred years pass, you will be born in the worldly realm of the Blissful [Pure Land] (*bde ba can, sukhāvatī*). At that time you will emit many great magical emanations. Staying on the eighth ground, you will set one body in the Blissful [Pure Land], and, upon emanating one body, you will set it in the Joyous [Pure Land] (*dga' ldan, tuṣita*), questioning the Undaunted Protector [Maitreya] about this sutra.

Jam-yang-shay-ba creatively puts together these passages and many others in the *Great Cloud Sutra* and *Great Drum Sutra* in his *Great Exposition of Tenets* (*ca* 3a.2-6b.7) and *Great Exposition of the Middle Way* (193a.4-197a.1) into a coherent story. (Jeffrey Hopkins plans to publish a detailed analysis of this material and thus gives only a summary here.)

Nāgārjuna's history begins, so to speak, with wishes made in the presence of an earlier Buddha, Lamp-Of-The-Nāga-Lineage (*klu rigs sgron me, nāgakulapradīpa*), to proclaim three proclamations of the excellent doctrine during the time of the teaching of Śākyamuni. Śākyamuni Buddha himself identifies a Licchavi youth in his audience, called Liked-When-Seen-By-All-The-World (*'jig rten thams cad kyis mthong na dga' ba, sarvalokapriyadarśana*), as a rebirth of a Nāga king called Nāga-Of-Great-Effort (*brtson 'grus chen po'i klu*) who lived at the time of Lamp-Of-The-Nāga-Lineage. Also in his audience are Vimalaprabhā and Kauṇḍinya; Śākyamuni Buddha identifies Vimalaprabhā as the rebirth of the wife of King Nāga-Of-Great-Effort and foretells that in the future she will be reborn as a princess in a family of King Udayana (*bde spyod*) in a city that Nāgārjuna will visit. He foretells that Kauṇḍinya will become the great Buddhist king Aśoka.

Also, another Buddha called Lamp-Maker (*mar me mdzad, dīpaṃkara*), foretells that a prince who is in his audience will later take birth in the Licchavi clan and be called Liked-When-Seen-By-All-The-World, at which time he will come to be in the retinue of Śākyamuni Buddha. The Buddha Lamp-Maker explains that after the death of Śākyamuni and at a time when the teaching of the Mahāyāna has deteriorated, the prince will take birth (as Nāgārjuna) and take the vows of monkhood, at which point he will be called Mindful (*blo 'chang*).

In another setting, in the presence of a group of Bodhisattvas including Liked-When-Seen-By-All-The-World, Śākyamuni Buddha speaks to Mahākāśyapa about the future rebirth of Liked-When-Seen-By-All-The-World as Nāgārjuna. He explains that Liked-When-Seen-By-All-The-World will be born in the Śākya clan in the family lineage called Kayāgaurī (*ka yo ri*) in a village called Base-Of-The-Great-Garland (*phreng ba chen po rten*) in a district called Ayodhyā (*dmag gis mi tshugs pa*) on the banks of a river in a southern area called *Ru mun de*. Śākyamuni explains that Nāgārjuna actually will be a seventh-ground Bodhisattva, attaining the eighth ground in that lifetime, but will assume the aspect of a common being who newly attains the first Bodhisattva ground in that lifetime. He also foretells Nāgārjuna's three proclamations of doctrine and their content, as well as his death, which, given his high spiritual attainments, is merely a display.

Thus, four hundred years after Śākyamuni Buddha passed away, the prince Liked-When-Seen-By-All-The-World—to fulfill his earlier wish to assist the teaching made in the presence of the Buddha Lamp-Of-The-Nāga-Lineage—took birth in South India (the first of three appearances in South India) and became a monk under Saraha. He was given the name Glorious Mindful One (*dpal ldan blo 'chang*) and was called Nāgārjuna. In his first proclamation of doctrine Nāgārjuna protected the monks at Nālanda from famine through alchemy, exhorting the indolent and expelling the wayward. Then, having gained adepthood, somewhere between his fiftieth and hundredth year he went to the land of dragons *(klu, nāga)* and, bringing back the *One Hundred Thousand Stanza Perfection of Wisdom Sutra*, appeared in South India a second time. Having composed the *Treatise on the Middle Way, the Fundamental Text Called "Wisdom,"* he proclaimed the second proclamation of the Mahāyāna doctrine of emptiness for up to a hundred years. Then, he went to the northern continent called Unpleasant Sound (*sgra mi nyan, kuru*), furthering the interests of sentient beings for two hundred years, and again appeared in South India for a third time. During this final period, he brought back the *Great Drum Sutra*, the *Great Cloud Sutra*, and so forth, from the northern continent and proclaimed the third proclamation of doctrine, a discourse examining the basic constituent of the Buddha nature. During this final period of a hundred years, he taught about the existence of the Buddha nature in all sentient beings in such works as his *Praise of the Element of Reality* (*chos dbyings bstod pa, dharmadhātustotra*).

Śākyamuni foretells that after Liked-When-Seen-By-All-The-World's life as Nāgārjuna, he will be reborn in the Blissful Pure Land (*bde ba can, sukhāvatī*), from which he will emit a magical emanation to the Joyous Pure Land (*dga' ldan, tuṣita*) in order to question the Undaunted Protector Maitreya about the *Great Drum Sutra*. Śākyamuni then prophesies Nāgārjuna's enlightenment after more than sixty-two eons in the land known as Very Pure Light (*rab tu dang ba'i 'od, suviśuddhaprabhābhumi* or *prasannaprabhā*). About the Buddha whom Nāgārjuna will become, Śākyamuni says:

1. that his lifespan will be fifteen intermediate eons
2. that he will be born in lands called Manifestly Liking Doctrine, and so forth
3. that those places will be without Hearers, Solitary Realizers, and Forders, will be without absence of leisure for the practice of doctrine, and will have many Bodhisattvas and be adorned always with pleasant sounds
4. that even after that Buddha passes away, his teaching will remain for one thousand ten million years.

The continuum of the being who became Nāgārjuna is thereby said to have had an illustrious history dating back to the earlier Buddha Lamp-Of-The-Nāga-Lineage, through the time of Śākyamuni Buddha, through his six hundred year lifetime as Nāgārjuna, and stretching long into the future when he will become a Buddha.

That the saga begins with a promise and a wish illustrates the power of intentions, the epochal importance of individual initiative. That the saga takes place over such a long period of time illustrates the doctrine of gradual development over many lifetimes. That the teaching of emptiness about to be presented comes from this illustrious being indicates that for this tradition Nāgārjuna is both an intelligent scholar and also a highly altruistic special being.

46. Candrakīrti quotes the prophecies of Nāgārjuna in the *Descent into Laṅkā Sutra* and the *Great Cloud Sutra*, and Tsong-kha-pa refers to, but does not quote, two more, in the *Mañjuśrī Root Tantra* and the *Great Drum Sutra*. Tsong-kha-pa does not explicitly state why he expands on Candrakīrti's citation of prophecies, but the reason is clear when the remarks of his predecessor, the great scholar Bu-dön Rin-chen-drup (*bu ston rin chen grub*) of the Sa-gya (*sa skya*) order, are juxtaposed. Bu-dön questions in his *History of Buddhism* (see Obermiller, Part Two, p. 129) the very existence of the passage in the *Great Cloud Superior Sutra of Twelve Thousand Stanzas* that Candrakīrti cites:

> Someone [namely, Candrakīrti] says that the *Great Cloud Sutra* explains that ". . . four hundred years after I [Śākyamuni Buddha] pass away, this Licchavi Liked-When-Seen-By-All-The-World will become a monk known as Nāga and will disseminate my teaching. Finally, in the land known as the Very Pure Light he will become a One Gone Thus, a Foe Destroyer, a completely perfect Buddha named Light-Which-Is-A-Source-of-All-Wisdom." However, what appears in the *Great Cloud Sutra* is the following with no clear [mention] of Nāgārjuna:
>
>> In the south, in the country called Ṛṣila (*drang srong byi bo'i yul*) a king named Vipatticikitsaka (*rgud pa gso ba*) will emerge. In the eightieth year of his lifespan when the excellent doctrine will have become such that there will be only remnants of its destruction, in an area of the merchant class (*rje rigs, vaiśya*) Dra-go-jen (*'bra go can*) on the northern bank of the Sundarabhuti (*mdzes 'byor*) River of the city called Mahāvāluka (*bye ma chen po*), [a place] of meritorious beings, the Licchavi youth Liked-When-Seen-By-All-The-World will be born with my name for the sake of bringing out the doctrine of the One Gone Thus. Having made a promise in the presence of the Buddha Lamp-Of-The-Nāga-Lineage to give his life for the sake of the doctrine during the teaching of [Śākya]muni, he will spread the teaching.
>
> [That this passage prophesies Nāgārjuna] should be analyzed in accordance with a certain [scholar's] assertion that Nāgārjuna's name was Śākyamitra [in an attempt to account for the statement that the Licchavi youth Liked-When-Seen-By-All-The-World would have Śākyamuni's name. The claim] that the *Great Drum Sutra* sets forth an extensive prophecy of Nāgārjuna also should be analyzed.

The passage is translated from The Collected Works of Bu-ston *bde bar gshegs pa'i bstan pa'i gsal byed chos kyi 'byung gnas gsung rab rin po che'i mdzod*, Part 24, ed. Lokesh Chandra (New Delhi, 1971), 833.3-834.1. For E. Obermiller's translation of the same passage, see his *History of Buddhism by Bu-ston*, Part 2, 129-30; I have taken the Sanskrit equivalents from Obermiller's translation.

Jam-yang-shay-ba (*Great Exposition of the Middle Way*, 194b.2) challenges Bu-dön's qualm that the passage supposedly mentioning Nāgārjuna by name (i.e., Nāga) is not to be found in the *Great Cloud Sutra* by suggesting that Bu-dön did not realize that Candrakīrti could have been dealing with an edition of the *Great Cloud Sutra* different from the one translated into Tibetan. Thereby, Jam-yang-shay-ba weakly disposes of this challenge to Candrakīrti by saying that its absence in that sutra as translated into Tibetan does not mean that it is not in the (longer) version that Candrakīrti cites. This is undoubtedly the reason why Jam-yang-shay-ba cites the title of the text as the *Great Cloud Superior Sutra of Twelve Thousand Stanzas*, to distinguish it from the one translated into Tibetan.

Tsong-kha-pa indirectly answers Bu-dön's challenge that "[The claim] that the *Great Drum Sutra* sets forth an extensive prophecy of Nāgārjuna also should be analyzed." He appeals to authority, simply saying that both Bodhibhadra and Atīśa accept the *Great Drum Sutra* as prophesying Nāgārjuna. When he says about these Indian scholars that "they are relying on the explanation that the Licchavi Liked-When-Seen and Nāgārjuna are of one continuum," he also suggests that since Bodhibhadra and Atīśa accept the *Great Drum Sutra* as prophesying Nāgārjuna even though it does not mention him by name but speaks of the Licchavi Liked-When-Seen, one should also accept the passage in the *Great Cloud Sutra* that speaks of the Licchavi Liked-When-Seen as prophesying Nāgārjuna, whether or not Nāgārjuna's name is given.

Tsong-kha-pa does not address Bu-dön's qualm about Nāgārjuna's having Śākyamuni's name, but the *Great Cloud Sutra* indicates in several places that having Śākyamuni's name means to be born in the Śākya clan; see, for instance, *The Great Cloud Sutra* 250.5.3 for *śākya'i rus*. In this vein, Jam-yang-shay-ba (*Great Exposition of Tenets*, *ca* 4a.2) says:

> When four hundred years had elapsed after the Teacher passed away, the Licchavi Liked-When-Seen-By-All-The-World—who had conversation about relics with the Brahmin Kauṇḍinya at the time of the Teacher [Buddha Śākyamuni] and who [was the rebirth of] King Nāga-Of-Great-Effort during the age of an earlier Buddha, Lamp-Of-The-Nāga-Lineage—was born again, as explained earlier, *in a clan in South [India] of the Śākya lineage*.

The highly creative implication is that since Nāgārjuna's clan was Śākya—the addition of this information being sudden, to say the least—it is not necessary to find that Śākya was part of his name, as in "Śākyamitra."

47. P888, vol. 35, 97.5.4.

48. Gön-chok-jik-may-wang-bo, *Lamp of Scripture and Reasoning*, 185.6-186.1. Jam-yang-shay-ba (*Great Exposition of the Middle Way*, 195b.6) holds that in fact Nāgārjuna, in that lifetime, was a seventh-ground Bodhisattva who attained the eighth ground. From the viewpoint of Highest Yoga Mantra, he is held to have achieved Buddhahood in that lifetime. See the next note.

49. Here Tsong-kha-pa answers another objection to accepting the *Great Drum Sutra* as a valid prophecy of Nāgārjuna, this being because it says that Nāgārjuna is a

seventh-ground Bodhisattva whereas the *Descent into Laṅkā Sutra* indicates that he will become a first-ground Bodhisattva in that lifetime. By cryptically saying, ". . . variations among scriptures do occur," Tsong-kha-pa dismisses the objection.

Jam-yang-shay-ba expands on this answer in his *Great Exposition of Tenets* (*ca* 4a.8-5a.2) and *Great Exposition of the Middle Way* (195b.4-196b.1) by showing that Tsong-kha-pa's meaning is not that a variety of *incompatible* expositions are to be found in sutra but that variations *understandable as fitting into a coherent picture* are often found in sutra. After much creatively constructive consideration of sources, Jam-yang-shay-ba concludes that the various prophecies and descriptions fit together well if, from the sutra point of view, Nāgārjuna is considered to be a seventh-ground Bodhisattva who assumed the manner of an ordinary common being who newly attained the first ground in that lifetime.

From this perspective, the explanation given even by the Indian scholar Avalokitavrata, that Nāgārjuna attained the first ground—as well as the prophecies of the same in the *Descent into Laṅkā* and the *Mañjuśrī Root Tantra*—are interpreted as according merely with common appearance and not the actual fact. This interpretation is based on the *Great Drum Sutra* itself (P888, vol. 35, 97.5.4) where it says, "Having set him in the seventh ground, I will bless him *as an ordinary being*," indicating that although Nāgārjuna was a seventh-ground Bodhisattva (who attained the eighth ground in that lifetime), he appeared to be an ordinary being who attained the path of seeing and thus the first ground in that lifetime.

The seeming conflict in the scriptures is explained by adopting a double view of Nāgārjuna—that is, as a higher being who put on a show of attaining a lower achievement for the sake of helping others. The situation is further complicated because in tantra, as Tsong-kha-pa's *Ocean of Reasoning, Explanation of (Nāgārjuna's) "Treatise on the Middle Way"* (5.1-5.6) reports, Nāgārjuna is considered to have attained Buddhahood in that very lifetime. Tsong-kha-pa refers to Candrakīrti's *Lamp Illuminating (Nāgārjuna's) "Five Stages"* (*sgron ma gsal bar byed pa zhes bya ba'i rgya cher bshad pa, pradīpoddyotananāmaṭīkā*) which says that Nāgārjuna attained the status of a Vajradhara, a Buddha, in that very lifetime through the path of Highest Yoga Tantra. He compares this to Śākyamuni Buddha's *display* of enlightenment in this world-system even though he had actually attained enlightenment many eons earlier. Thus, in what is considered the final presentation there is a triple view of Nāgārjuna—he made a double display, as a common being who attained the first Bodhisattva ground and as a seventh-ground Bodhisattva who attained the eighth, whereas actually he attained Buddhahood by practicing Highest Yoga Tantra.

50. Yeshey Tupden's commentary, chapter 3; Peking edition, vol. 154, 28; Sarnath edition, 119.12; Dharamsala edition, 65.1-66.4.

51. This is an abbreviation for *dbu ma'i bstan bcos* (*madhyamakaśāstra*).

52. The Tibetan Cultural Printing Press edition (65.1), the Sarnath edition (119.12), the Peking (28.4.8), and Guru Deva (132.6) read *goms par* whereas Candrakīrti's commentary (Poussin, Osnabrück, 77.7, and Dharamsala, 64.7) and Jayānanda (P5271, vol. 99, 119.4.7) read *goms pas*; the latter is preferable.

53. The material from here up to the question and answer leading into stanza 4 is not found in Candrakīrti's commentary. It repeats a theme found throughout Tsong-kha-pa's writings on the Middle Way School. Jayānanda (P5271, vol. 99, 119.5.8) cites this and XXIV.12 from Nāgārjuna's *Treatise.*

54. Tsong-kha-pa is saying that to hold that something does not exist and that it is not existent amount to the same thing. The verbal difference does not yield a difference in meaning. Therefore, one cannot hold that something is not existent and is not nonexistent. He makes a similar point in his "Middling Exposition of Special Insight":

> Differentiating between the two—"is not existent" and "does not exist"—and between the two—"is not nonexistent" and "exists" [in order to propound that an object is not existent, is not nonexistent, is not both, and is not either] with respect to a base [i.e., an object] is exhausted as merely a difference in the mode of expression. No matter how much one analyzes how the meanings of both appear to the mind, there is no difference at all. Hence, to propound that one falls or does not fall to an extreme through [how] those words [are used] is exhausted as an unfounded fixation on mere words. (Jeffrey Hopkins, unpublished translation, 43.)

55. XII.12: *apāyam eva yāty ekaḥ śivam eva tu netaraḥ*. See Karen Lang, *Āryadeva's Catuḥśataka: On the Bodhisattva's Cultivation of Merit and Knowledge*, Indiske Studier VII (Copenhagen: Akademisk Forlag, 1986), p. 114.

56. Yeshey Tupden (oral commentary) identified the nonordinary as a person without the conception of inherent existence.

57. The material in this paragraph is not found in Candrakīrti's commentary.

58. Yeshey Tupden's commentary, chapter 4; Peking edition, vol. 154, 29.2.2; Sarnath edition, 121.14; Dharamsala edition, 66.5.

59. The material in this paragraph is not found in Candrakīrti's commentary.

60. Not translated here; see Hopkins, *Compassion*, pp. 182-91.

61. Not translated here; see Hopkins, *Compassion*, pp. 101-25.

62. Yeshey Tupden, oral commentary.

63. Yeshey Tupden, oral commentary.

64. The rest of this section is not found in Candrakīrti's commentary.

65. In the late eighth century a Chinese monk by the name of Ha-shang Mahāyāna purportedly presented in Tibet the view that all thoughts are equally obstructive of enlightenment; his view was superceded in Tibet by that of Kamalaśīla, an Indian proponent of gradual enlightenment (see n. 20, chapter 3, pp. 236-237). For bibliography on this debate see Elizabeth Napper, *Dependent-Arising and Emptiness* (London: Wisdom Publications, 1989), n. 36, p. 656. See also chapter 3, n. 17, p. 235.

66. Yeshey Tupden's commentary, chapter 5; Peking edition, vol. 154, 29.4.6; Sarnath edition, 124.14-127.2; Dharamsala edition, 67.1.

67. The rest of this section is not found in Candrakīrti's commentary.

68. Yeshey Tupden, oral commentary.

69. Yeshey Tupden, oral commentary.

70. The four modes of gathering students are by way of giving gifts, giving doctrine, teaching others to fulfill their aims, and oneself acting according to that teaching. Nāgārjuna's *Precious Garland* (stanza 133) says:

> You should cause the religious
> And the worldly to assemble
> Through giving, speaking pleasantly,
> Behaving with purpose, and concordance.

"Behaving with purpose" refers to causing others to practice what is helpful; "concordance" is for one to practice what one teaches others. See Jeffrey Hopkins, tr., in Nāgārjuna and the Seventh Dalai Lama, *The Precious Garland and the Song of the Four Mindfulnesses* (New York, Harper and Row, 1975); reprinted in *The Buddhism of Tibet* (London: George Allen and Unwin, 1983, and Ithaca: Snow Lion Publications, 1987).

71. This could be done, for example, by leading a student gradually through the views of the Vaibhāṣika, Sautrāntika, Cittamātra, and Svātantrika Schools before introducing the Prāsaṅgika School doctrines.

72. P5330, vol. 102, 108.5.4-109.1.4.

73. Translation doubtful.

74. Yeshey Tupden (oral commentary) explained this as lacking an understanding of emptiness.

75. Yeshey Tupden, oral commentary.

76. Paraphrasing a citation in Nāgārjuna's *Compendium of Sutra* (P5330, vol. 102, 109.2.2-109.3.2). This is perhaps the *āryatathāgatagarbhanāmamahāyānasūtra* referred to as *tathāgatakośagarbhasūtra.*

77. Paraphrasing the next citation in Nāgārjuna's *Compendium of Sutra* (P5330, vol. 102, 109.3.4-109.3.6).

78. Killing one's father, killing one's mother, causing blood to flow from a Buddha's body with evil intent, killing an Arhat (*dgra bcom pa, arhan*), and causing dissent in the spiritual community.

79. Quoting Nāgārjuna's *Compendium of Sutra* (P5330, vol. 102, 109.4.5-109.4.6).

## 2. Dependent Arising and Reality

1. Yeshey Tupden's commentary, chapter 6; Peking edition, vol. 154, 30.21; Sarnath edition, 127.2; Dharamsala edition, 69.

2. The translation here includes the first of these three.

3. None of the material after this citation is found in Candrakīrti's text. Candrakīrti directly proceeds to the refutation of inherently existence production, whereas Tsong-kha-pa has a long excursus on the object negated in the view of selflessness in the Mādhyamika Schools.

4. Yeshey Tupden's commentary, chapter 7; Peking edition, vol. 154, 30.4.1; Sarnath edition, 128.20; Dharamsala edition, 70.2.

5. The Sanskrit is:

*kalpitaṃ bhāvamaspṛṣṭvā tadabhāvo na gṛhyate//*

See Vidhushekara Bhattacharya, ed., *Bodhicaryāvatāra*, Bibliotheca Indica, vol. 280 (Calcutta: the Asiatic Society, 1960), p. 221.

6. Read *shes dgos kyi* for *shes kyi* in accordance with P6143, vol. 154, 30.5.7.

## 3. The Svātantrika School on True Existence

1. Yeshey Tupden's commentary, chap. 8; Peking edition, vol. 154, 30.5.8-31.3.5; Sarnath edition, 129.19-132.8; Dharamsala edition, 70.15-71.24.

2. The translation accords with the explanation in Nga-wang-bel-den's *Annotations for (Jam-yang-shay-ba's) "Great Exposition of Tenets"* (*dbu* 37a.4-38a.1). Nga-wang-bel-den (*dbu* 37a.8-37b.8) recasts the meaning of this passage as follows:

> The subject, the innate conception of true existence which conceives that phenomena ultimately inherently exist whereas they do not, is called a "concealer" (*kun rdzob, saṃvṛti*) or obstructor (*sgrib byed*) because the conception of true existence, like an eye obstructed by cataracts, obstructs itself from seeing suchness, [or] this conception of true existence veils other awarenesses from seeing suchness, like covering something with a cloth. This is because the *Descent into Laṅkā Sutra* says:
>
> > Things are produced conventionally (*kun rdzob tu, saṃvṛtitas*).
> > Ultimately they are without inherent existence.
> > That which is mistaken about the lack of inherent existence
> > Is asserted as the concealer (*kun rdzob, saṃvṛti*) of reality.
>
> . . . Since an artificial awareness in the continuum of a Proponent of True Existence arises from that conception of true existence, all false things such as forms, and so forth—which are the observed objects of such an artificial awareness that sees them displayed by that conception of true existence as if they are

truly existent—exist only conventionally, not ultimately. Not only does that artificial awareness arise from the conception of true existence but also that conception of true existence arises through the maturation of beginningless predispositions for error. That conception of true existence displays truly established phenomena to all living beings as if they exist, whether their awarenesses are affected by systems of tenets or not, and those living beings also perceive them that way. Therefore, since it would not be suitable to posit phenomena as existing through the force of appearing to a consciousness conceiving true existence, existence which is posited through the force of appearing to a nondefective awareness—its factors of appearance and conception not being affected by the force of the conception of true existence—is the meaning of existing conventionally. Hence, the object of negation—true existence—does not appear to sense consciousnesses.

3. Yeshey Tupden's commentary, chapter 9; Peking edition, vol. 154, 31.3.5; Sarnath edition, 132.8; Dharamsala edition, 71.24.

4. "True establishment *in terms of a conventional ordinary awareness*" does not refer to the object of negation as the term "true establishment" usually does but to something that is true on the conventional level. Tsong-kha-pa is saying that even on the conventional level, if something is true, there will be no conflict between how it appears and how it is; it will not appear to be something and yet not be that, and correspondingly, if it is empty of something—that is, if it is not something—it will not appear to be that. Therefore, a magician's illusion, since it appears to be a real object and yet is not, cannot be true (or truly established) in a conventional sense of that term and thus must be a falsity, appearing one way and existing another.

5. Yeshey Tupden's commentary, chapter 9; Peking edition, vol. 154, 32.3.4; Sarnath edition, 136.19; Dharamsala edition, 74.11.

## 4. The Prāsaṅgika School on True Existence

1. For the Sanskrit see Karen Lang, *Āryadeva's Catuḥśataka*, 78.

2. P5266, vol. 98, 229.5.3, commenting on VIII.3.

3. *gzhir* here means *mtshan gzhir.*

4. *kun gzhi rnam par shes pa, ālayavijñāna.*

5. Perhaps the meaning of this cryptic conclusion is that if a mind-basis-of-all were a person, then since a mind-basis-of-all is held not to realize anything, it could not be a Superior, and thus one could not reasonably assert Superiors in such a system.

6. Tsong-kha-pa cites this twice in his "Middling Exposition of Special Insight" (Jeffrey Hopkins, unpublished translation, pp. 33 and 63), in terms of extending knowledge of the absence of true existence of persons to other phenomena. However, here he cites it in the context of extending understanding of the imputed nature of the person to other phenomena.

7. The bracketed material is from Nga-wang-bel-den's *Annotations for (Jam-yang-shay-ba's) "Great Exposition of Tenets"* (*dbu* 67b.4-67b.8).

8. If the person were the composite or aggregation of the mental and physical aggregates or even if it were designated *to* the composite or aggregation of the mental and physical aggregates, that composite would be the person. Rather, the person is designated *in dependence upon* the mental and physical aggregates.

9. Nga-wang-bel-den (*Annotations*, *dbu* 67a.1 ff.) recasts the first stanza as follows:

> Because the phenomena of forms [which have the obstructiveness of which space is the absence] are only names, space also is just a name [and does not exist inherently. If someone said that forms exist inherently, then] when the elements do not exist [inherently], how could form exist [inherently]? Therefore, even name-only-ness does not exist [inherently because that which possesses a name does not exist inherently].

10. P5266, vol. 98, 103.4.4, chapter XII.

11. VI.127-128.

12. P5263, vol. 98, 141.1.2, commenting on VI.120: "The object of observation of [a consciousness viewing the transitory collection as an inherently existent self] is the [nominally existent] self. For, that which conceives an [inherently existent] I has as its object [an inherently existent] self." Bracketed material is from Tsong-kha-pa's *Illumination*, P6143, vol. 154, 82.2.8.

13. Commenting on VI.120.

14. See Hopkins, *Compassion*, p. 116.

15. The Sanskrit is not extant. See also Karen Lang, *Āryadeva's Catuḥśataka*, 134.

16. The Sanskrit is not extant. See also Karen Lang, *Āryadeva's Catuḥśataka*, 66.

# Bibliography of Works Cited

## WORKS IN WESTERN LANGUAGES


Ackerman, Diane. 1991. *A Natural History of the Senses.* New York: Vintage.

Alper, Harvey P., ed. 1989. *Mantra.* Albany: State University of New York Press.

Bakhtin, M. M. 1990. *Art and Answerability: Early Philosophical Essays.* (Austin: University of Texas Press).

Batchelor, Stephen. 1979. *Guide to the Bodhisattva's Way of Life.* Dharamsala: Library of Tibetan Works and Archives.

Bhattacharya, Vidhushekhara, ed. 1960. *Bodhicaryāvatāra.* Bibliotheca Indica, vol. 280. Calcutta: The Asiatic Society.

Broughton, Jeffrey. 1983. "Early Ch'an Schools in Tibet" in *Studies in Ch'an and Hua-yen,* Robert M. Gimello and Peter M. Gregory, eds., Honolulu: University of Hawaii Press.

Buddhaghosa. 1976. *Path of Purification (Visuddhimagga).* tr. Bhikkhu Nyanamoli. Berkeley: Shambala.

Buswell, Robert. 1992. "The Wholesome Roots and Their Eradication: A Descent to the Bedrock of Buddhist Soteriology." In *Paths to Liberation.* Robert Buswell and Robert M. Gimello, eds. Kuroda Institute. Studies in East Asian Buddhism 7. Honolulu: University of Hawaii Press.

Buswell, Robert, and Gimello, Robert M., eds. 1992. *Paths to Liberation: The Mārga and its Transformations in Buddhist Thought.* Kuroda Institute. Studies in East Asian Buddhism 7. Honolulu: University of Hawaii Press.

Carothers, J. C. 1959. "Culture, Psychiatry, and the Written Word" in *Psychiatry,* 22.

Cozort, Daniel. 1986. *Highest Yoga Tantra.* Ithaca: Snow Lion.

Das, Sarat Chandra. 1902. *A Tibetan-English Dictionary.* Calcutta:Bengal Secretariat Book Dept.; reprint, Compact Edition: Kyoto: Rinsen Book Company, 1977.

Demieville, Paul. 1954. *Le Concile de Lhasa.* Paris: Imprimerie Nationale de France.

Dhargyey, Geshey Ngawang. 1974. *Tibetan Tradition of Mental Development.* Dharamsala: Library of Tibetan Works and Archives.

Eckel, David M. 1986. *Jñānagarbha's Commentary on the Distinction Between the Two Truths.* Albany: State University of New York Press.

Edgerton, Franklin. 1972. *Buddhist Hybrid Sanskrit Grammar and Dictionary.* New Haven: Yale University Press, 1953; reprint, Delhi: Motilal.

Fenner, Peter. 1984. "A Study of the Relationship between Analysis *(vicāra)* and Insight *(prañā).* Based on the Madhyamakāvatāra" in *Journal of Indian Philosophy* 12: 139-97.

Gallop, Jane. 1985. *Reading Lacan.* Ithaca: Cornell University Press.

Gimello, Robert M., and Gregory, Peter N., eds. 1983. *Studies in Ch'an and Hua-Yen.* Kuroda Institute Studies in East Asian Buddhism. Honolulu: University of Hawaii Press.

Gleick, James. 1987. *Chaos.* New York: Viking.

Gomez, Luis O. 1983. "The Direct and Gradual Approaches of Zen Master Mahāyāna: Fragments of the Teachings of Mo-Ho-Yen." In *Studies in Ch'an and Hua'yen,* Robert M. Gimello and Peter N. Gregory, eds. Honolulu: Kuroda Institute, University of Hawaii Press.

———. 1983a. "Indian Materials on the Doctrine of Sudden Enlightenment." In *Early Ch'an in China and Tibet.* Whalen Lai and Lewis Lancaster, eds. Berkeley: Buddhist Studies Series 5, pp. 351-66.

———. 1987. "Purifying Gold: The Metaphor of Effort and Intuition in Buddhist Thought and Practice." In *Sudden and Gradual Approaches to Enlightenment in Chinese Thought.* Peter N. Gregory, ed. Honolulu: Kuroda Institute, University of Hawaii Press.

Gonda, Jan. 1963. "The Indian Mantra." *Oriens,* XVI, pp. 244-97.

Goodman, Steven D., and Davidson, Ronald M. 1992. *Tibetan Buddhism: Reason and Revelation.* Albany: State University of New York Press.

Goody, Jack, and Watt, Ian. 1968. "The Consequences of Literacy." In *Literacy in Traditional Societies.* J. R. Goody, ed. Cambridge: Oxford University Press.

Griffiths, Paul. 1986. *Being Mindless.* La Salle, Illinois: Open Court Press.

Guenther, Herbert. 1983. "Meditation Trends in Early Tibet." In *Early Ch'an in China and Tibet.* Whalen Lai and Louis Lancaster, eds. Berkeley: Berkeley Buddhist Studies Series, no. 5.

Gyatso, Geshe Kelsang. 1982. *Clear Light of Bliss.* London: Wisdom Publications.

Gyatso, Janet. 1992. "Letter Magic." In *the Mirror of Memory*. ed. Janet Gyatso. Albany: State University of New York Press.

Hopkins, Jeffrey. 1977. *Tantra in Tibet.* London: George, Allen & Unwin.

———. 1980. *Compassion in Tibetan Buddhism.* Ithaca: Snow Lion.

———. 1983. *Meditation on Emptiness.* London: Wisdom Publications.

———. 1987. *Emptiness Yoga: The Middle Way Consequence School.* Joe B. Wilson, ed. Ithaca: Snow Lion.

———. 1989. *Cutting Through Appearances.* Ithaca: Snow Lion.

Hopkins, Jeffrey, tr. 1974. *Practice of Emptiness: The Perfection of Wisdom Chapter of the Fifth Dalai Lama's "Sacred Word of Mañjuśrī" (jam dpal shal lung).* Dharamsala: Library of Tibetan Works and Archives.

———. 1975. *The Precious Garland and the Song of the Four Mindfulnesses.* Nāgārjuna and the Seventh Dalai Lama. New York: Harper and Row.

Hopkins, Jeffrey, tr., with Lati Rinbochay. 1986. *Death, the Intermediate State, and Rebirth.* Ithaca: Snow Lion.

Huntington, C. W.; and Geshe Namgyal Wangchen. 1989. *The Emptiness of Emptiness: An Introduction to Early Indian Mādhyamika.* Honolulu: University of Hawaii Press.

Ihde, Don. 1976. *Listening and Voice.* Athens, Ohio: Ohio University Press.

Jousse, Marcel. 1990. *The Oral Style.* Tr. Edgard Sienaert and Richard Whitaker. The Alfred Bates Lord Studies in Oral Tradition. New York: Garland Publishing.

Kapstein, Matthew. 1986. "Collins, Parfit, and the Problem of Personal Identity in Two Philosophical Traditions—a review of *Selfless Persons* in *Philosophy East and West* 36, no. 3, July.

Klein, Anne C. 1986. *Knowledge and Liberation.* Ithaca: Snow Lion.

———. 1991. *Knowing, Naming, and Negation.* Ithaca: Snow Lion.

———. 1992. "Mental Concentration and the Unconditioned: A Buddhist Case for Unmediated Experience." In *Paths to Liberation.* Robert Buswell and Robert M. Gimello, eds. Kuroda Institute. Studies in East Asian Buddhism 7. Honolulu: University of Hawaii Press.

Lalou, Marcelle. 1939, 1950, 1950, and 1961. *Inventaire des manuscrits tibétains de Touenhouang conservés à la Bibliothèque Nationale.* Paris: Bibliothèque Nationale.

Lati Rinbochay, Lochö Rinbochay, Leah Zahler, and Jeffrey Hopkins. 1983. *Meditatitve States in Tibetan Buddhism.* London: Wisdom Publications.

Lipman, Kennard. 1992. "What is Buddhist Logic?" in *Tibetan Buddhism: Reason and Revelation*. Steven D. Goodman and Ronald M. Davidson, eds. Albany: State University of New York Press.

Lodrö, Geshe Gedun. 1992. *Walking Through Walls*. Ithaca: Snow Lion.

Lopez, Donald S. , Jr. 1987. *A Study of Svātantrika*. Ithaca: Snow Lion.

Lumpp, Randolph Franklin. 1976. "Culture, Religion, and The Presence of the Word: A Study of the Thought of Walter Jackson Ong." Ph. D. Dissertation, University of Ottowa.

Mimaki, Katsumi. 1982. *Blo gsal grub mtha*. Kyoto: Zinbun Kagaku Kenkyusyo, Université de Kyoto.

Nagatomi, Masatoshi. 1980. "Mānasa-pratyakṣa: A Conundrum in the Buddhist Pramāṇa System." In *Sanskrit and Indian Studies*. M. Nagatoi, B.K. Matilal, J.M. Masson, and R. Dimock, eds. Boston: D. Reidel.

Napper, Elizabeth. 1989. *Dependent-Arising and Emptiness*. London:Wisdom Publications.

———. 1980. *Mind in Tibetan Buddhism*. Ithaca: Snow Lion.

Newland, Guy. 1992. *The Two Truths in the Mādhyamika Philosophy of the Ge-luk-ba Order of Tibetan Buddhism*. Ithaca: Snow Lion.

Nobel, Johannes, ed. 1944. *Suvarṇaprabhāsottamasūtra, Das Goldglanz-Sūtra*. Leiden: Brill.

Norbu, Namkhai. 1984. *Dzog Chen and Zen*, Kennard Lipman, ed. Oakland, CA: Zhang Zhung Editions.

Obermiller, E., tr. 1931. *History of Buddhism by Bu-ston (Chos 'byung)*. Heidelberg: Harrassowitz.

Ong, Walter J., S. J. 1982. *Orality and Literacy: The Technologizing of the Word*. London and New York: Methuen & Co.

———. 1967. *The Presence of the Word*. New Haven and London: Yale University Press.

Perdue, Daniel E. 1992. *Debate in Tibetan Buddhism*. Ithaca: Snow Lion.

Poussin, Louis de la Vallé, *Madhyamakāvatāra*. *Muséon* 8 (1907): 249-317; 11 (1910): 271-358; 12 (1911): 235-328.

Rizzi, Cesare. 1988. *Candrakīrti*. Delhi: Motilal Banarsidass.

Robinson, Richard. 1972. "Did Nāgārjuna Really Refute All Views?" In *Philosophy East and West* 22 (1972), pp. 325-31.

Ruegg, David S. 1981. *La Traité sur le Tathāgatha Garbha de Bu-ston*. Paris: École française d'Extrême-Orient, A. Maissonneuve.

———. 1981. *The Literature of the Madhyamaka School of Philosophy in India*. Wiesbaden: Otto Harrassowitz.

———. 1969. *La Théorie du Tathagathagarbha et du Gotra*. Paris: École Française d'Extrême-Orient.

Stein, R.A. 1961. *Une chronique ancienne de bSam-yas: sba bzed*. Paris: n.p.

Tauscher, Helmut. 1981. *Candrakīrti Madhyamakāvatāraḥ und Madhyamakāvatāra-bhāṣyam*. Wien: Wiener Studien zur Tibetologie und Buddhismuskunde, Heft 5.

Tāranātha. 1980. *History of Buddhism in India*. Tr. by Lama Chimpa and Alaka Chattopadhyaya. Calcutta: Bagchi.

Thurman, Robert A. F. 1984. *Tsong-ka-ba's Speech of Gold in the Essence of True Eloquence*. Princeton: Princeton University Press.

———. 1982. *The Life and Teachings of Tsong Khapa*. Dharamsala: Library of Tibetan Works and Archives.

Giuseppe Tucci, ed. and tr. 1971. *The New Red Annals* by Pan-chen So-nam Drak-pa (reproduced and translated as *Deb t'er dmar po gsar ma)*. Serie Orientale Roma. Roma: Istituto Italiano Per Il Medio Ed Estremo Oriente.

Ueyama, Daishun. 1983. "The Study of Tibetan Ch'an Manuscripts Recovered from Tun-huang: A Review of the Field and its Prospects." In *Early Ch'an in China and Tibet*. Whalen Lai and Lewis Lancaster, eds. Berkeley: Buddhist Studies Series 5.

Vaidya, P. L., ed. 1963. *Saddharmalaṅkāvatārasūtram*. Buddhist Sanskrit Texts No. 3. Darbhanga: Mithila Institute.

Walleser, M. 1979. "The Life of Nāgārjuna from Tibetan and Chinese Sources." *Asia Major*. Introductory Volume; Hirth Anniversary Volume. Leipzig (1923): 421-55. Reprint: Delhi: Nag Publishers.

Yampolsky, Philip B., tr. 1967. *The Platform Sutra of the Sixth Patriarch*. New York: Columbia University Press.

## WORKS IN TIBETAN AND SANSKRIT

Indian and Tibetan treatises are listed alphabetically by author in the second section, using the root letter for names of Tibetan authors.

"P" stands for "Peking edition" and refers to the Tibetan Tripiṭaka (Tokyo-Kyoto: Tibetan Tripiṭaka Research Foundation, 1956.

"Toh" refers to the *Complete Catalogue of the Tibetan Buddhist Canons*, Prof. Hukuju Ui, ed., and *A Catalogue of the Tohuku University Collection of Tibetan Works on Buddhism*, Prof. Yensho Kanakura, ed. (Sendai, Japan: 1934 and 1953).

## 1. Sūtras and Tantras

*Condensed Perfection of Wisdom Sūtra*
sañcayagāthāprajñāpāramitāsūtra
'phags pa sdud pa
P735, vol. 21
Also: *Prajñā-Pāramitā-Ratna-Guṇa-Saṃcaya-Gāthā*; Sanskrit and Tibetan Text ed. by E. Obermiller. 'S-Gravenhage, 1960; or as edited by Akira Yuyama. Cambridge University Press, 1976

*Descent Into Laṅkā Sūtra*
laṅkāvatārasūtra
lang kar gshegs pa'i mdo
P775, vol. 29
Sanskrit: *Saddharmalaṅkāvatārasūtram*. P. L. Vaidya, ed. Buddhist Sanskrit Texts. No. 3. Darbhanga: Mithila Institute, 1963; also: Bunyiu Nanjio, ed. Bibl. Otaniensis, vol. I. Kyoto: Otani University Press, 1923
English translation: D.T. Suzuki. *The Lankavatara Sutra*. London: Routledge and Kegan Paul, 1932

*Diamond Cutter Sūtra*
āryavajrachchedikānāmamahāyānasūtra
'phags pa shes rab kyi pha rol tu phyin pa rdo rje gcod pa zhes bya ba theg pa chen po'i mdo
P739, vol. 21

*Excellent Golden Light*
āryasuvarṇaprabhāsottamasūtrendrarājanāmamahāyānasūtra
'phags pa gser 'od dam pa mdo sde dbang po'i rgyal po zhes bya ba theg pa chen po'i mdo
P175, vol. 7
Also: *Suvarnaprabhāsottamasūtra, Das Goldglanz-Sūtra*. ed. Johannes Nobel. Leiden: Brill, 1944

*Great Cloud Superior Sūtra of Twelve Thousand Stanzas*
āryadvādaśasahasramahāmegha
'phags pa sprin chen po stong phrag bcu gnyis pa
See next entry

*Great Cloud Sūtra*
āryamahāmeghanāmamahāyānasūtra
'phags pa sprin chen po zhes bya ba theg pa chen po'i mdo
P898, vol. 35

*Great Drum Sūtra*
āryamahābherīharakaparivartanāmamahāyānasūtra
'phags pa rnga bo che chen po'i le'u zhes bya ba theg pa chen po'i mdo
P888, vol. 35

*King of Meditative Stabilizations Sūtra*
samādhirājasūtra/ sarvadharmasvabhāvasamatāvipañcatasamādhirājasūtra
ting nge 'dzin rgyal po'i mdo/ chos thams cad kyi rang bzhin mnyam pa nyid rnam par spros pa ting nge 'dzin gyi rgyal po'i mdo
P795, vol. 31-2; Toh 127; Dharma, vol. 20
Sanskrit: *Samādhirājasūtram.* P. L. Vaidya, ed. Buddhist Sanskrit Texts, no. 2. Darbhanga: Mithila Institute, 1961
Partial English translation (of chapters 8, 19, and 22): K. Regamey. *Three Chapters from the Samādhirājasūtra.* Warsaw: Publications of the Oriental Commission, 1938

*Mañjuśrī Root Tantra*
mañjuśrīmūlakalpa
'jam dpal tsa ba'i rtog pa
P162, vol. 6

*Questions of Upāli Sūtra*
upālipariprcchā
nye bar 'khor gyis zhus pa
[?]

*Sūtra of Ajātaśatru*
āryājātaśatrukaukṛttyavinodananāmamahāyānasūtra
'phags pa ma skyes dgra'i 'gyod pa bsal ba zhes bya ba theg pa chen po'i mdo
P882, vol. 35

*Sūtra on the Ten Grounds*
daśabhūmikasūtra
mdo sde sa bcu pa
P761.31, vol. 25
Sanskrit: *Daśabhūmikasūtram.* P. L. Vaidya, ed. Buddhist Sanskrit Texts, no. 7. Darbhanga: Mithila Institute, 1967
English translation: M. Honda. "An Annotated Translation of the 'Daśabhūmika.'" In D. Sinor, ed. *Studies in Southeast and Central Asia.* Śatapiṭaka Series 74. New Delhi: 1968, pp.115-276

## Treatises

Āryadeva ('phags pa lha, second to third century C.E. )
*Four Hundred/Treatise of Four Hundred Stanzas*
catuḥśatakaśāstrakārikā
bstan bcos bzhi brgya pa zhes bya ba'i tshig le'ur byas pa
P5246, vol. 95

Edited Tibetan and Sanskrit fragments along with English translation: Karen Lang, Āryadeva's *Catuḥśataka: On the Bodhisattva's Cultivation of Merit and Knowledge.* Cophenhagen: Akademisk Forlag, 1986

Asaṅga (*thogs med*, fourth century)
*Grounds of Bodhisattvas*
bodhisattvabhūmi
byang chub sems pa'i sa
P5538, vol. 110
Sanskrit edition: *Bodhisattvabhūmi (being the XVth Section of Asangapada's Yogacārabhūmi).* Nalinaksha Dutt, ed. Tibetan Sanskrit Works Series, vol. 7. Patna: K. P. Jayaswal Research Institue, 1966
English translation of the "Chapter on Suchness," chapter 4 of Part I, which is the fifteenth volume of the *Grounds of Yogic Practice*: Janice D. Willis. *On Knowing Reality.* Delhi: Motilal, 1979
French translation by Johannes Rahder. *Daśabhūmikasūtra et Bodhisattvabhūmi: Chapitres Vihāra et Bhūmi* Paris and Louvain, 1926.

Explanation of (Maitreya's) 'Sublime Continuum of the Great Vehicle'
Mahāyānottaratantraśāstravyākhyā
Theg pa chen po'i rgyud bla ma'i bstan bcos kyi rnam par bshad pa
P5526, vol. 108

Bu-dön (*bu ston rin chen grub*, 1290-1364)
*History of the Doctrine*
bde bar gshegs pa'i bstan pa'i gsal byed chos kyi 'byung gnas gsung rab rin po che'i mdzod
Lha-sa: zhol bka' 'gyur spar khang, n.d.
English translation: E. Obermiller. *History of Buddhism.* Heidleberg: Harrasowitz, rpt. Suzuki Reprint Series, 1931.

Candrakīrti (*zla ba grags pa*, seventh century)
*[Auto]Commentary on the "Entrance to (Nāgārjuna's) Treatise on the Middle Way"*
madhyamakāvatārabhāṣya
dbu ma la 'jug pa'i bshad pa/dbu ma la 'jug pa'i rang 'grel
P5263, vol. 98
Also: Dharamsala: Council of Religious and Cultural Affairs, 1968
Edited Tibetan: Louis de la Vallée Poussin. *Madhyamakāvatāra par Candrakīrti.* Bibliotheca Buddhica IX. Osnabrück: Biblio Verlag, 1970
French translation (up to VI.165): Louis de la Vallée Poussin. *Muséon* 8 (1907): 249-317; ii (1910): 271-358; 12 (1911): 235-328
German translation (VI. 166-226: Helmut Tauscher. *Candrakīrti-Madhyamakāvatāraḥ und Madhyamakāvatārabhāṣyam.* Wien: Wiener Studien zur Tibetologie und Buddhismuskunde, 1981

*Brilliant Lamp, Extensive Commentary [on the Guhyasamāja Tantra]*
pradīpoddyotananāmaṭīkā
sgron ma gsal bar byed pa zhes bya ba'i rgya cher bshad pa
P5709, vol. 60

*Clear Words, Commentary on (Nāgārjuna's) "Treatise on the Middle Way"*
mūlamadhyamakavṛttiprasannapadā
dbu ma rtsa ba'i 'grel pa tshig gsal ba
P5260, vol. 98
Also: Dharamsala: Tibetan Publishing House, 1968
Sanskrit: *Mūlamadhyamakakārikās de Nāgārjuna avec la Prasannapadā Commentaire de Candrakīrti*. Louis de la Vallée Poussin, ed. Bibliotheca Buddhica IV. Osnabrück: Biblio Verlag, 1970
English translation (chap. 1, 25): T. Stcherbatsky. *Conception of Buddhist Nirvāṇa*. Leningrad: Office of the Academy of Sciences of the USSR, 1927; revised reprint: Delhi: Motilal Banarsidass, 1978, pp. 77-222
English translation (chap. 2): Jeffrey Hopkins. "Analysis of Going and Coming." Dharamsala: Library of Tibetan Works and Archives, 1974
Partial English translation: Mervyn Sprung. *Lucid Exposition of the Middle Way, the Essential Chapters from the Prasannapadā of Candrakīrti translated from the Sanskrit*. London: Routledge, 1979, and Boulder: Prajñā Press, 1979
French translation (chap. 2-4, 6-9, 11, 23, 24, 26, 28): Jacques May. *Prasannapadā Madhyamaka-vṛtti, douze chapitres traduits du sanscrit et du tibétain*. Paris: Adrien-Maisonneuve, 1959
French translation (chap. 18-22): J. W. de Jong. *Cinq chapitres de la Prasannapadā*. Paris: Geuthner, 1949
French translation (chap. 17): É. Lamotte. "Le Traité de l'acte de Vasubandhu, Karmasiddhiprakaraṇa." *Mélanges Chinois et Bouddhiques* 4 (1936), 265-288
German translation (chap. 5, 12-16): St. Schayer. *Ausgewhälte Kapitel aus der Prasannapadā*. Krakow: Naktadem Polskiej Akademji Umiejetnosci, 1931
German translation (chap. 10): St. Schayer. "Feuer und Brennstoff." *Rocznik Orjentalistyczny* 7 (1931), pp. 26-52

*Commentary on (Āryadeva's) "Four Hundred Stanzas on the Yogic Deeds of Bodhisattvas"*
bodhisattvayogacaryācatuḥśatakaṭīkā
byang chub sems dpa'i rnal 'byor spyod pa bzhi brgya pa'i rgya cher 'grel pa
P5266, vol. 98; Toh 3865, Tokyo *sde dge* vol. 8
Edited Sanskrit fragments: Haraprasād Shāstri, ed. "Catuḥśatika of Ārya Deva." Memoirs of the Asiatic Society of Bengal, 3: 8 (1914): 449-514
Also (chap. 8-16): Vidhusekhara Bhattacarya, ed. *The Catuḥśataka of Āryadeva: Sanskrit and Tibetan texts with copious extracts from the commentary of Candrakīrtti*, Part II. Calcutta: Visva-Bharati Bookshop, 1931

*Entrance to (Nāgārjuna's) "Treatise on the Middle Way"*
madhyamakāvatāra
dbu ma la 'jug pa
P5261, P5262, vol. 98
Edited Tibetan: Louis de la Vallée Poussin. *Madhyamakāvtāra par Candrakīrti*. Bibliotheca Buddhica IX. Osnabrück: Biblio Verlag, 1970

Partial English translation (chap. 1-5): Jeffrey Hopkins, in *Compassion in Tibetan Buddhism.* Ithaca: NY: Snow Lion, 1980.
Partial English translation (chap. 1-5): Huntington and Geshe Namgyal, in *The Emptiness of Emptiness.* Honolulu: University of Hawaii Press 1989
Partial English translation of chap. 6: Stephen Batchelor, in Geshé Rabten's *Echoes of Voidness.* London: Wisdom, 1983
See also references under Candrakīrti's *[Auto]Commentary on the "Entrance..."*

Dharmakīrti (*chos kyi grags pa*, seventh century)
*Commentary on (Dignāga's) "Compendium on Valid Cognition"*
tshad ma rnam 'grel gyi tshig le'ur byas pa
pramāṇavārttikakārikā
P5709, vol. 130

Gön-chok-jig-may-wang-bo (*dkon mchog 'jigs med dbang po*, known also as the second *'jam dbyangs bzhad pa*, 1728-1791)

*Analysis of the Great Treatise, (Candrakīrti's) Entrance to (Nāgārjuna's) "Treatise on the Middle Way": Lamp of Scripture and Reasoning: Oral Transmission of the Omniscient Lama, Jam-yang-shay-bay-dor-jay*
bstan gcos chen po dbu ma la 'jug pa'i mtha' dpyod lung rigs sgron me zhes bya ba kun mkhyen bla ma 'jam dbyangs bzhad pa'i rdo rje'i gsung rgyun
*The Collected Works of dkon-mchog-'jigs-med-dbaṅ-po.* New Delhi: Ngawang Gelek Demo, 1972. Vol. 6: 1-484

*Precious Garland of Tenets/Presentation of Tenets, A Precious Garland*
Grub pa'i mtha'i rnam par bzhag pa rin po che'i phreng ba
Mundgod, India: Dre-Gomang Buddhist Cultural Association (Printed by Dre-Loseling Press), 1980

*Presentation of the Grounds and Paths, Beautiful Ornament of the Three Vehicles*
sa lam gyi rnam bzhag theg gsum mdzes rgyan. New Delhi: Ngawang Gelek Demo
*The Collected Works of dkon-mchog-'jigs-med-dbaṅ-po.* 1972. Vol. 7

Jam-yang-shay-ba (*'jam dbyangs bzhad pa*, 1648-1721)
*Great Exposition of Tenets/ Explanation of Tenets, Sun of the Land of Samantabhadra Brilliantly Illuminating All of Our Own and Others' Tenets and the Meaning of the Profound [Emptiness], Ocean of Scripture and Reasoning Fulfilling All Hopes of All Beings*
grub mtha' chen mo/ grub mtha'i rnam bshad rang gzhan grub mtha' kun dang zab don mchog tu gsal ba kun bzang zhing gi nyi ma lung rigs rgya mtsho skye dgu'i re ba kun skong
Musoorie: Dalama, 1962
English translation from the chapter on the Prāsaṅgika [Consequence] School): Jeffrey Hopkins. In *Meditation on Emptiness.* London: Wisdom Publications, 1983

*Great Exposition of the Concentrations and Formless Absorptions/Treatise on the Presentations of the Concentrations and Formless Absorptions, Adornment Beautifying the Subduer's Teaching, Ocean of Scripture and Delighting the Fortunate*
bsam gzugs kyi snyoms 'jug rnams kyi rnam par bzhag pa'i bstan bcos thub bstan mdzes gyan lung dang rigs pa'i rgya mtsho skal bzang dga' byed
Folio printing in India: n.p., n.d.

*Great Exposition of the Middle Way/ Analysis of (Candrakīrti's) "Entrance to (Nāgārjuna's) 'Treatise on the Middle Way'" Treasury of Scripture and Reasoning, Thoroughly Illuminating the Profound Meaning [of Emptiness], Entrance for the Fortunate*
dbu ma chen mo/ dbu ma 'jug pa'i mtha' dpyod lung rigs gter mdzod zab don kun gsal skal bzang 'jug ngogs
Buxaduor: Gomang, 1967

Jam-yang-shay-ba, et. al. [Ba-so Chö-gyi-gyel-tsen *(ba so chos kyi rgyal mtshan)*, De-druk-ken-chen Nga-wang-rap-den *(sde drug mkhan chen ngag dbang rab brtan)*, and Da-di-ge-shay Rin-chen-don-drup *(bra sti dge bshes rin chen don grub)*]
*Four Interwoven Annotations to (Tsong-kha-pa's) "Great Exposition of the Stages of the Path"*
lam rim mchan bzhi sbrags ma
New Delhi: Chophen Lekden, 1972. (Discussed and partly translated in Napper 1989)

Jang-gya (*lcang skya rol ba'i rdo rje*, 1717-86)
*Presentation of Tenets*
grub pa'i mtha'i rnam bzhag
Varanasi: Pleasure of Elegant Sayings Press, 1970): 126.10-128.4 (Sautrāntika chapter tr. in Klein, *Knowing Naming and Negation,* and discussed in Mimaki, *blo gsal grub mtha;* Svātantrika chapter tr. in Lopez, *A Study of Svātantrika*

Jayānanda (12th century)
*Explanation of (Candrakīrti's) "Entrance to (Nāgārjuna's) Middle Way"*
madhyamakāvatāraṭīka
dbu ma la 'jug pa'i grel bshad
P5271, vol. 99

Jetsun Chö-gyi-gyal-tsen (*rje btsun chos kyi rgyal mtshan*, 1469-1544)
*Clarifying the Difficult Points of (Tsong-kha-pa's) "Illumination"*
dgongs pa rab gsal dak' bnad gsal bar byed pa
Woodblock print, n.p; n.d.

Jñānagarbha (*ye shes snying po*, early eighth century)
*Commentary on Distinguishing the Two Truths*
satyadvayavibhaṅgavṛtti
bden pa gnyis rnam par 'byed pa'i 'grel pa

[Not in P] Toh 3882.
Discussed and translated by David M. Eckel in *Jñānagarbha's Commentary on the Distinction Between the Two Truths*. Albany: State University of New York Press, 1986

Kamalaśīla (c. 740-795)
*Illumination of the Middle Way*
madhyamakāloka
dbu ma snang ba
P5287, vol.101

*Stages of Meditation*
bhāvanākrama
sgom pa'i rim pa
P5310-12, Vol. 102; Toh 3915-17; Dharma vol. 73; Tokyo *sde dge* vol. 15
Sanskrit: *First Bhāvanākrama*. G. Tucci, ed. *Minor Buddhist texts, II, Serie Orientale Roma IX: 2* (Rome: I.S.M.E.O, 1958): 185-229. Third Bhāvanākrama. Go Tucci, ed., *Minor Buddhist texts, III, Serie Orientale Roma: XLIII*. Rome. I.S.M.E.O., 1971

Lo-sang Chö-gyi-gyal-tsen (*blo bzang chos kyi rgyal mtsan,* 1567-1662)
*The Path of Well-Being/ The Path of Well-Being for Those Travelling to Omniscience: Essential Guide to the Stages of the Path to Enlightenment*
byang chub lam gyi rim pa'i dmar khrid thams cad mkhyen par 'brod ba'i bde lam
sbag-sa s.n. 1967?

Lo-sang-da-yang (*blo bzang rta dbyangs*, also known as *blo bzang rta mgrin*, 1867-1937)
*Presentation of Grounds and Paths in the Prāsaṅgika System*
thal 'gyur pa'i sa lam
*Collected Works of rJe-btsun blo-bzaṅg-rta-mgrin,* New Delhi: Guru Deva

Lo-sang-dam-chö (*blo bzang dam chos*)
ten 'brel bstod pa'i tikka mkhas mang dgyes pa
Blockprint in possession of Kensur Yeshey Tupden, n.p., n.d.

*Annotations on [Panchen Sönam Drakba's] "General Meaning of Mādhyamika," A Lamp Illuminating the Profound Meaning*
dbu ma'i spyi don gyi mchan 'grel
New Delhi: Tibet House, 1974

Maitreya *(byams pa)*
*Differentiation of the Middle Way and the Extremes*
madhyāntavibhaṅga
dbus dang mtha' rnam par 'byed pa
P5522, vol. 108
Sanskrit: *Madhyānta-vibhāga-śāstra.* Ramchandra Pandeya ed. Delhi: Motilal Banarsidass, 1971

Partial English translation: T. Stcherbatsky. *Madhyānta-Vibhaṅga.* Calcutta: Indian Studies Past and Present, 1971

*Ornament for Clear Realization*
Abhisamayālaṃkāra
mngon par rtogs pa'i rgyan, P5184, Vol. 88, translated by E. Conze, *Abhisamāyalaṅkāra*, Serie Orientale Roma. VI (Rome: I.S.M.E.O., July 1954); also translated by E. Obermiller
*Analysis of the Abhisamayālaṃkāra* (Calcutta Oriental Series, No. 27, Fasc. I, II, III, London: Luzac & Co. 1933, 1936 and 1943)

Mipham (*mi pham rnam rgyal/'ju mi-pham rgya mtsho*, 1846-1912)
*Word Commentary on the "Wisdom" Chapter, "The Norbu Ketaka"*
shes rab le'ui tshig don go sla bar rnam par bshad pa nor bu ke da ka
Varanasi: Tarthang Tulku, Sanskrit University, 1966

brgal lan nyin byed snang ba.
Varanasi: Tarthang Tulku, Sanskrit University, 1967

Nāgārjuna (*klu sgrub*, first to second century)

*Compendium of Sūtra*
sūtrasamuccaya
mdo kun las btus pa
P5330, vol. 102

*Essay on the Mind of Enlightenment*
bodhicittavivaraṇa
byang chub sems 'grel
P2665, vol. 61; P2666, vol. 61

*Praise of the Element of Reality*
dharmadhātustotra
chos kyi dbyings su bstod pa
P2010, vol. 46

*Precious Garland of Advice for the King*
rājaparikathāratnāvalī
rgyal po la gtam bya ba rin po che'i phreng ba
P5658, vol. 129
Sanskrit, Tibetan, and Chinese: In Michael Hahn. *Nāgārjuna's Ratnāvalī.* Vol.1: *The Basic Texts (Sanskrit, Tibetan, and Chinese).* Bonn, Indica et Tibetica Verlag, 1982
English translation: Jeffrey Hopkins. In Nāgārjuna and the Seventh Dalai Lama, *The Precious Garland and the Song of the Four Mindfulnesses.* New York: Harper and Row, 1975

*Seventy Stanzas on Emptiness*
śūnyatāsaptatikārikā

stong pa nyid bdun cu pa'i tshig le'ur byas pa
P5227, vol. 95; Toh 3827, Tokyo *sde dge* vol. 1
Edited Tibetan and English translation: Chr. Lindtner. In *Nagarjuniana.* Indiske Studier 4: 34-69. Copenhagen: Akademisk Forlag, 1982
English translation: David Ross Komito. *Nāgārjuna's "Seventy Stanzas": A Buddhist Psychology of Emptiness.* Ithaca: Snow Lion, 1987

*Sixty Stanzas of Reasoning*
yuktiṣaṣṭikākārikā
rigs pa drug cu pa'i tshig le'ur byas pa
P5225, vol. 95; Toh 3825, Tokyo *sde dge* vol. 1
Edited Tibetan with Sanskrit fragments and English translation: Chr. Lindtner. In *Nagarjuniana.* Indiske Studier 4: 100-119. Copenhagen: Akademisk Forlag, 1982

*Treatise on the Middle Way/ Fundamental Treatise on the Middle, Called "Wisdom"*
madhyamakaśāstra/prajñānāmamūlamadhyamakakārikā
dbu ma'i bstan bcos/ dbu ma rtsa ba'i tshig le'ur byas pa shes rab ces bya ba
P5224, vol. 95
Edited Sanskrit: *Nāgārjuna, Mūlamadhyamakakārikāḥ.* J. W. de Jong, ed. Adyar: Adyar Library and Research Centre, 1977. Also: Chr. Lindtner in *Nāgārjuna's Filosofiske Vaerker.* Indiske Studier 2: 177-215. Copenhagen: Akademisk Forlag, 1982
English translation: Frederick Streng. *Emptiness: A Study in Religious Meaning.* Nashville and New York: Abingdon Press, 1967. Also: Kenneth Inada. *Nāgārjuna: A Translation of His Mūlamadhyamakakārikā.* Tokyo: The Hokuseido Press, 1970. Also: David J. Kalupahana. *Nāgārjuna: The Philosophy of the Middle Way.* Albany: State University Press of New York, 1986
Italian translation: R. Gnoli. *Nāgārjuna: Madhyamaka Kārikā, Le stanze del cammino di mezzo.* Enciclopedia di autori classici 61. Turin: P. Boringhieri, 1961
Danish translation: Chr. Lindtner in *Nāgārjuna's Filosofiske Vaerker.* Indiske Studier 2: 67-135. Copenhagen: Akademisk Forlag, 1982

Ngawang Belden (*ngag dbang dpal ldan*, b. 1797), also known as Bel-den-chö-jay (*dpal ldan chos rje*)
*Annotations for (Jam-yang-shay-ba's) "Great Exposition of Tenets," Freeing the Knots of the Difficult Points, Precious Jewel of Clear Thought*
grub mtha' chen mo'i mchan 'grel dka' gnad mdud grol blo gsal gces nor
Sarnath: Pleasure of Elegant Sayings Press, 1964

Panchen Sönam Drakba (*paṇ chen bsod nams grags pa*, 1478-1554)

*Analysis of (Candrakīrti's) "Entrance to the Middle Way"*
dbu ma 'jug pa'i mtha' dpyod/dbu ma 'jug pa'i mtha' dpyod lung rigs gter mdzod zab don kun gsal skal bzang 'jug ngogs
Gomang College Library, Mundgod, India. n.d.

*General Meaning of (Maitreya's) "Ornament for Clear Realization"*
phar phyin spyi don/ shes rab kyi pha rol tu phyin pa'i man ngag gi bstan bcos mngon par rtogs pa'i rgyan 'grel pa dang bcas pa'i rnam bshad snying po rgyan gyi don legs par bshad pa yum don gsal ba'i sgron me
Buxaduor: Nang bstan shes rig 'dzin skyong slob gnyer khang, 1963

*General Meaning of the Middle Way*
dbu ma'i spyi don
*Collected Works (gsung 'bum) of Pan-chen bsod-nams-grags-pa*, vol. 7. Mundgod, Karnataka: Drebung Loseling Library Society, 1985

*The New Red Annals*
Reproduced and translated as *Deb t'er dmar po gsar ma.* G. Tucci. Serie Orientale Roma. Roma: Istituto Italiano Per Il Medio Ed Estremo Oriente

*Response to Queries Regarding [Candrakīrti's] "Entrance to the Middle Way," A Lamp Fully Iluminating the Profound Meaning*
dbu ma la 'jug ba'i brgal lan zab don yang gsal sgron me
The Collected Works *(gsung 'bum)* of Pan-chen bsod-nams-grags-pa, vol. 7. Mundgod, Karnataka: Drebung Loseling Library Society, 1985
Lamp Illuminating the Meaning of the Mother/ Lamp Illuminating the Profound Meaning

*Yum don gsal ba'i sgron me* [also known as *zab don gsal ba'i sgron ma*]
Collected Works *(gsung 'bum)* of Pan-chen bsod-nams-grags pa, vol. 3 (Mundgod, Karnataka, and Delhi: Jayyed Press Ballimaran, 1983

Pur-bu-jok (*phur bu lcog byams pa rgya mtsho*, 1825-1901)
*Explanation of the Lesser Path of Reasoning*
rigs lam chung ngu'i rnam par bshad pa
In *Magical Key to the Path of Reasoning, Presentation of the Collected Topics Revealing the Meaning of the Treatises on Valid Cognition*
tshad ma'i gzhung don 'byed pa'i bsdus brva'i rnam bzhag rigs lam 'phrul gyi sde mig
Translated in Perdue, 1992

*Explanation of the Presentation of Objects and Object Possessors as well as Awareness and Knowledge* (yul yul can dang blo rig gi rnam par bshad pa). *Magical Key to the path of Reasoning, Presentation of the Collected Topics Revealing the Meaning of the Treatises on Valid Cognition*
tshad ma'i gzhung don 'byed pa'i bsdus grva'i rnam bzhag rigs lam 'phrul gyi sde mig
Buxa: n.p., 1965
Translated and discussed in Napper, 1980

Nga-wang-dra-shi (*ngag dbang bkra shis*, 1648-1721)
*Collected Topics from a Spiritual Son of Jam-yang-shay-ba*
gomang yig cha/kun mkhyen 'jam dbyangs bzhad pa'i thugs sras ngag dbang bkra

shis kyis mdzad pa'i bsdus grva. Gomang College, Mundgod, India: n.p., n.d.

Ren-da-wa (*red mda' ba gzhon nu blo gros*, 1349-1412)
*Explanation of [Candrakīrti's] "Entrance to the Middle Way," A Lamp Illuminating Reality*
dbu ma la 'jug pa'i rnam bshad de kho na nyid gsal ba'i sgron ma. Delhi: Ngawang Topgay, 1974

Śāntideva (*zhi ba lha*, eighth century)
*Engaging in the Bodhisattva Deeds*
bodhi[sattva]caryāvatāra
byang chub sems dpa'i spyod pa la 'jug pa
P5272, vol. 99
Sanskrit and Tibetan texts: Vidhushekara Bhattacharya, ed. *Bodhicaryāvatāra.* Bibliotheca Indica, vol. 280. Calcutta: The Asiatic Society, 1960
English translation: Stephen Batchelor. *A Guide to the Bodhisattva's Way of Life.* Dharamsala: Library of Tibetan Works and Archives, 1979. Also: Marion Matics. *Entering the Path of Enlightenment.* New York: Macmillan Co., 1970
Contemporary commentary by Geshe Kelsang Gyatso. *Meaningful to Behold.* London: Wisdom Publications, 1980

*Compendium of Learning*
śikṣāsamuccayakārikā
bslab pa kun las btus pa'i tshig le'ur byas pa
P5336, Vol. 102
Translated by C. Bendall and W. H. D. Rouse. *Śikṣā Samuccaya.* Delhi, Motilal, 1971

Sum-ba Khen-bo (*sumbha mkhan po dpal 'byor*, 1702-1775)
*Sumpakhampo's History of Tibet*
sumbha mkhan po dpal 'byor gyi gsung rgya gar 'phags yul rgya nag chen po gangs can bod yul sogs yul rnam su dam chas rin chen byung tshul dpag bsam lcon bzang las gang can bod kyi yul du dam chos dang tshul gyi dpe deb
Sarnath, Varanasi, U.P.: Mongolian Lama Guru Deva, Pleasure of Elegant Sayings Press, 1985

Tsong-kha-pa (*tsong kha pa blo bzang grags pa*, 1357-1419).
*Explaining Eight Difficult Points in [Nāgārjuna's] "Treatise on the Middle Way"*
rtsa ba shes rab kyi dka' gnas chen po brgyad kyi bshad pa
Sarnath: Pleasure of Elegant Sayings Press, 1970.

*Four Interwoven Annotations on (Tsong-kha-pa's) "Great Exposition of the Stages of the Path"*
In *The Lam rim chen mo of the incomparable Tsong-kha-pa, with the interlineal notes of Ba-so Chos-kyi-rgyal-mtshan, Sde-drug Mkhan-chenNgag-dbang-*

*rab-rtan, 'Jam-dbyangs-bshad-pa'i-rdo-rje, and Bra-sti Dge-bshes Rin-chen-don-grub.* New Delhi: Chos-'phel-legs-ldan, 1972

*Great Exposition of the Stages of the Path/ Stages of the Path to Enlightenment Thoroughly Teaching All the Stages of Practice of the Three Types of Beings*
lam rim chen mo/ skyes bu gsum gyi rnyams su blang ba'i rim pa thams cad tshang bar ston pa'i byang chub lam gyi rim pa
P6001, vol. 152
Also: Dharamsala: Shes rig par khang, 1964
Also: Delhi: Ngawang Gelek, 1975-
English translation of section on the object negated *(dgag bya)* in Elizabeth Napper, *Dependent-Arising and Emptiness.* London: Wisdom Publications, 1989
English translation of the parts on calm abiding and special insight in Alex Wayman, *Calming the Mind and Discerning the Real.* New York: Columbia University Press, 1978; reprint New Delhi, Motilal Banarsidass, 1979

*Illumination of the Thought, Extensive Explanation of (Candrakīrti's) "Entrance to (Nāgārjuna's) 'Treatise on the Middle'"*
dbu ma la 'jug pa'i rgya cher bshad pa dgongs pa rab gsal
P6143, vol. 154
Also: Sarnath, India: Pleasure of Elegant Sayings Press, 1973
Also: Dharamsala, India: Tibetan Cultural Printing Press, n.d.
Also: The Collected Works (gsuṅ 'bum) of the Incomparable Lord Tsoṅ-kha-pa Blo-bzaṅ-grags-pa, vol. 16 *ma* [photographic reprint of the "1897 old źol *(dga'-ldan-phun-tshogs-gliṅ)* blocks"]. New Delhi: Guru Deva, 1979
English translation (first five chapters): Jeffrey Hopkins. In *Compassion in Tibetan Buddhism.* Ithaca, New York: Snow Lion, 1980

*Ocean of Reasoning, Explanation of (Nāgārjuna's) "Treatise on the Middle Way"/ Great Commentary on (Nāgārjuna's) "Treatise on the Middle Way"*
dbu ma rtsa ba'i tshig le'ur byas pa shes rab ces bya ba'i rnam bshad rigs pa'i rgya mtsho
P6153, vol. 156
Also: Sarnath, India: Pleasure of Elegant Sayings Printing Press, n.d.
Also: in *rje tsong kha pa'i gsung dbu ma'i lta ba'i skor*, vol. 1 and 2, Sarnath, India: Pleasure of Elegant Sayings Press, 1975

"Middling Exposition of Special Insight"
lhag mthong 'bring
In *rje tsong kha pa'i gsung dbu ma'i lta ba'i skor*, Vol. 2, Sarnath, India, Pleasure of Elegant Sayings Press, 1975
English translation: "The Middle Transcendent Insight." In Thurman, 1982

*Songs of the Stages of the Path*
lam rim mnyam mgur bshugs
In *zhal 'don nyer mkho phyogs bsdebs bshugs.* Sarnath: Gelukba Students Welfare Committee, 1979

Vasubandhu (*dbyig gnyen*, fourth century)
*Treasury of Knowledge*
chos mngon pa mdzod kyi tshig le'ur byas pa
abhidharmakośakārikā
P5590, Vol. 115
Sanskrit: *Abhidharmakośa & Bhāṣya of Ācārya Vasubandhu with Sphuṭārtha Commentary of Ācārya Yaśomitra.* Swami Dwarikadas Shastri, ed. Bauddha Bharati Series no. 5. Banaras: Bauddha Bharati, 1970
French translation: Louis de la Vallée Poussin. *L'Abhidharmakośa de Vasubandhu.* Paris: Geuthner, 1923-31

# Index


abiding mode of subsistence, 96, 249n.17
absorption, 13, 15
absorption of cessation, 40-41, 55, 223n.62, 255n.17
  common and uncommon, 38, 39, 229n.18, 230n.24
actions, 54, 73, 133-134
  cause and effect of, 74, 75, 76
  motivation for, 54
  power of, 83
  uncontaminated, 89
actuality, 66, 86
adherence to the true existence of, 104
  *See also* conception of true existence
advisory speech, 6-8, 21
afflictions, 73
  true cessation of, 87
aggregates, 176
  appearance of, 142, 270n.4
  disintegrating, 139, 143
  five mental, 109, 135, 141
  understood as real I, 139-145
*Ajātaśatru*
  *Sutra of*, 162
analysis of conventionalities, 34, 46, 48, 106, 107, 108, 113, 145
*Analysis of (Candrakīrti's) "Entrance to the Middle Way,"* 3
Ānanda, 260n.39
anger, 62, 73, 74, 127, 158, 241n.9
  and emptiness, 62
appearance
  dualistic, 32, 95, 96, 173
  mistaken, 69, 111
  of emptiness, 99
  of true existence, 98, 110
Approaching, 18, 149, 150, 152
  *See also* Manifest
Arhat, 54, 87, 98, 244n.2
*The Arising of the Dharma*, 78
artist
  meditation as, 25
Āryadeva, 77, 178
  *Four Hundred*, 156, 176, 182, 271n.15-16
āryan, 12
Asaṅga, 65, 93
  *Bodhissatva Grounds*, 164
Aśoka, 259n.35
aspect, 34, 35
  casting of, 35, 95, 227n.13
  conceptualized, 34, 35
  of inherent existence, 143
Atīśa, 155
attachment, 53
Avalokiteśvara, 219n.19

Bakhtin, 225n.75
Banaras Sanskrit University, xiv
Barthes, Roland, 26, 225n.77
bases of designation, 45, 138, 140
Bhāvaviveka, 78, 87, 120, 125, 238n.27, 241n.15, 248n.10
blessings, 8, 9
Bodhissatva, 12, 14, 16, 18, 19, 22, 63, 67, 76, 86, 87, 88, 89, 98, 151, 152, 158, 241n.7, 256n.26
  deeds, 74, 75
  path, 13
  and rebirth, 87
  Superior, 42

# Epilogue

During a 1980 audience with His Holiness the Dalai Lama, I mentioned the work on Tshong-kha-pa's *Illumination* I was doing with Kensur Yeshey Tupden. He took this in with a thunderous, Vimalakīrti-like silence for a moment and then declared, in his heartfelt way and strong voice, "Excellent." I reported this conversation to Kensur, first describing the scene in Tibetan, and then repeating for him the Dalai Lama's own word. Thoughtfully, slowly, as if moved at making this oral connection with the Dalai Lama, Yeshey Tupden repeated, in clear articulation of the three syllables he was pronouncing for the first time, the English word "Excellent."

Thinking once again of the many teachers and friends who connect me with this textual tradition and others, I am inspired to hope that whatever excellence comes about through the interplay between the reader and this text may magically or materially help nourish and make flourish by whatever means required the happiness and good will of beings everywhere.